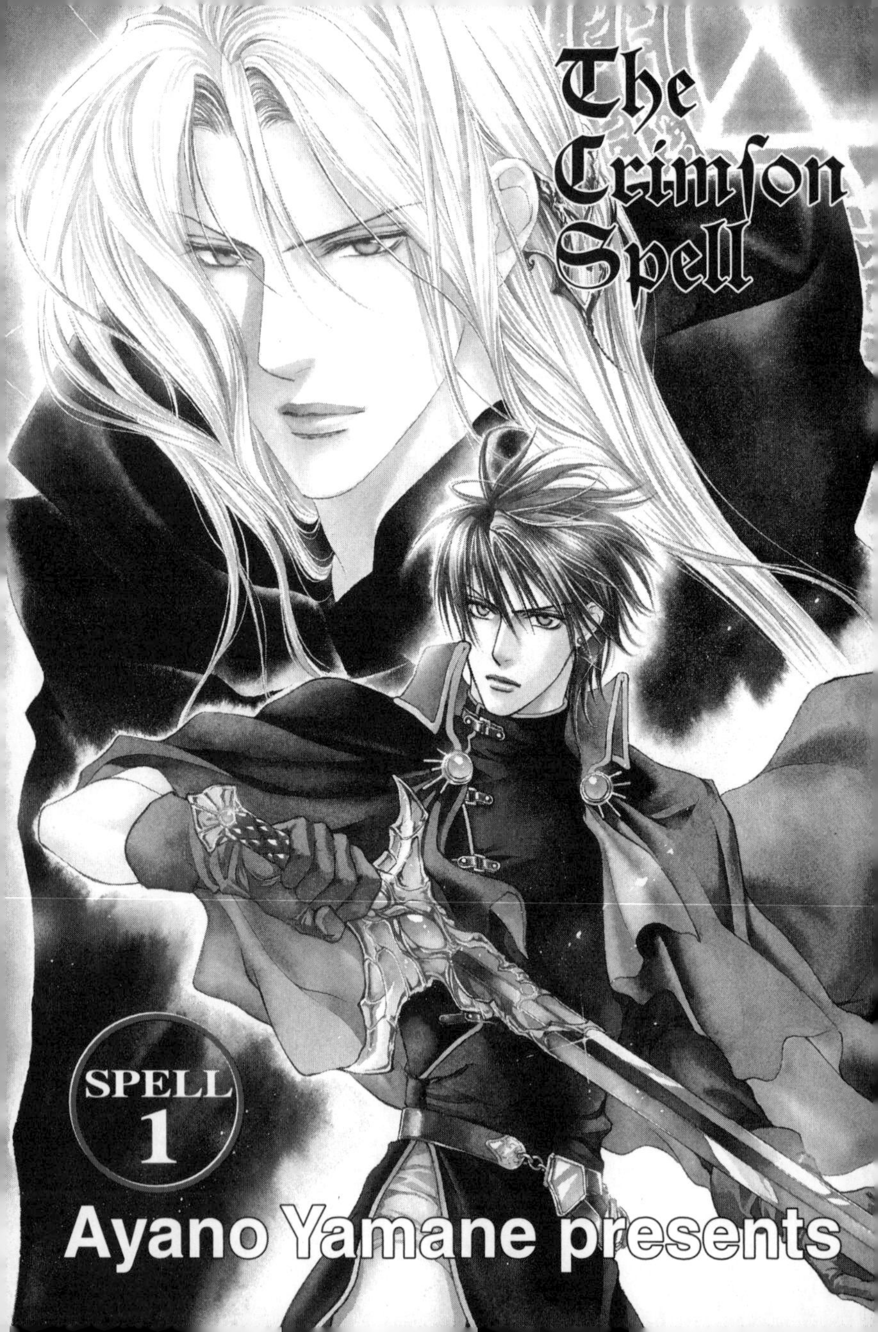
The Crimson Spell
SPELL 1
Ayano Yamane presents

Ayano Yamane Presents

The
Crimson
Spell

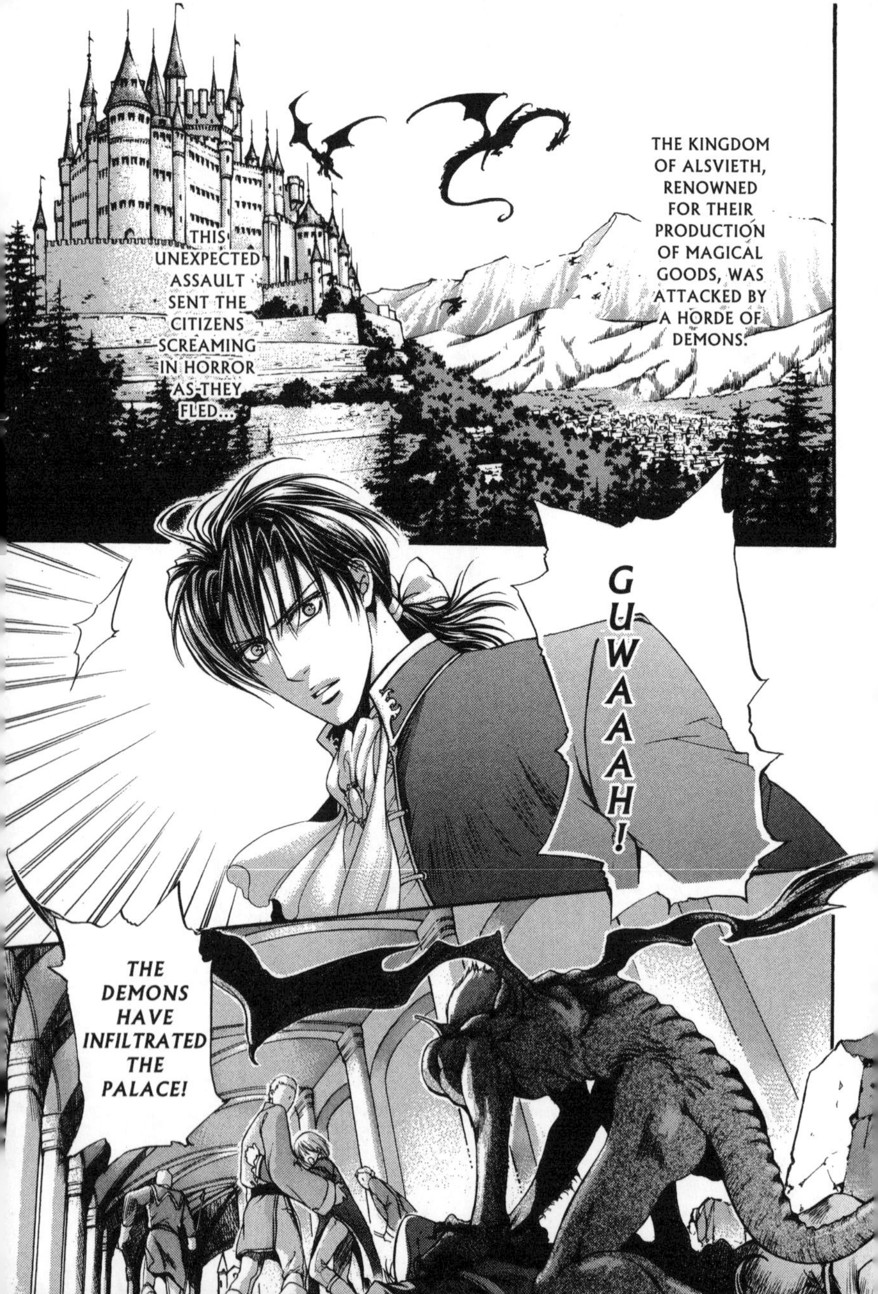
THE KINGDOM OF ALSVIETH, RENOWNED FOR THEIR PRODUCTION OF MAGICAL GOODS, WAS ATTACKED BY A HORDE OF DEMONS.
THIS UNEXPECTED ASSAULT SENT THE CITIZENS SCREAMING IN HORROR AS THEY FLED...
GUWAAAAH!
THE DEMONS HAVE INFILTRATED THE PALACE!

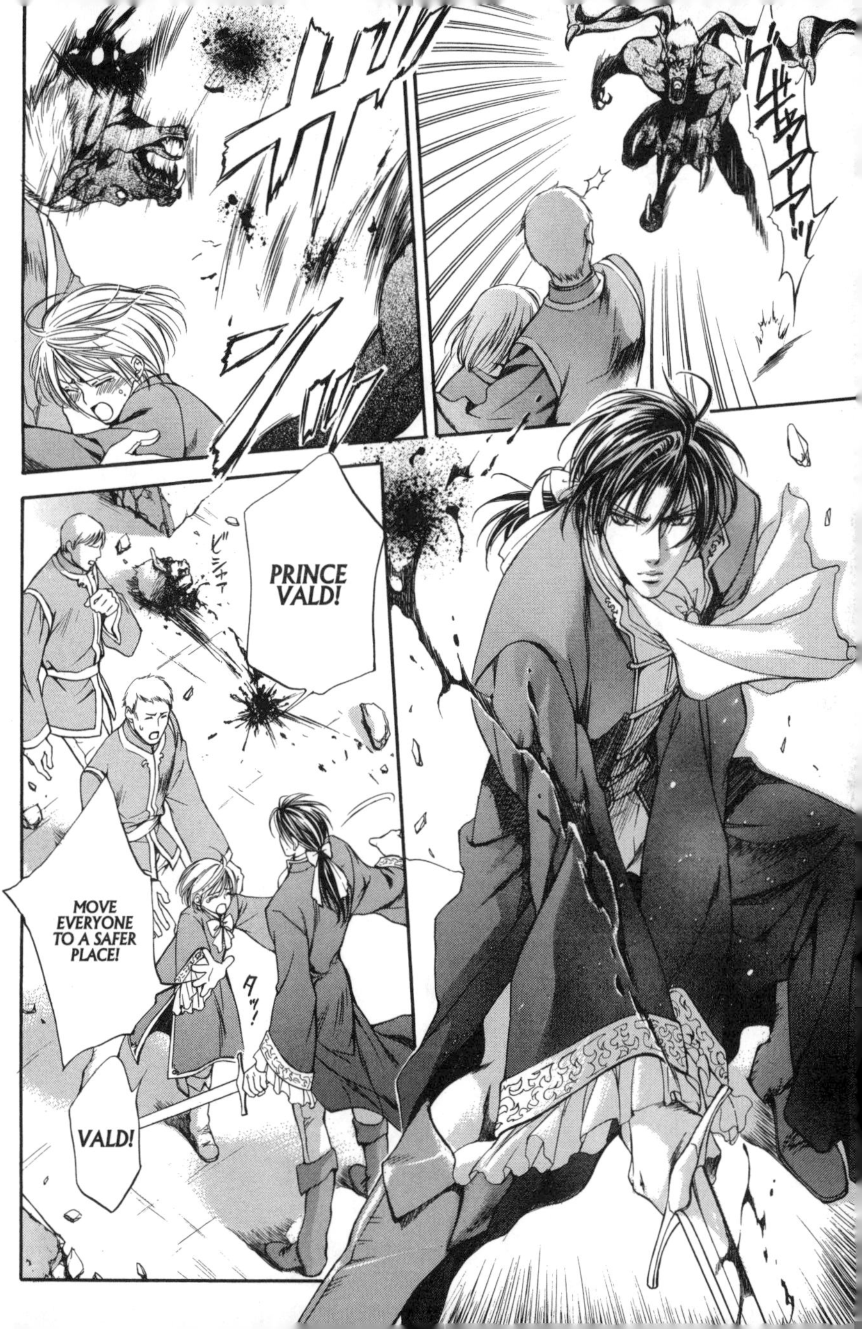
PRINCE VALD!
MOVE EVERYONE TO A SAFER PLACE!
VALD!

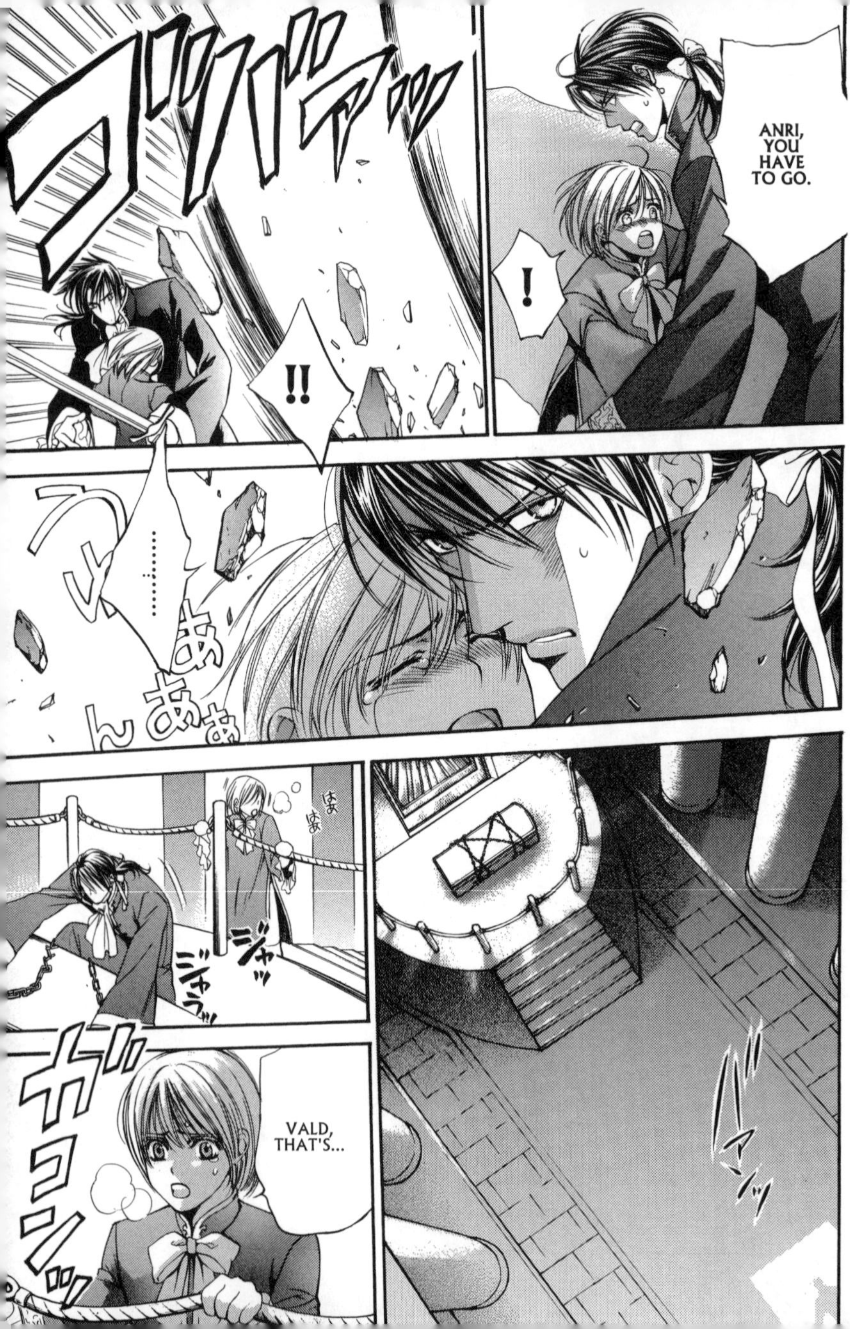
ANRI, YOU HAVE TO GO.
!
!!
……
はぁ はぁ
VALD, THAT'S...

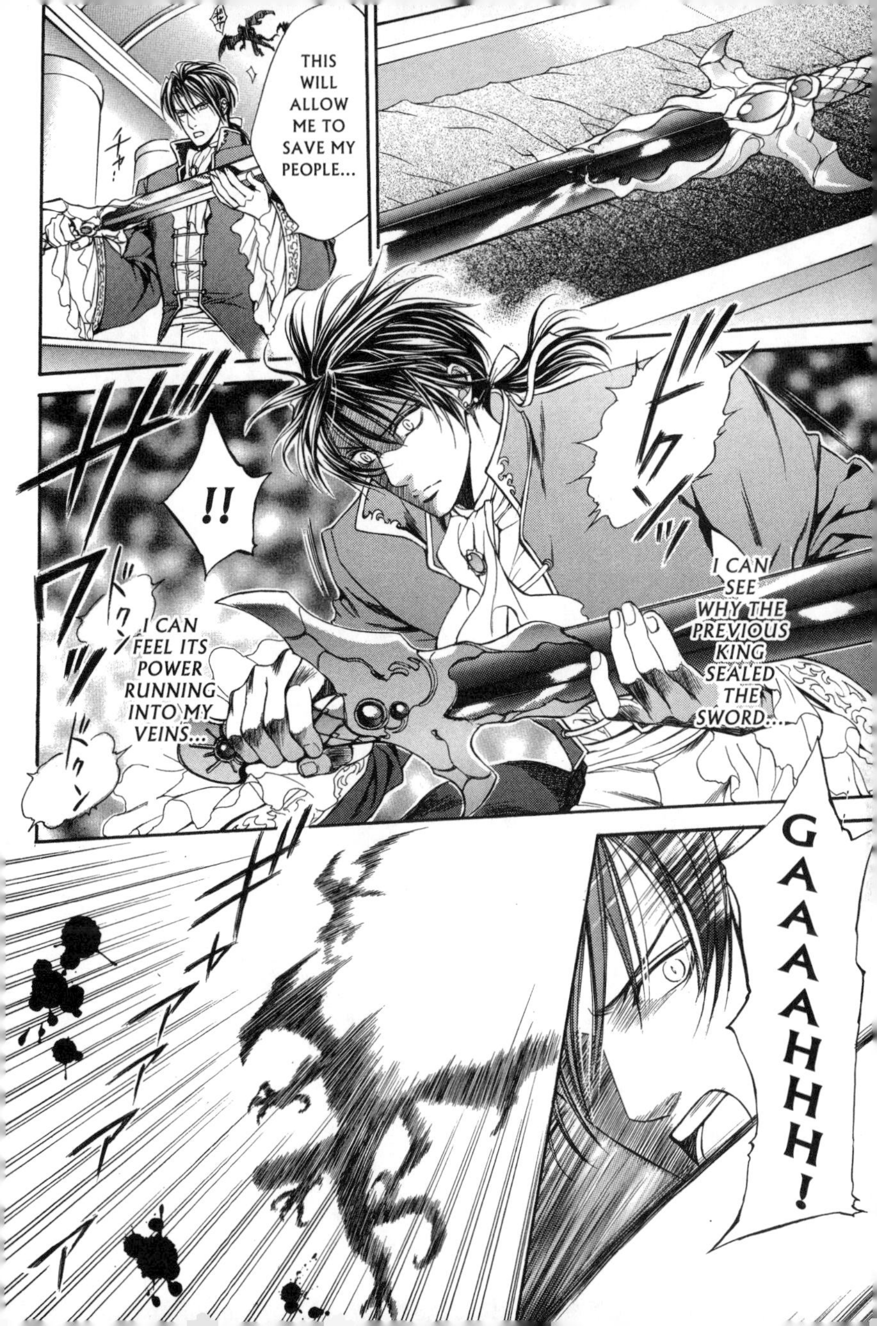
THIS WILL ALLOW ME TO SAVE MY PEOPLE...
I CAN SEE WHY THE PREVIOUS KING SEALED THE SWORD...
!!
I CAN FEEL ITS POWER RUNNING INTO MY VEINS...
GAAAAHHH!

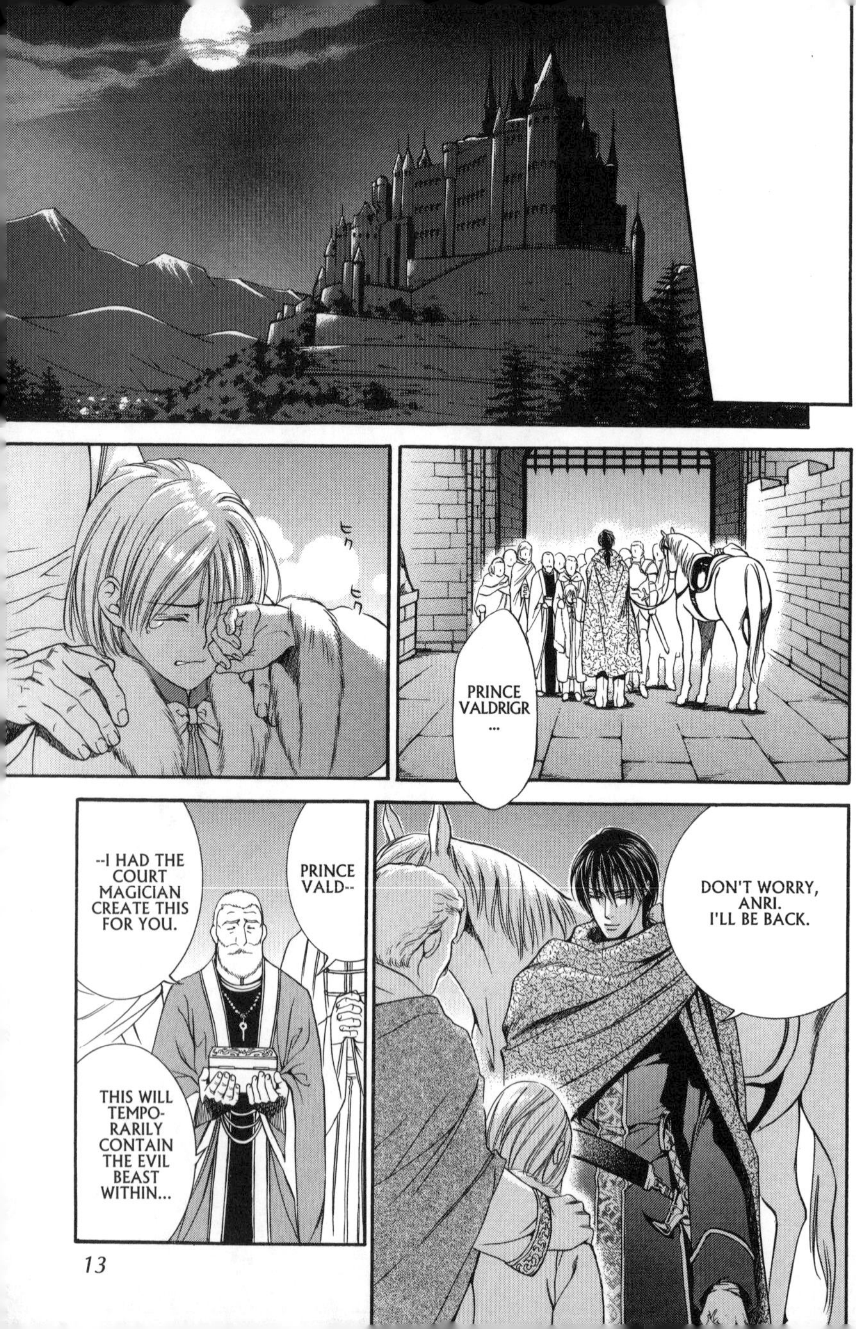
PRINCE VALDRIGR ...
DON'T WORRY, ANRI. I'LL BE BACK.
PRINCE VALD--
--I HAD THE COURT MAGICIAN CREATE THIS FOR YOU.
THIS WILL TEMPO-RARILY CONTAIN THE EVIL BEAST WITHIN...

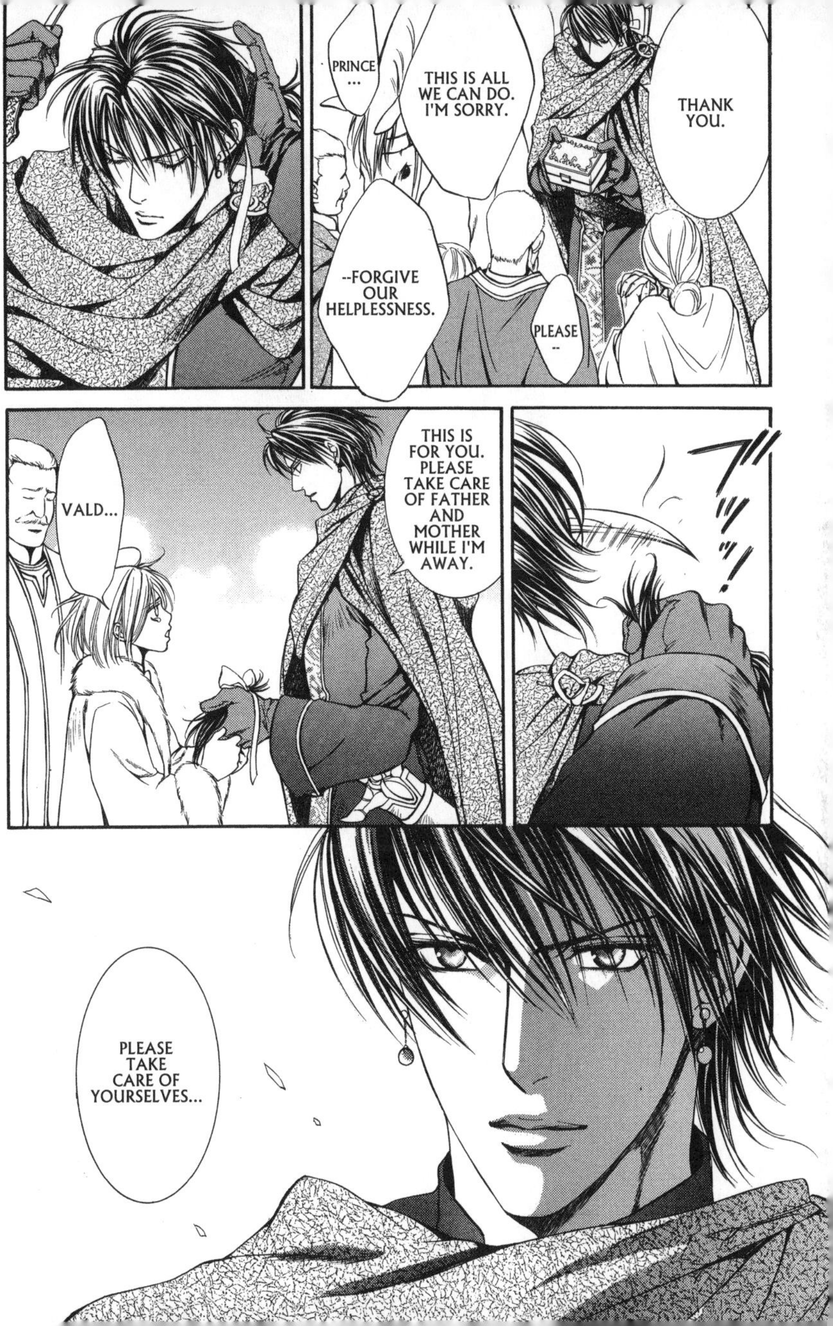
THANK YOU.
THIS IS ALL WE CAN DO. I'M SORRY.
PRINCE ...
PLEASE --
--FORGIVE OUR HELPLESSNESS.
ブツッ!
THIS IS FOR YOU. PLEASE TAKE CARE OF FATHER AND MOTHER WHILE I'M AWAY.
VALD...
PLEASE TAKE CARE OF YOURSELVES...

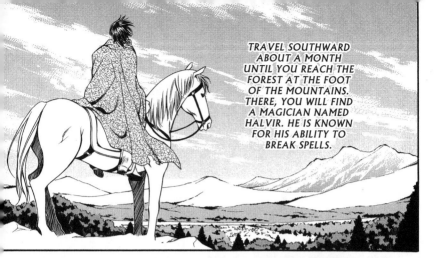

TRAVEL SOUTHWARD ABOUT A MONTH UNTIL YOU REACH THE FOREST AT THE FOOT OF THE MOUNTAINS. THERE, YOU WILL FIND A MAGICIAN NAMED HALVIR. HE IS KNOWN FOR HIS ABILITY TO BREAK SPELLS.

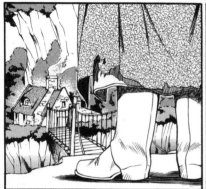

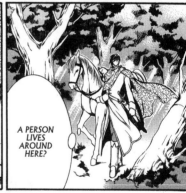

A PERSON LIVES AROUND HERE?

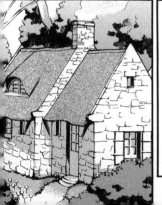

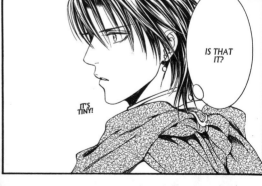

IS THAT IT?

IT'S TINY!

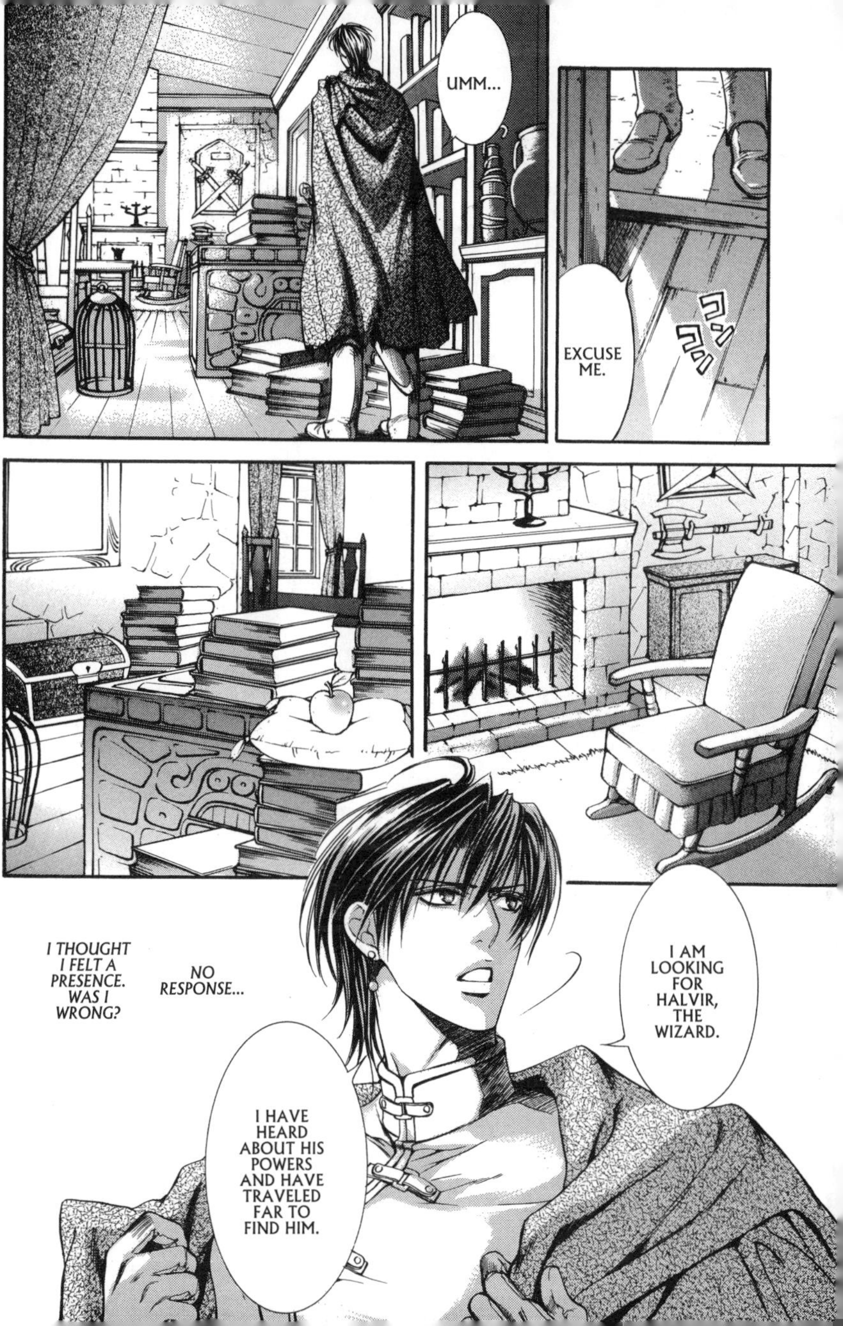
コンコン
EXCUSE ME.
UMM...
I AM LOOKING FOR HALVIR, THE WIZARD.
I HAVE HEARD ABOUT HIS POWERS AND HAVE TRAVELED FAR TO FIND HIM.
NO RESPONSE...
I THOUGHT I FELT A PRESENCE. WAS I WRONG?

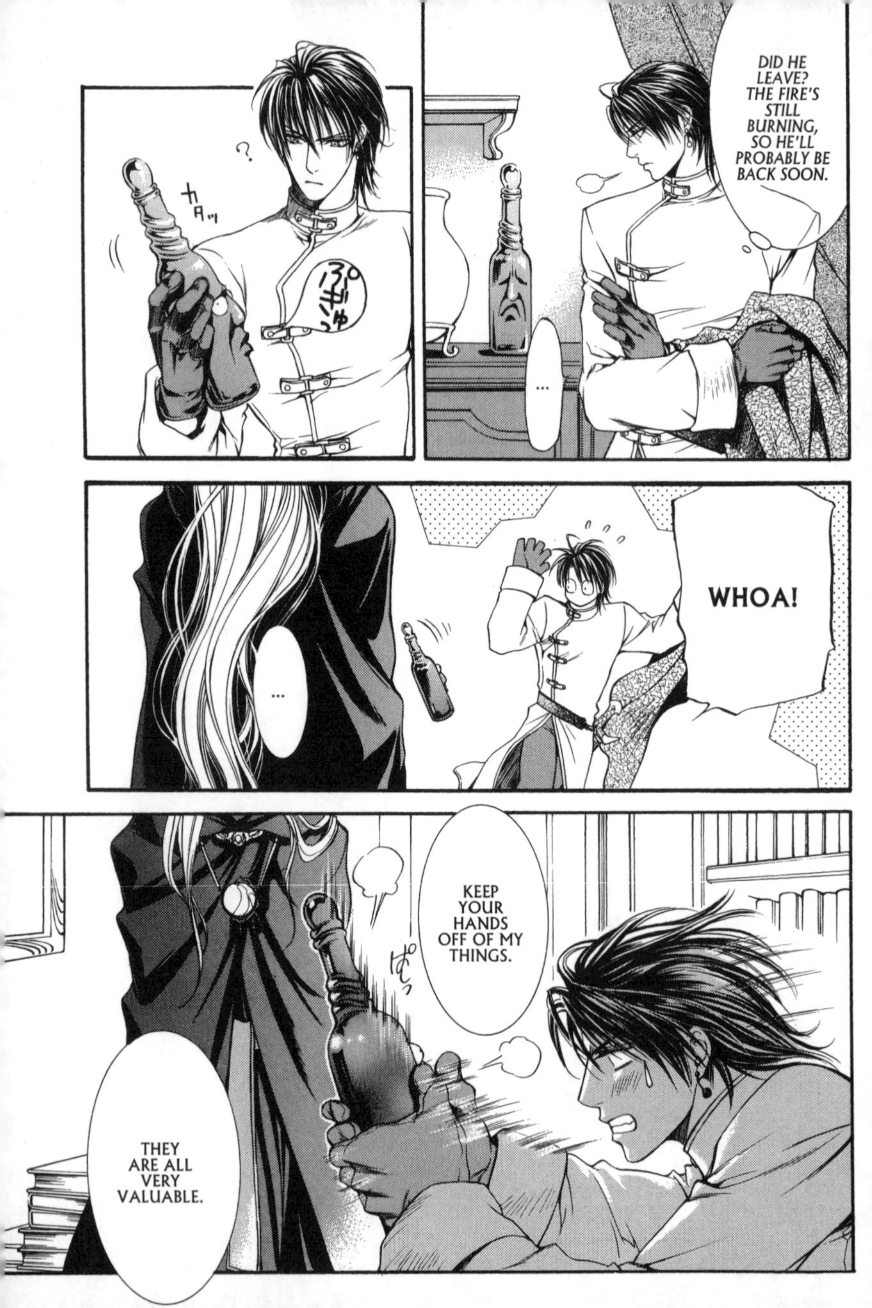
DID HE LEAVE? THE FIRE'S STILL BURNING, SO HE'LL PROBABLY BE BACK SOON.
...
カタッ
?
WHOA!
...
KEEP YOUR HANDS OFF OF MY THINGS.
THEY ARE ALL VERY VALUABLE.

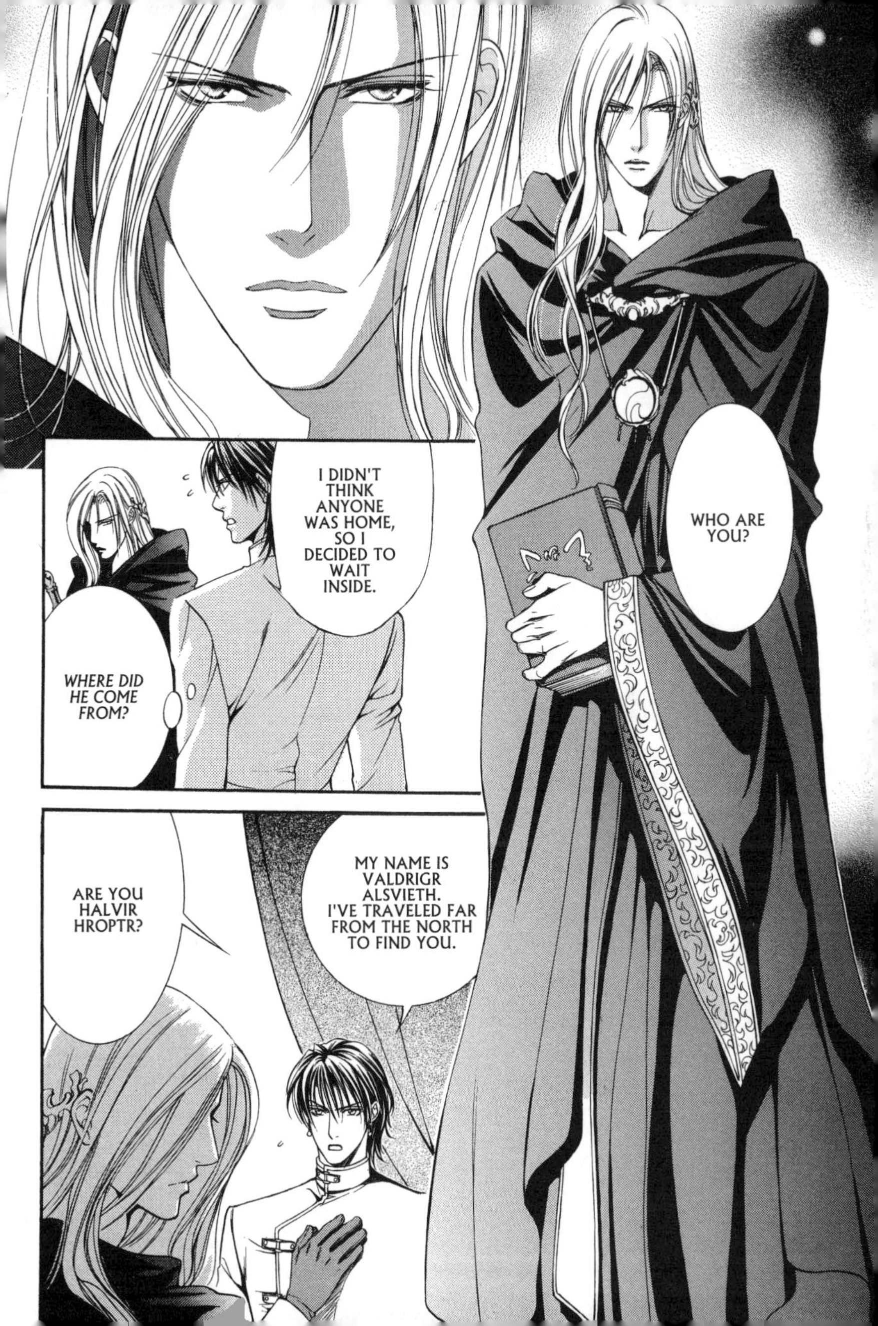
WHO ARE YOU?
I DIDN'T THINK ANYONE WAS HOME, SO I DECIDED TO WAIT INSIDE.
WHERE DID HE COME FROM?
MY NAME IS VALDRIGR ALSVIETH. I'VE TRAVELED FAR FROM THE NORTH TO FIND YOU.
ARE YOU HALVIR HROPTR?

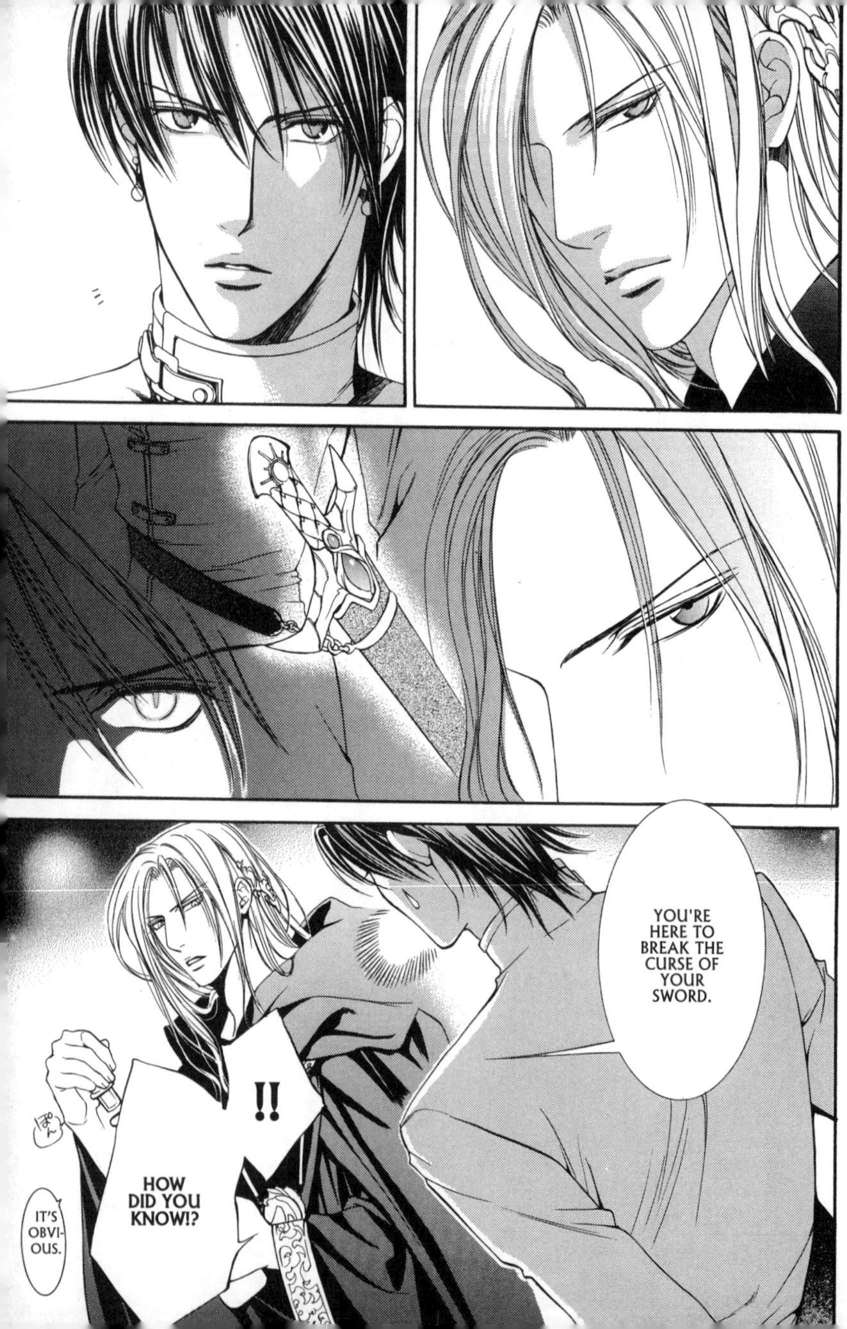
YOU'RE HERE TO BREAK THE CURSE OF YOUR SWORD.
!!
HOW DID YOU KNOW!?
IT'S OBVIOUS.

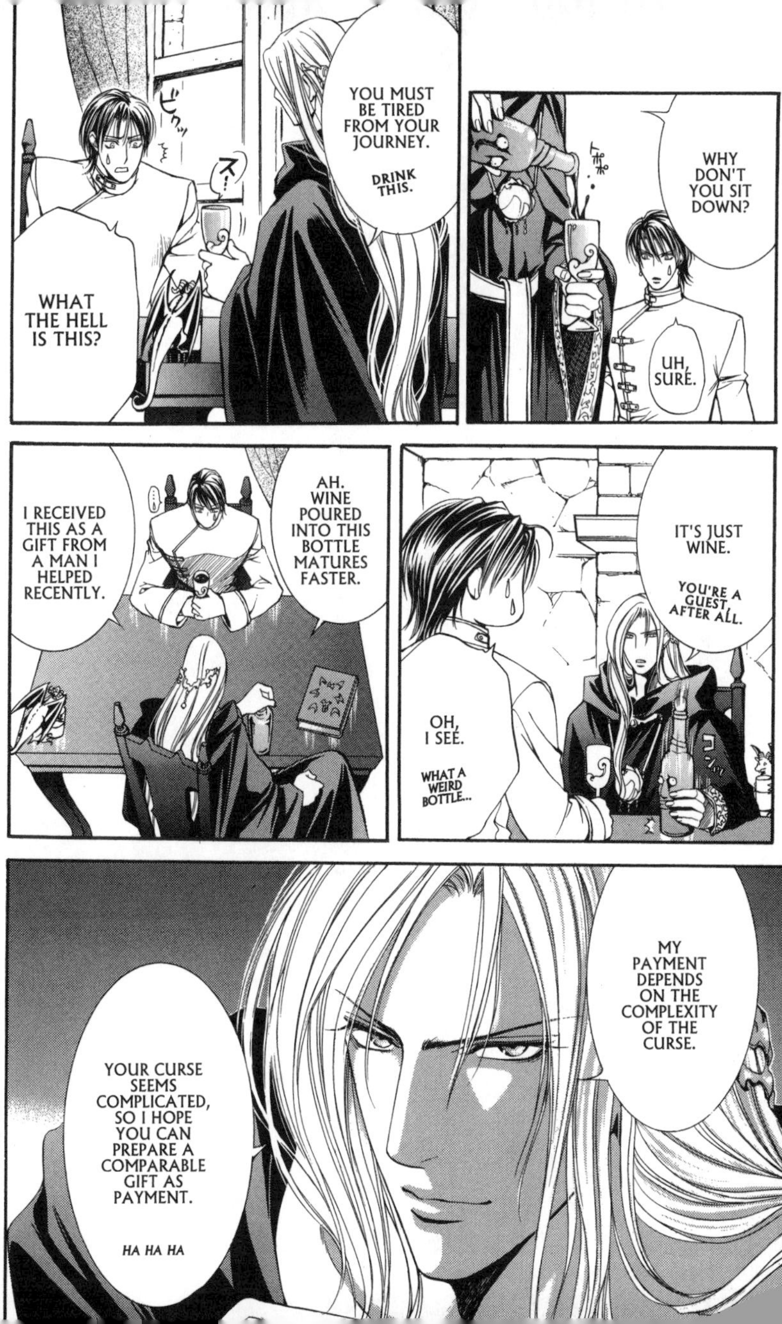
WHY DON'T YOU SIT DOWN?
UH, SURE.
YOU MUST BE TIRED FROM YOUR JOURNEY.
DRINK THIS.
WHAT THE HELL IS THIS?
IT'S JUST WINE.
YOU'RE A GUEST, AFTER ALL.
OH, I SEE.
WHAT A WEIRD BOTTLE...
AH. WINE POURED INTO THIS BOTTLE MATURES FASTER.
I RECEIVED THIS AS A GIFT FROM A MAN I HELPED RECENTLY.
MY PAYMENT DEPENDS ON THE COMPLEXITY OF THE CURSE.
YOUR CURSE SEEMS COMPLICATED, SO I HOPE YOU CAN PREPARE A COMPARABLE GIFT AS PAYMENT.
HA HA HA

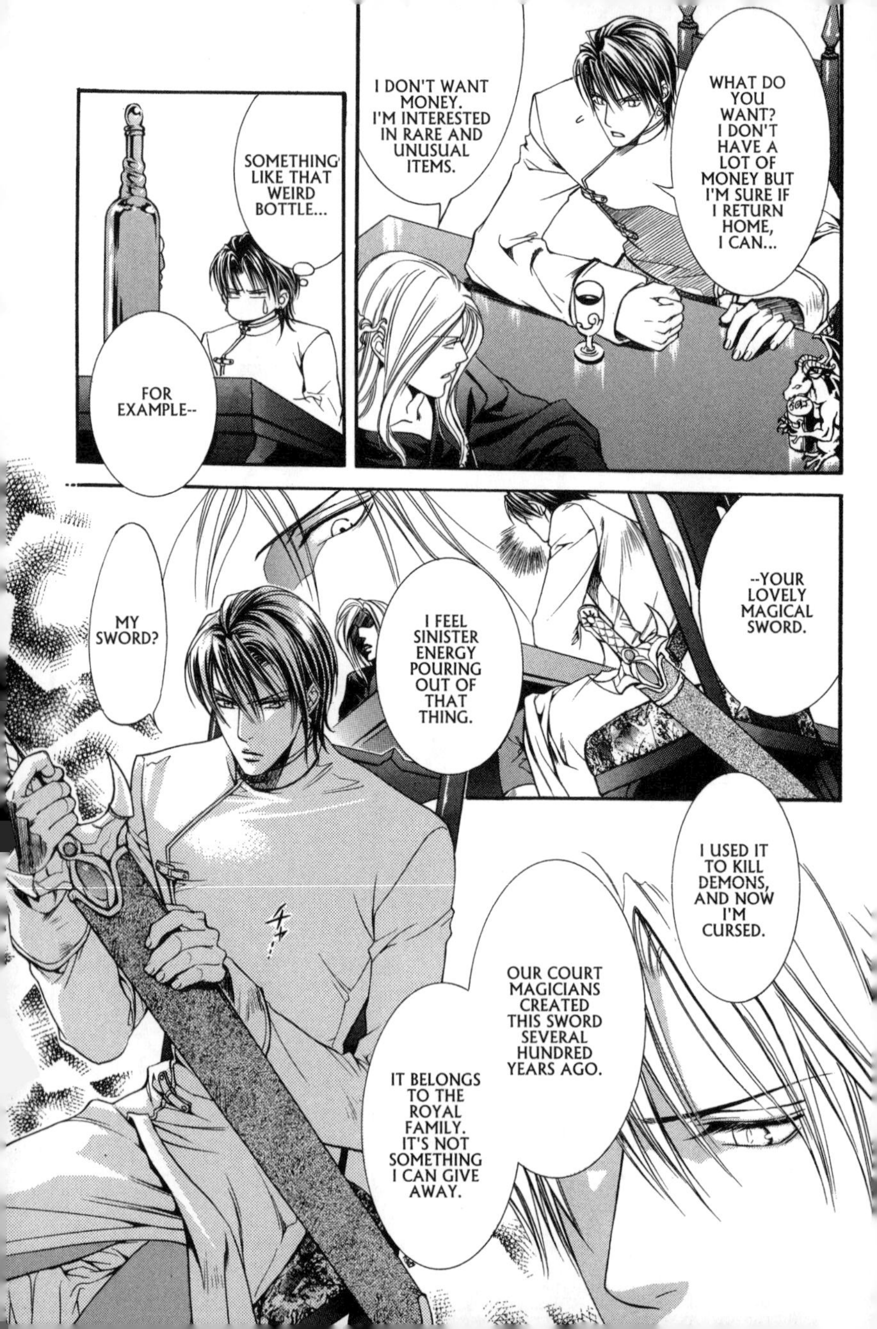
WHAT DO YOU WANT? I DON'T HAVE A LOT OF MONEY BUT I'M SURE IF I RETURN HOME, I CAN...
I DON'T WANT MONEY. I'M INTERESTED IN RARE AND UNUSUAL ITEMS.
SOMETHING LIKE THAT WEIRD BOTTLE...
FOR EXAMPLE--
--YOUR LOVELY MAGICAL SWORD.
I FEEL SINISTER ENERGY POURING OUT OF THAT THING.
MY SWORD?
I USED IT TO KILL DEMONS, AND NOW I'M CURSED.
OUR COURT MAGICIANS CREATED THIS SWORD SEVERAL HUNDRED YEARS AGO.
IT BELONGS TO THE ROYAL FAMILY. IT'S NOT SOMETHING I CAN GIVE AWAY.

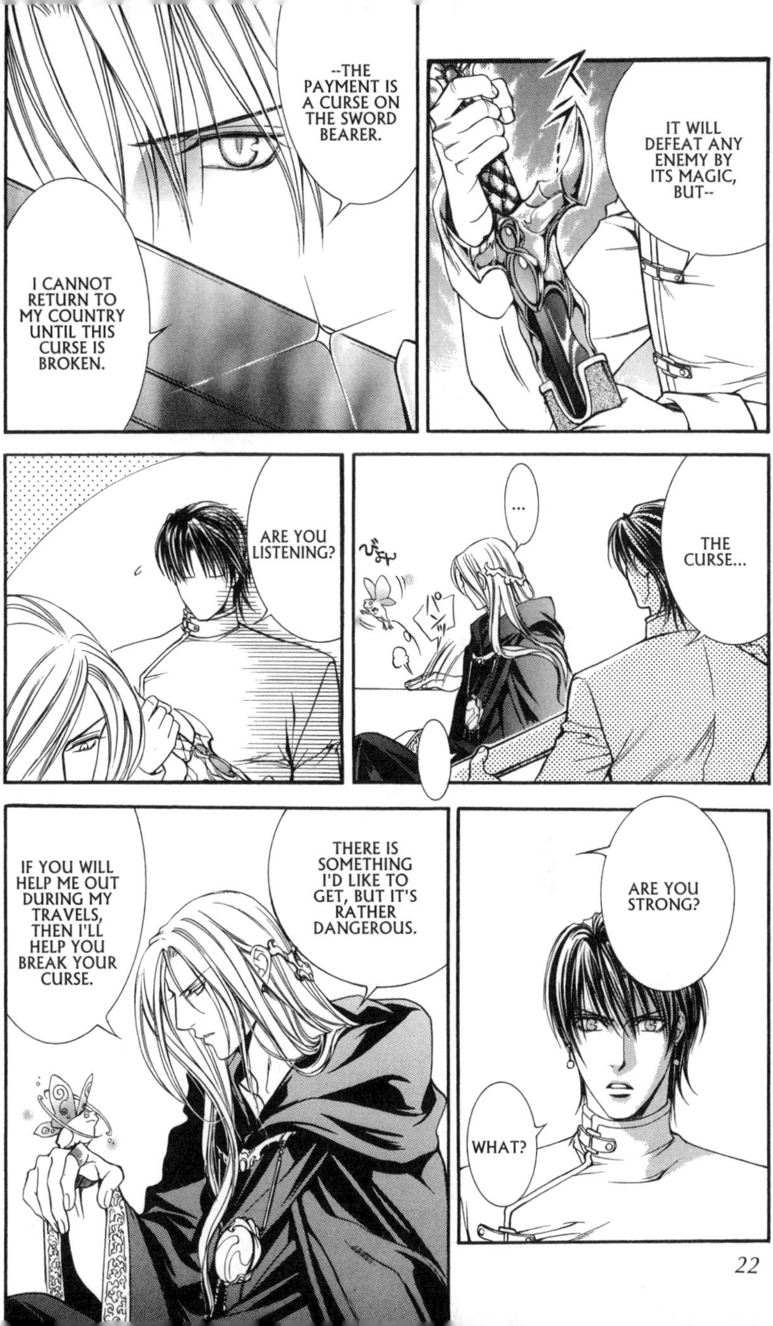
IT WILL DEFEAT ANY ENEMY BY ITS MAGIC, BUT--
--THE PAYMENT IS A CURSE ON THE SWORD BEARER.
I CANNOT RETURN TO MY COUNTRY UNTIL THIS CURSE IS BROKEN.
THE CURSE...
...
ARE YOU LISTENING?
ARE YOU STRONG?
WHAT?
THERE IS SOMETHING I'D LIKE TO GET, BUT IT'S RATHER DANGEROUS.
IF YOU WILL HELP ME OUT DURING MY TRAVELS, THEN I'LL HELP YOU BREAK YOUR CURSE.

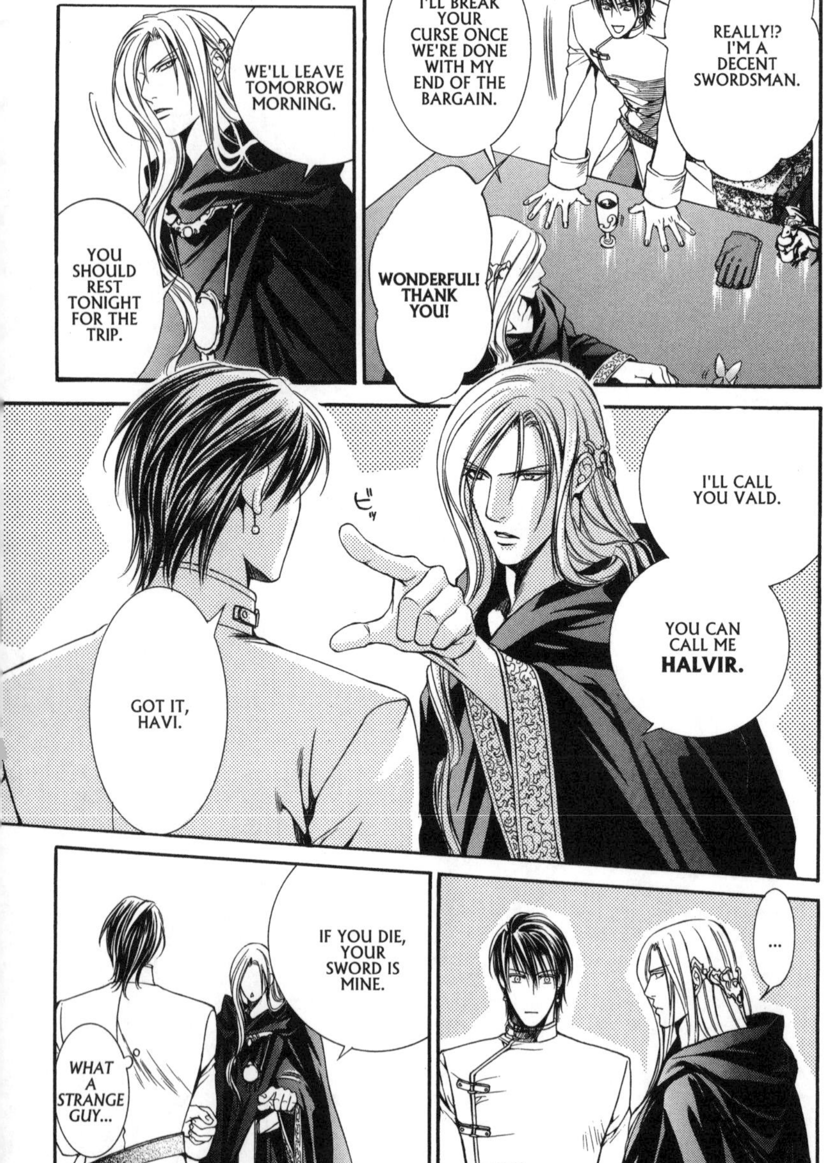
REALLY!? I'M A DECENT SWORDSMAN.
ガタッ
I'LL BREAK YOUR CURSE ONCE WE'RE DONE WITH MY END OF THE BARGAIN.
WONDERFUL! THANK YOU!
WE'LL LEAVE TOMORROW MORNING.
YOU SHOULD REST TONIGHT FOR THE TRIP.
I'LL CALL YOU VALD.
YOU CAN CALL ME HALVIR.
ビッ
GOT IT, HAVI.
...
IF YOU DIE, YOUR SWORD IS MINE.
WHAT A STRANGE GUY...

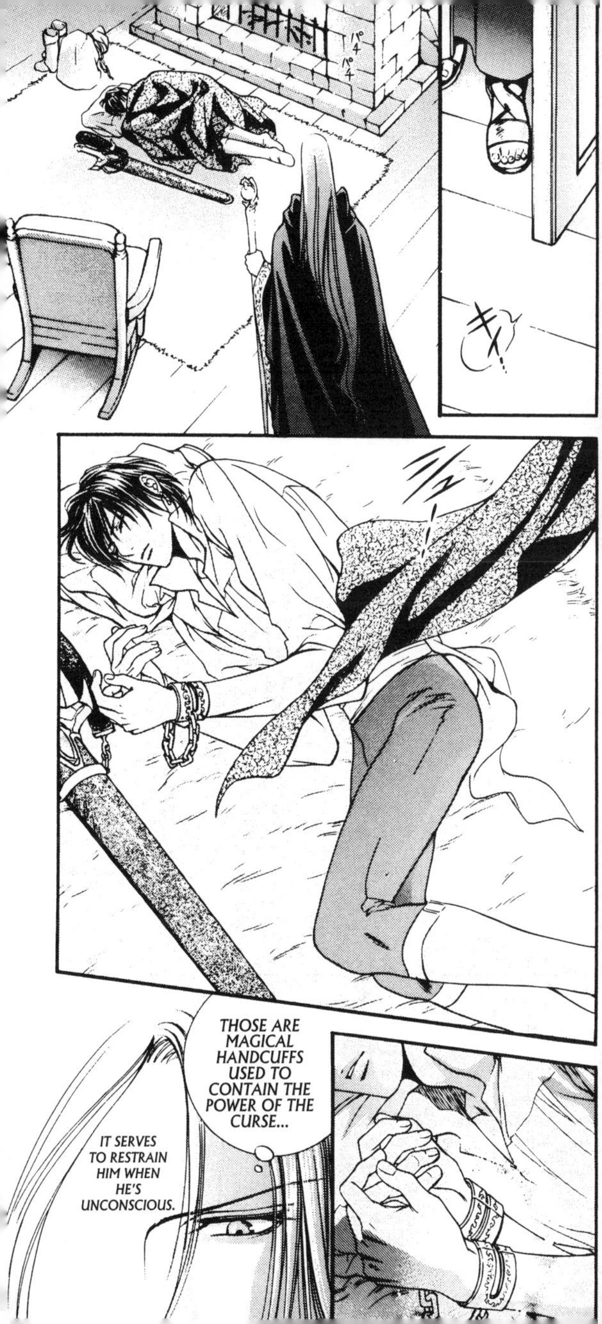
THOSE ARE MAGICAL HANDCUFFS USED TO CONTAIN THE POWER OF THE CURSE...
IT SERVES TO RESTRAIN HIM WHEN HE'S UNCONSCIOUS.

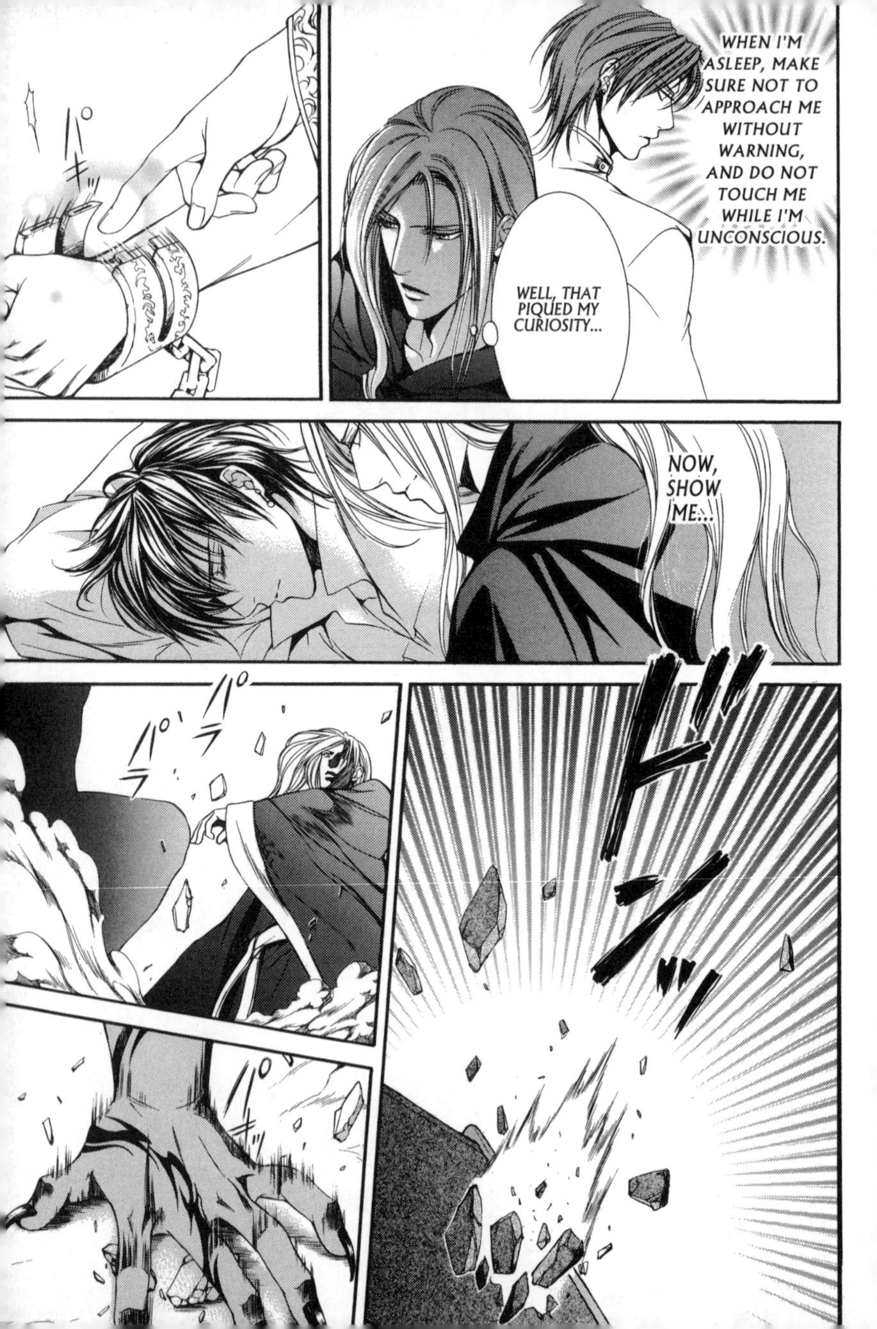
WHEN I'M ASLEEP, MAKE SURE NOT TO APPROACH ME WITHOUT WARNING, AND DO NOT TOUCH ME WHILE I'M UNCONSCIOUS.
WELL, THAT PIQUED MY CURIOSITY...
パキッ
NOW, SHOW ME...
パラ
パラ

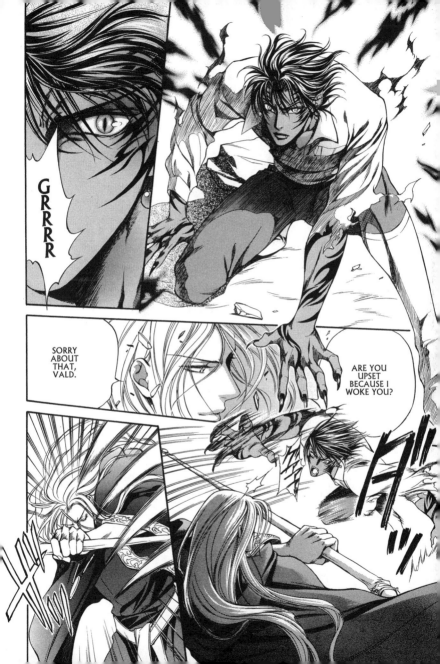

GRRRR

SORRY ABOUT THAT, VALD.

ARE YOU UPSET BECAUSE I WOKE YOU?

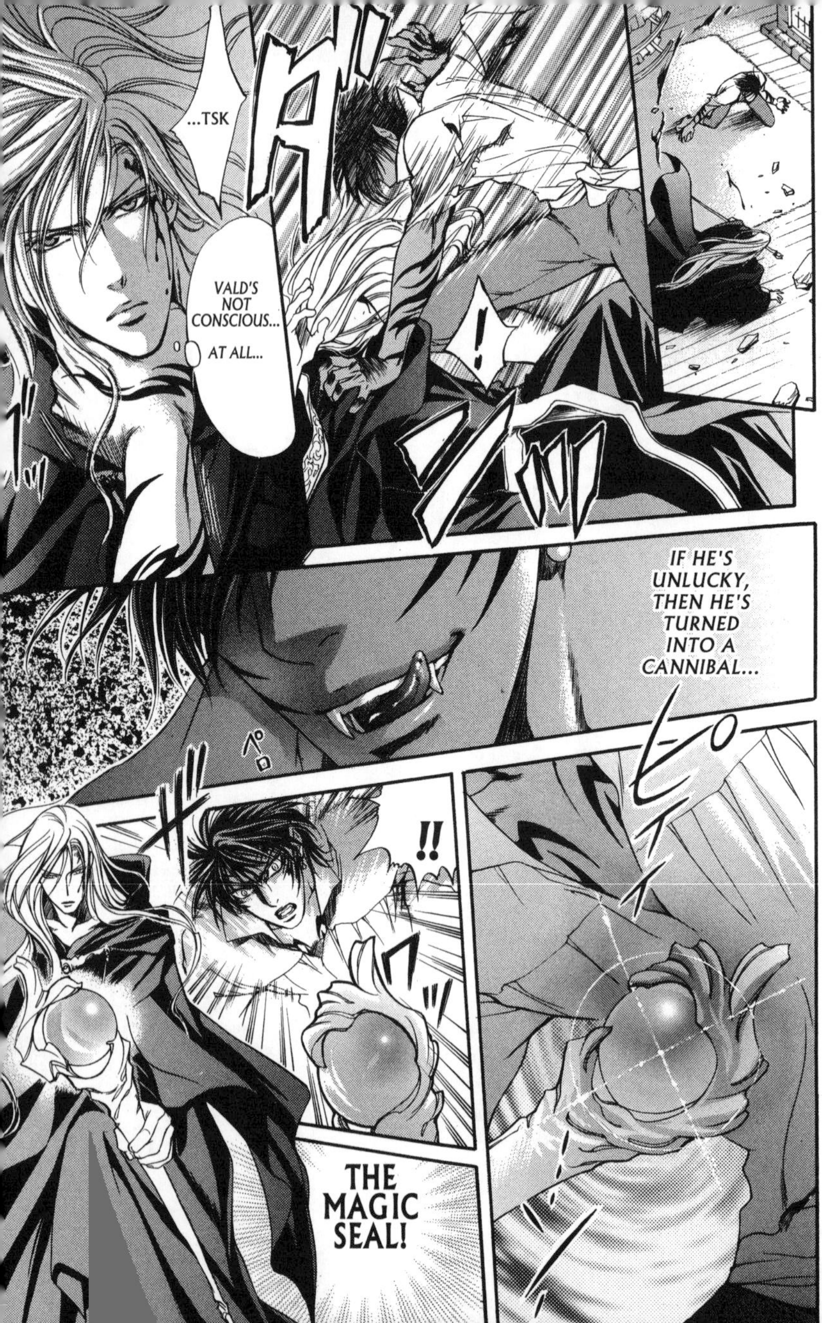
!
...TSK
VALD'S NOT CONSCIOUS...
AT ALL...
IF HE'S UNLUCKY, THEN HE'S TURNED INTO A CANNIBAL...
!!
THE MAGIC SEAL!

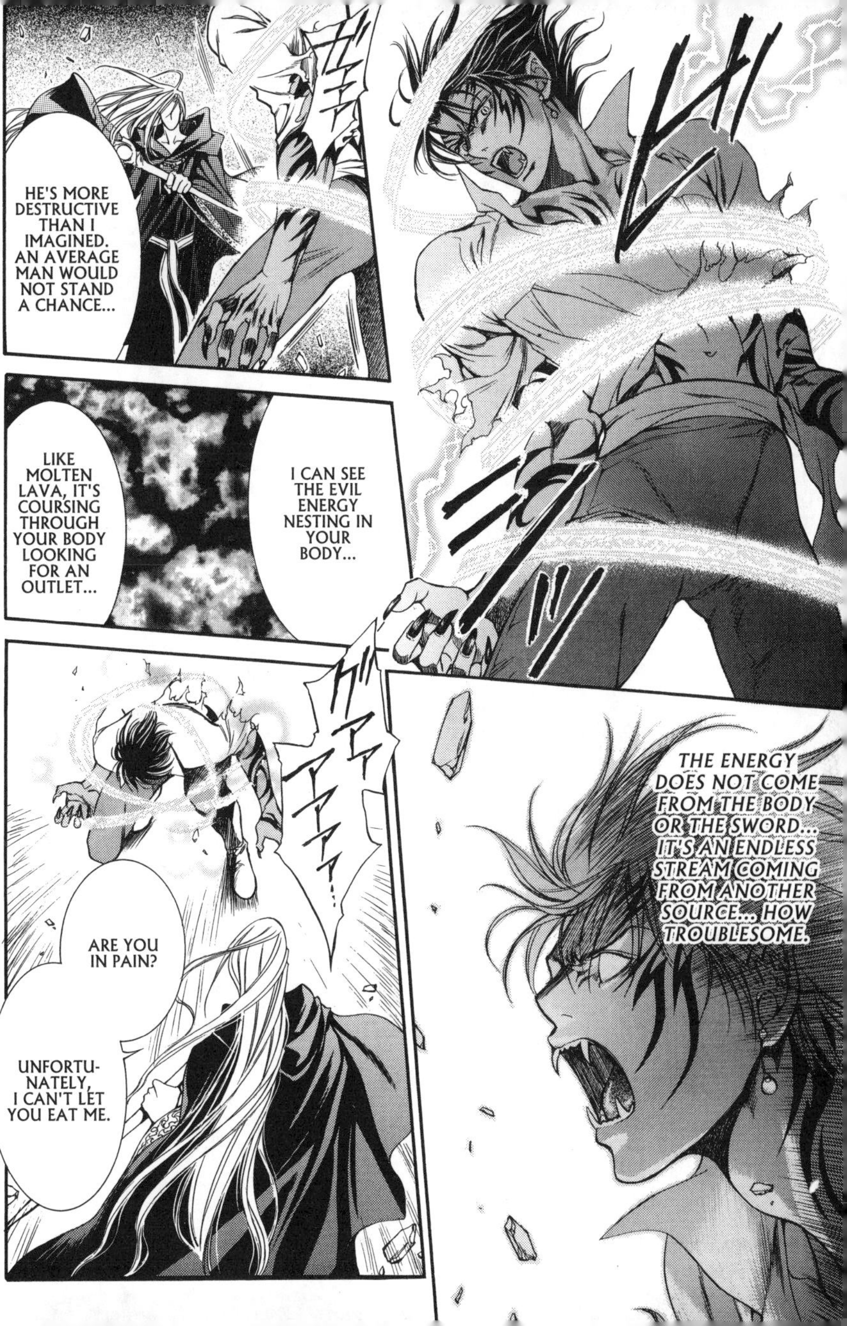
HE'S MORE DESTRUCTIVE THAN I IMAGINED. AN AVERAGE MAN WOULD NOT STAND A CHANCE...
I CAN SEE THE EVIL ENERGY NESTING IN YOUR BODY...
LIKE MOLTEN LAVA, IT'S COURSING THROUGH YOUR BODY LOOKING FOR AN OUTLET...
THE ENERGY DOES NOT COME FROM THE BODY OR THE SWORD... IT'S AN ENDLESS STREAM COMING FROM ANOTHER SOURCE... HOW TROUBLESOME.
ARE YOU IN PAIN?
UNFORTU-NATELY, I CAN'T LET YOU EAT ME.

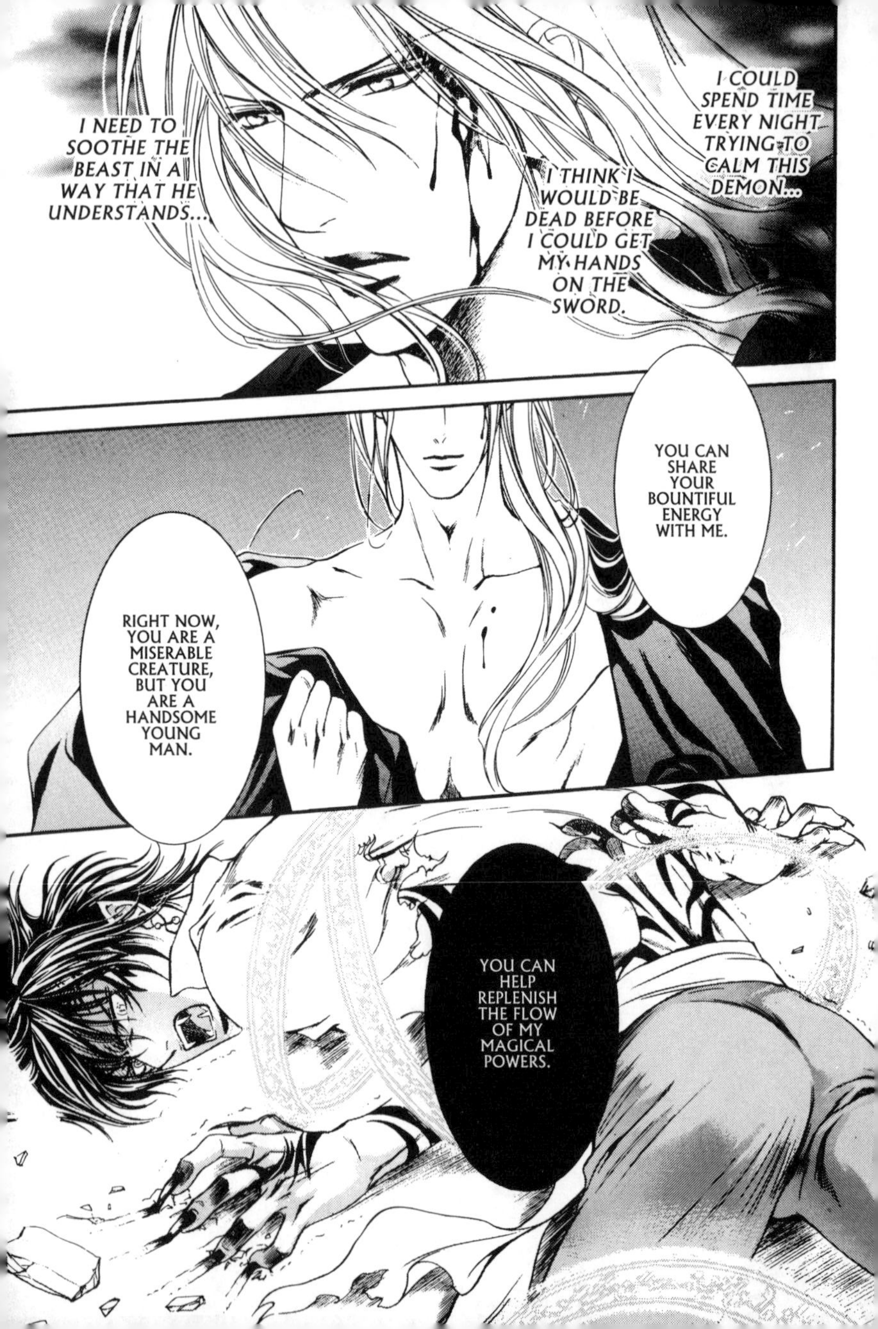
I COULD SPEND TIME EVERY NIGHT TRYING TO CALM THIS DEMON...
I THINK I WOULD BE DEAD BEFORE I COULD GET MY HANDS ON THE SWORD.
I NEED TO SOOTHE THE BEAST IN A WAY THAT HE UNDERSTANDS...
YOU CAN SHARE YOUR BOUNTIFUL ENERGY WITH ME.
RIGHT NOW, YOU ARE A MISERABLE CREATURE, BUT YOU ARE A HANDSOME YOUNG MAN.
YOU CAN HELP REPLENISH THE FLOW OF MY MAGICAL POWERS.

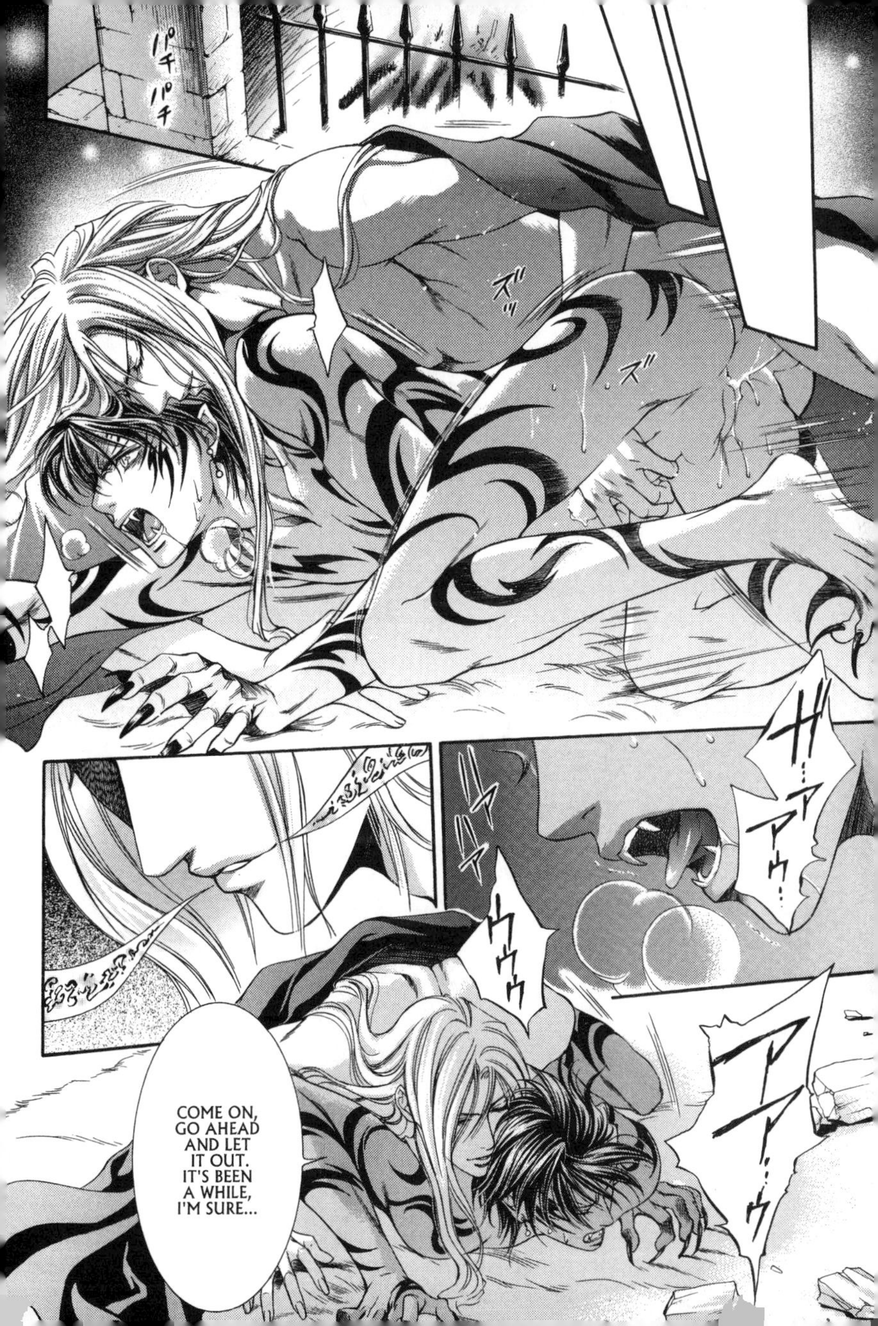
ズッ
ズ
パチ
パチ
ウウウ
COME ON, GO AHEAD AND LET IT OUT. IT'S BEEN A WHILE, I'M SURE...

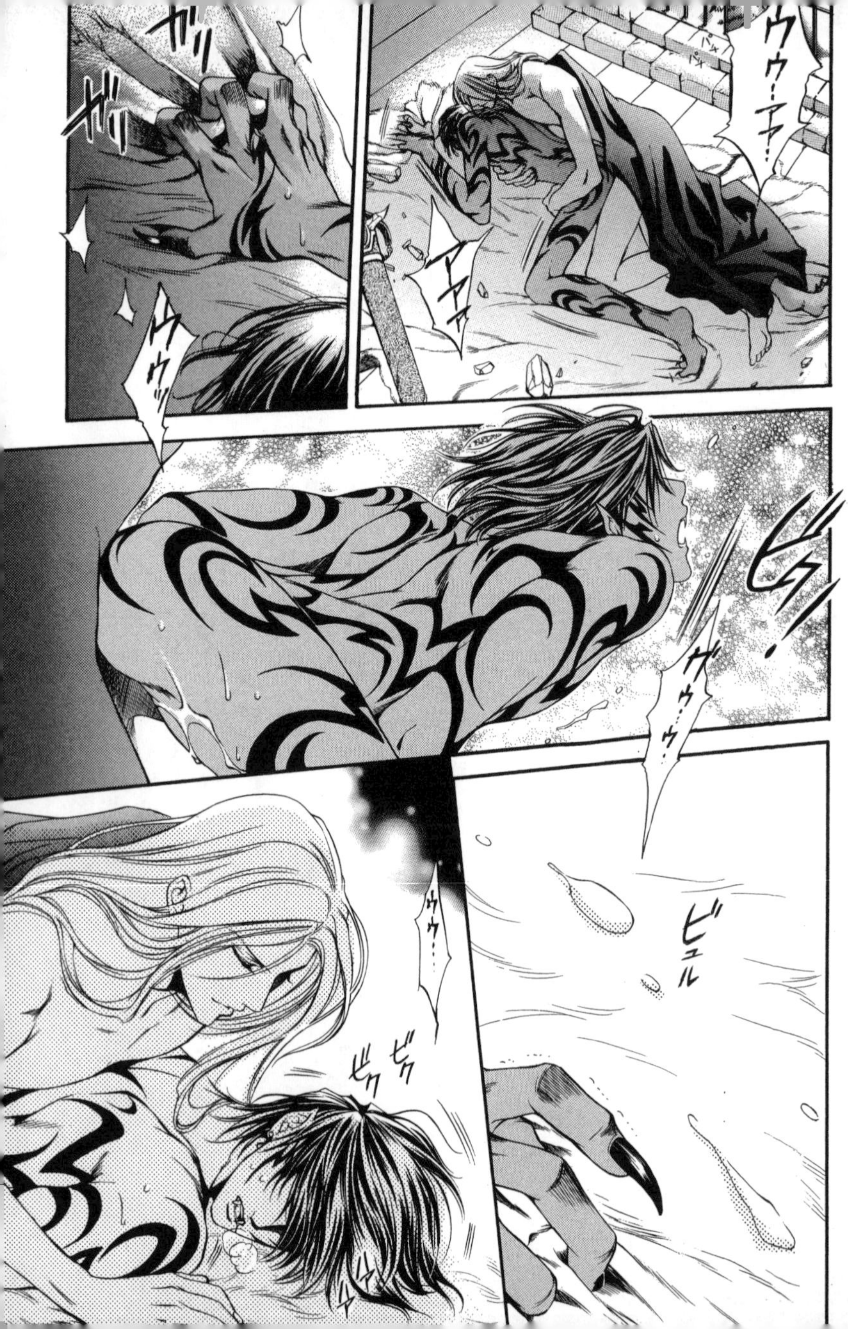

ウウ…アア…
アアア
ガリ
ガリ
ウウッ
ビクッ!!
ヴウ…ウ…
ビュル
ウウ…
ビク ビク

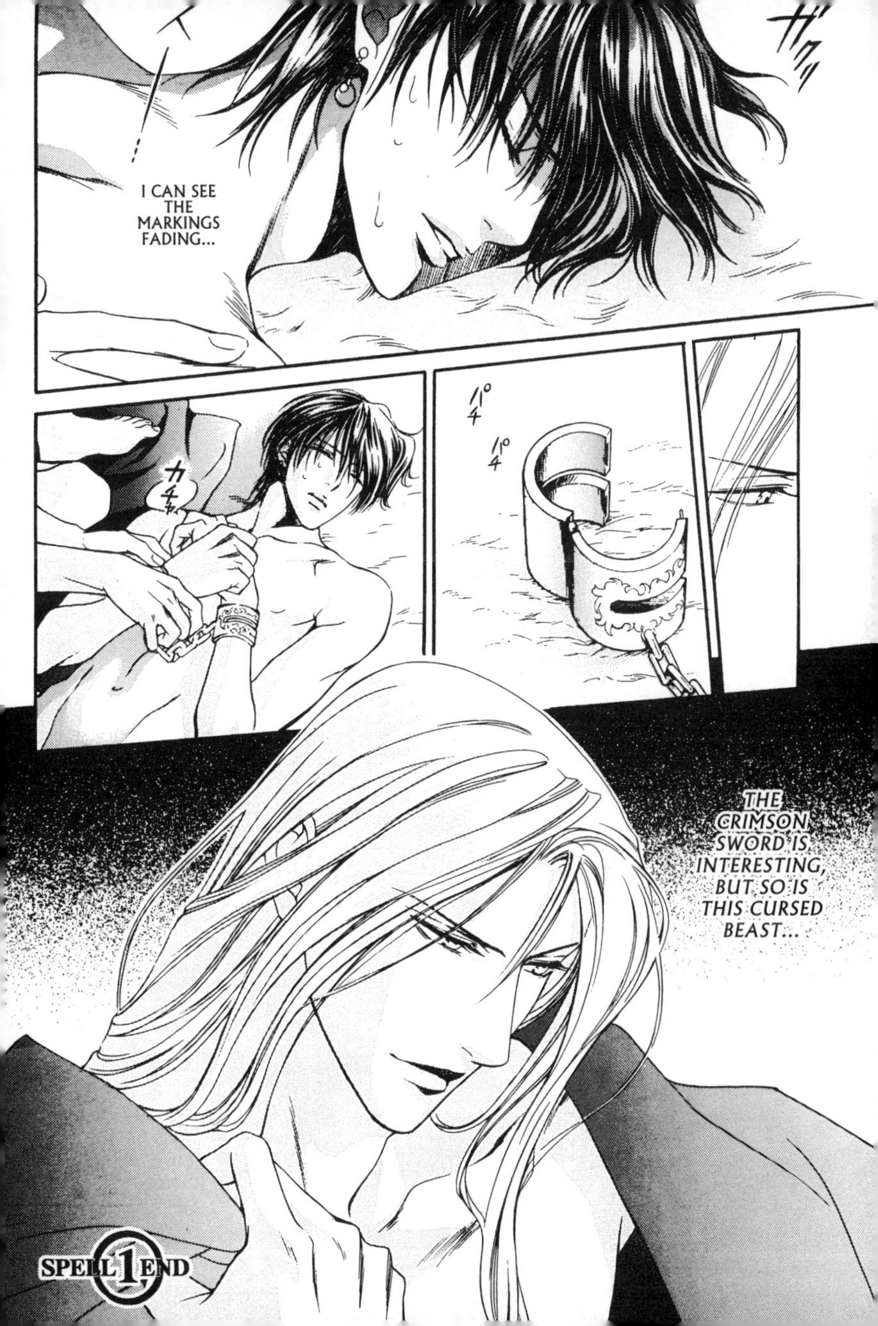
I CAN SEE THE MARKINGS FADING...
THE CRIMSON SWORD IS INTERESTING, BUT SO IS THIS CURSED BEAST...
SPELL 1 END

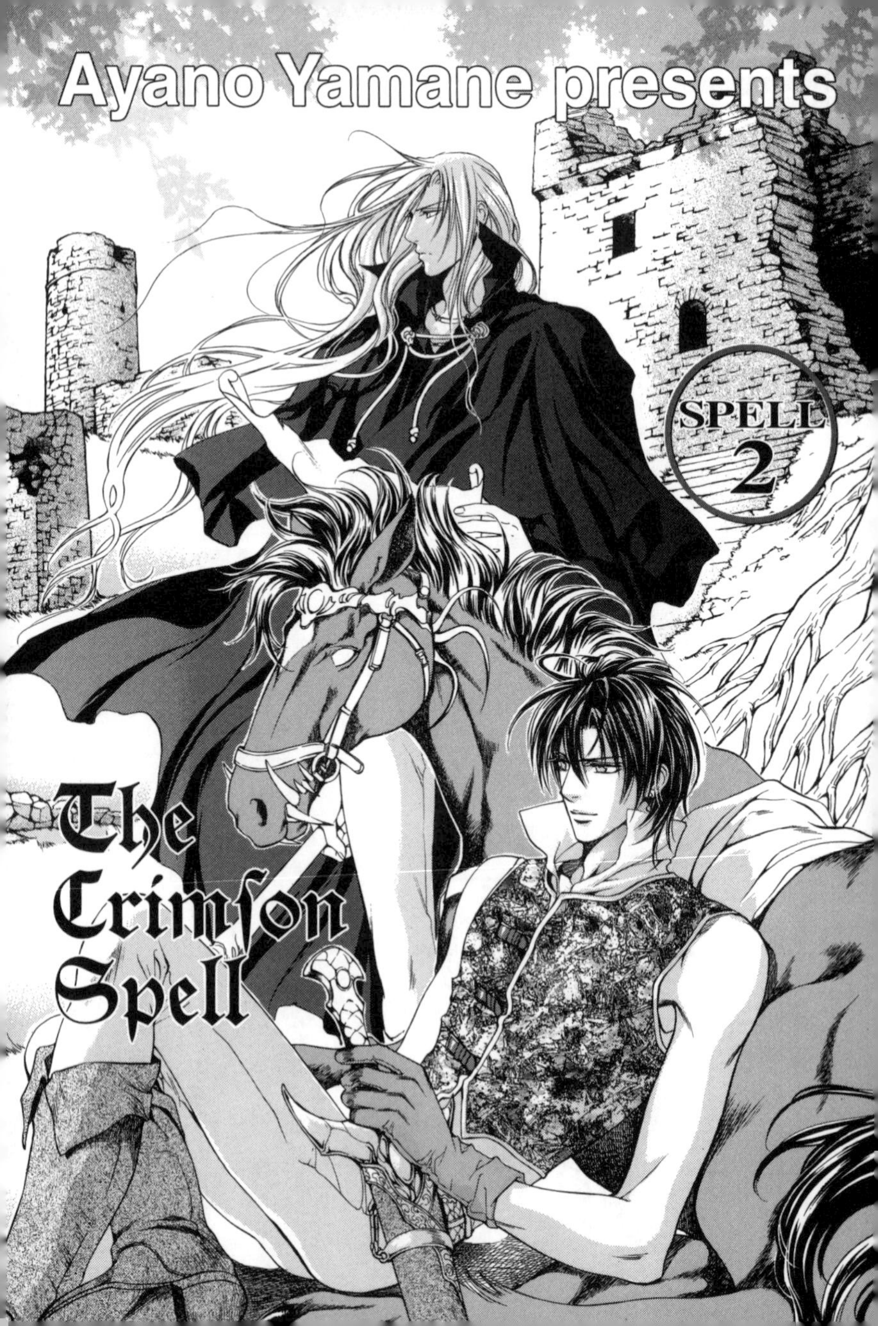

Ayano Yamane presents
SPELL 2
The Crimson Spell

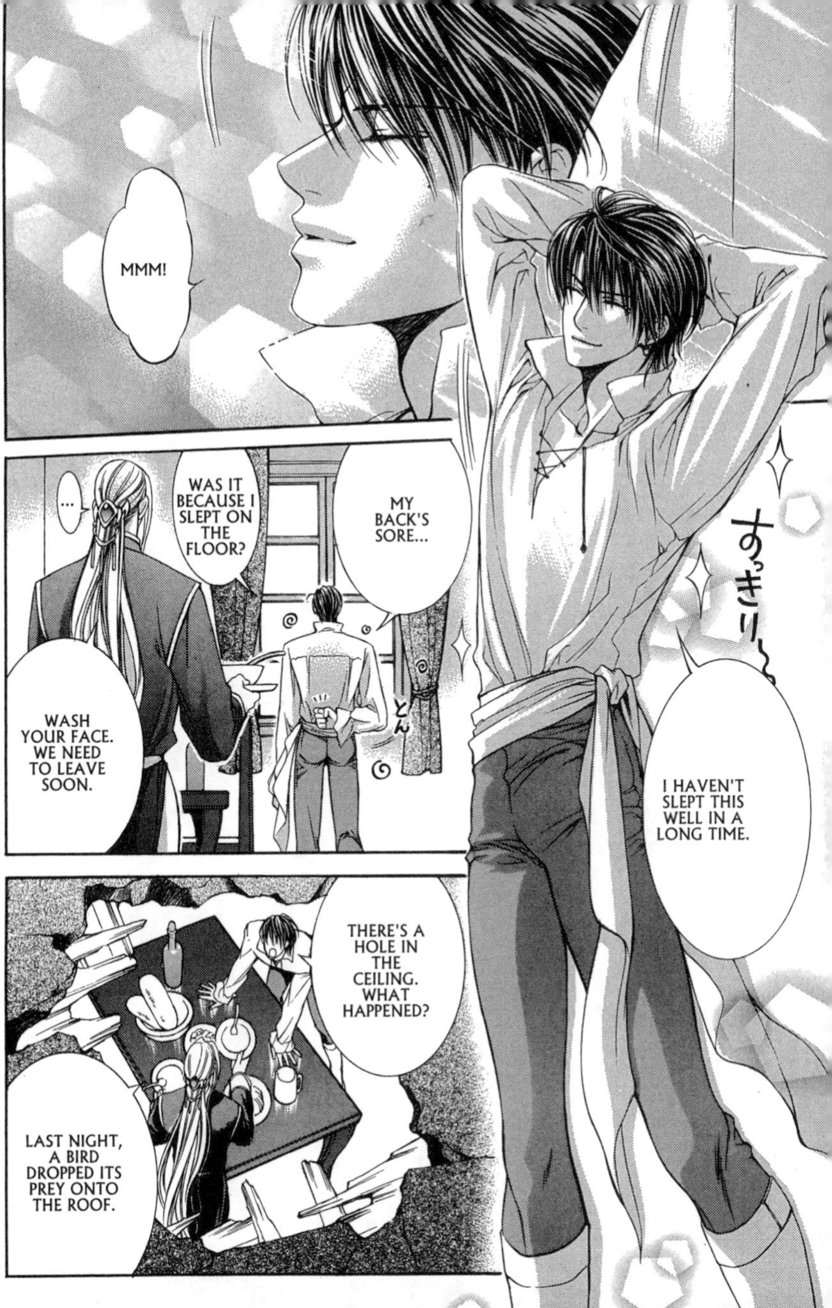
すっきり〜
I HAVEN'T SLEPT THIS WELL IN A LONG TIME.
MMM!
MY BACK'S SORE...
とん
WAS IT BECAUSE I SLEPT ON THE FLOOR?
...
WASH YOUR FACE. WE NEED TO LEAVE SOON.
THERE'S A HOLE IN THE CEILING. WHAT HAPPENED?
LAST NIGHT, A BIRD DROPPED ITS PREY ONTO THE ROOF.

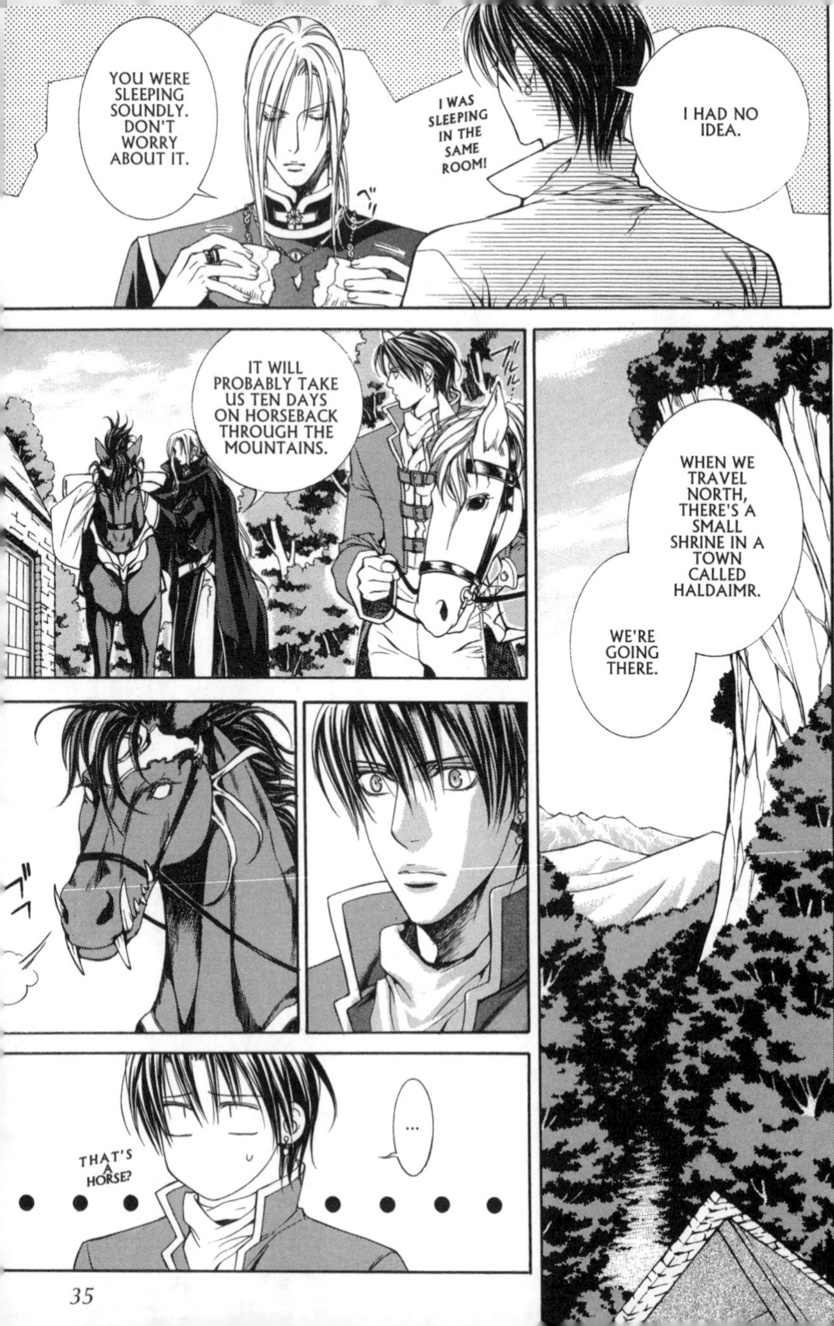
I HAD NO IDEA.
I WAS SLEEPING IN THE SAME ROOM!
YOU WERE SLEEPING SOUNDLY. DON'T WORRY ABOUT IT.
WHEN WE TRAVEL NORTH, THERE'S A SMALL SHRINE IN A TOWN CALLED HALDAIMR.
WE'RE GOING THERE.
IT WILL PROBABLY TAKE US TEN DAYS ON HORSEBACK THROUGH THE MOUNTAINS.
...
THAT'S A HORSE?

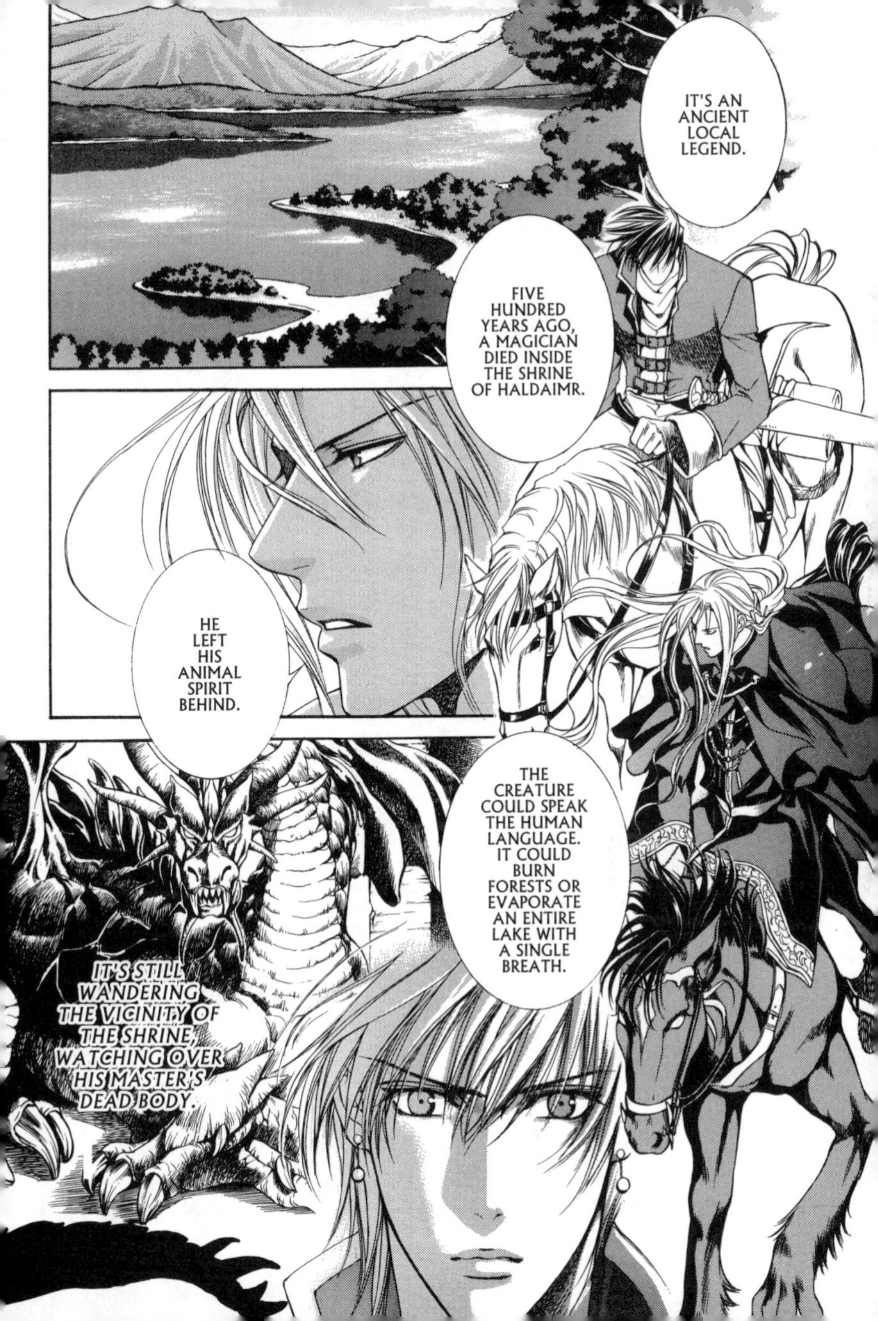
IT'S AN ANCIENT LOCAL LEGEND.
FIVE HUNDRED YEARS AGO, A MAGICIAN DIED INSIDE THE SHRINE OF HALDAIMR.
HE LEFT HIS ANIMAL SPIRIT BEHIND.
THE CREATURE COULD SPEAK THE HUMAN LANGUAGE. IT COULD BURN FORESTS OR EVAPORATE AN ENTIRE LAKE WITH A SINGLE BREATH.
IT'S STILL WANDERING THE VICINITY OF THE SHRINE, WATCHING OVER HIS MASTER'S DEAD BODY.

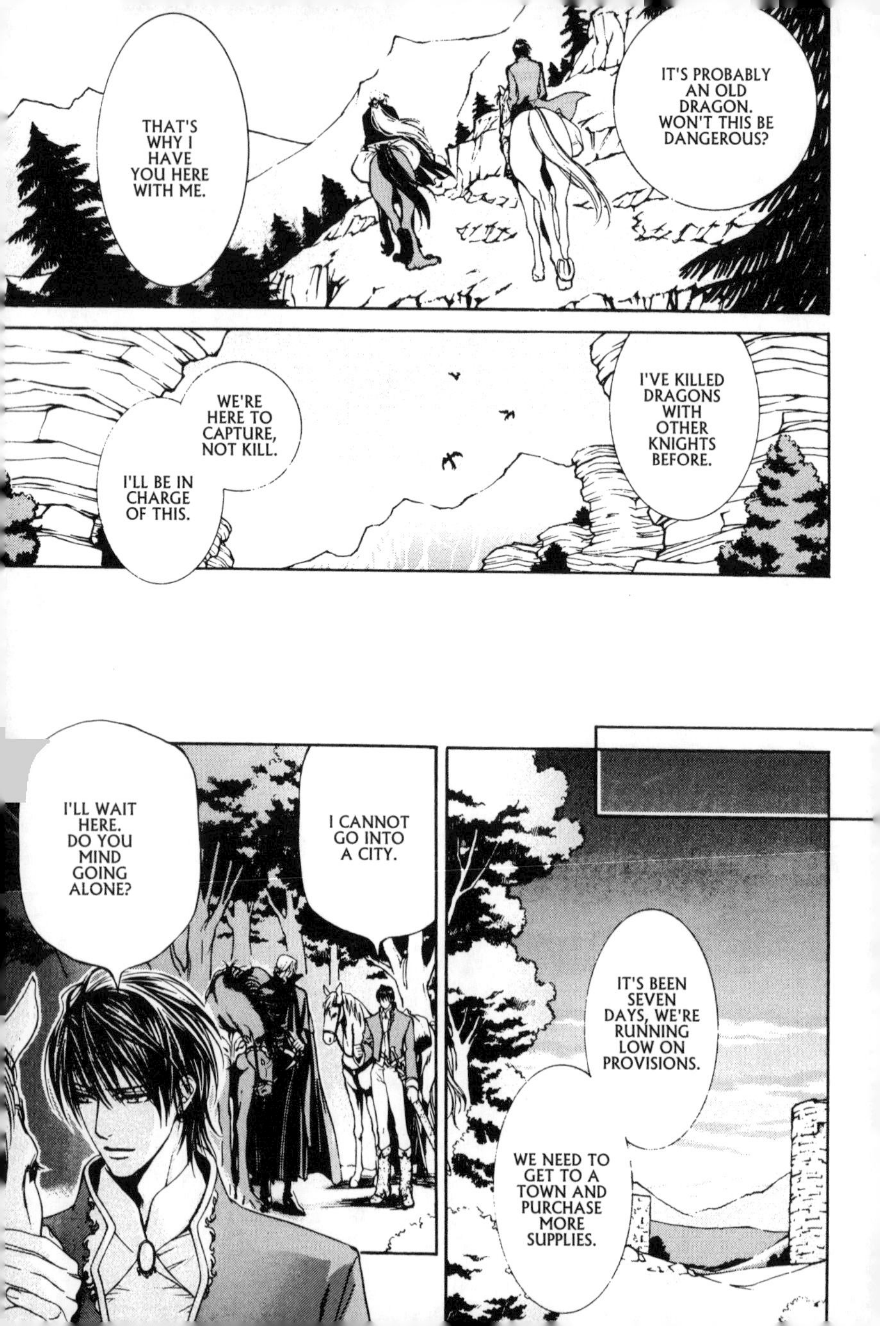
IT'S PROBABLY AN OLD DRAGON. WON'T THIS BE DANGEROUS?
THAT'S WHY I HAVE YOU HERE WITH ME.
I'VE KILLED DRAGONS WITH OTHER KNIGHTS BEFORE.
WE'RE HERE TO CAPTURE, NOT KILL.
I'LL BE IN CHARGE OF THIS.
IT'S BEEN SEVEN DAYS, WE'RE RUNNING LOW ON PROVISIONS.
WE NEED TO GET TO A TOWN AND PURCHASE MORE SUPPLIES.
I CANNOT GO INTO A CITY.
I'LL WAIT HERE. DO YOU MIND GOING ALONE?

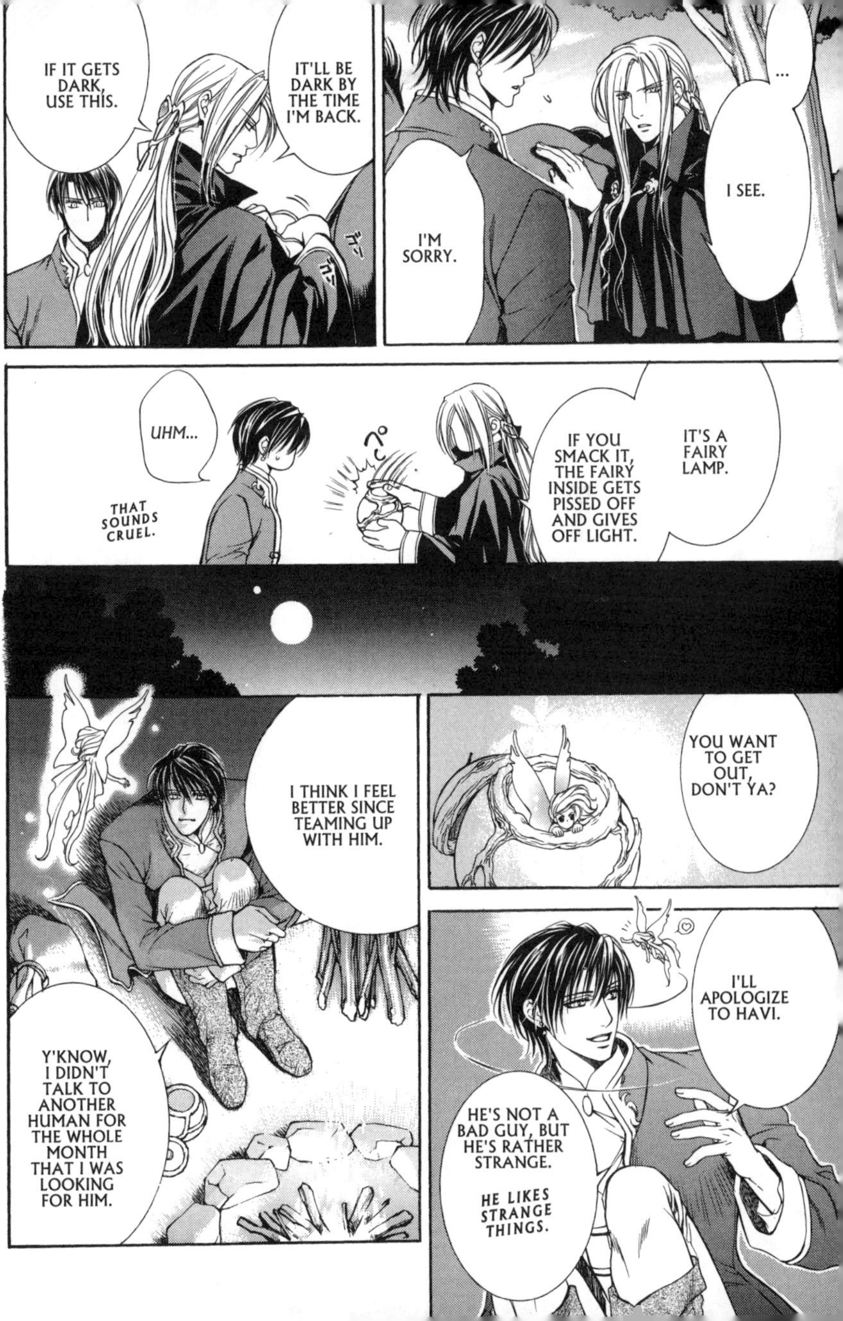
...
I SEE.
I'M SORRY.
IT'LL BE DARK BY THE TIME I'M BACK.
IF IT GETS DARK, USE THIS.
IT'S A FAIRY LAMP.
IF YOU SMACK IT, THE FAIRY INSIDE GETS PISSED OFF AND GIVES OFF LIGHT.
UHM...
THAT SOUNDS CRUEL.
YOU WANT TO GET OUT, DON'T YA?
I'LL APOLOGIZE TO HAVI.
HE'S NOT A BAD GUY, BUT HE'S RATHER STRANGE.
HE LIKES STRANGE THINGS.
I THINK I FEEL BETTER SINCE TEAMING UP WITH HIM.
Y'KNOW, I DIDN'T TALK TO ANOTHER HUMAN FOR THE WHOLE MONTH THAT I WAS LOOKING FOR HIM.

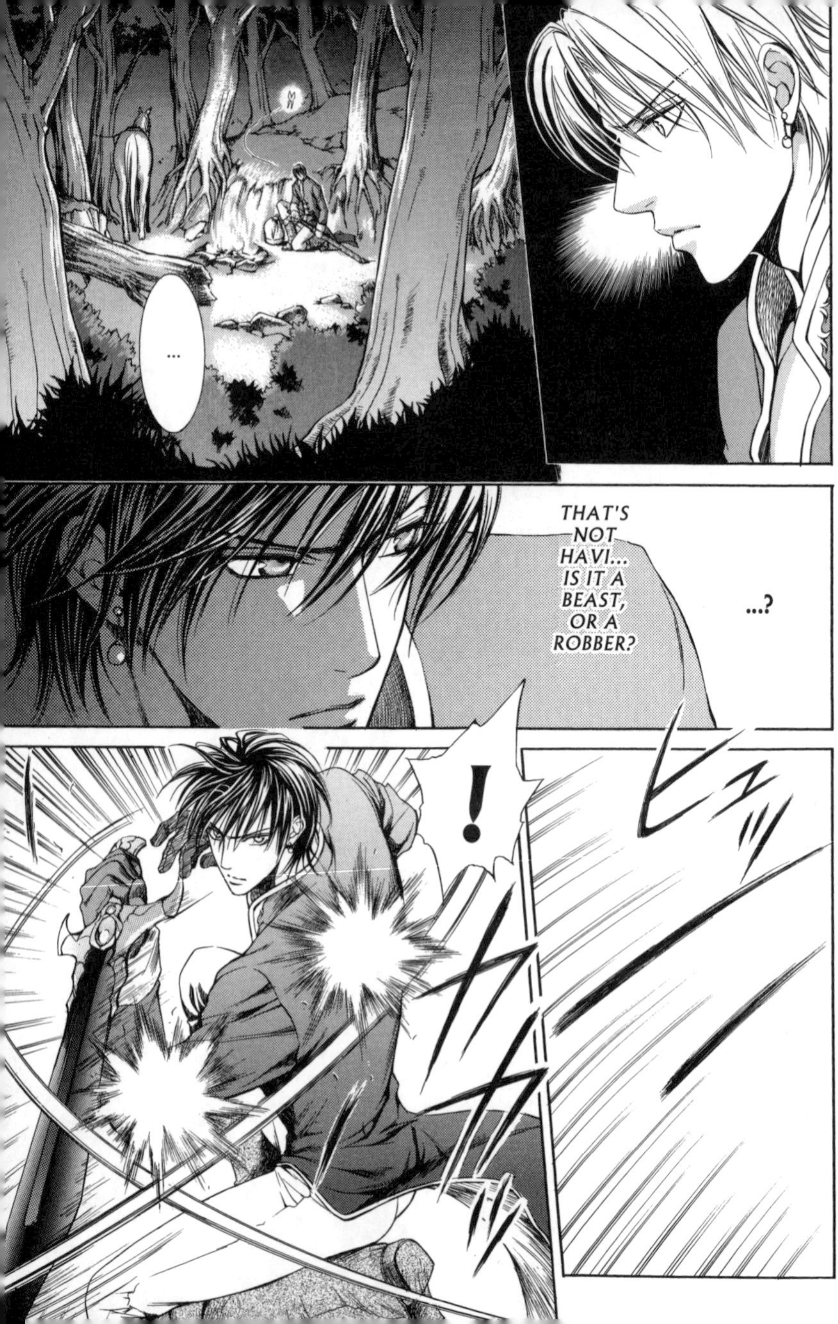
...
...?
THAT'S NOT HAVI... IS IT A BEAST, OR A ROBBER?
!

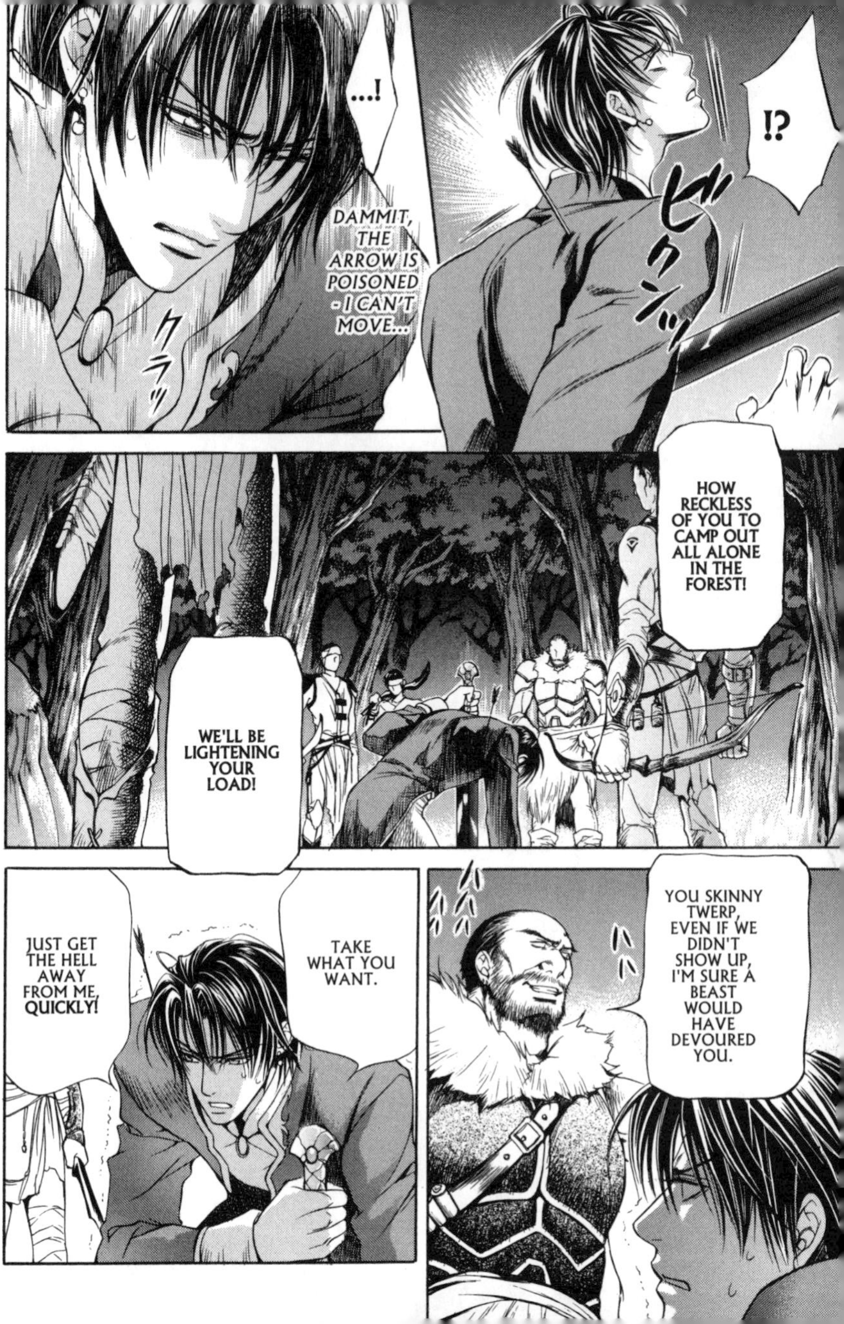
!?
ビクンッ
...!
DAMMIT, THE ARROW IS POISONED - I CAN'T MOVE...
クラッ
HOW RECKLESS OF YOU TO CAMP OUT ALL ALONE IN THE FOREST!
WE'LL BE LIGHTENING YOUR LOAD!
ハハハ
ハハ
YOU SKINNY TWERP, EVEN IF WE DIDN'T SHOW UP, I'M SURE A BEAST WOULD HAVE DEVOURED YOU.
TAKE WHAT YOU WANT.
JUST GET THE HELL AWAY FROM ME, **QUICKLY!**

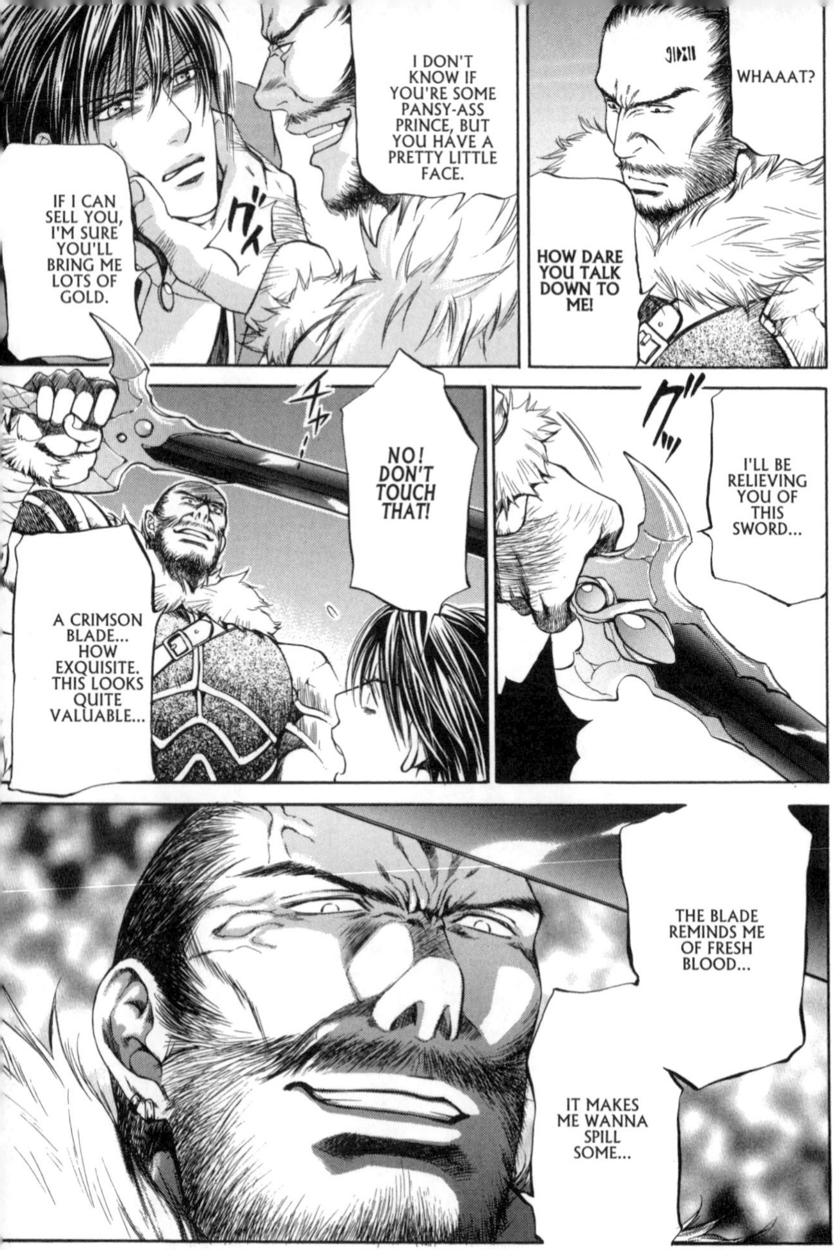
WHAAAT?
HOW DARE YOU TALK DOWN TO ME!
I DON'T KNOW IF YOU'RE SOME PANSY-ASS PRINCE, BUT YOU HAVE A PRETTY LITTLE FACE.
グイ
IF I CAN SELL YOU, I'M SURE YOU'LL BRING ME LOTS OF GOLD.
グッ
I'LL BE RELIEVING YOU OF THIS SWORD...
チャ…
NO! DON'T TOUCH THAT!
A CRIMSON BLADE... HOW EXQUISITE. THIS LOOKS QUITE VALUABLE...
THE BLADE REMINDS ME OF FRESH BLOOD...
IT MAKES ME WANNA SPILL SOME...

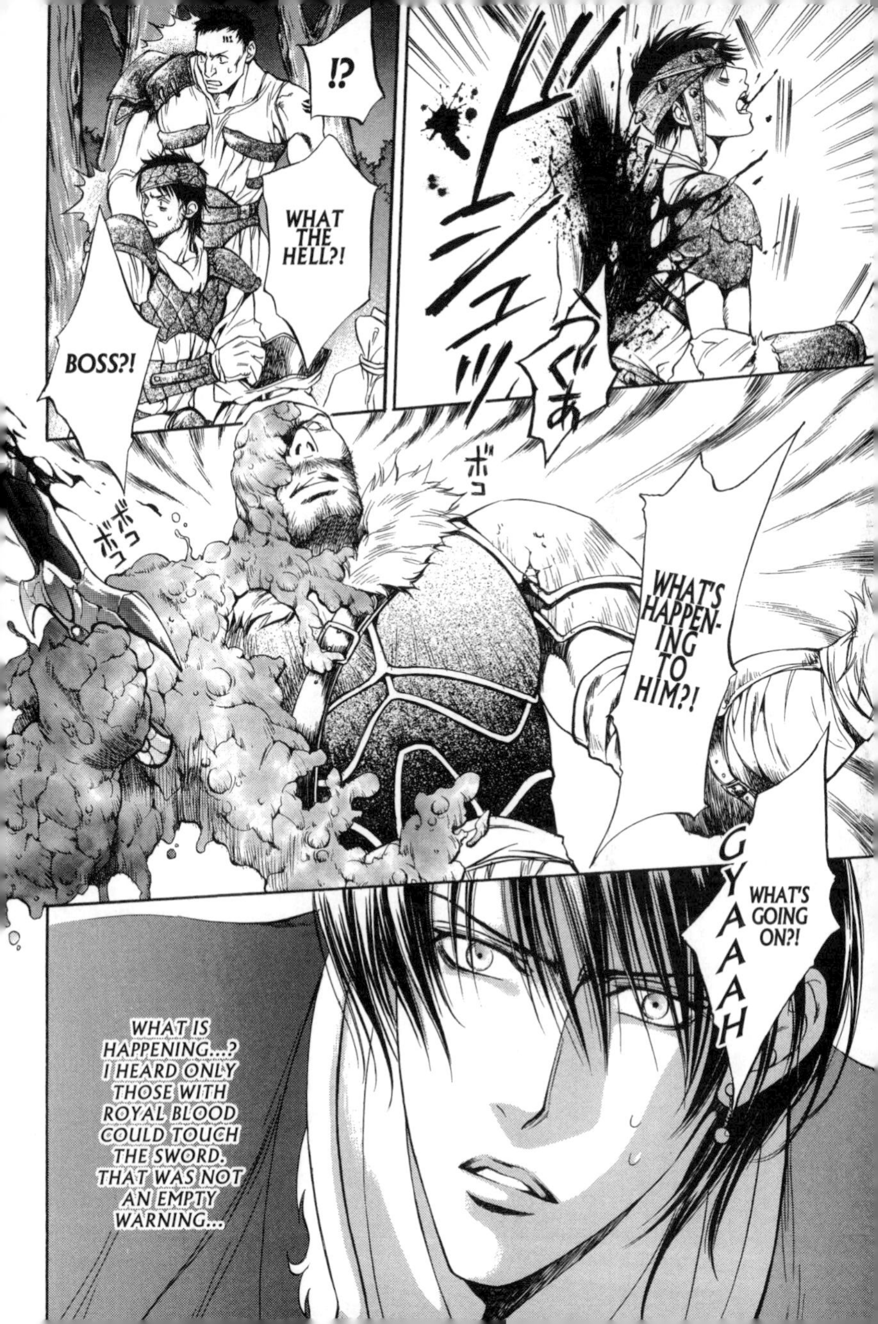
ドシュッ
うぐあ
!?
WHAT THE HELL?!
BOSS?!
WHAT'S HAPPENING TO HIM?!
GYAAAH
ボコ
ボコボコ
WHAT'S GOING ON?!
WHAT IS HAPPENING...? I HEARD ONLY THOSE WITH ROYAL BLOOD COULD TOUCH THE SWORD. THAT WAS NOT AN EMPTY WARNING...

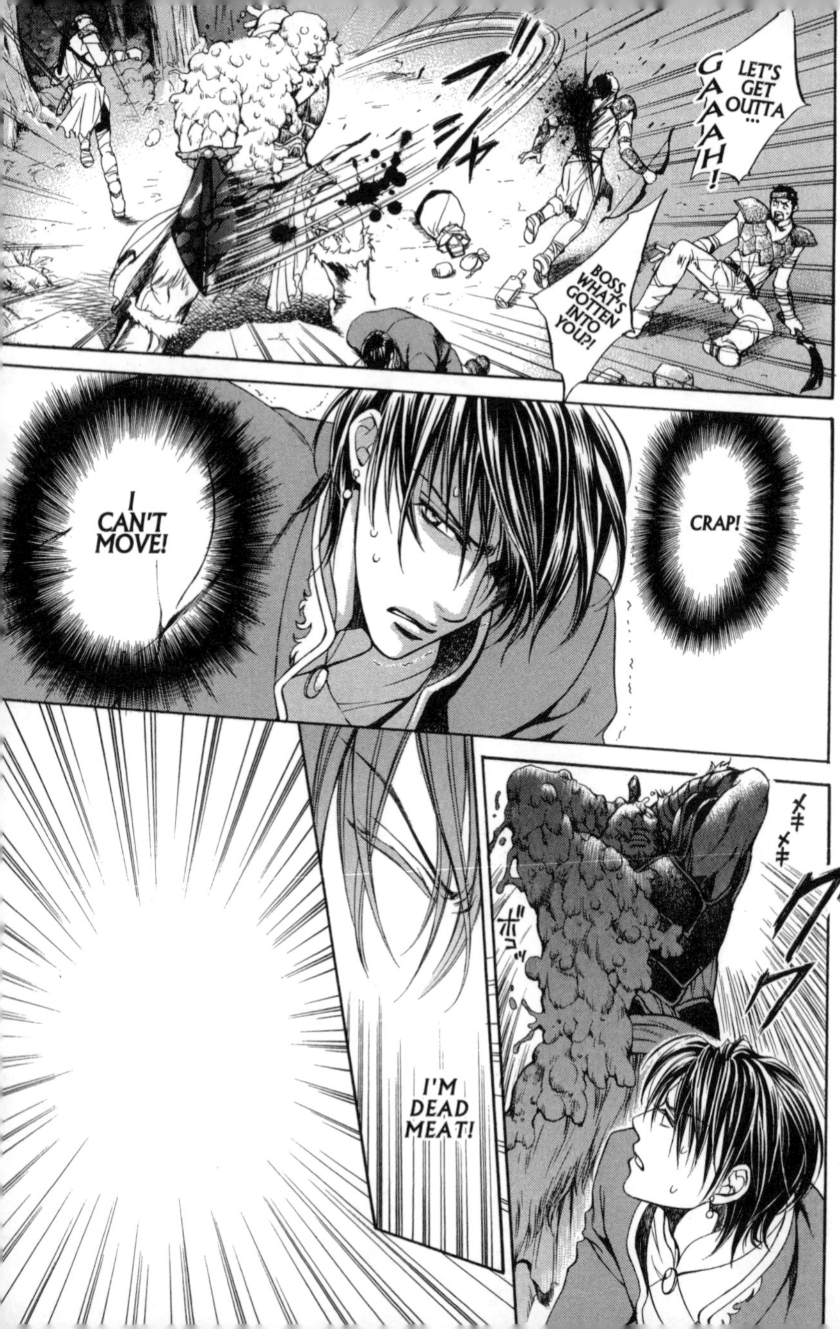
LET'S GET OUTTA...
GAAAAH!
BOSS, WHAT'S GOTTEN INTO YOU?!
CRAP!
I CAN'T MOVE!
I'M DEAD MEAT!

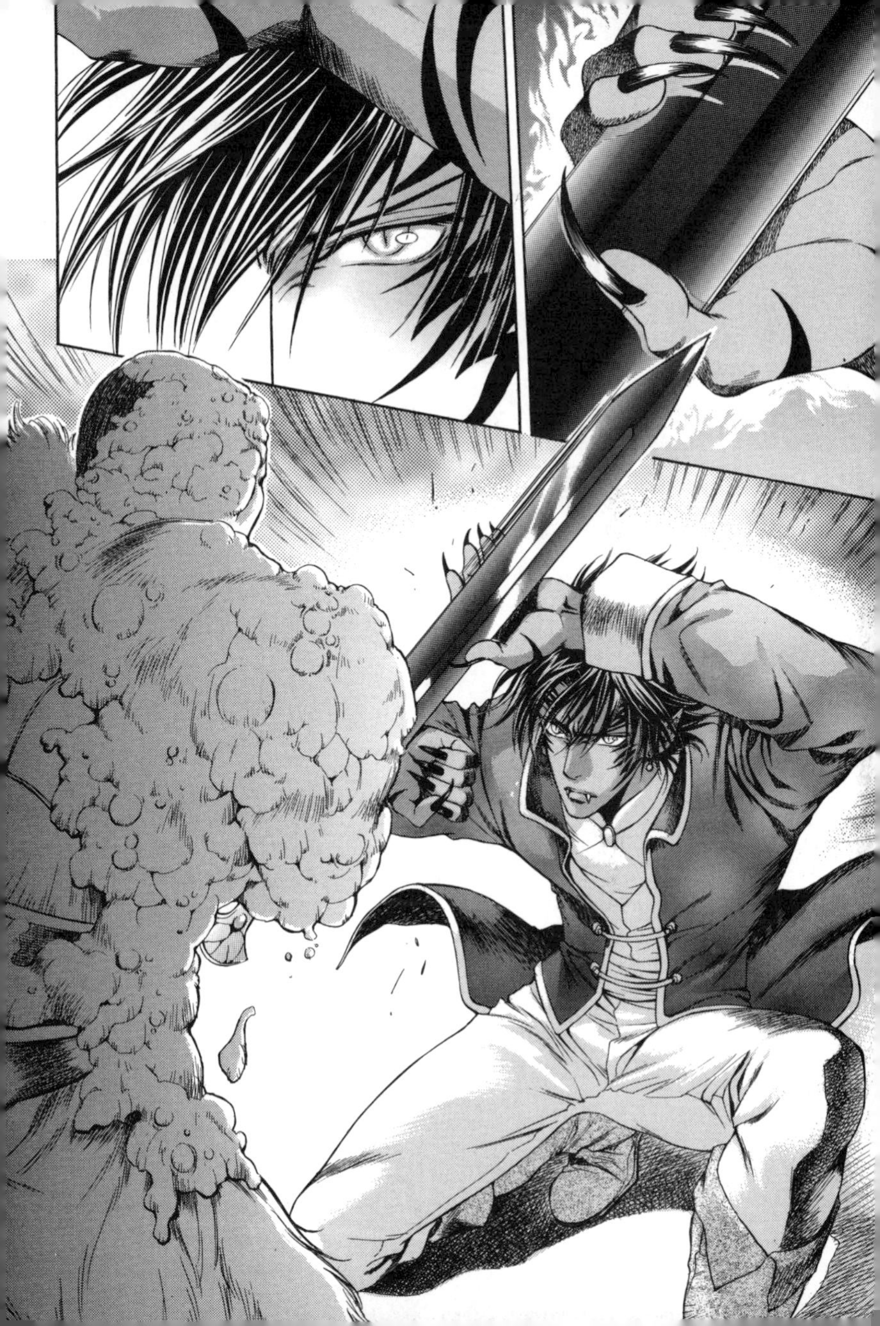

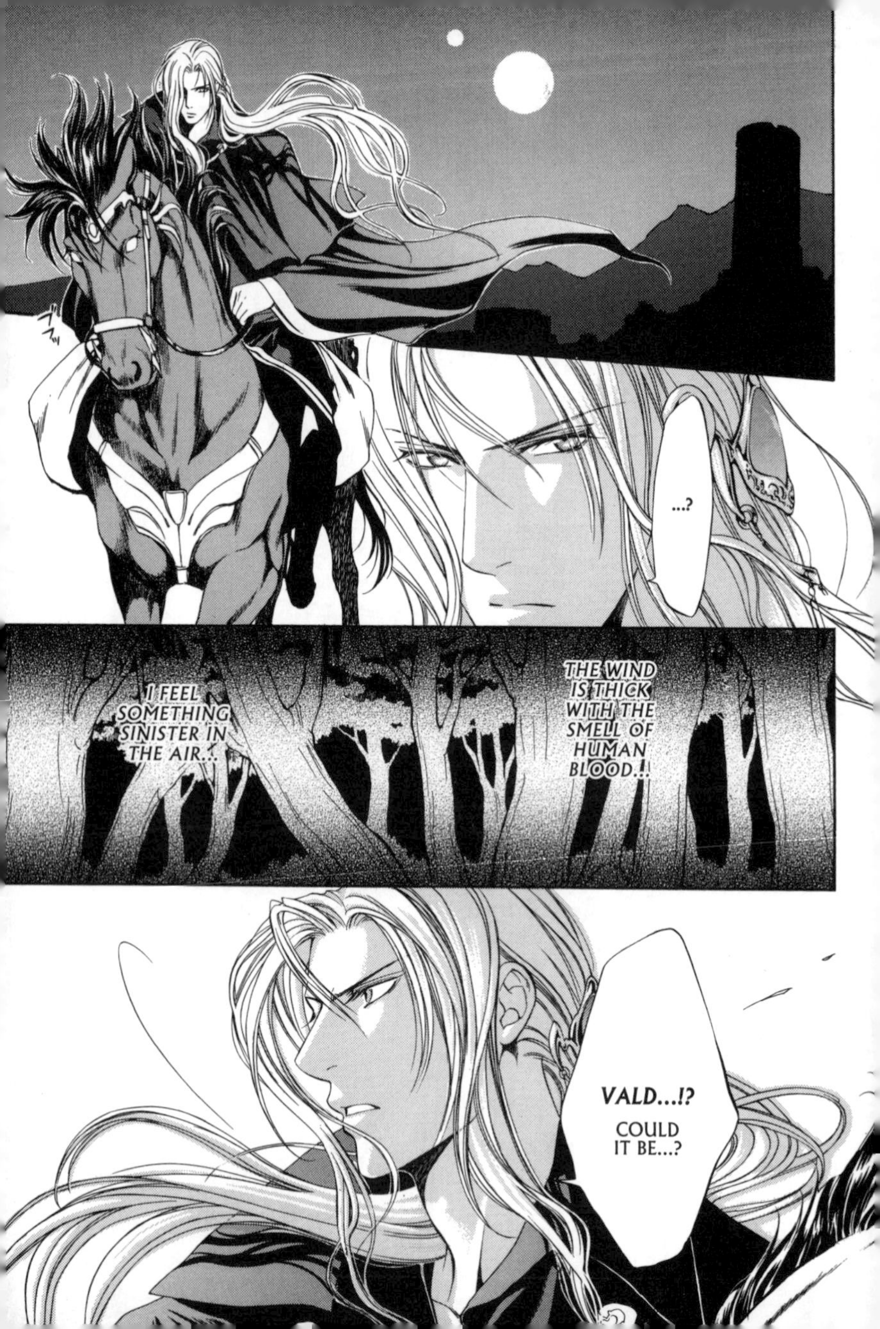
...?
THE WIND IS THICK WITH THE SMELL OF HUMAN BLOOD...
I FEEL SOMETHING SINISTER IN THE AIR...
VALD...!?
COULD IT BE...?

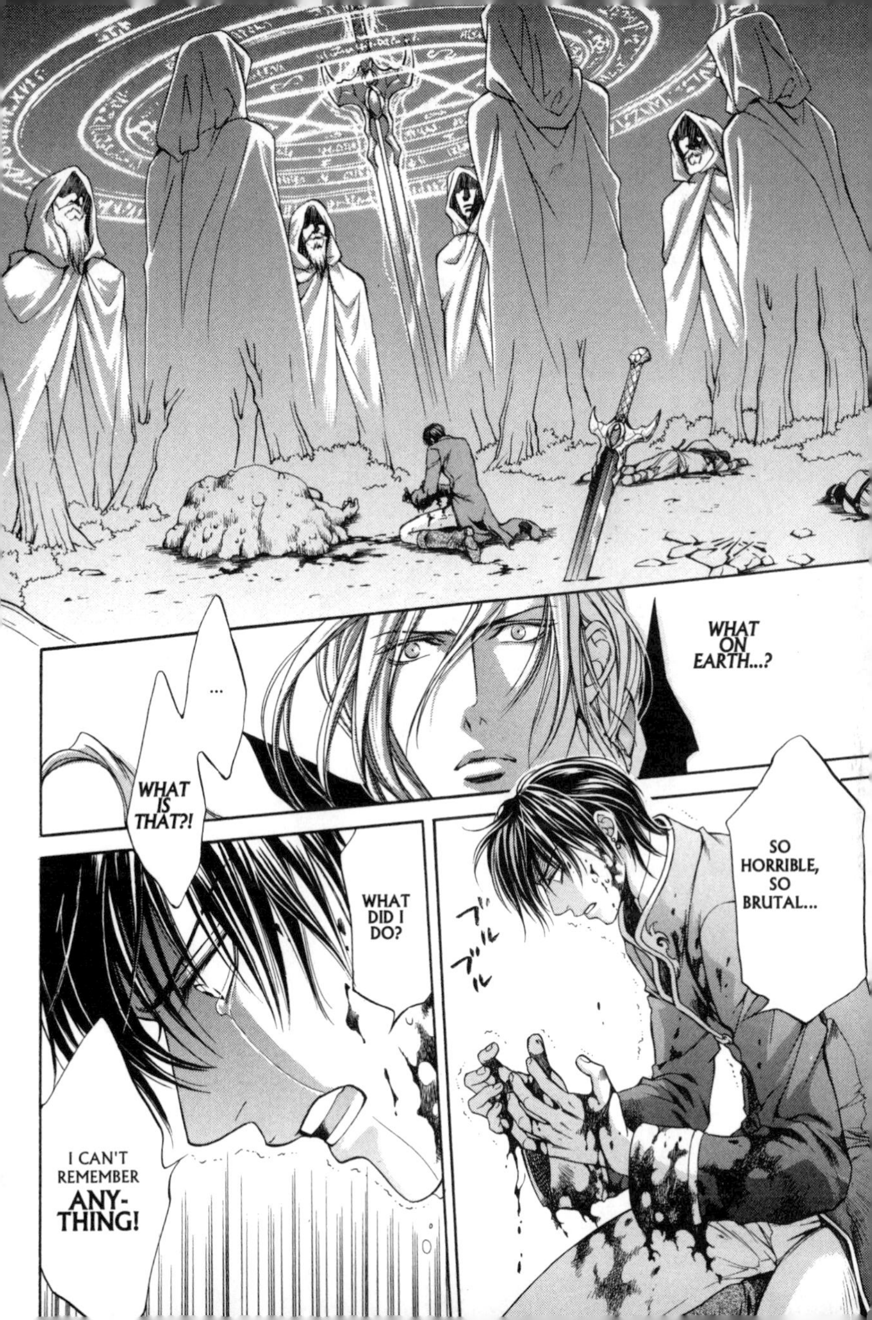
WHAT ON EARTH...?
...
WHAT IS THAT?!
SO HORRIBLE, SO BRUTAL...
ブル
ブル
WHAT DID I DO?
I CAN'T REMEMBER ANY-THING!

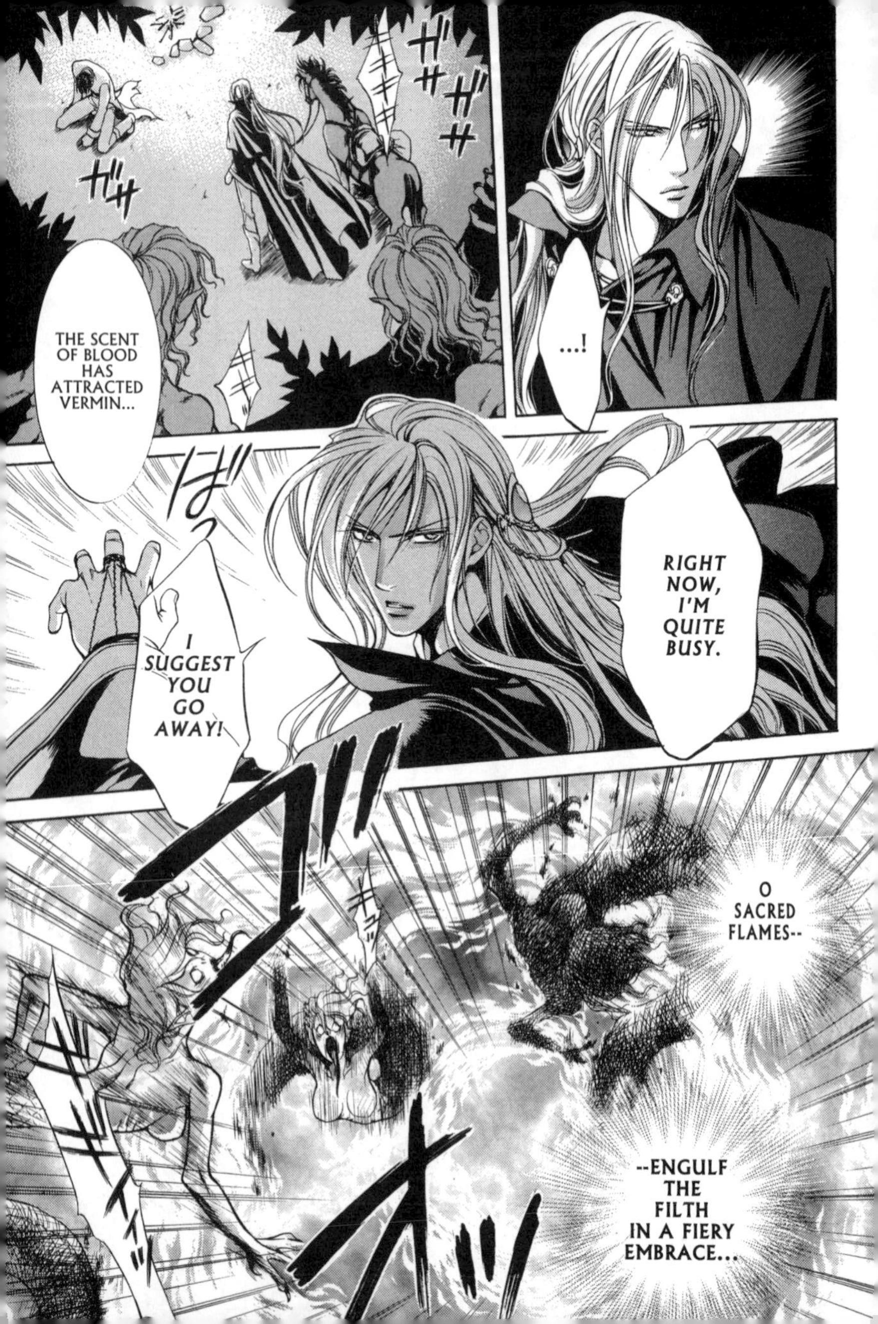
...!
THE SCENT OF BLOOD HAS ATTRACTED VERMIN...
RIGHT NOW, I'M QUITE BUSY.
I SUGGEST YOU GO AWAY!
O SACRED FLAMES--
--ENGULF THE FILTH IN A FIERY EMBRACE...

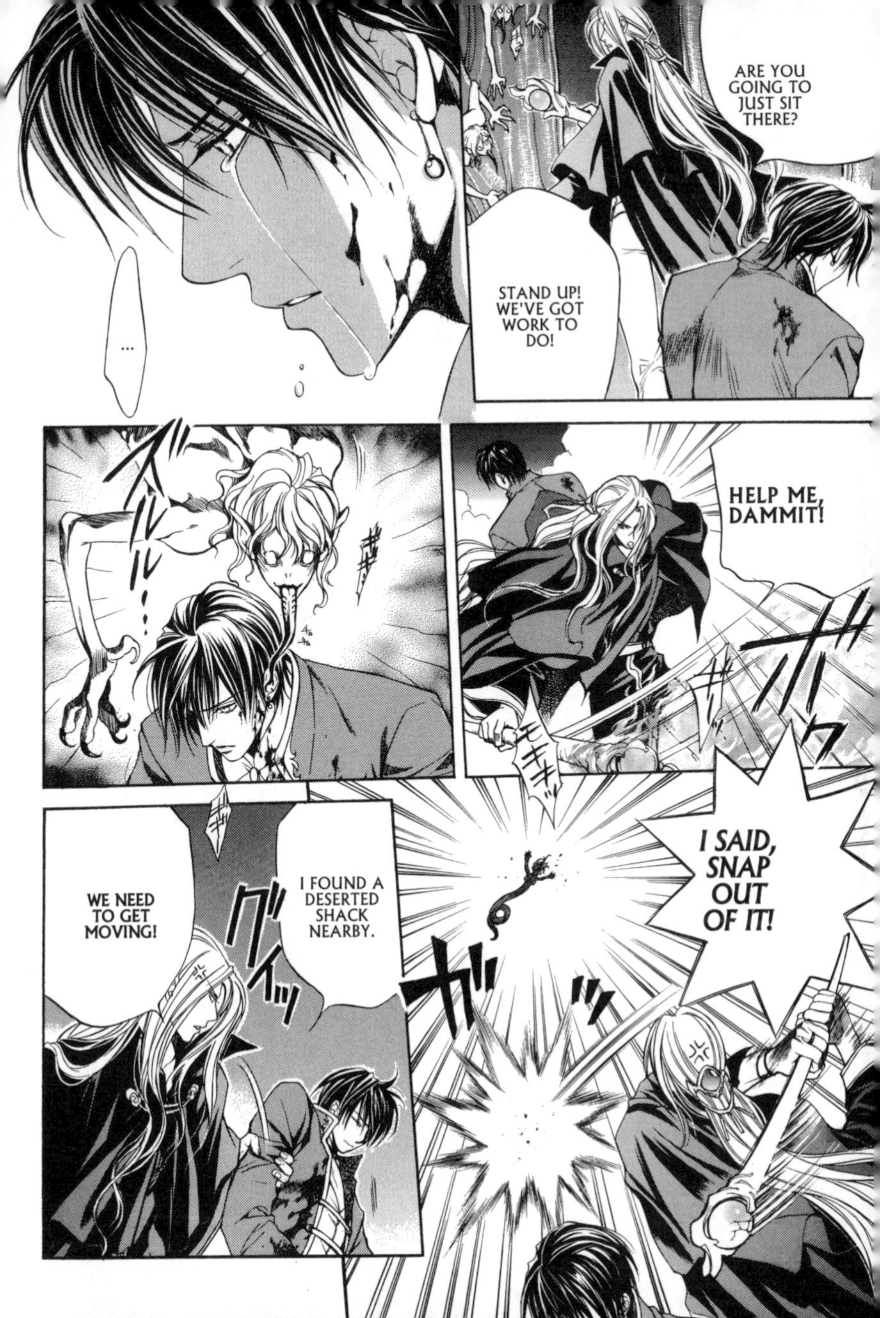
ARE YOU GOING TO JUST SIT THERE?
STAND UP! WE'VE GOT WORK TO DO!
...
HELP ME, DAMMIT!
I SAID, SNAP OUT OF IT!
I FOUND A DESERTED SHACK NEARBY.
WE NEED TO GET MOVING!

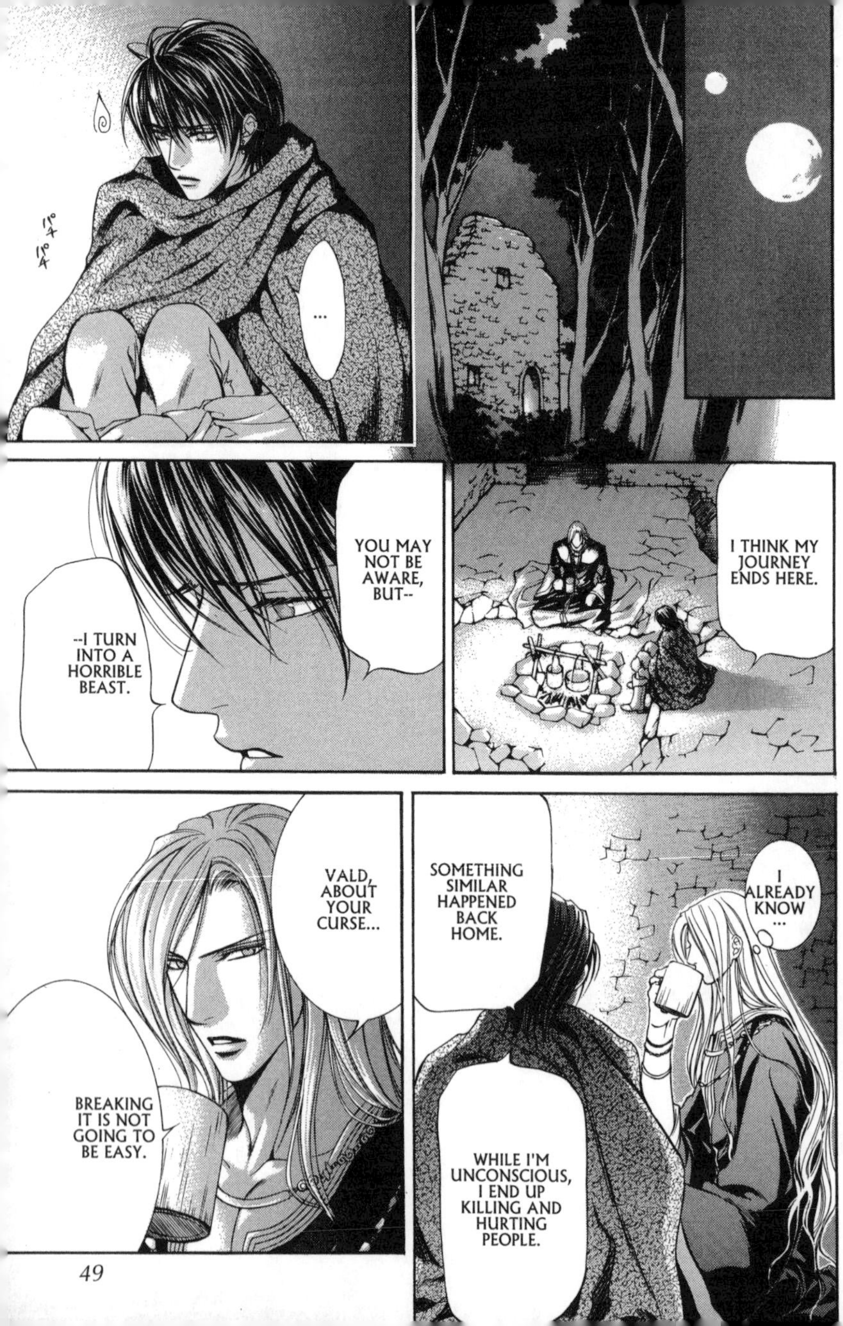
...
I THINK MY JOURNEY ENDS HERE.
YOU MAY NOT BE AWARE, BUT--
--I TURN INTO A HORRIBLE BEAST.
I ALREADY KNOW ...
SOMETHING SIMILAR HAPPENED BACK HOME.
WHILE I'M UNCONSCIOUS, I END UP KILLING AND HURTING PEOPLE.
VALD, ABOUT YOUR CURSE...
BREAKING IT IS NOT GOING TO BE EASY.

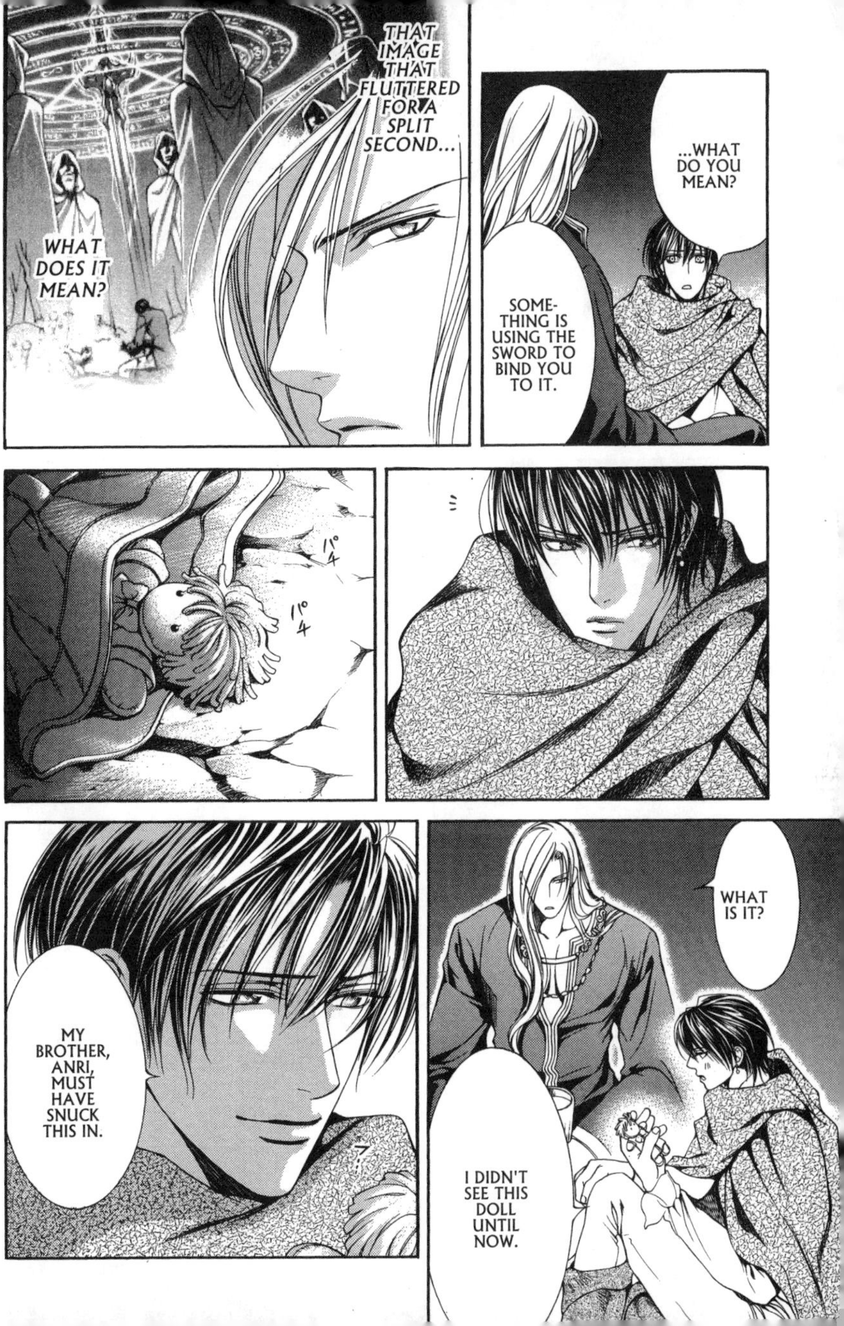
...WHAT DO YOU MEAN?
SOME-THING IS USING THE SWORD TO BIND YOU TO IT.
THAT IMAGE THAT FLUTTERED FOR A SPLIT SECOND...
WHAT DOES IT MEAN?
WHAT IS IT?
I DIDN'T SEE THIS DOLL UNTIL NOW.
MY BROTHER, ANRI, MUST HAVE SNUCK THIS IN.

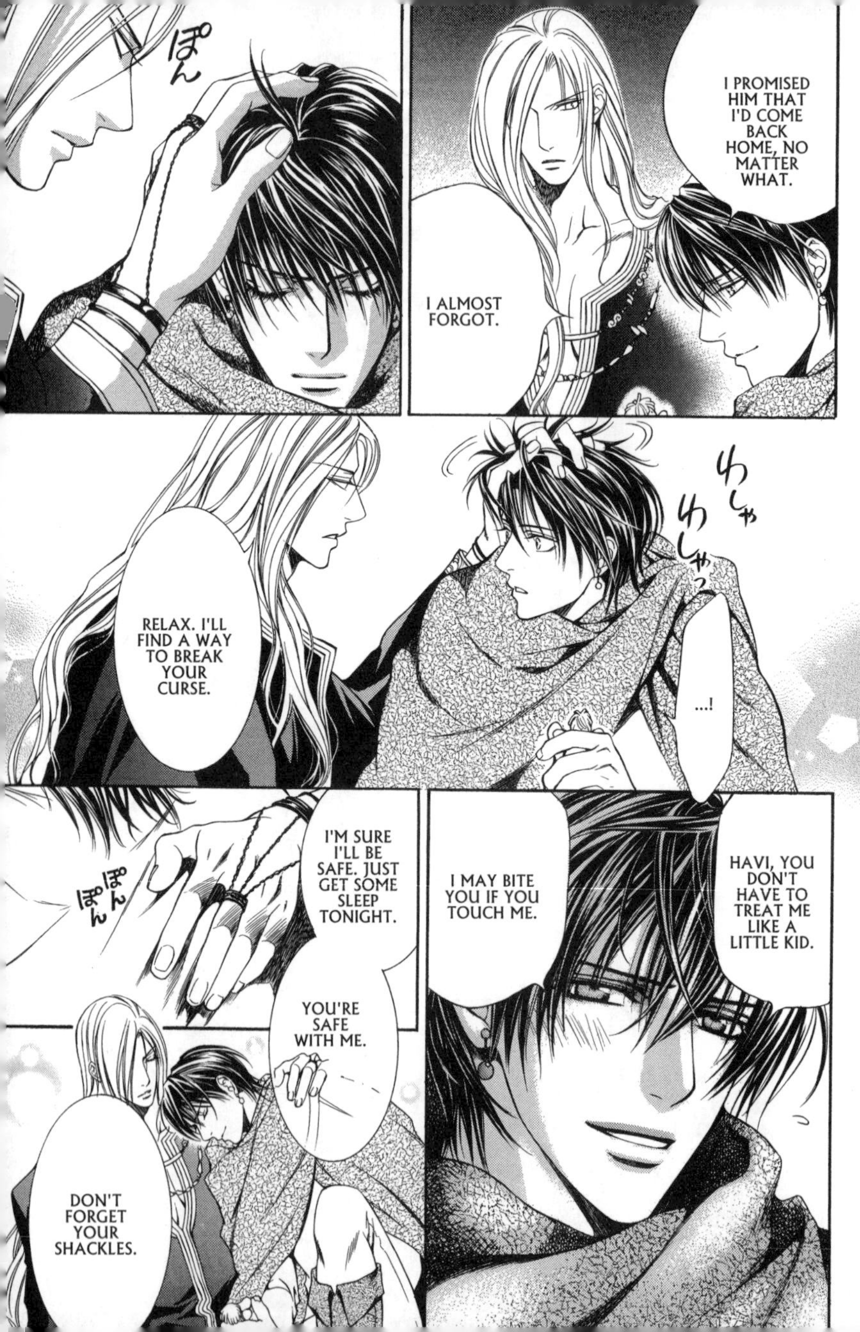
I PROMISED HIM THAT I'D COME BACK HOME, NO MATTER WHAT.
I ALMOST FORGOT.
ぽん
わしゃ わしゃっ
...!
RELAX. I'LL FIND A WAY TO BREAK YOUR CURSE.
HAVI, YOU DON'T HAVE TO TREAT ME LIKE A LITTLE KID.
I MAY BITE YOU IF YOU TOUCH ME.
I'M SURE I'LL BE SAFE. JUST GET SOME SLEEP TONIGHT.
ぽんぽん
YOU'RE SAFE WITH ME.
DON'T FORGET YOUR SHACKLES.

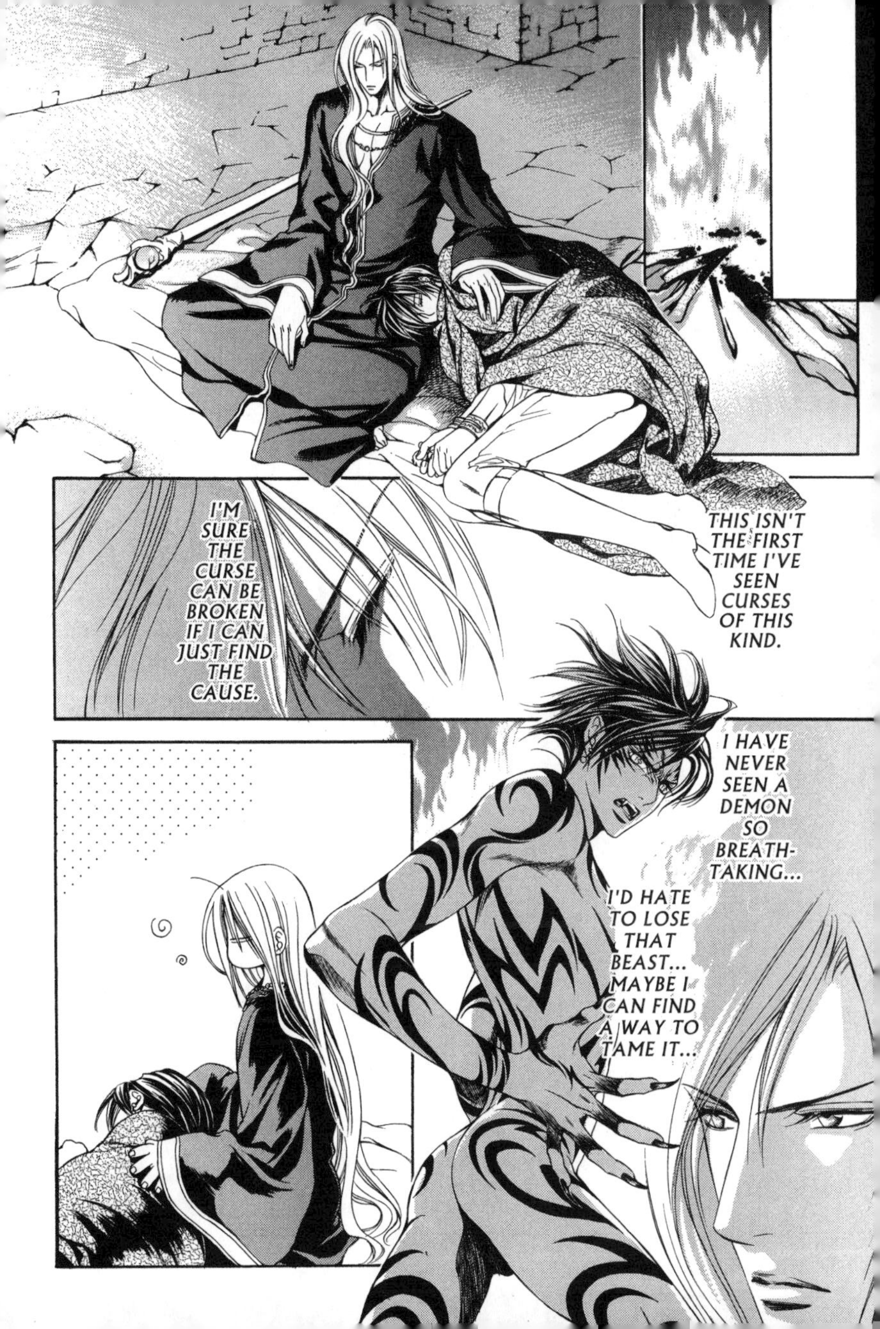
THIS ISN'T THE FIRST TIME I'VE SEEN CURSES OF THIS KIND.
I'M SURE THE CURSE CAN BE BROKEN IF I CAN JUST FIND THE CAUSE.
I HAVE NEVER SEEN A DEMON SO BREATH-TAKING...
I'D HATE TO LOSE THAT BEAST... MAYBE I CAN FIND A WAY TO TAME IT...

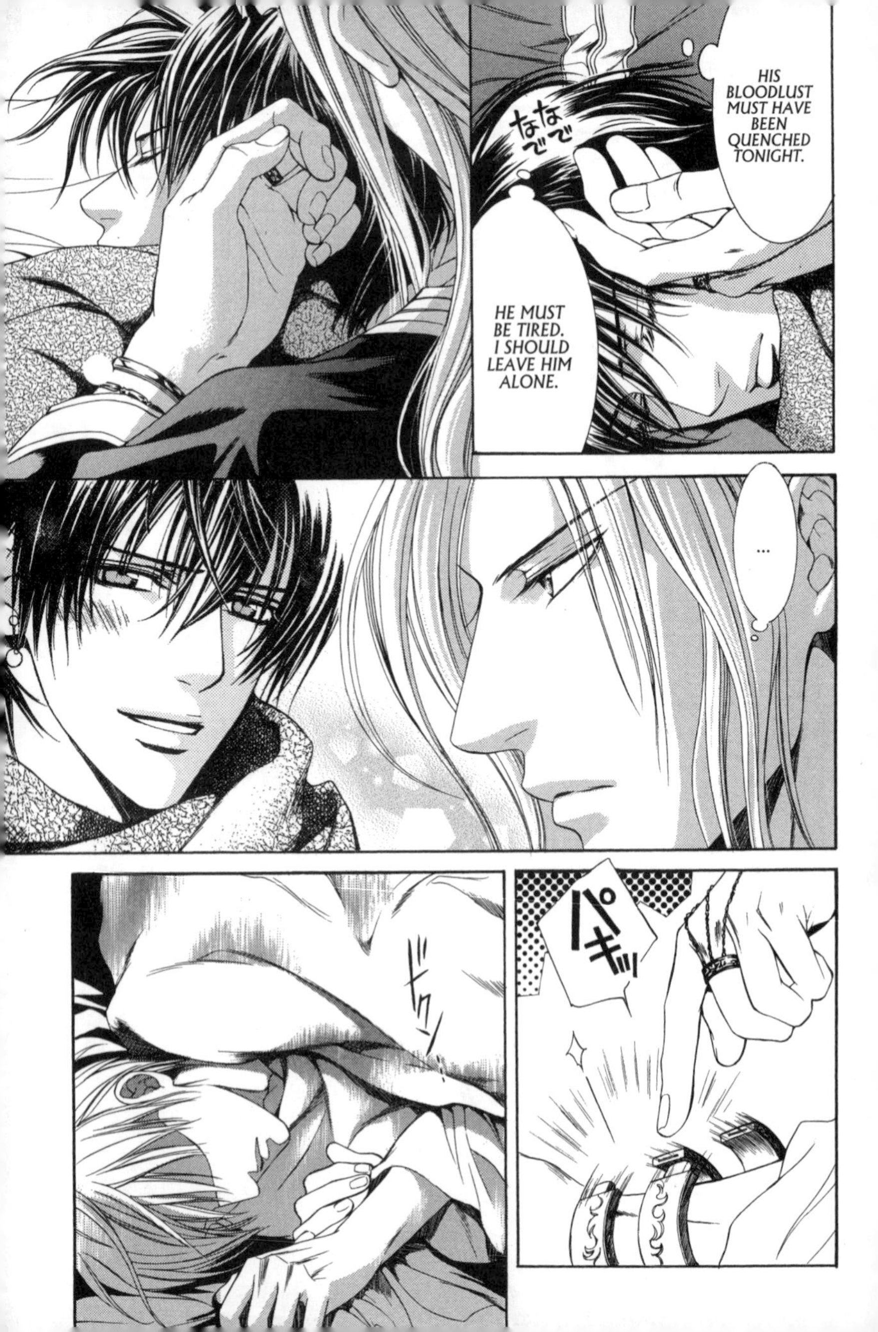
HIS BLOODLUST MUST HAVE BEEN QUENCHED TONIGHT.
なでなで
HE MUST BE TIRED. I SHOULD LEAVE HIM ALONE.
...
パキッ
ドクン

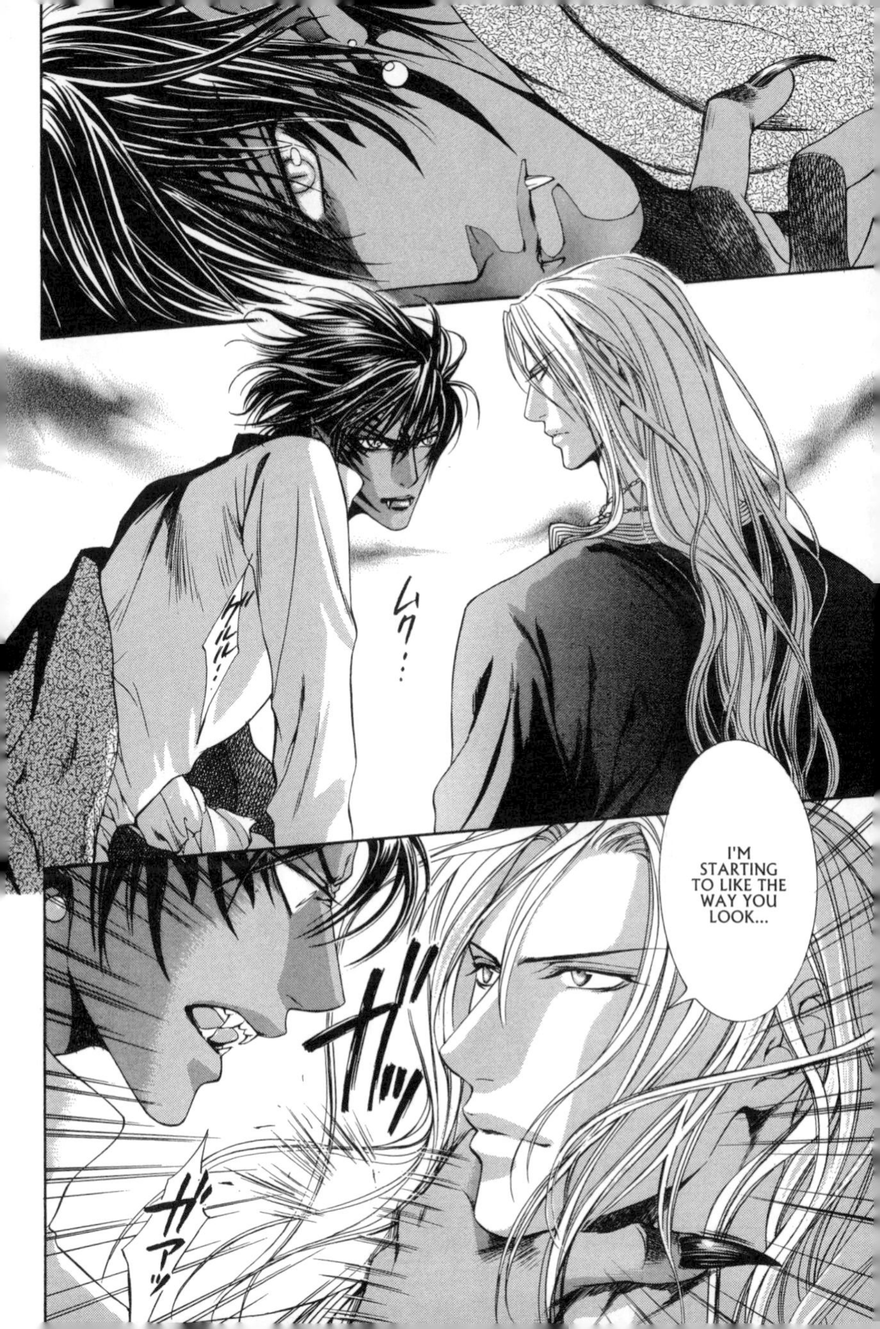
ムク…
グルル…
I'M STARTING TO LIKE THE WAY YOU LOOK...
ザッ
ザァッ

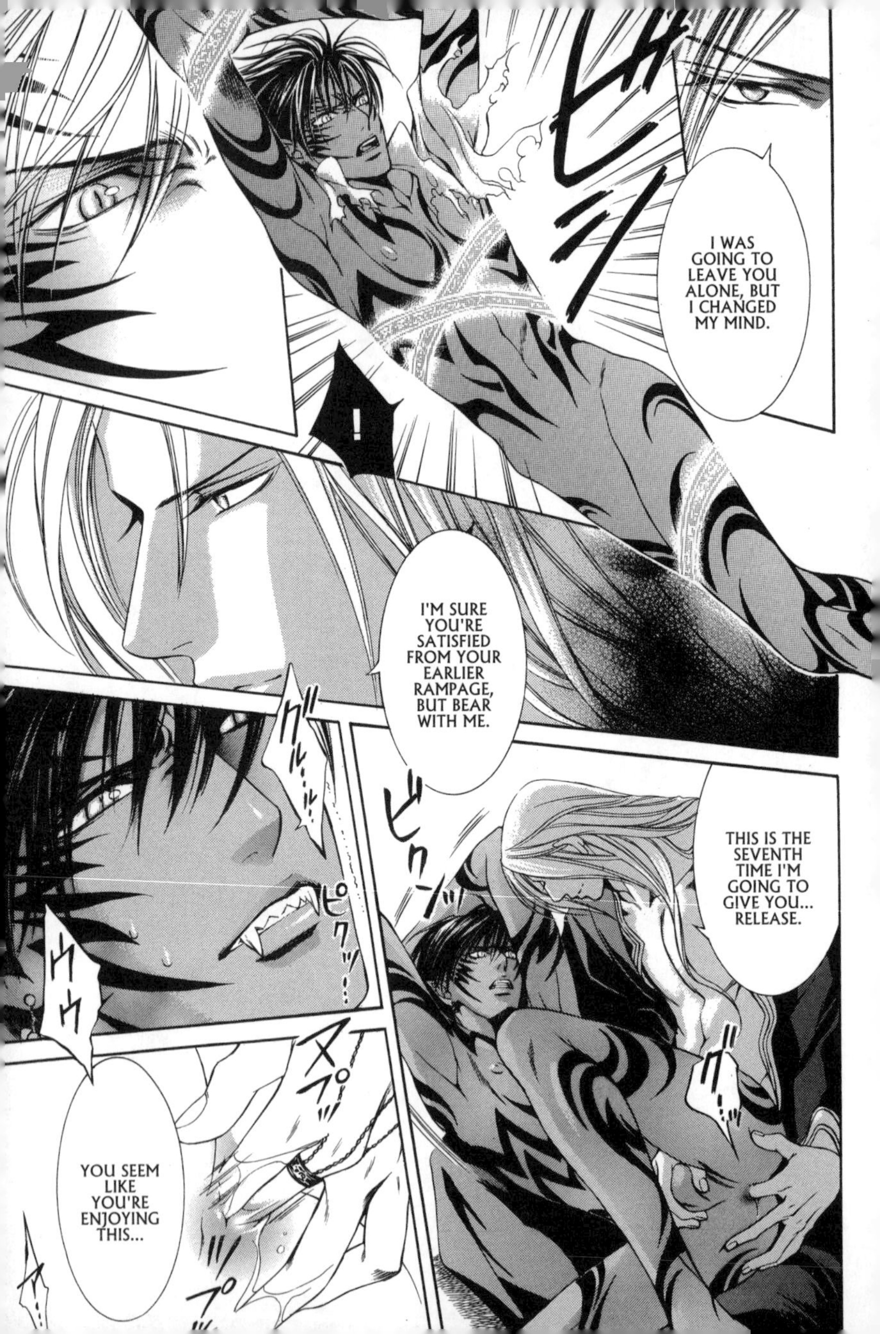
I WAS GOING TO LEAVE YOU ALONE, BUT I CHANGED MY MIND.
!
I'M SURE YOU'RE SATISFIED FROM YOUR EARLIER RAMPAGE, BUT BEAR WITH ME.
THIS IS THE SEVENTH TIME I'M GOING TO GIVE YOU... RELEASE.
YOU SEEM LIKE YOU'RE ENJOYING THIS...

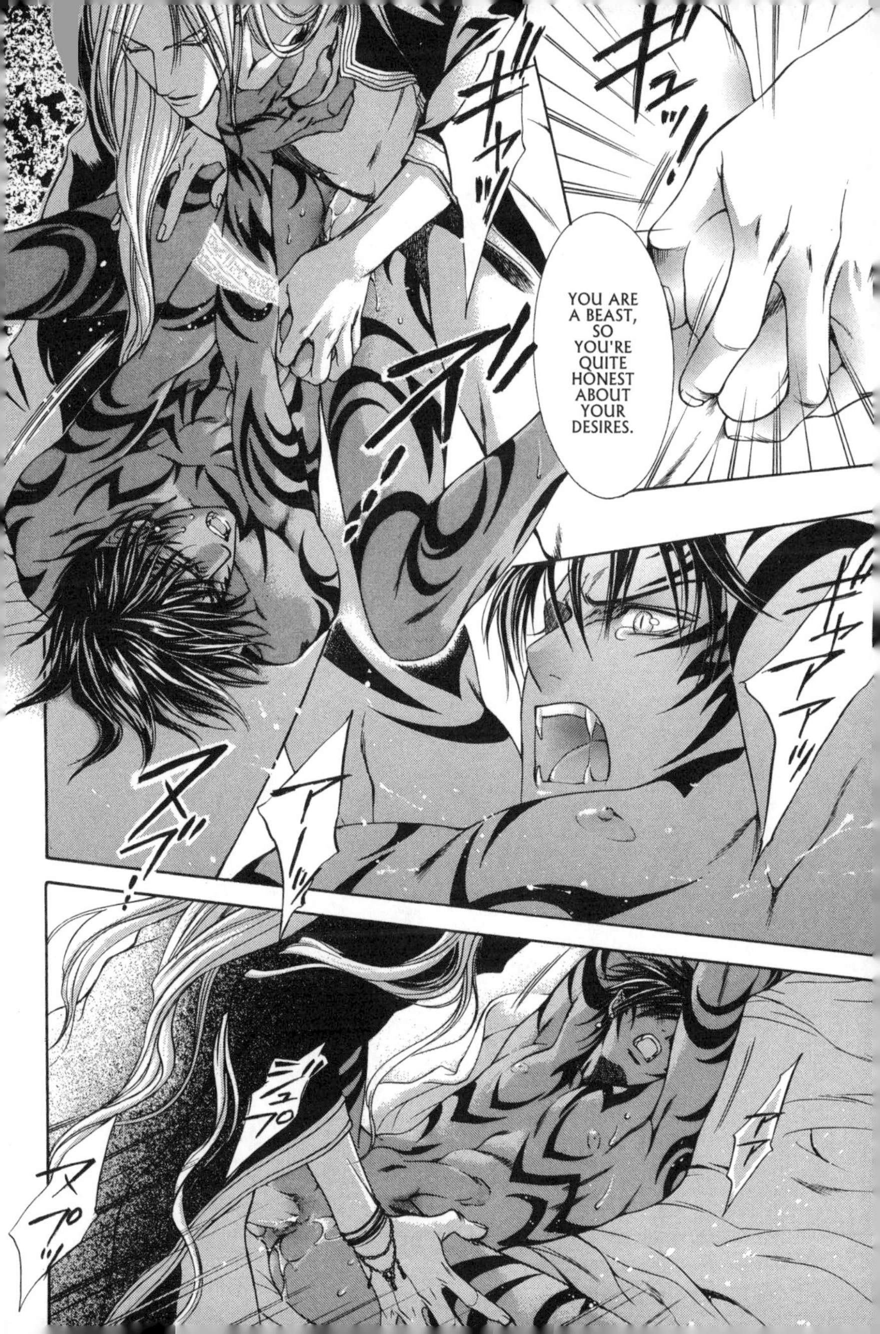
YOU ARE A BEAST, SO YOU'RE QUITE HONEST ABOUT YOUR DESIRES.

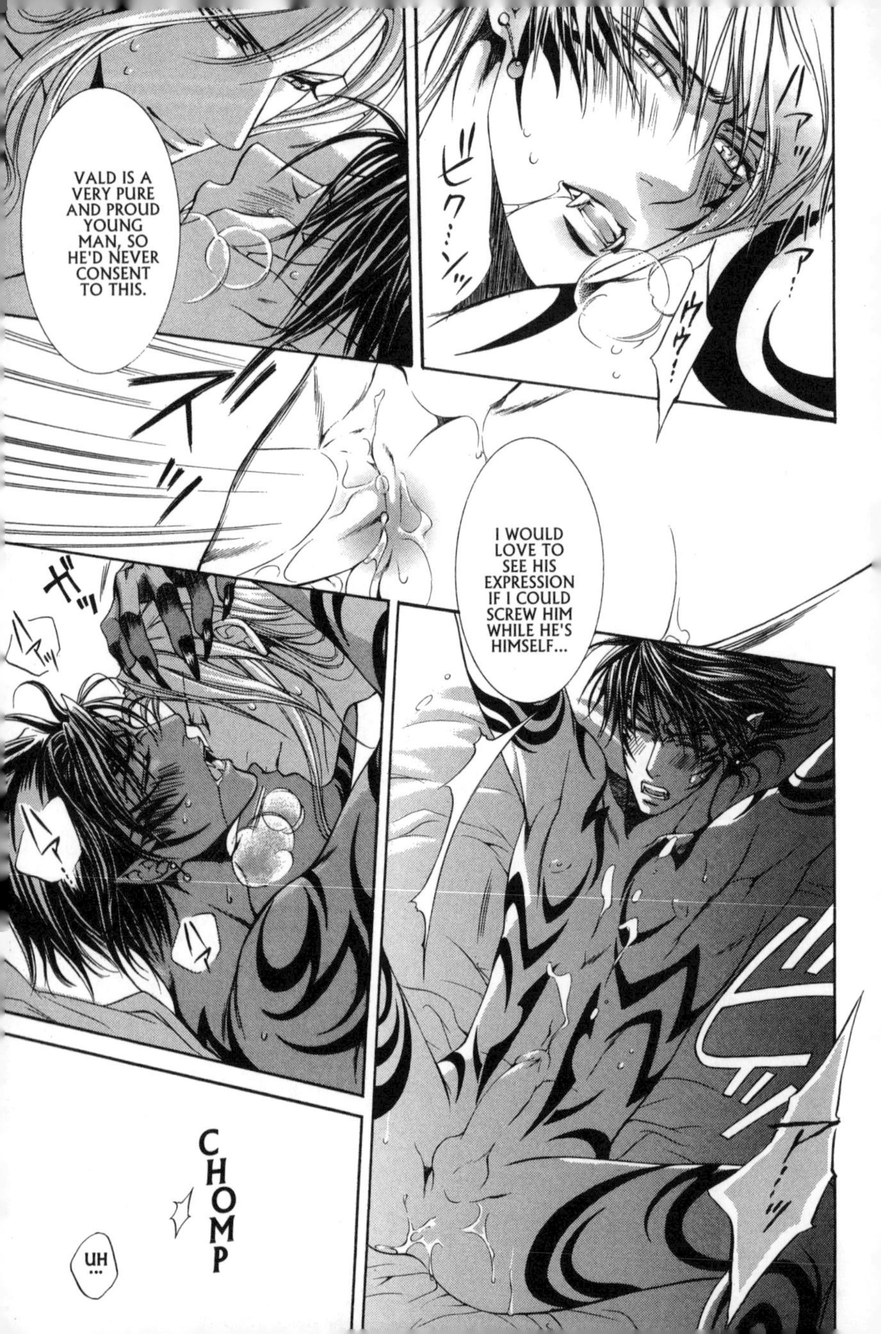
VALD IS A VERY PURE AND PROUD YOUNG MAN, SO HE'D NEVER CONSENT TO THIS.
I WOULD LOVE TO SEE HIS EXPRESSION IF I COULD SCREW HIM WHILE HE'S HIMSELF...
CHOMP
UH...

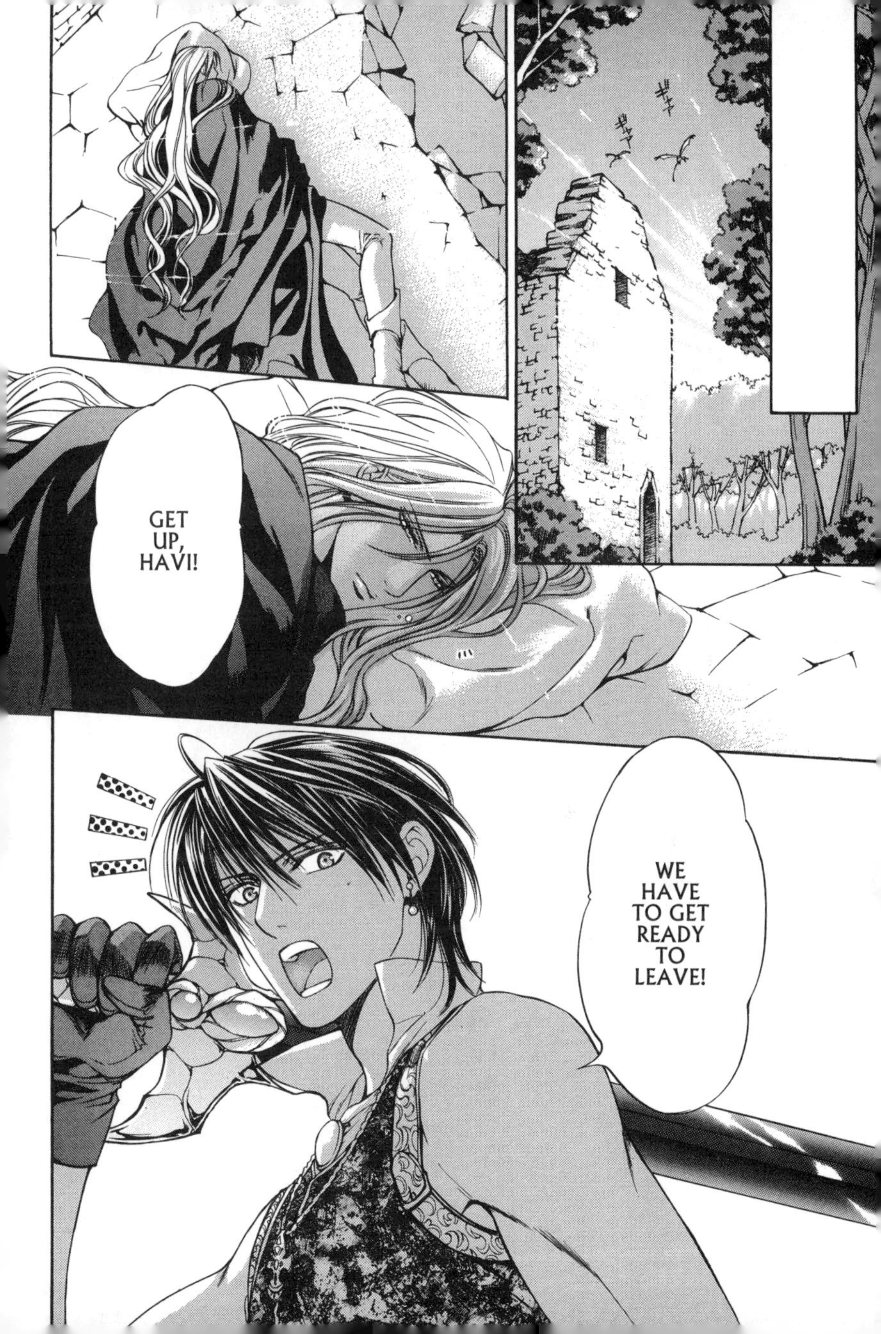
GET UP, HAVI!
WE HAVE TO GET READY TO LEAVE!

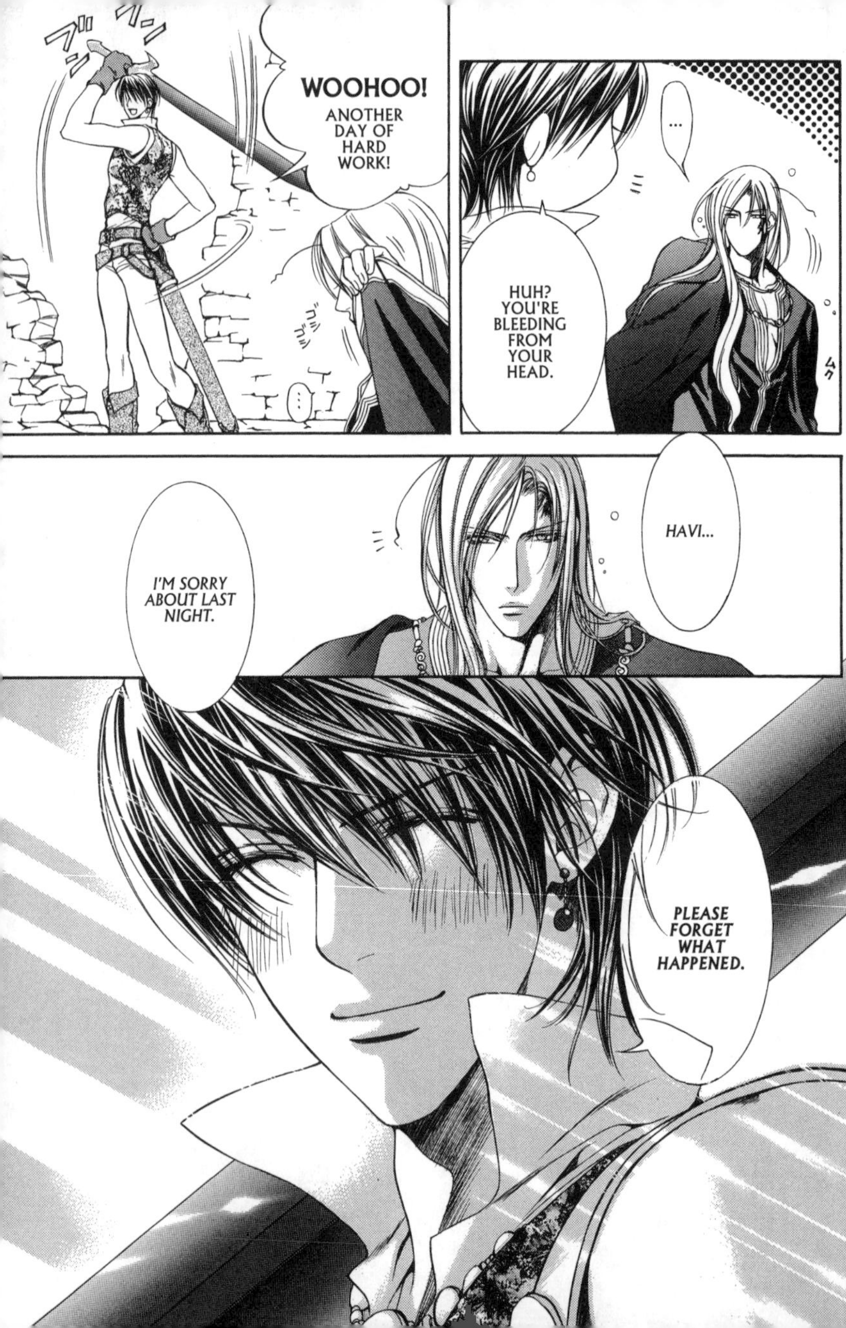
...
HUH? YOU'RE BLEEDING FROM YOUR HEAD.
ムク
WOOHOO! ANOTHER DAY OF HARD WORK!
ゴシゴシ
...
HAVI...
I'M SORRY ABOUT LAST NIGHT.
PLEASE FORGET WHAT HAPPENED.

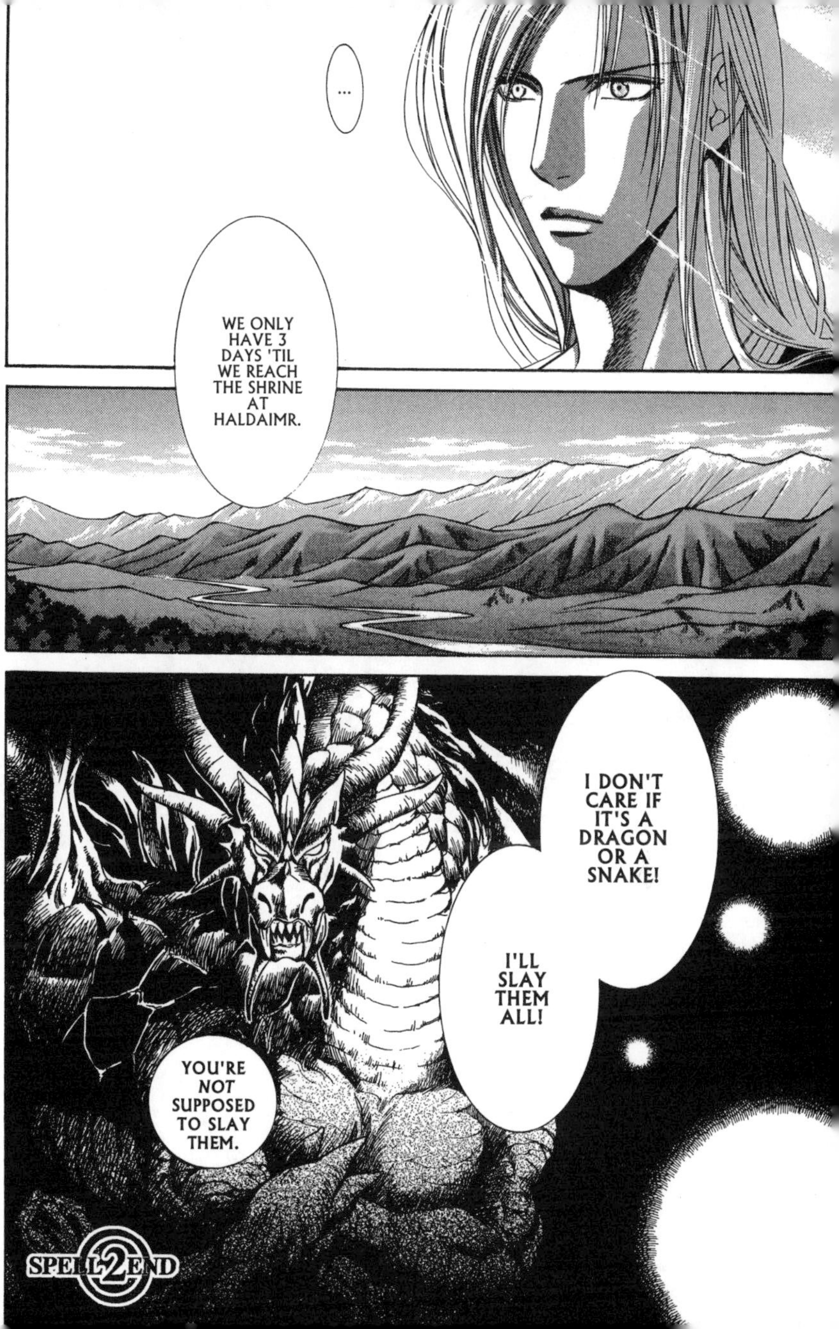
...
WE ONLY HAVE 3 DAYS 'TIL WE REACH THE SHRINE AT HALDAIMR.
I DON'T CARE IF IT'S A DRAGON OR A SNAKE!
I'LL SLAY THEM ALL!
YOU'RE *NOT* SUPPOSED TO SLAY THEM.
SPELL 2 END

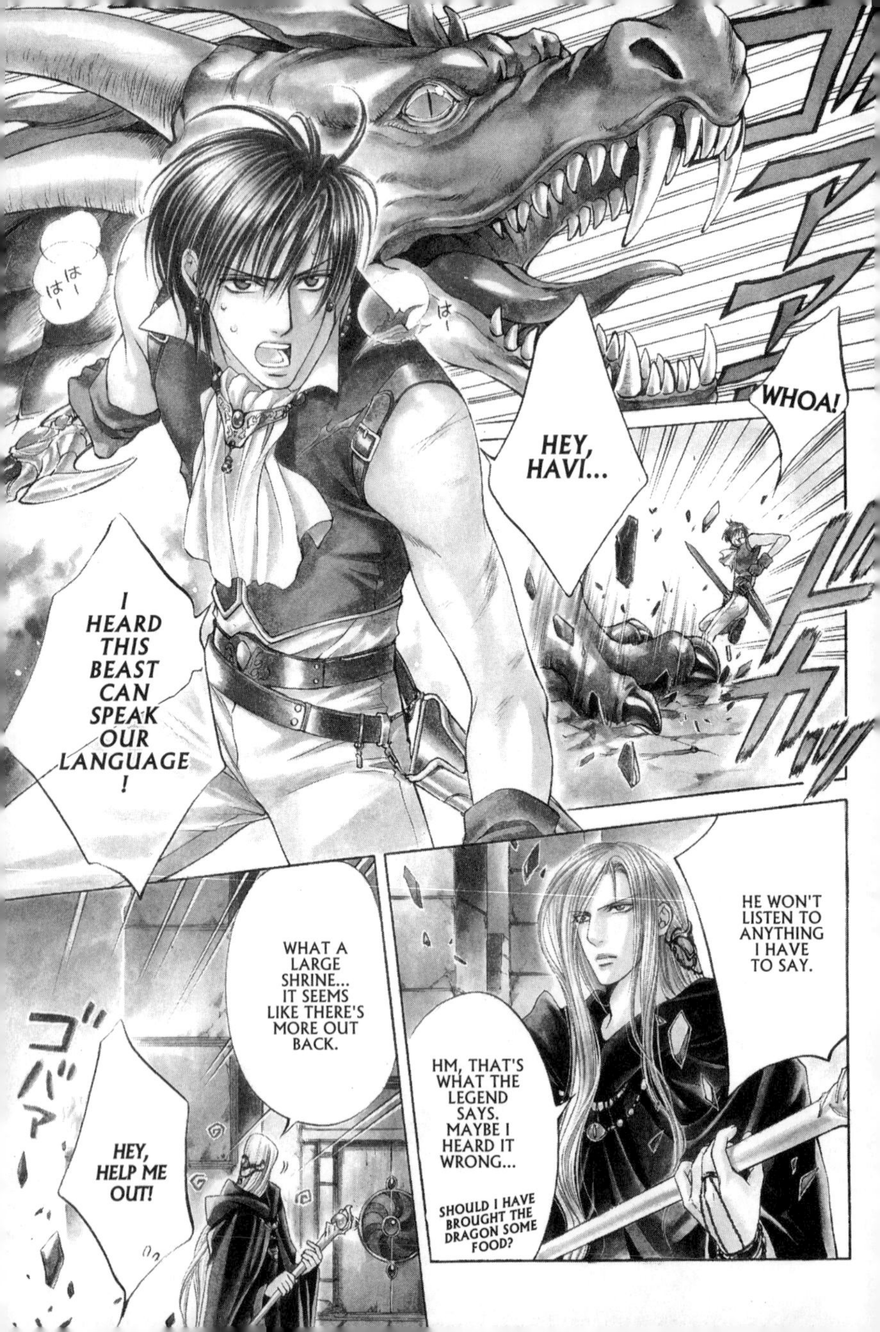
WHOA!
HEY, HAVI...
はーはー
はー
I HEARD THIS BEAST CAN SPEAK OUR LANGUAGE!
HE WON'T LISTEN TO ANYTHING I HAVE TO SAY.
HM, THAT'S WHAT THE LEGEND SAYS. MAYBE I HEARD IT WRONG...
SHOULD I HAVE BROUGHT THE DRAGON SOME FOOD?
WHAT A LARGE SHRINE... IT SEEMS LIKE THERE'S MORE OUT BACK.
HEY, HELP ME OUT!

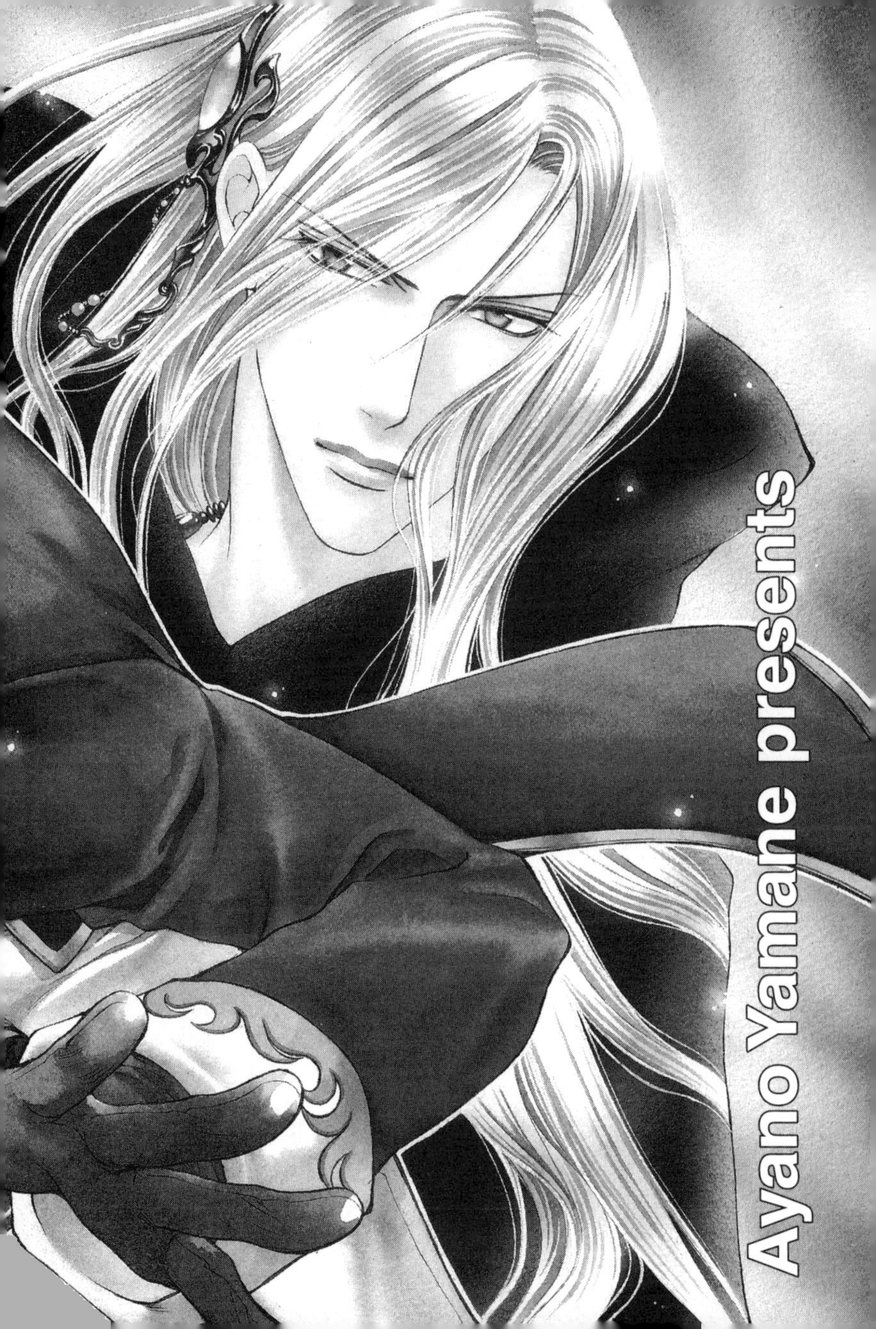
Ayano Yamane presents

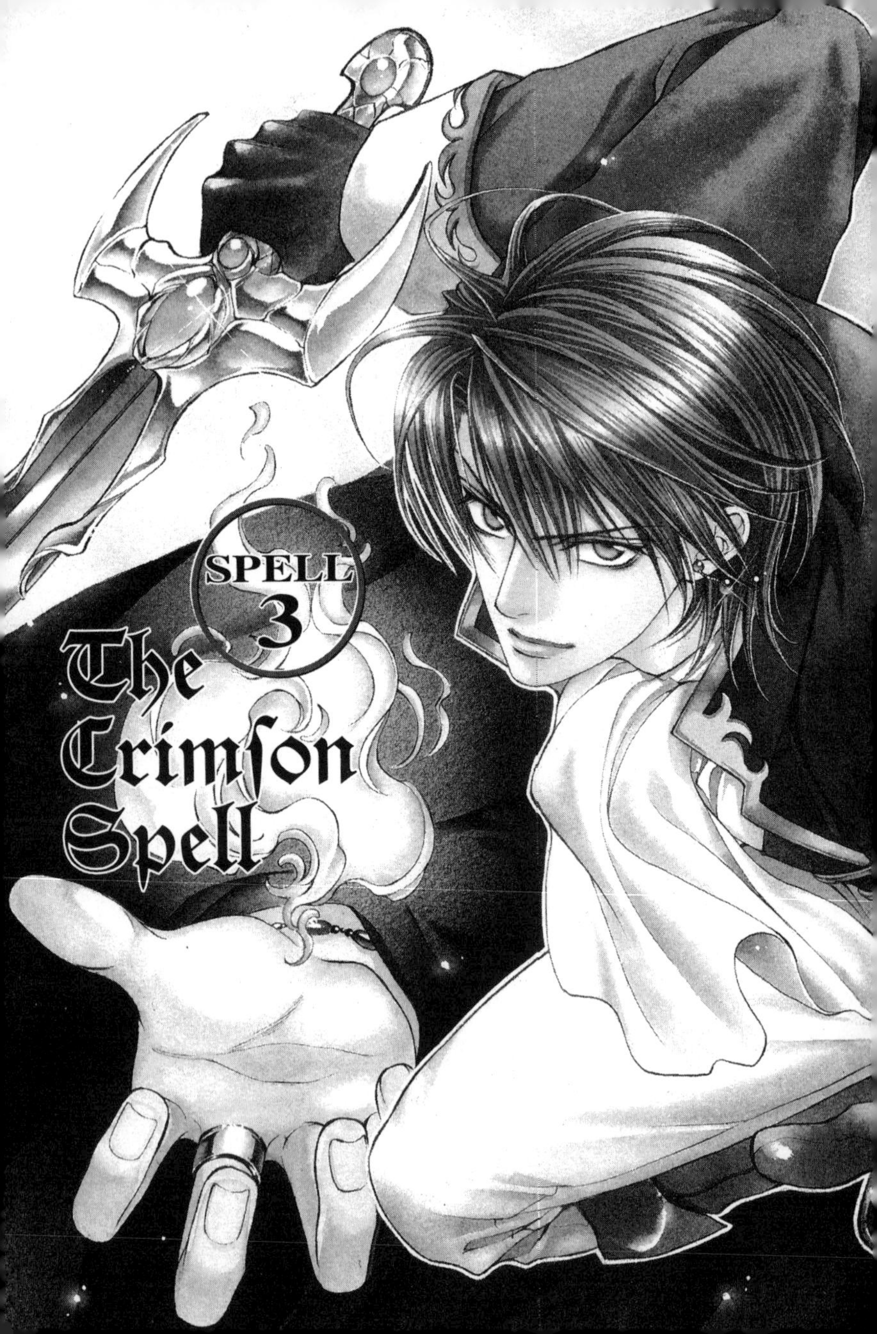
SPELL 3
The Crimson Spell

Ayano Yamane Presents

The
Crimson
Spell

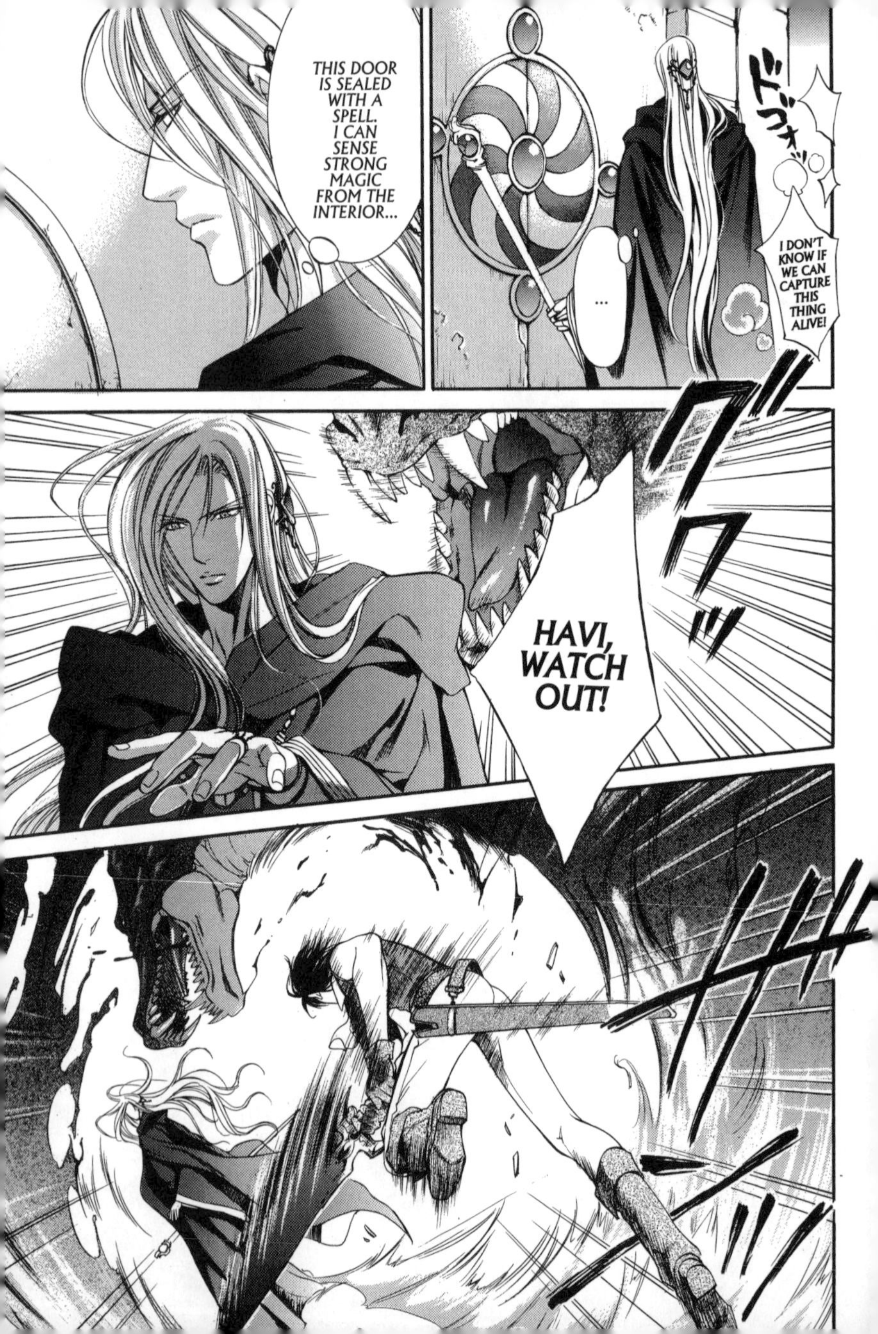
I DON'T KNOW IF WE CAN CAPTURE THIS THING ALIVE!
...
THIS DOOR IS SEALED WITH A SPELL. I CAN SENSE STRONG MAGIC FROM THE INTERIOR...
HAVI, WATCH OUT!

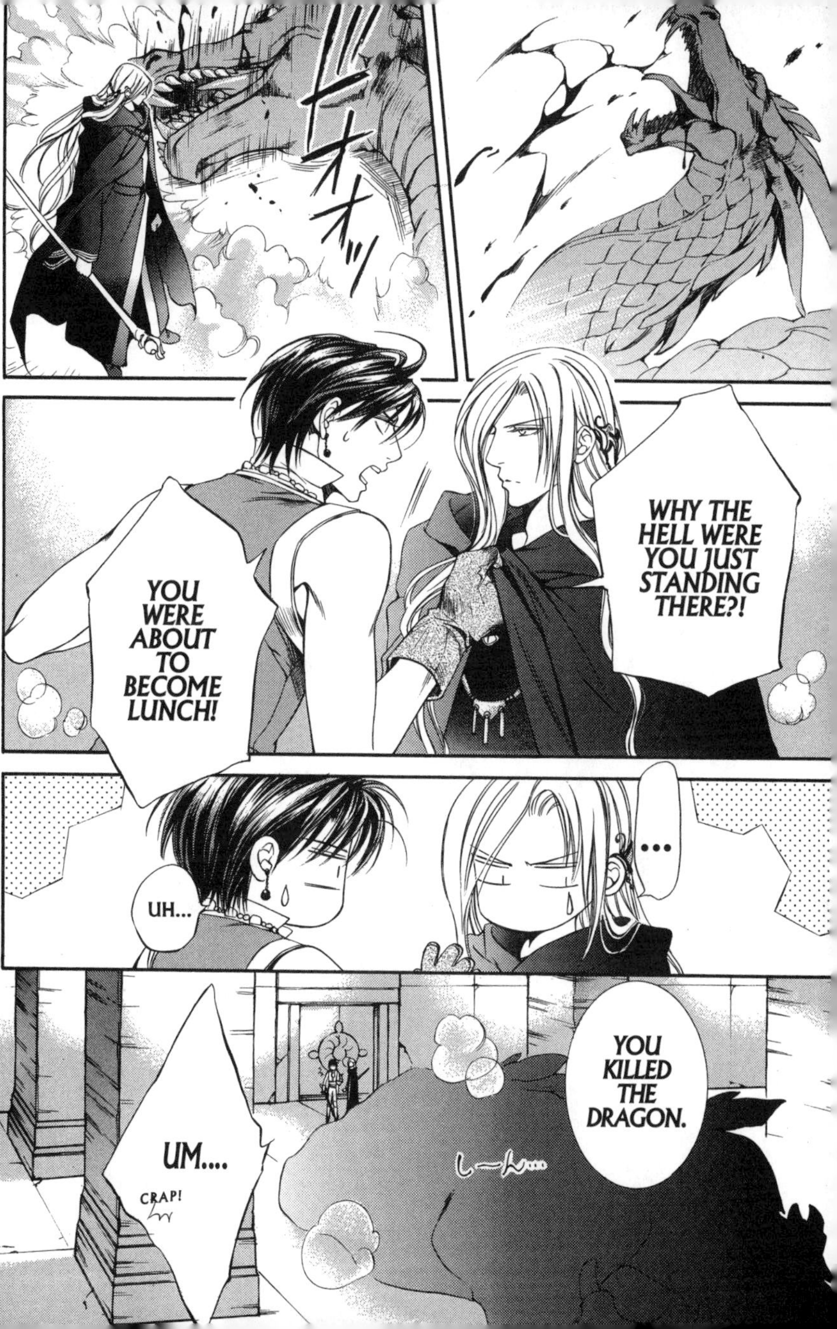
WHY THE HELL WERE YOU JUST STANDING THERE?!
YOU WERE ABOUT TO BECOME LUNCH!
...
UH...
YOU KILLED THE DRAGON.
しーん...
UM....
CRAP!

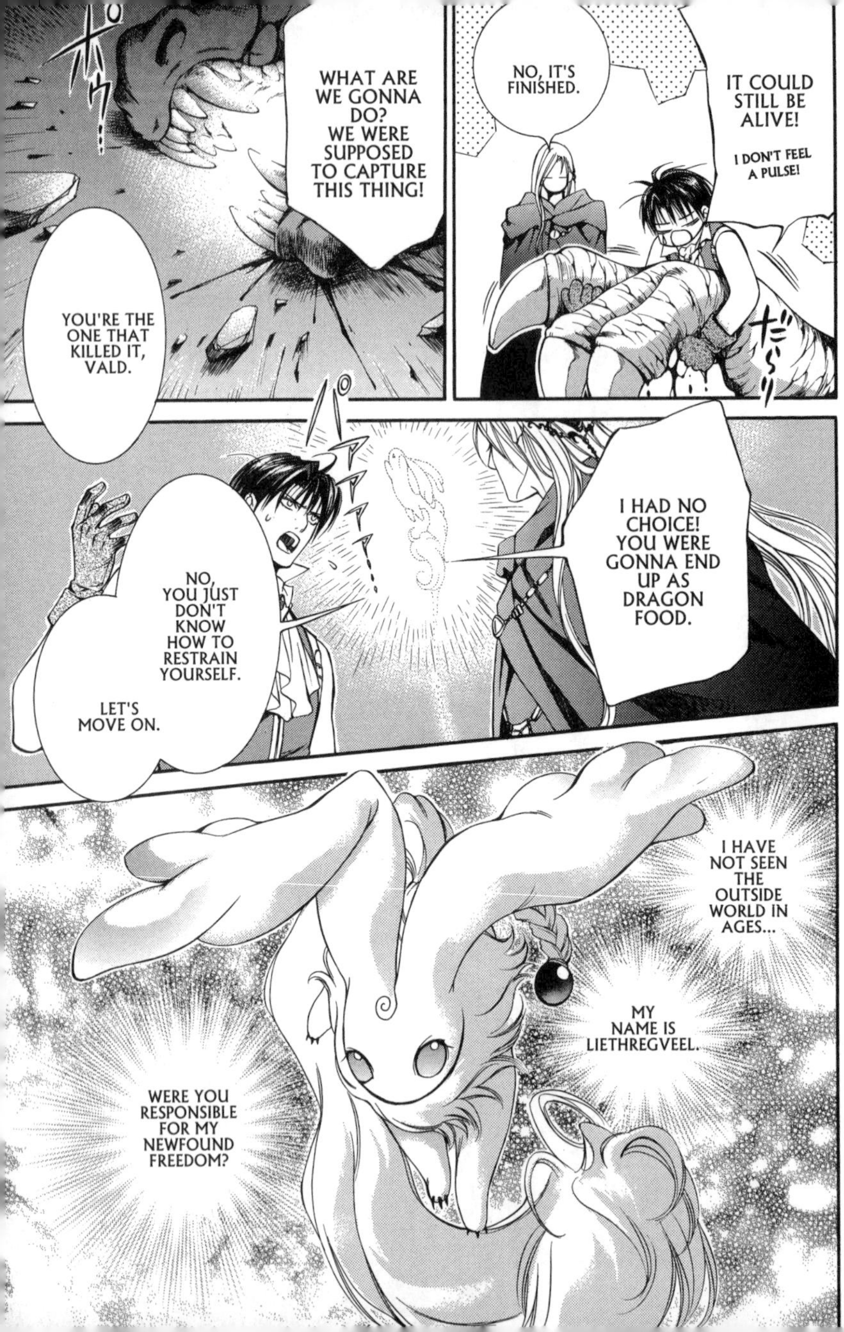
IT COULD STILL BE ALIVE!
I DON'T FEEL A PULSE!
NO, IT'S FINISHED.
WHAT ARE WE GONNA DO? WE WERE SUPPOSED TO CAPTURE THIS THING!
YOU'RE THE ONE THAT KILLED IT, VALD.
I HAD NO CHOICE! YOU WERE GONNA END UP AS DRAGON FOOD.
NO, YOU JUST DON'T KNOW HOW TO RESTRAIN YOURSELF.
LET'S MOVE ON.
I HAVE NOT SEEN THE OUTSIDE WORLD IN AGES...
MY NAME IS LIETHREGVEEL.
WERE YOU RESPONSIBLE FOR MY NEWFOUND FREEDOM?

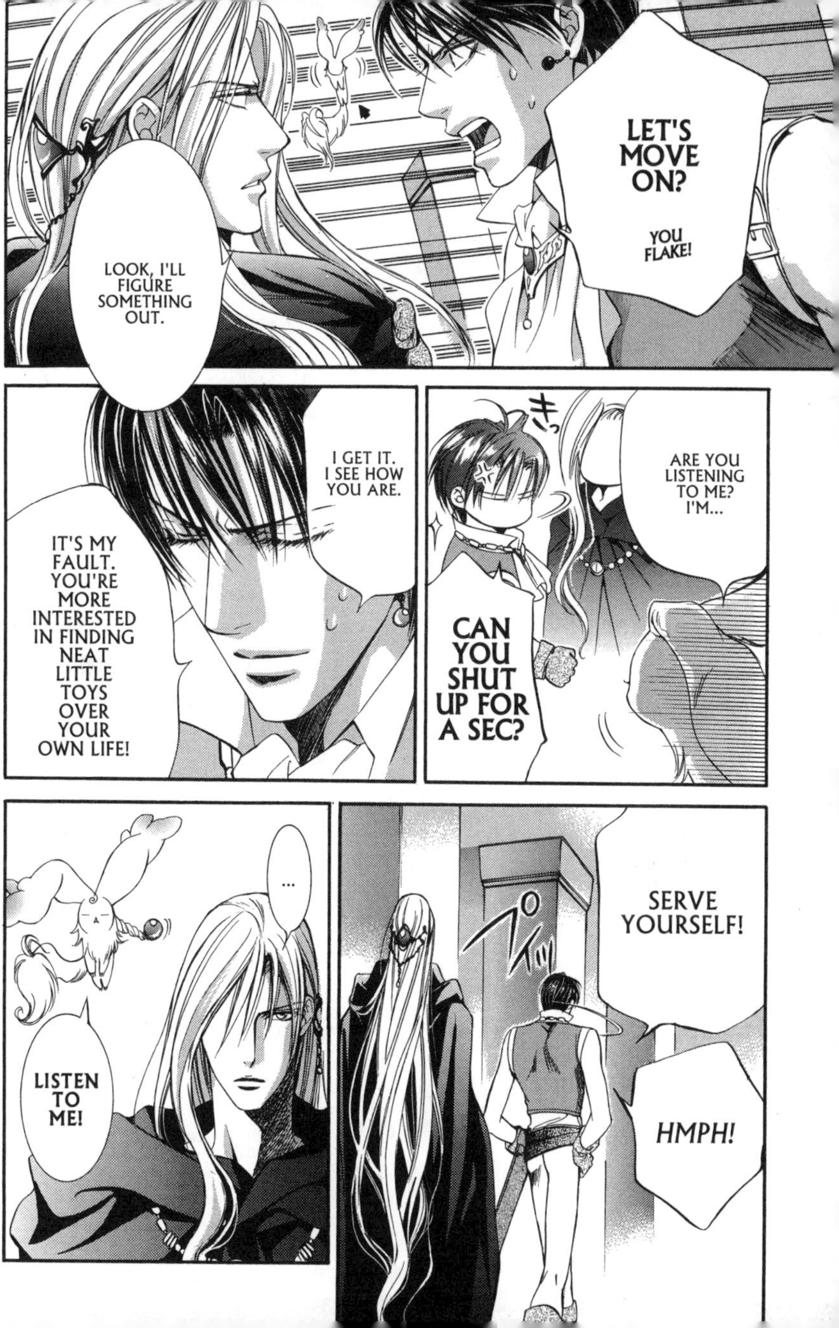
LET'S MOVE ON?
YOU FLAKE!
LOOK, I'LL FIGURE SOMETHING OUT.
きっ
ARE YOU LISTENING TO ME? I'M...
CAN YOU SHUT UP FOR A SEC?
I GET IT. I SEE HOW YOU ARE.
IT'S MY FAULT. YOU'RE MORE INTERESTED IN FINDING NEAT LITTLE TOYS OVER YOUR OWN LIFE!
SERVE YOURSELF!
プイッ
HMPH!
...
LISTEN TO ME!

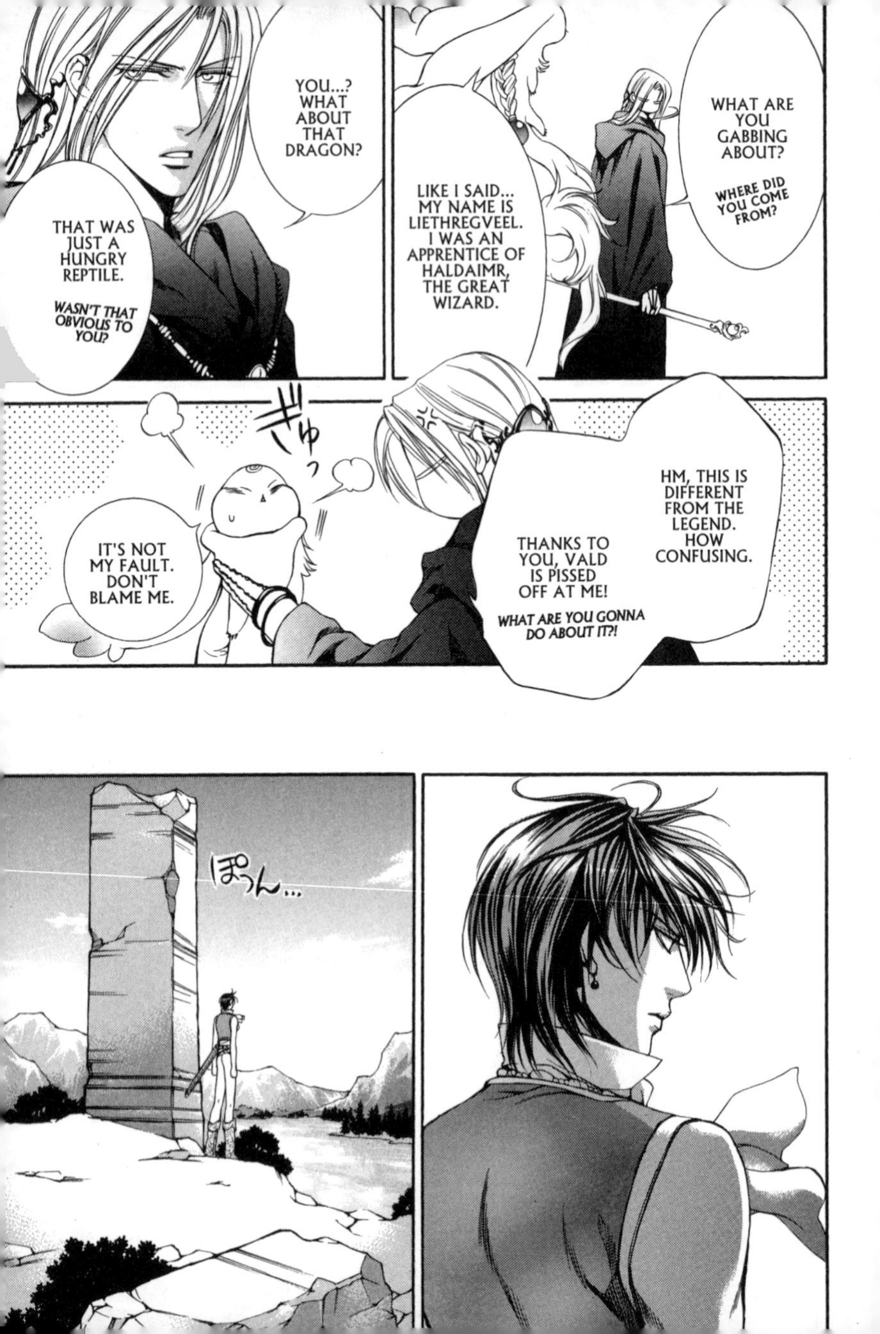
WHAT ARE YOU GABBING ABOUT?
WHERE DID YOU COME FROM?
LIKE I SAID... MY NAME IS LIETHREGVEEL. I WAS AN APPRENTICE OF HALDAIMR, THE GREAT WIZARD.
YOU...? WHAT ABOUT THAT DRAGON?
THAT WAS JUST A HUNGRY REPTILE.
WASN'T THAT OBVIOUS TO YOU?
HM, THIS IS DIFFERENT FROM THE LEGEND. HOW CONFUSING.
THANKS TO YOU, VALD IS PISSED OFF AT ME!
WHAT ARE YOU GONNA DO ABOUT IT?!
ぎゅっ
IT'S NOT MY FAULT. DON'T BLAME ME.
ぽつん...

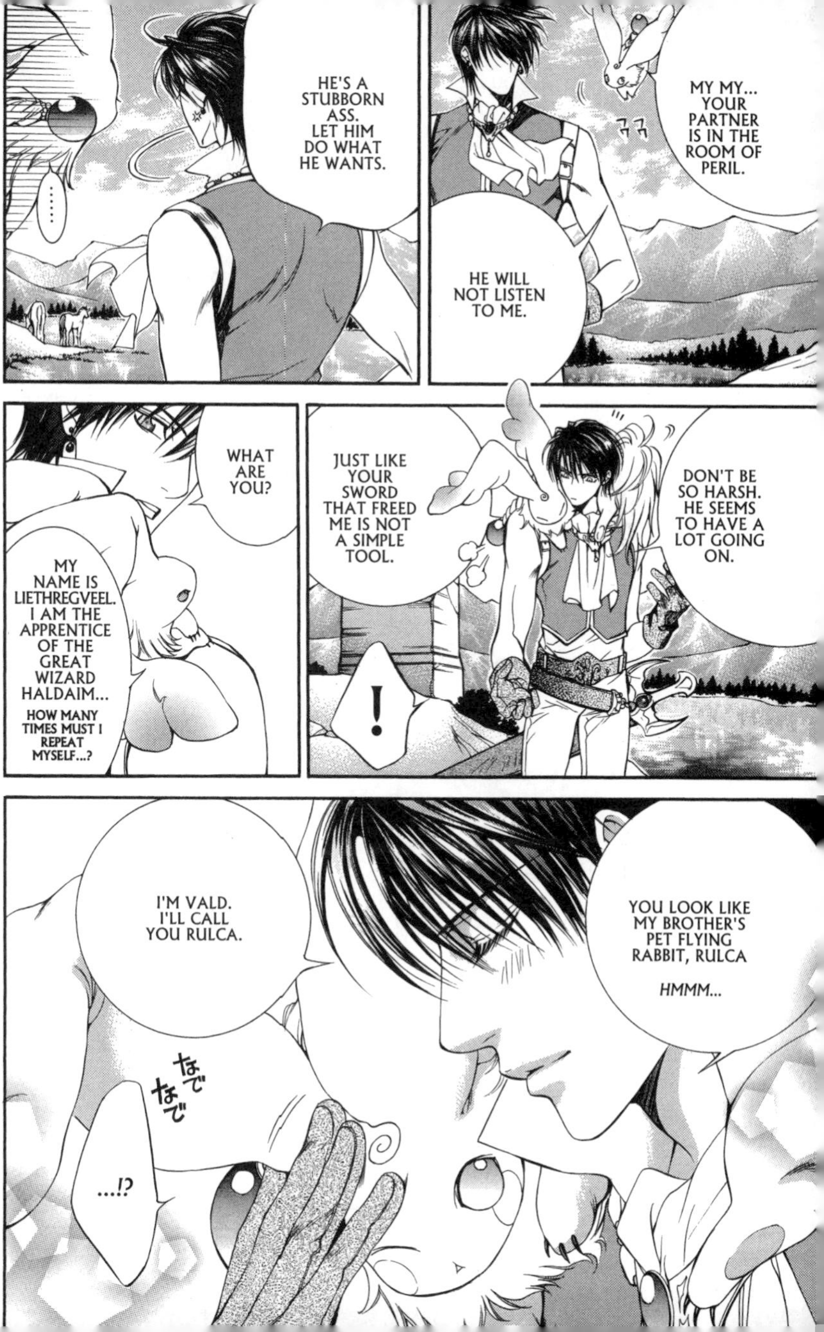
MY MY... YOUR PARTNER IS IN THE ROOM OF PERIL.
クク
HE WILL NOT LISTEN TO ME.
HE'S A STUBBORN ASS. LET HIM DO WHAT HE WANTS.
......
DON'T BE SO HARSH. HE SEEMS TO HAVE A LOT GOING ON.
JUST LIKE YOUR SWORD THAT FREED ME IS NOT A SIMPLE TOOL.
!
WHAT ARE YOU?
MY NAME IS LIETHREGVEEL. I AM THE APPRENTICE OF THE GREAT WIZARD HALDAIM...
HOW MANY TIMES MUST I REPEAT MYSELF...?
YOU LOOK LIKE MY BROTHER'S PET FLYING RABBIT, RULCA
HMMM...
I'M VALD. I'LL CALL YOU RULCA.
なでなで
...!?

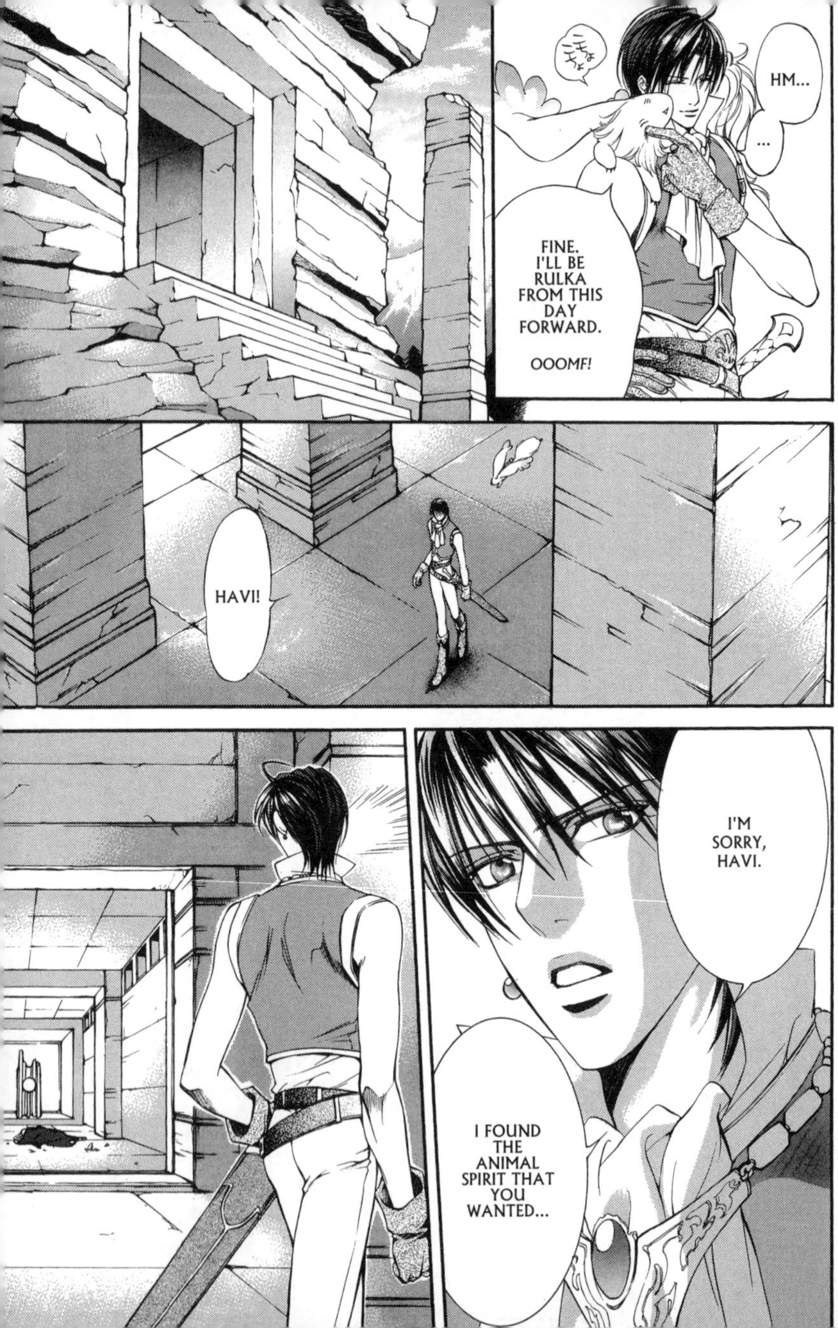
HM...
...
FINE. I'LL BE RULKA FROM THIS DAY FORWARD.
OOOMF!
HAVI!
I'M SORRY, HAVI.
I FOUND THE ANIMAL SPIRIT THAT YOU WANTED...

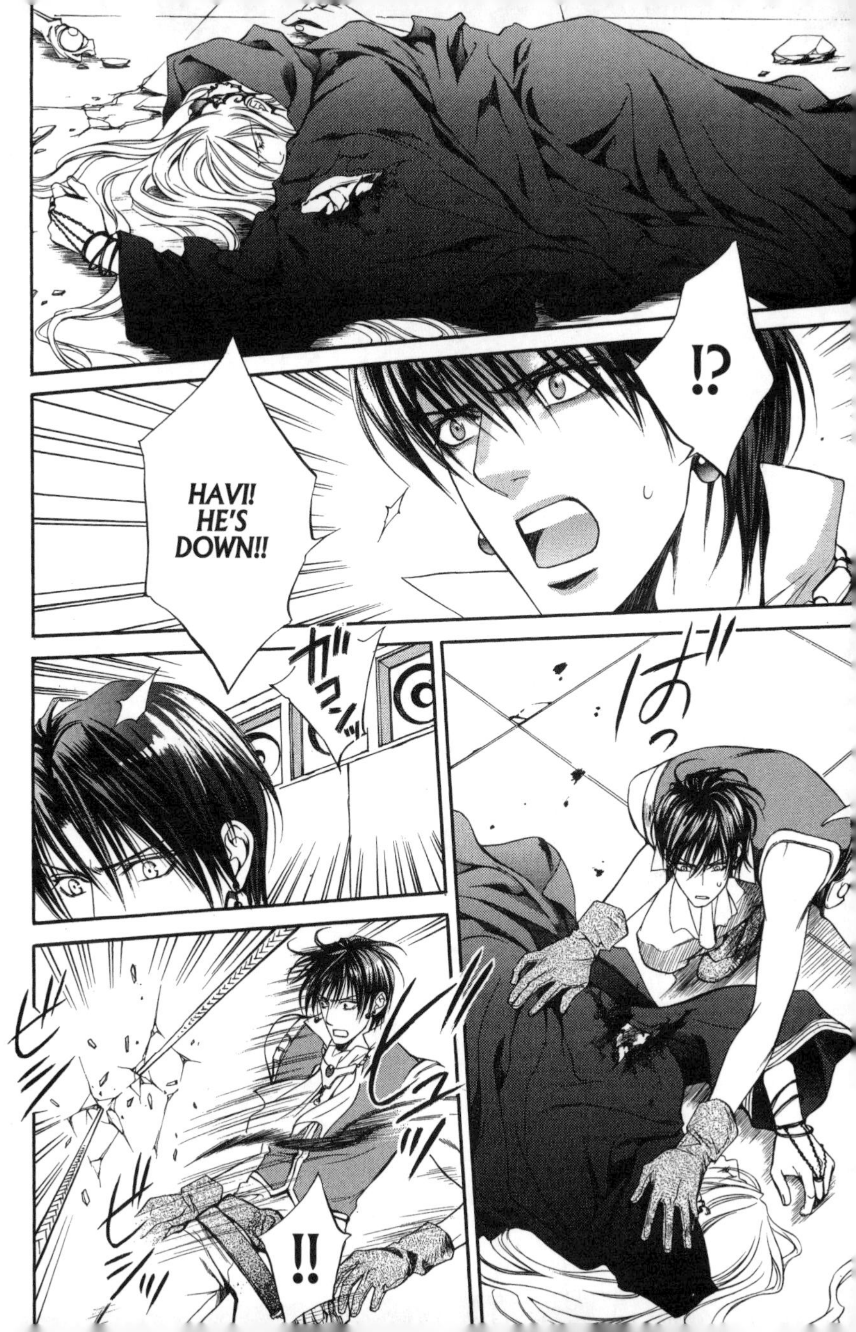
!?
HAVI! HE'S DOWN!!
ばっ
ガコンッ
!!

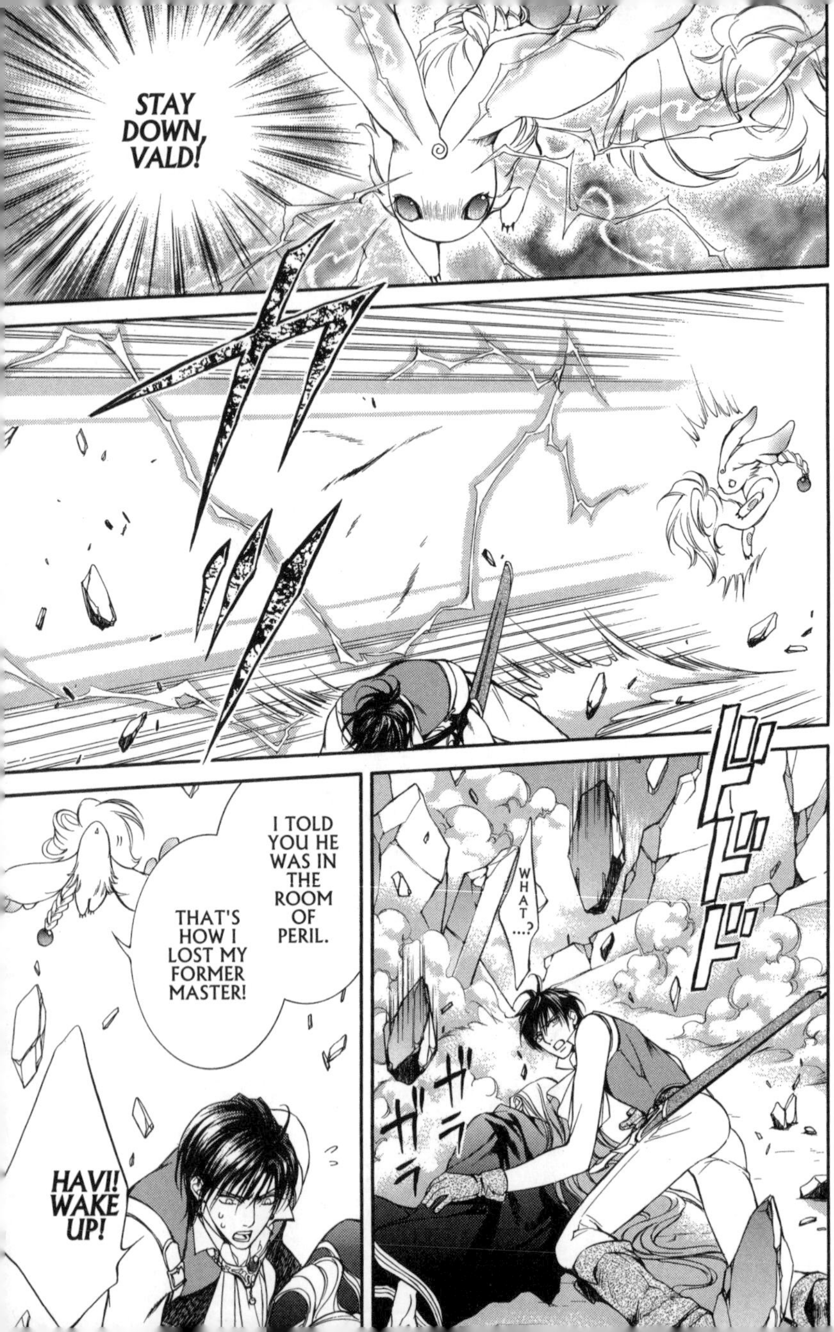
STAY DOWN, VALD!
WHAT ...?
I TOLD YOU HE WAS IN THE ROOM OF PERIL.
THAT'S HOW I LOST MY FORMER MASTER!
HAVI! WAKE UP!

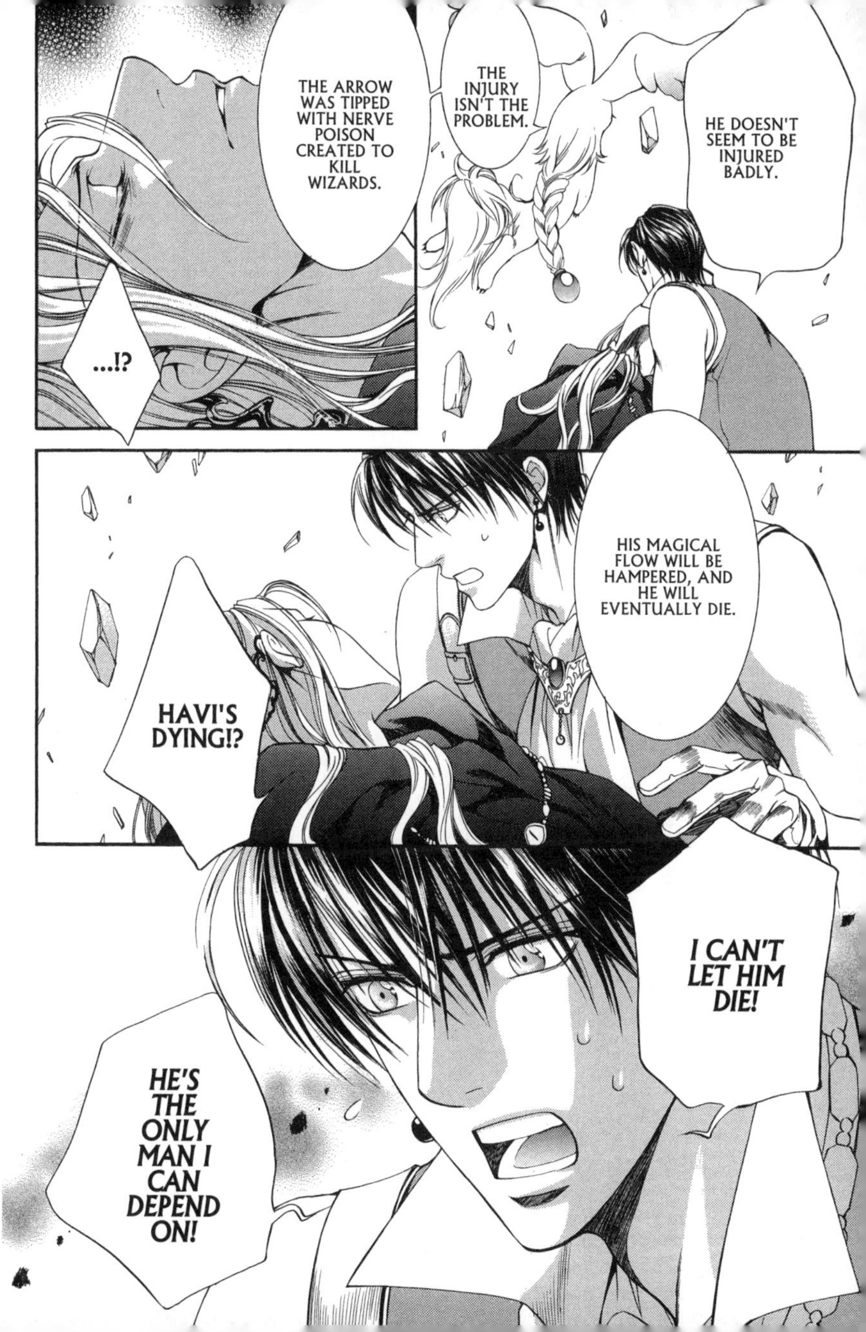
HE DOESN'T SEEM TO BE INJURED BADLY.
THE INJURY ISN'T THE PROBLEM.
THE ARROW WAS TIPPED WITH NERVE POISON CREATED TO KILL WIZARDS.
...!?
HIS MAGICAL FLOW WILL BE HAMPERED, AND HE WILL EVENTUALLY DIE.
HAVI'S DYING!?
I CAN'T LET HIM DIE!
HE'S THE ONLY MAN I CAN DEPEND ON!

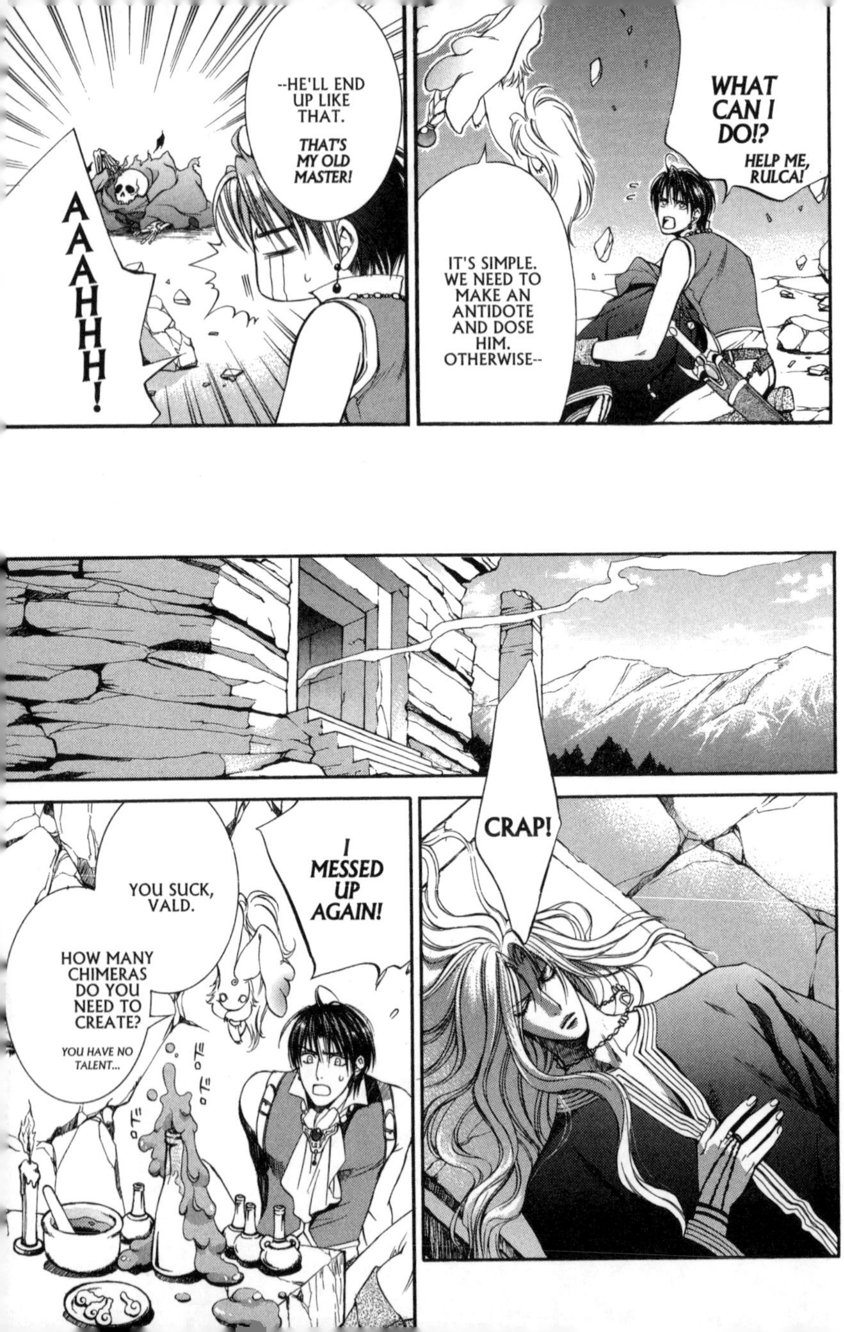
WHAT CAN I DO!?
HELP ME, RULCA!
IT'S SIMPLE. WE NEED TO MAKE AN ANTIDOTE AND DOSE HIM. OTHERWISE--
--HE'LL END UP LIKE THAT.
THAT'S MY OLD MASTER!
AAAHHH!
CRAP!
I MESSED UP AGAIN!
YOU SUCK, VALD.
HOW MANY CHIMERAS DO YOU NEED TO CREATE?
YOU HAVE NO TALENT...

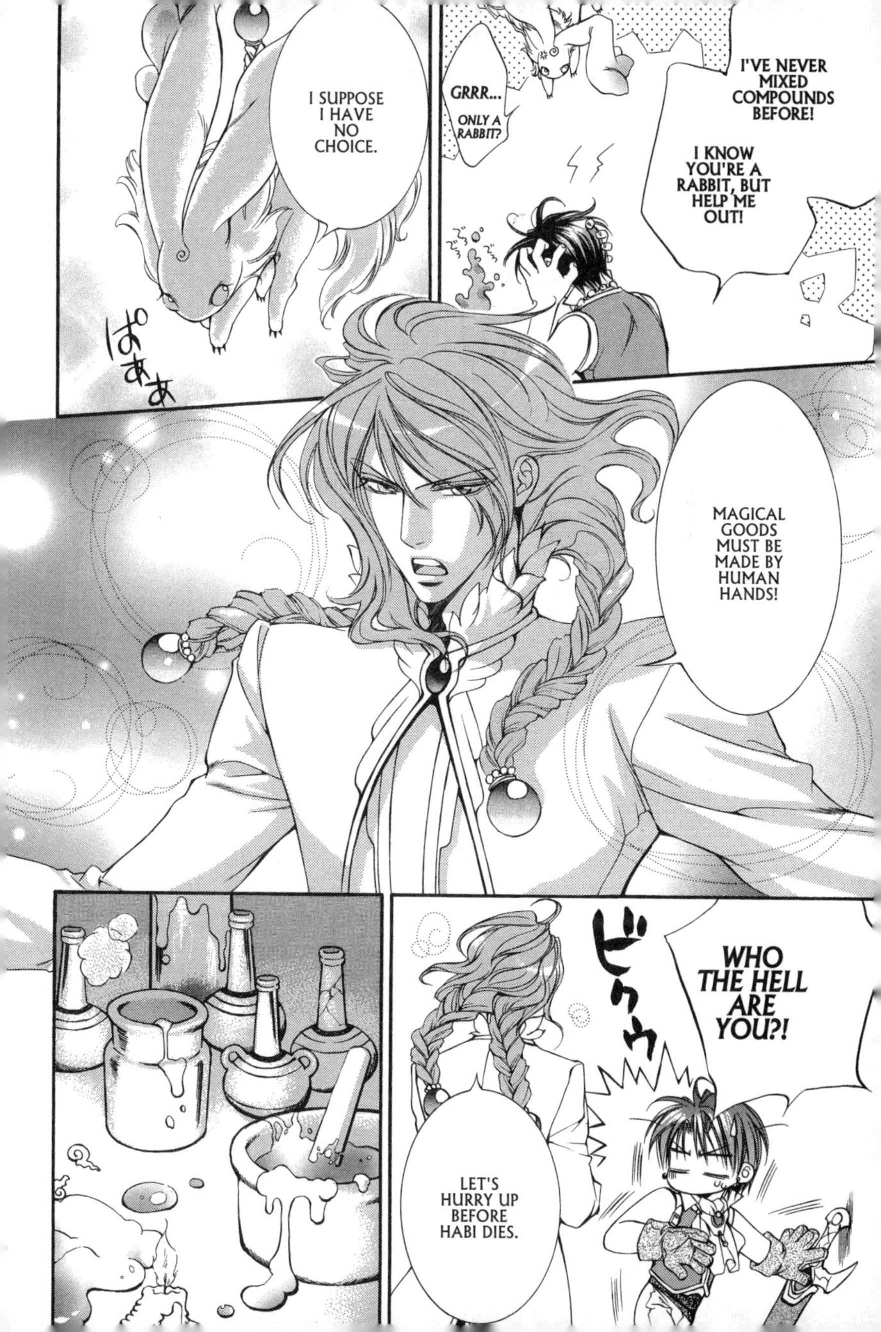

I'VE NEVER MIXED COMPOUNDS BEFORE!
I KNOW YOU'RE A RABBIT, BUT HELP ME OUT!
GRRR...
ONLY A RABBIT?
I SUPPOSE I HAVE NO CHOICE.
ぱああ
MAGICAL GOODS MUST BE MADE BY HUMAN HANDS!
WHO THE HELL ARE YOU?!
ビクゥ
LET'S HURRY UP BEFORE HABI DIES.

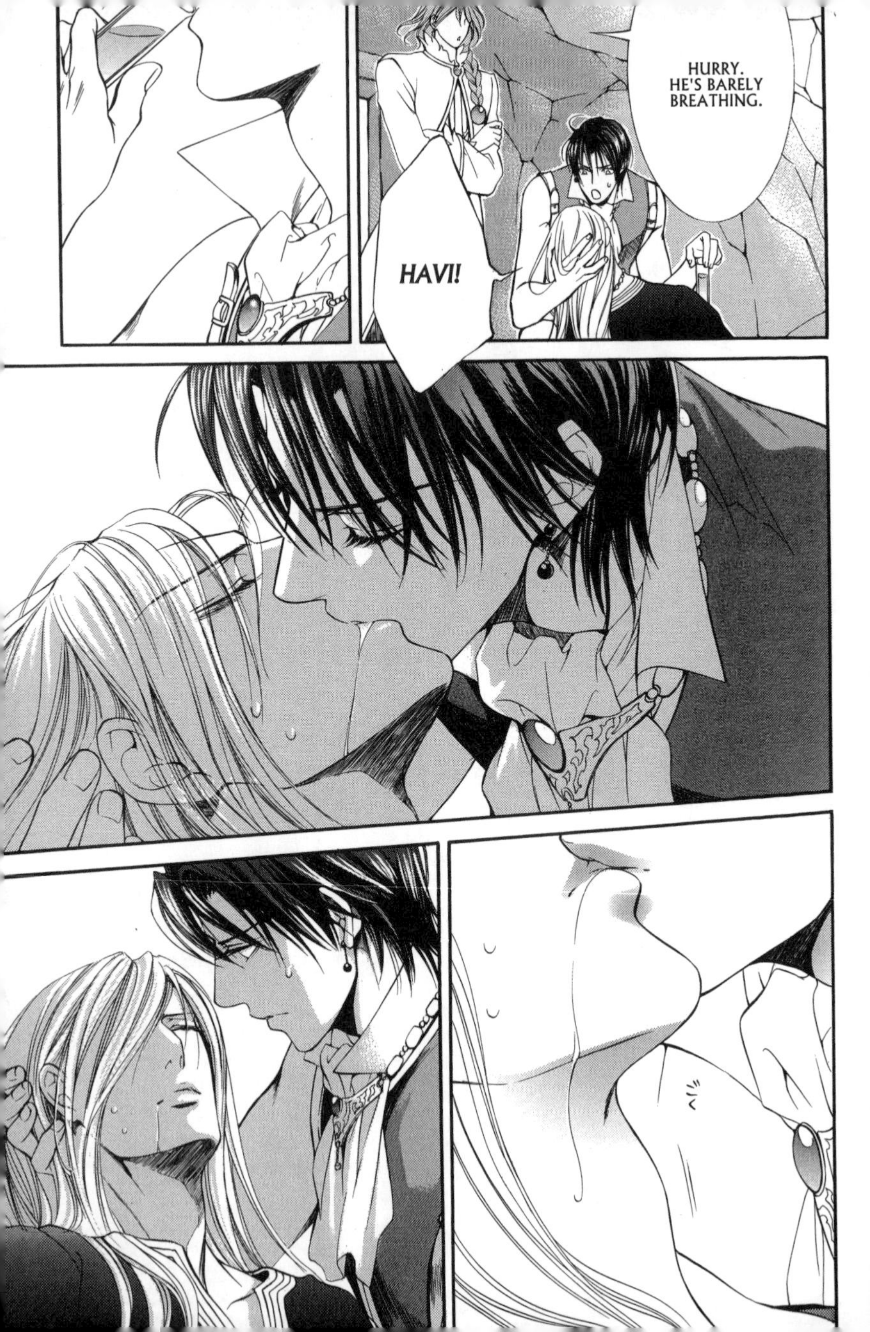
HURRY. HE'S BARELY BREATHING.
HAVI!

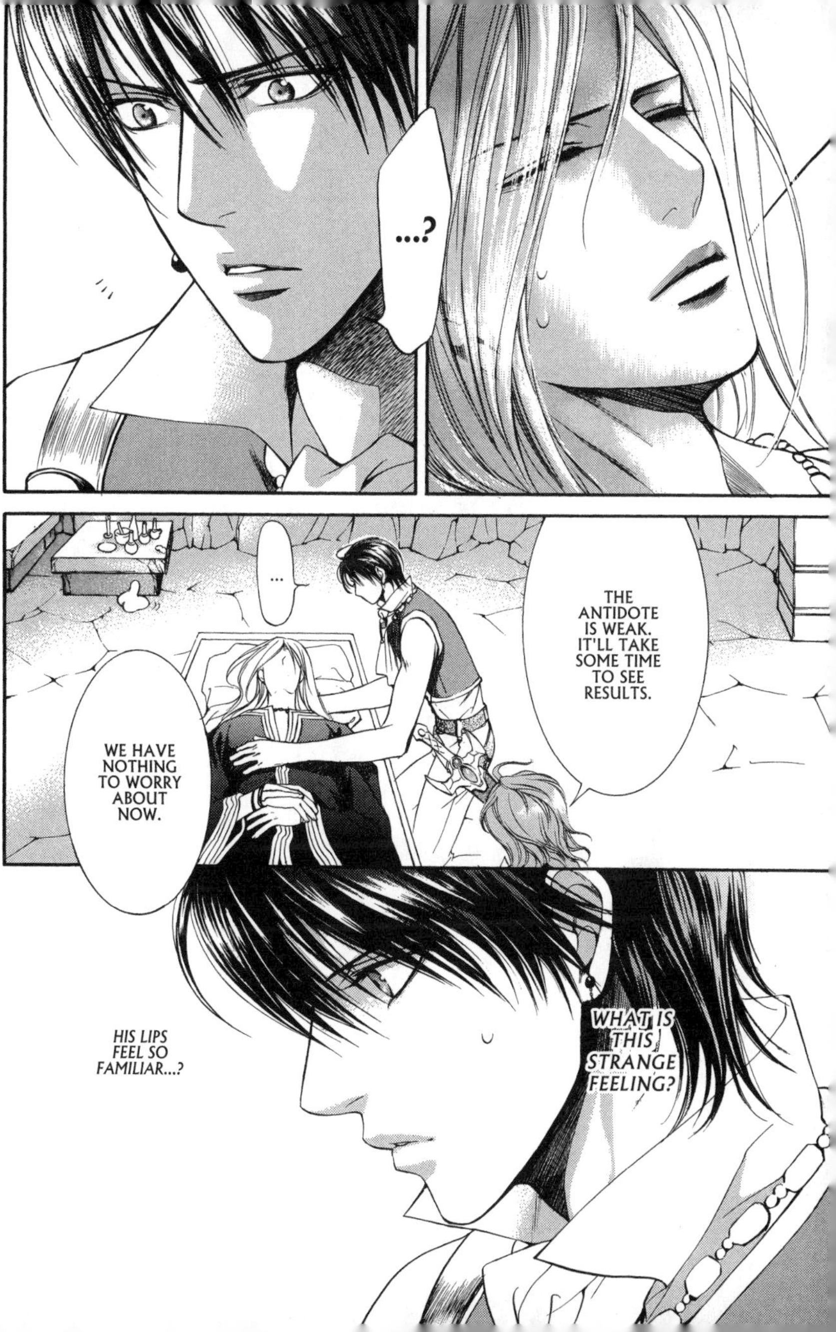
...?
THE ANTIDOTE IS WEAK. IT'LL TAKE SOME TIME TO SEE RESULTS.
...
WE HAVE NOTHING TO WORRY ABOUT NOW.
WHAT IS THIS STRANGE FEELING?
HIS LIPS FEEL SO FAMILIAR...?

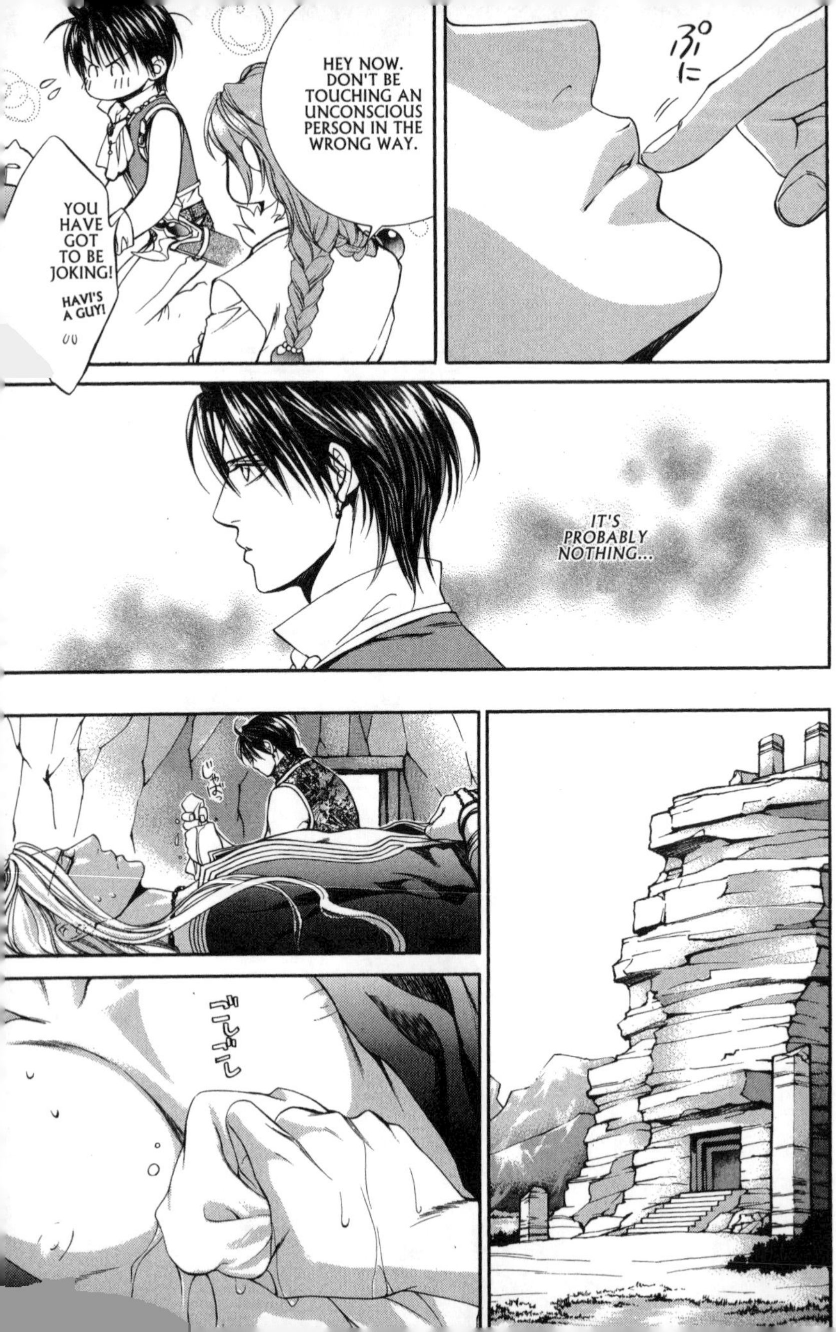
ぷに
HEY NOW. DON'T BE TOUCHING AN UNCONSCIOUS PERSON IN THE WRONG WAY.
YOU HAVE GOT TO BE JOKING!
HAVI'S A GUY!
IT'S PROBABLY NOTHING...

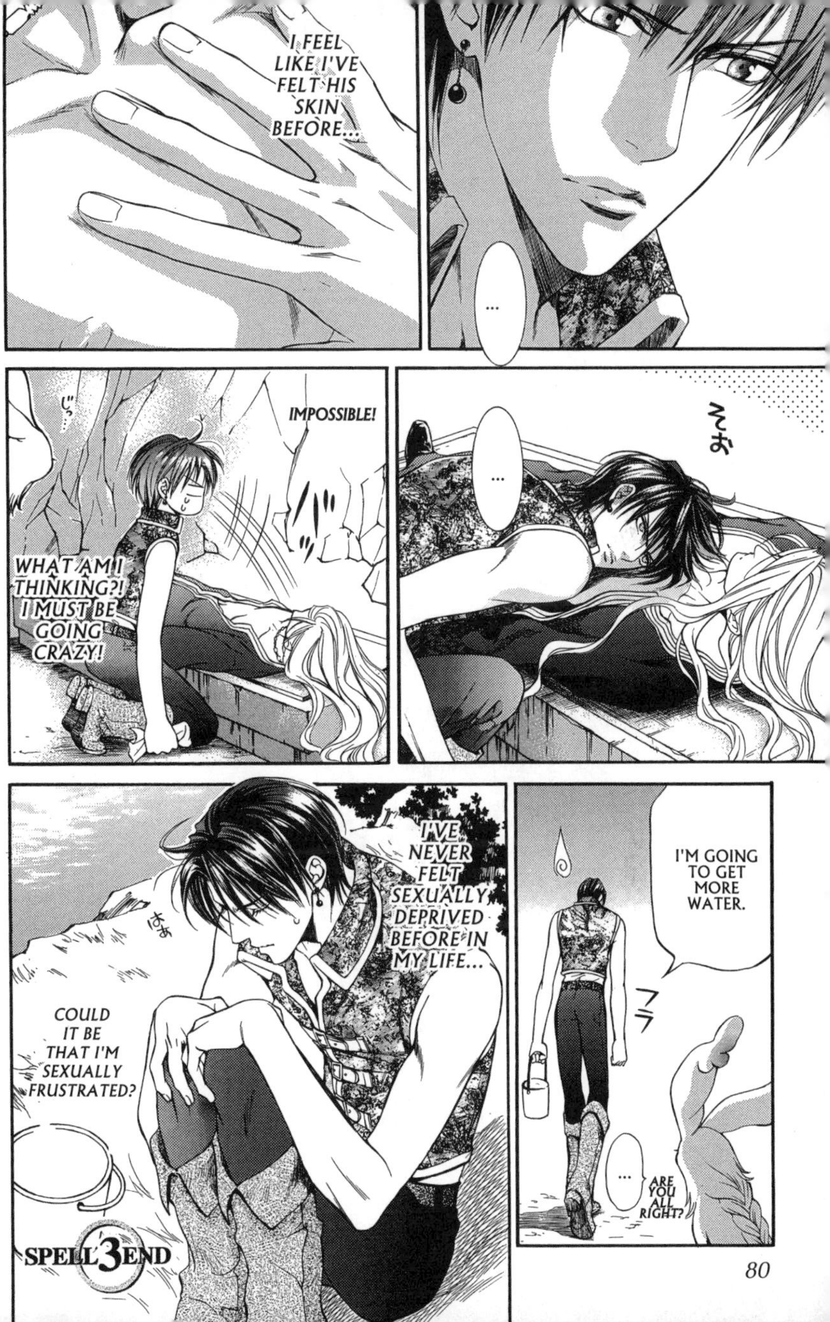
...
I FEEL LIKE I'VE FELT HIS SKIN BEFORE...
...
そお
じっ…
IMPOSSIBLE!
WHAT AM I THINKING?! I MUST BE GOING CRAZY!
I'M GOING TO GET MORE WATER.
フラ
...
ARE YOU ALL RIGHT?
I'VE NEVER FELT SEXUALLY DEPRIVED BEFORE IN MY LIFE...
はあ
COULD IT BE THAT I'M SEXUALLY FRUSTRATED?
SPELL 3 END

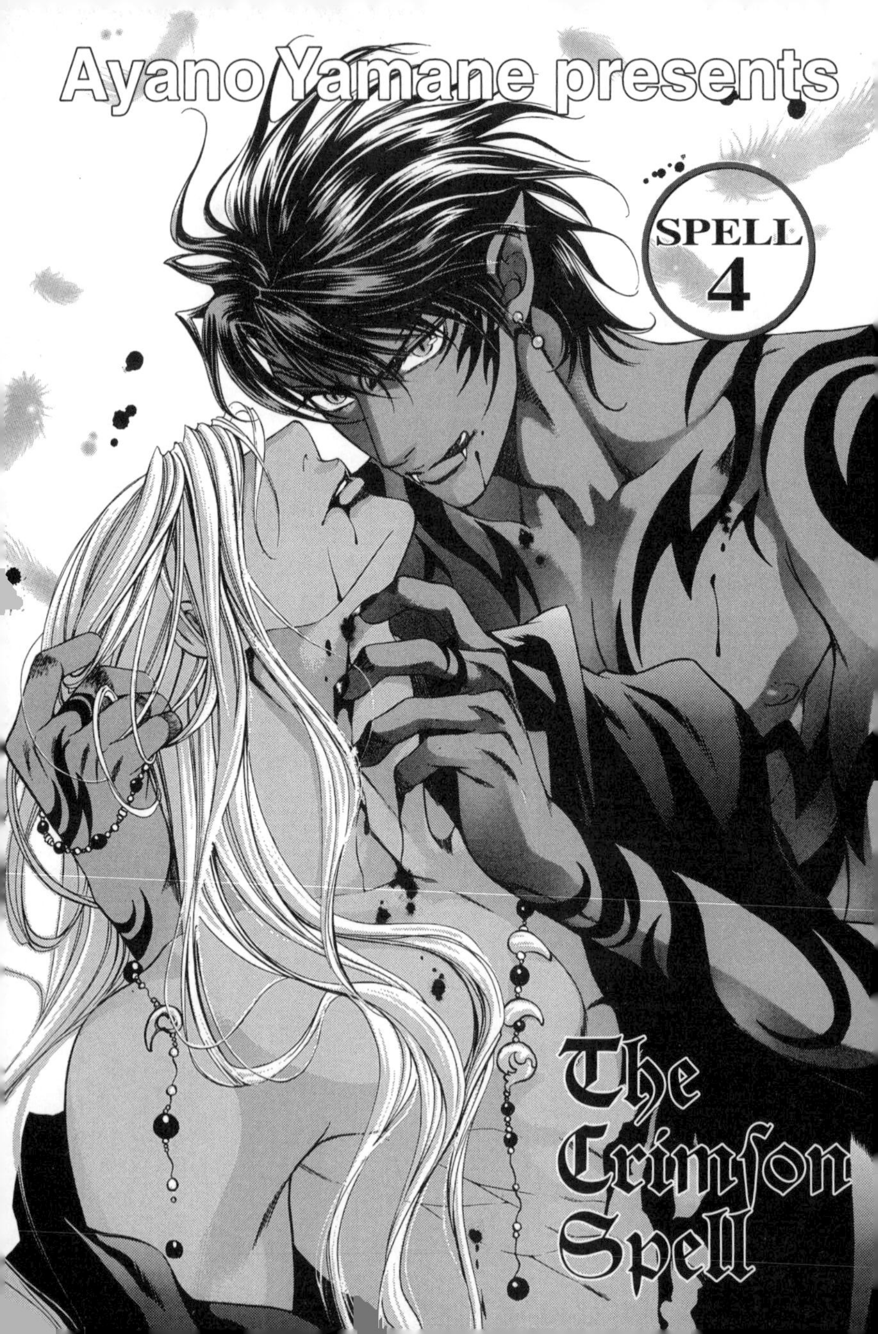
Ayano Yamane presents
SPELL 4
The Crimson Spell

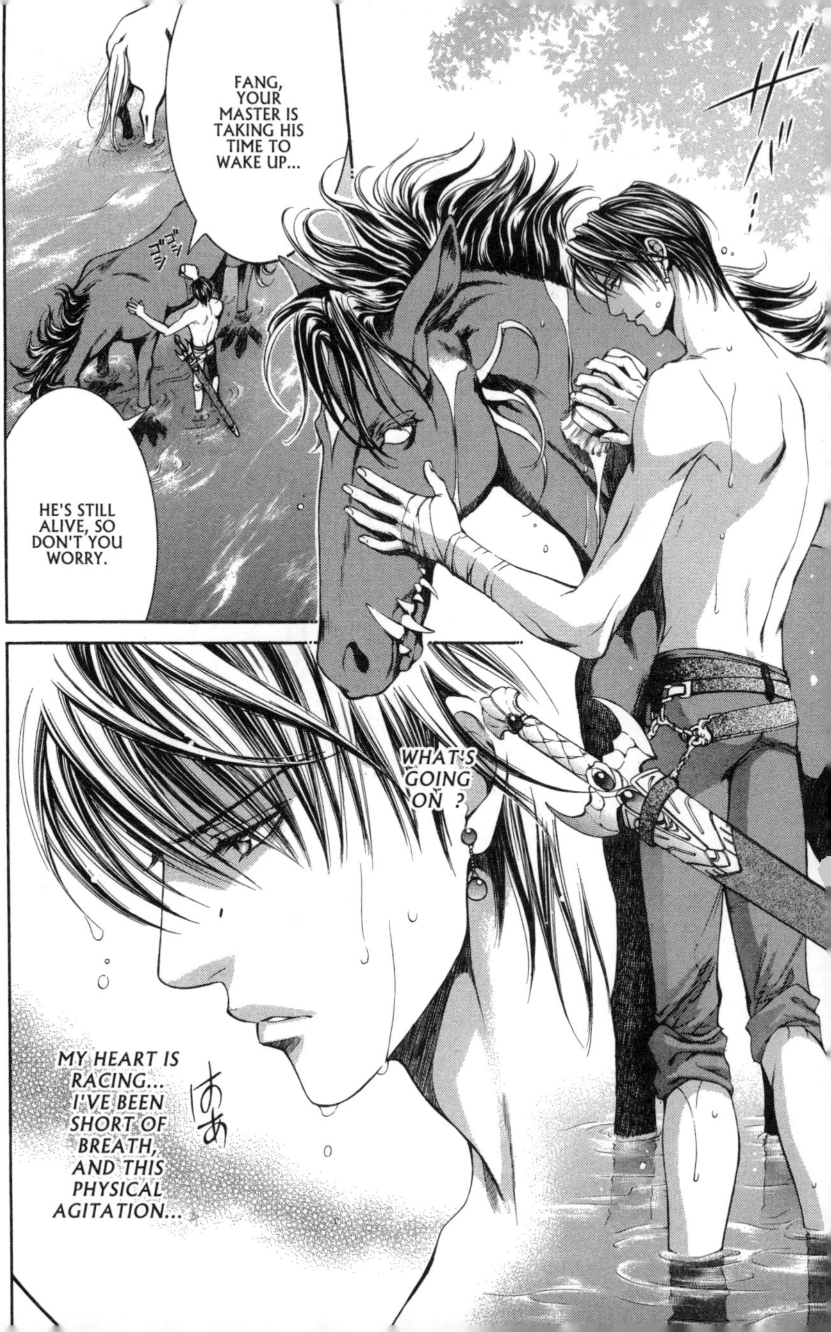
FANG, YOUR MASTER IS TAKING HIS TIME TO WAKE UP...
HE'S STILL ALIVE, SO DON'T YOU WORRY.
WHAT'S GOING ON ?
MY HEART IS RACING... I'VE BEEN SHORT OF BREATH, AND THIS PHYSICAL AGITATION...
はあ

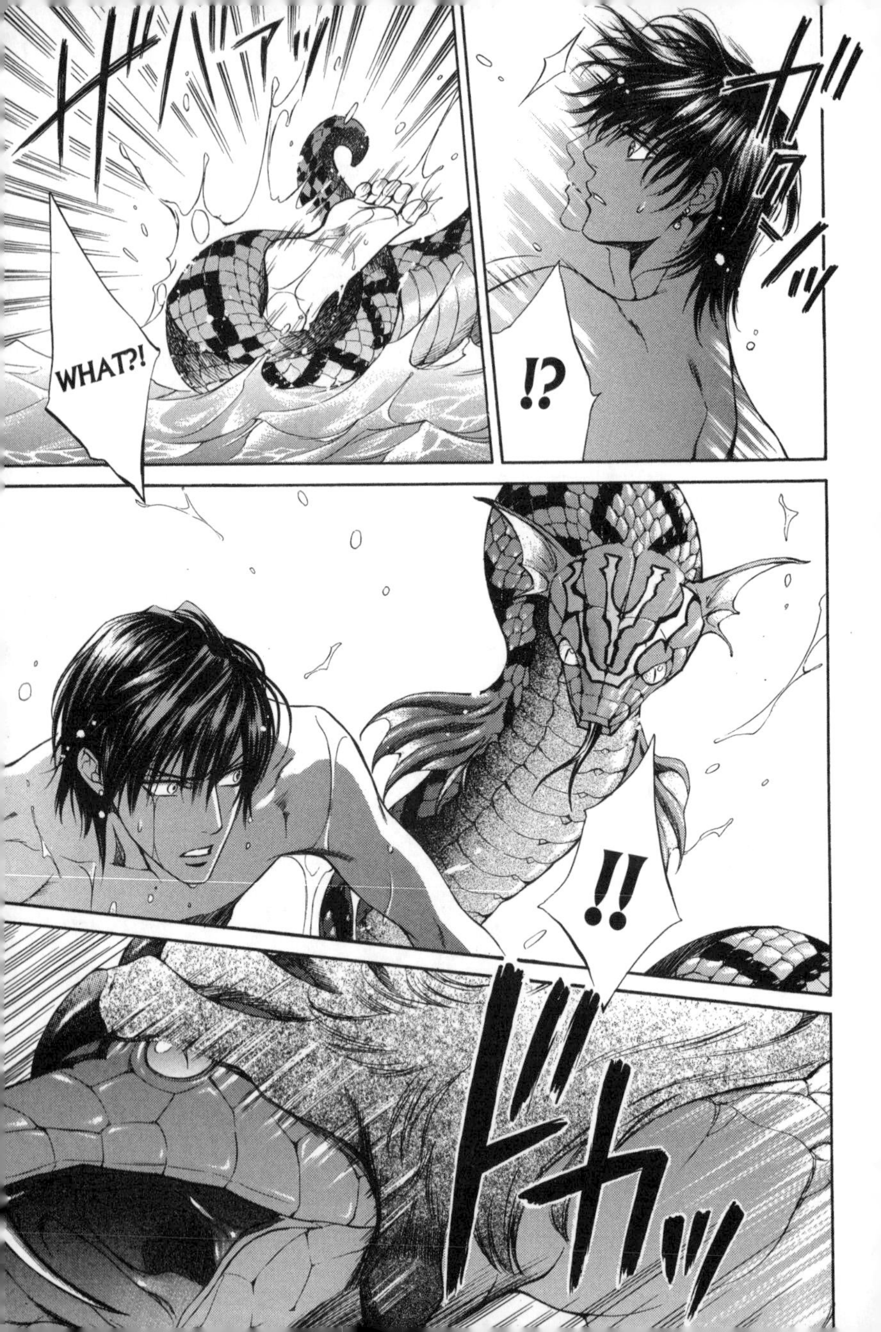
!?
WHAT?!
!!
ドカッ

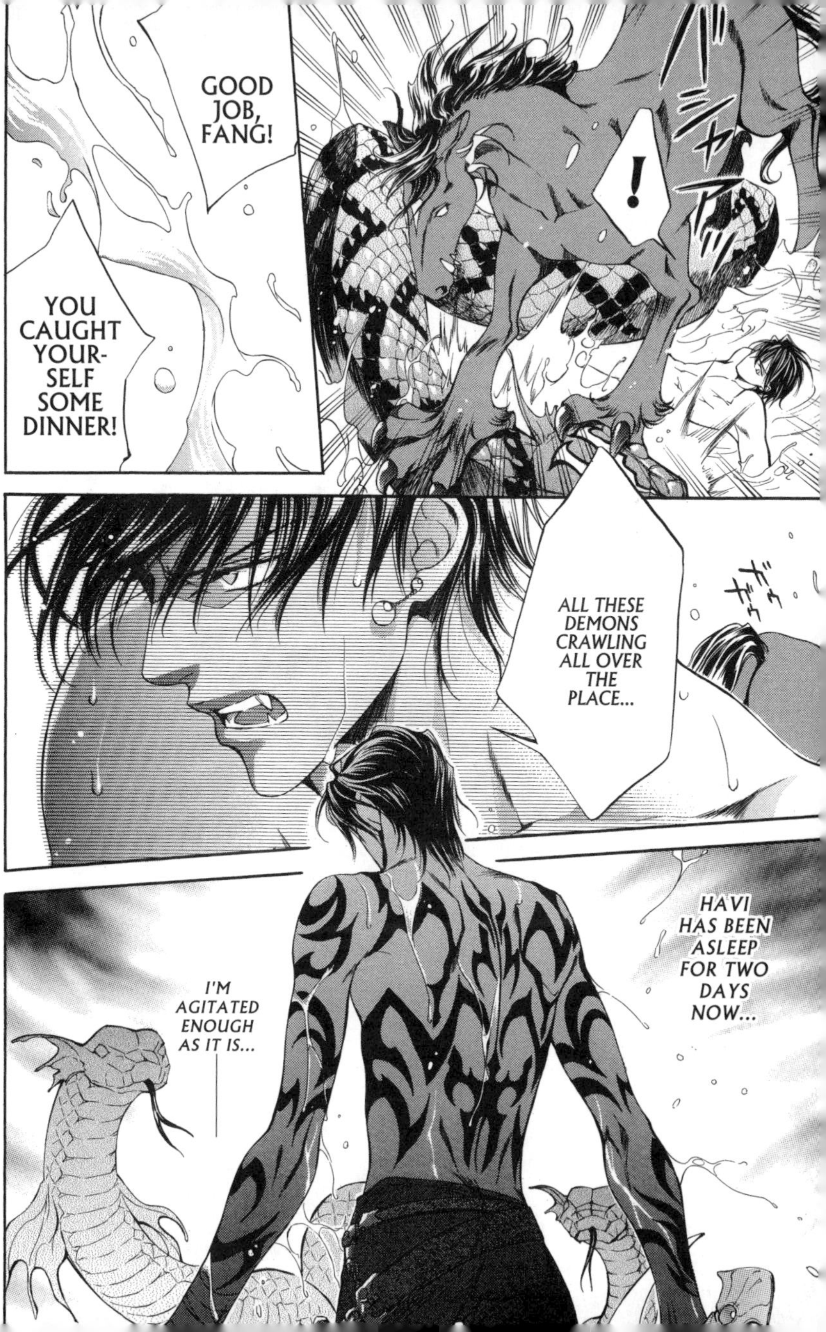
!
GOOD JOB, FANG!
YOU CAUGHT YOURSELF SOME DINNER!
ALL THESE DEMONS CRAWLING ALL OVER THE PLACE...
HAVI HAS BEEN ASLEEP FOR TWO DAYS NOW...
I'M AGITATED ENOUGH AS IT IS...

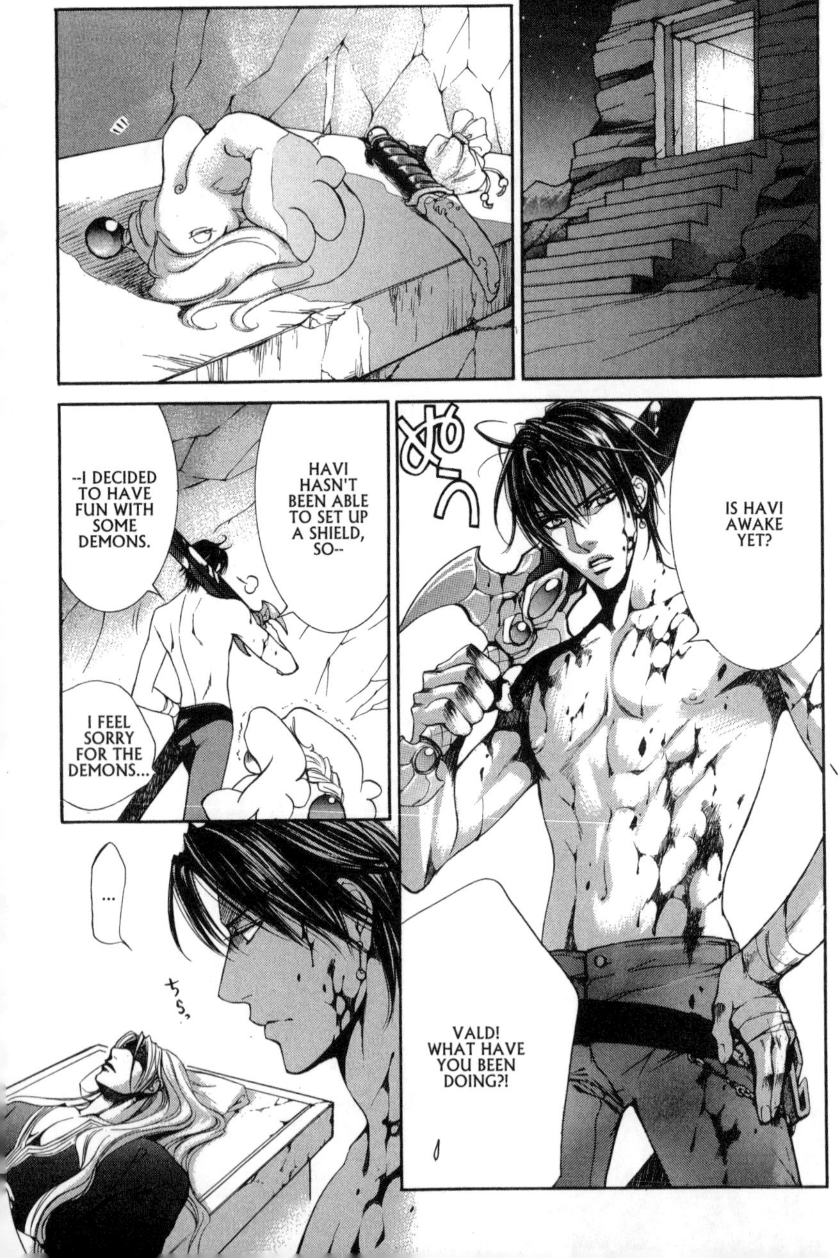
IS HAVI AWAKE YET?
VALD! WHAT HAVE YOU BEEN DOING?!
HAVI HASN'T BEEN ABLE TO SET UP A SHIELD, SO--
--I DECIDED TO HAVE FUN WITH SOME DEMONS.
I FEEL SORRY FOR THE DEMONS...
...

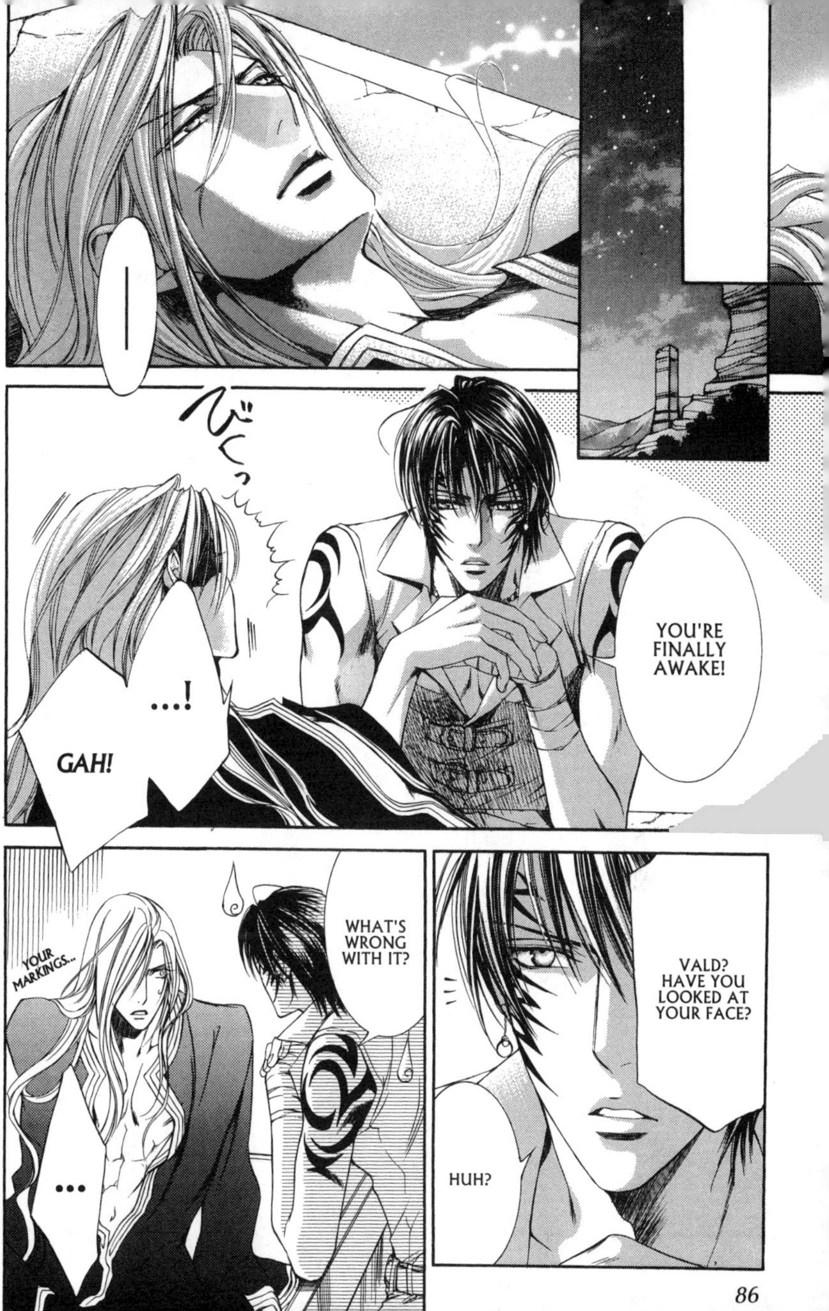
—
YOU'RE FINALLY AWAKE!
びくっ
...!
GAH!
VALD? HAVE YOU LOOKED AT YOUR FACE?
HUH?
WHAT'S WRONG WITH IT?
YOUR MARKINGS...
...

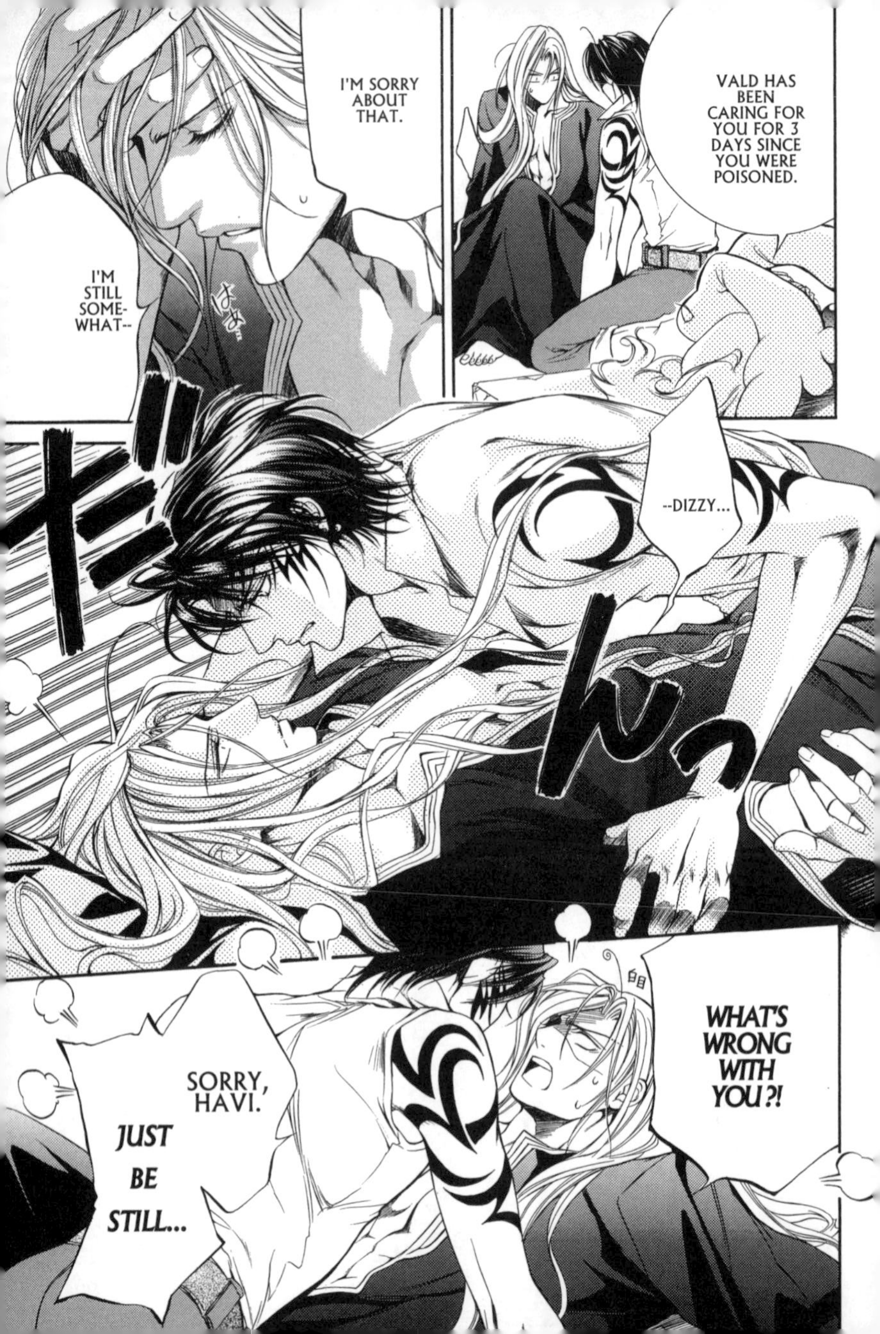
VALD HAS BEEN CARING FOR YOU FOR 3 DAYS SINCE YOU WERE POISONED.
I'M SORRY ABOUT THAT.
I'M STILL SOME-WHAT--
--DIZZY...
んっ
白目
WHAT'S WRONG WITH YOU?!
SORRY, HAVI.
JUST BE STILL...

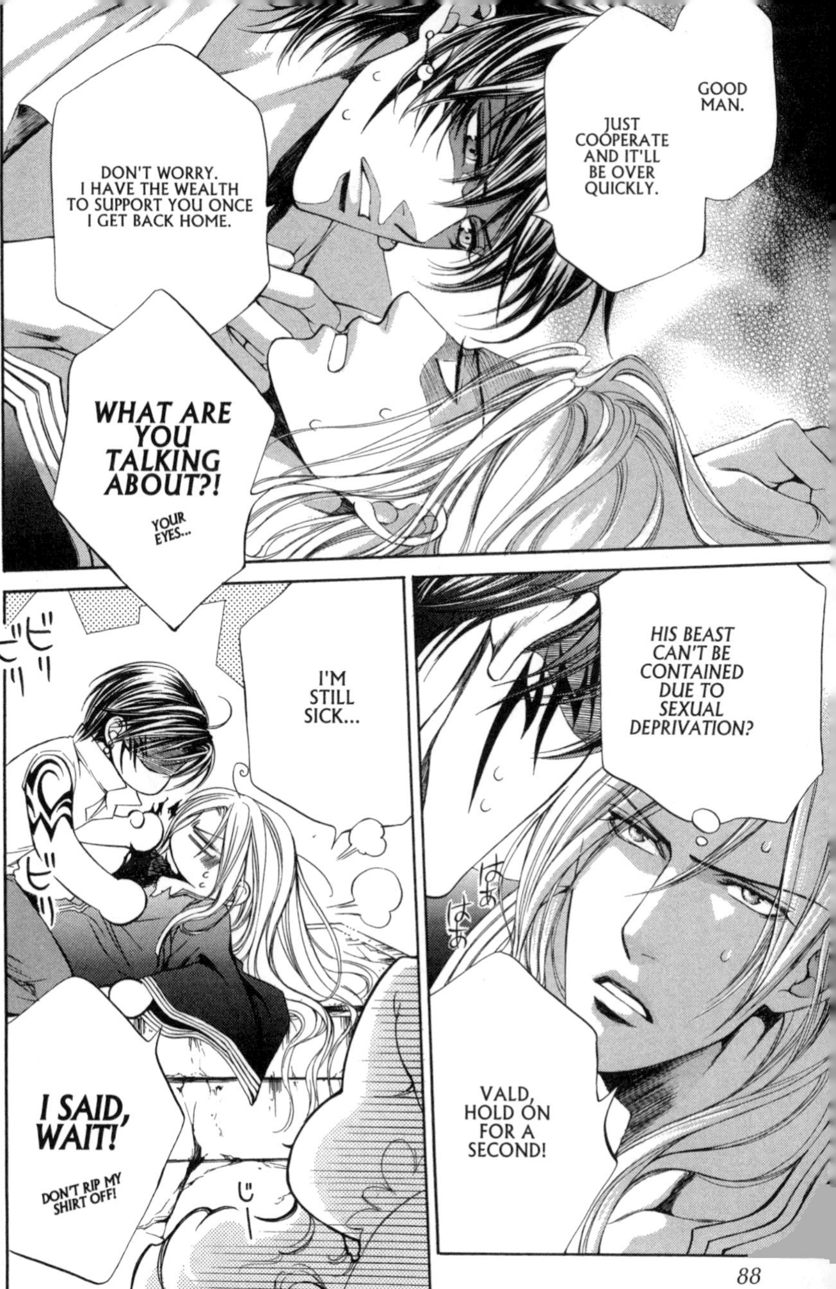
GOOD MAN.
JUST COOPERATE AND IT'LL BE OVER QUICKLY.
DON'T WORRY. I HAVE THE WEALTH TO SUPPORT YOU ONCE I GET BACK HOME.
WHAT ARE YOU TALKING ABOUT?!
YOUR EYES...
HIS BEAST CAN'T BE CONTAINED DUE TO SEXUAL DEPRIVATION?
はあ はあ
VALD, HOLD ON FOR A SECOND!
ビリビリ
I'M STILL SICK...
ビリ
I SAID, WAIT!
DON'T RIP MY SHIRT OFF!
じー

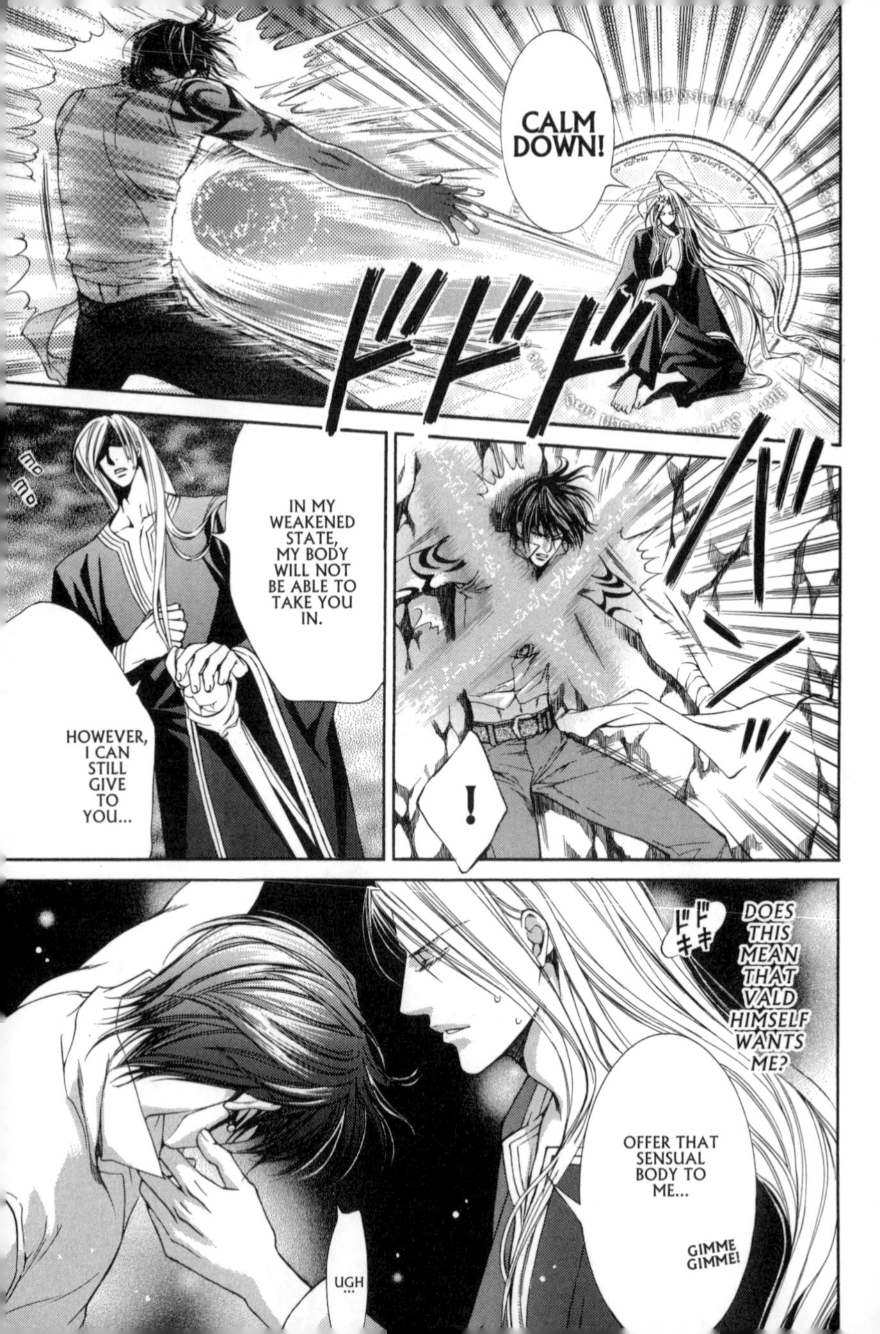
CALM DOWN!
ドドドド
!
IN MY WEAKENED STATE, MY BODY WILL NOT BE ABLE TO TAKE YOU IN.
HOWEVER, I CAN STILL GIVE TO YOU...
DOES THIS MEAN THAT VALD HIMSELF WANTS ME?
ドキドキ
OFFER THAT SENSUAL BODY TO ME...
GIMME GIMME!
UGH...

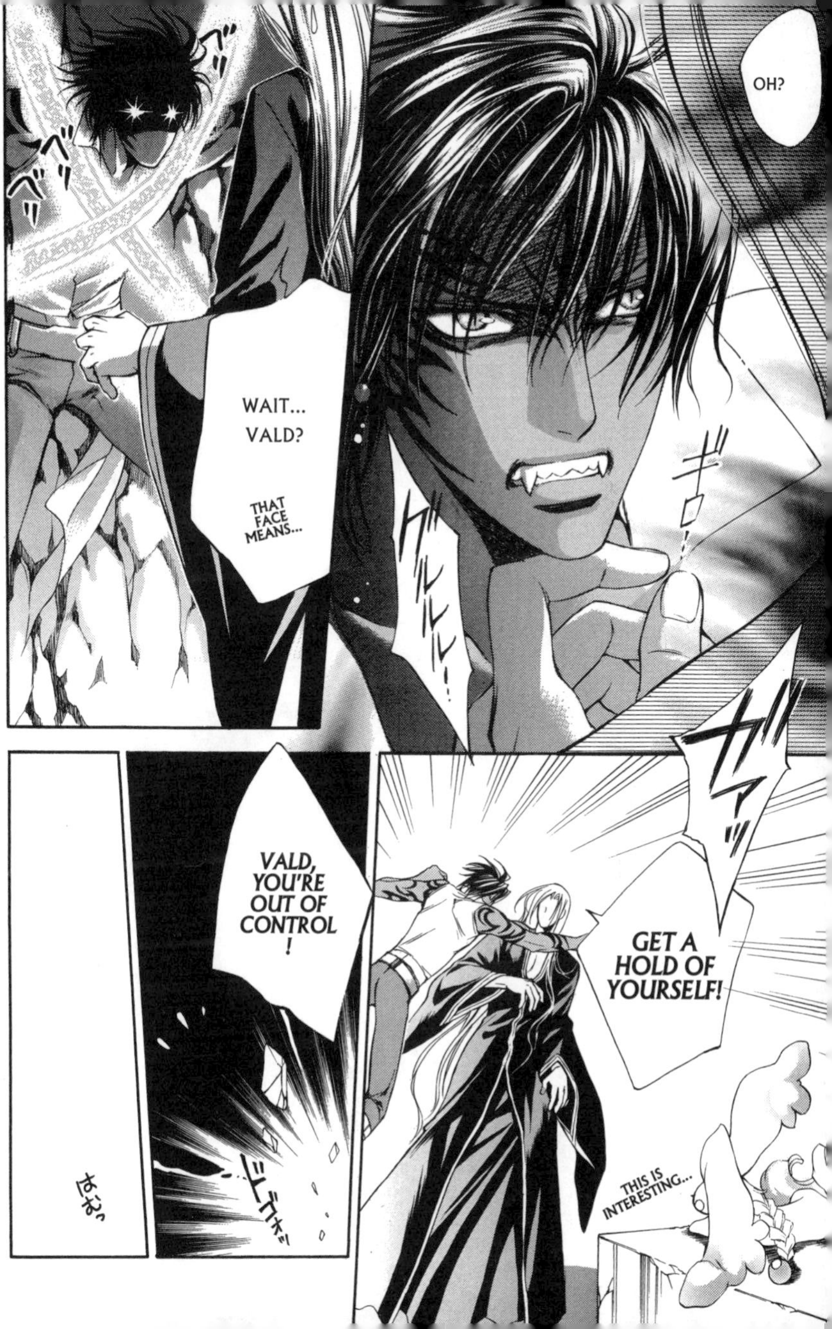
OH?
WAIT... VALD?
THAT FACE MEANS...
GET A HOLD OF YOURSELF!
THIS IS INTERESTING...
VALD, YOU'RE OUT OF CONTROL!
はむっ

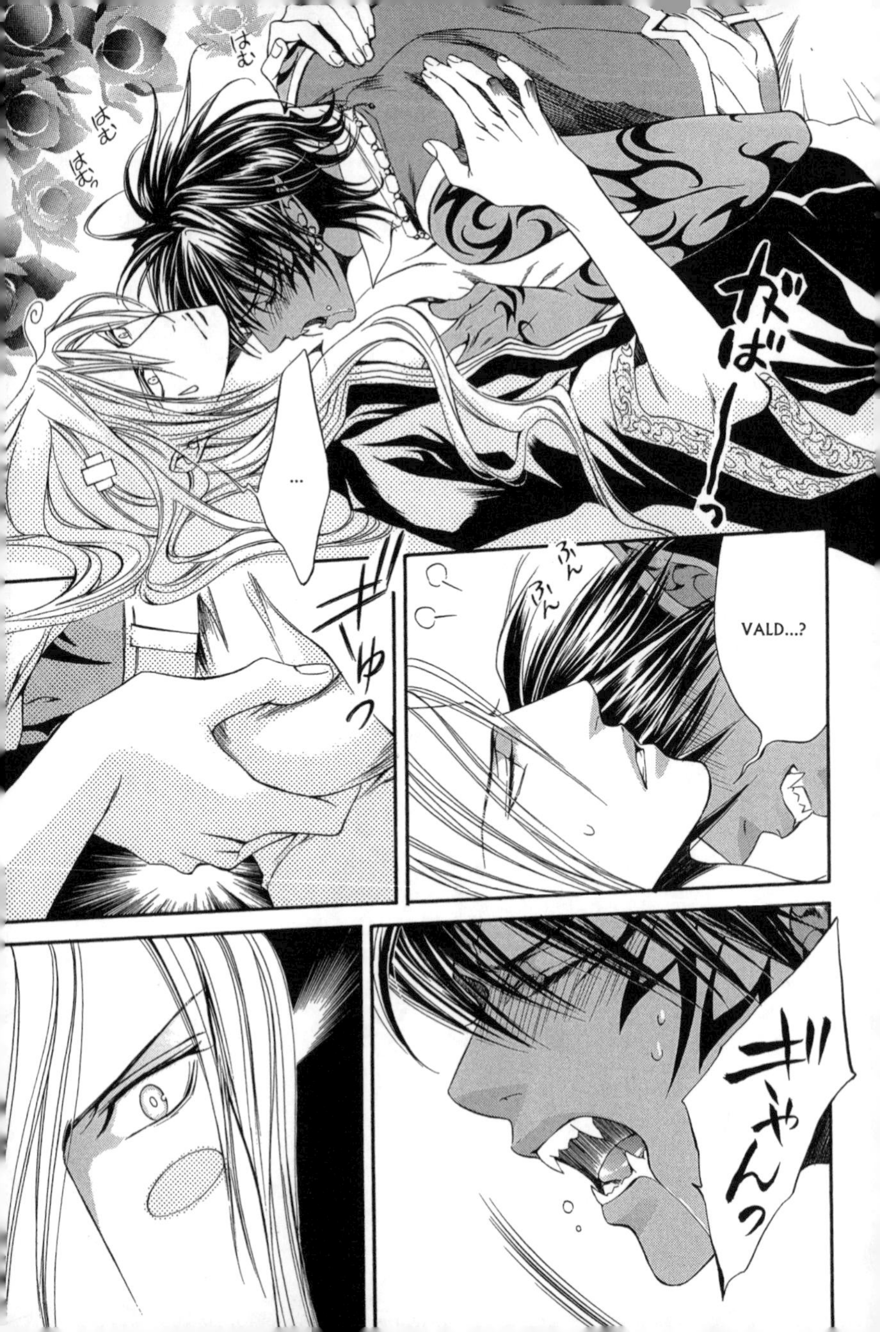
がばーっ
はむ はむ はむっ
...
ふん ふん
VALD...?
ギゅっ
ギゃんっ

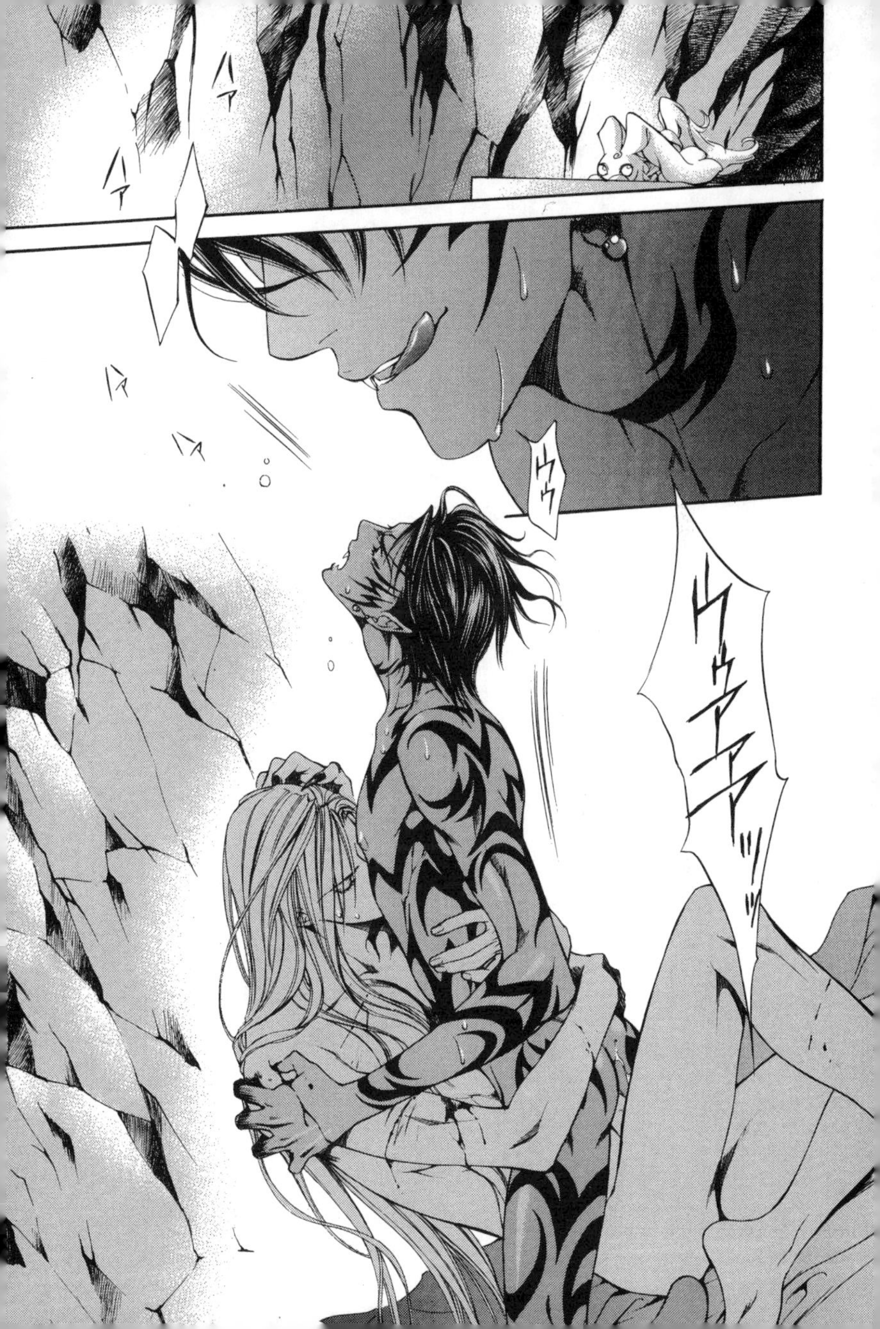
ハァ
ハァ
ウウ
ハァ
ハァ
ウウアアアッ

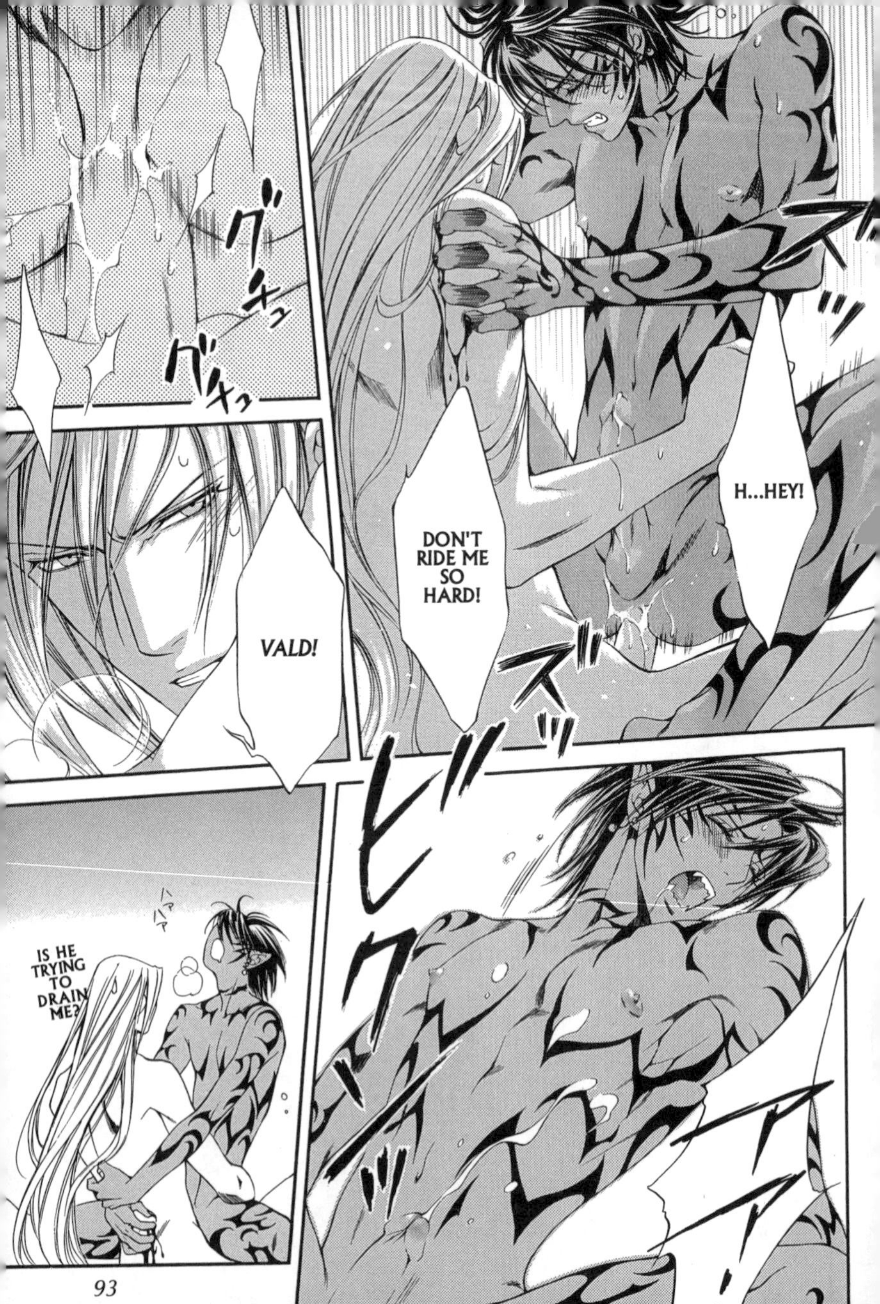
H...HEY!
DON'T RIDE ME SO HARD!
グチュ
グチュ
VALD!
IS HE TRYING TO DRAIN ME?
ハァハァ

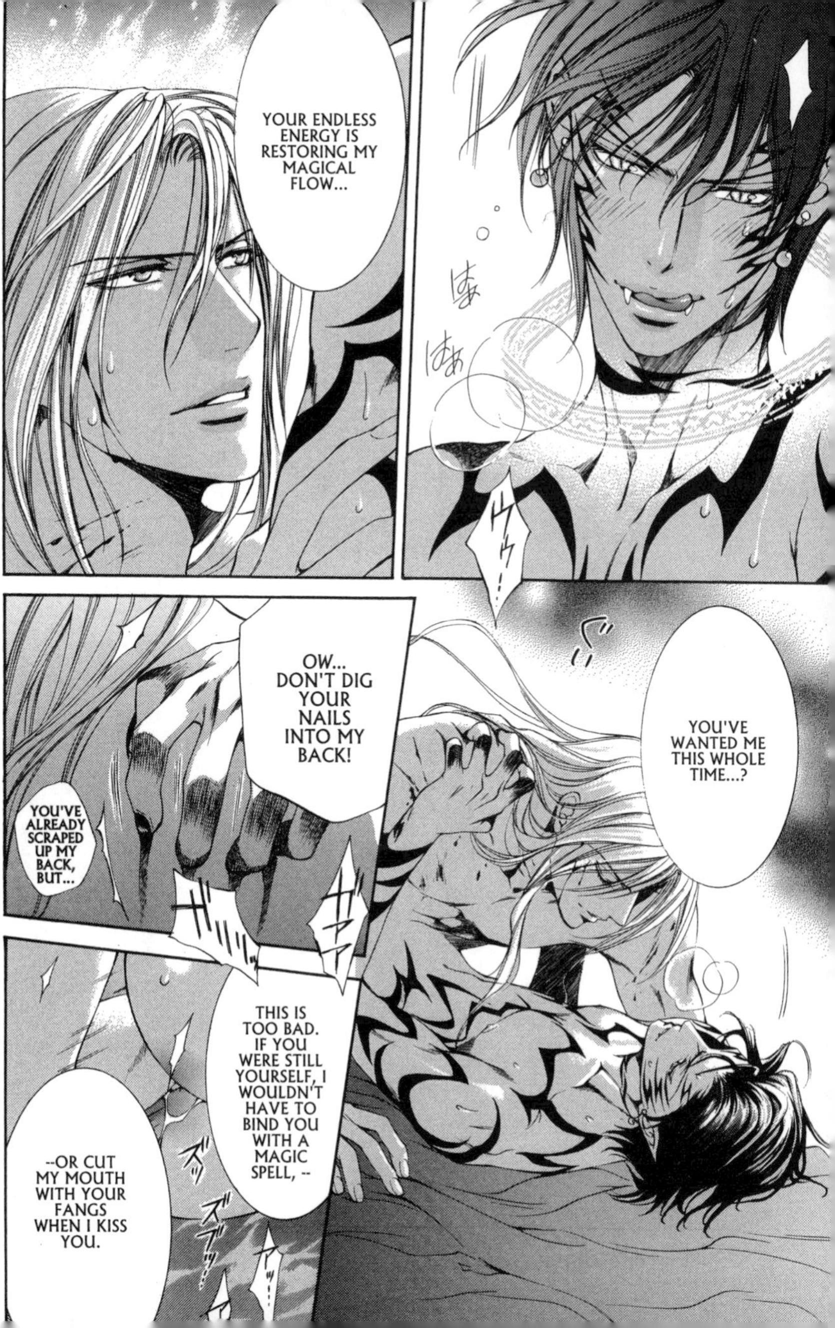
はぁ
はぁ
YOUR ENDLESS ENERGY IS RESTORING MY MAGICAL FLOW...
YOU'VE WANTED ME THIS WHOLE TIME...?
OW... DON'T DIG YOUR NAILS INTO MY BACK!
YOU'VE ALREADY SCRAPED UP MY BACK, BUT...
THIS IS TOO BAD. IF YOU WERE STILL YOURSELF, I WOULDN'T HAVE TO BIND YOU WITH A MAGIC SPELL, --
--OR CUT MY MOUTH WITH YOUR FANGS WHEN I KISS YOU.

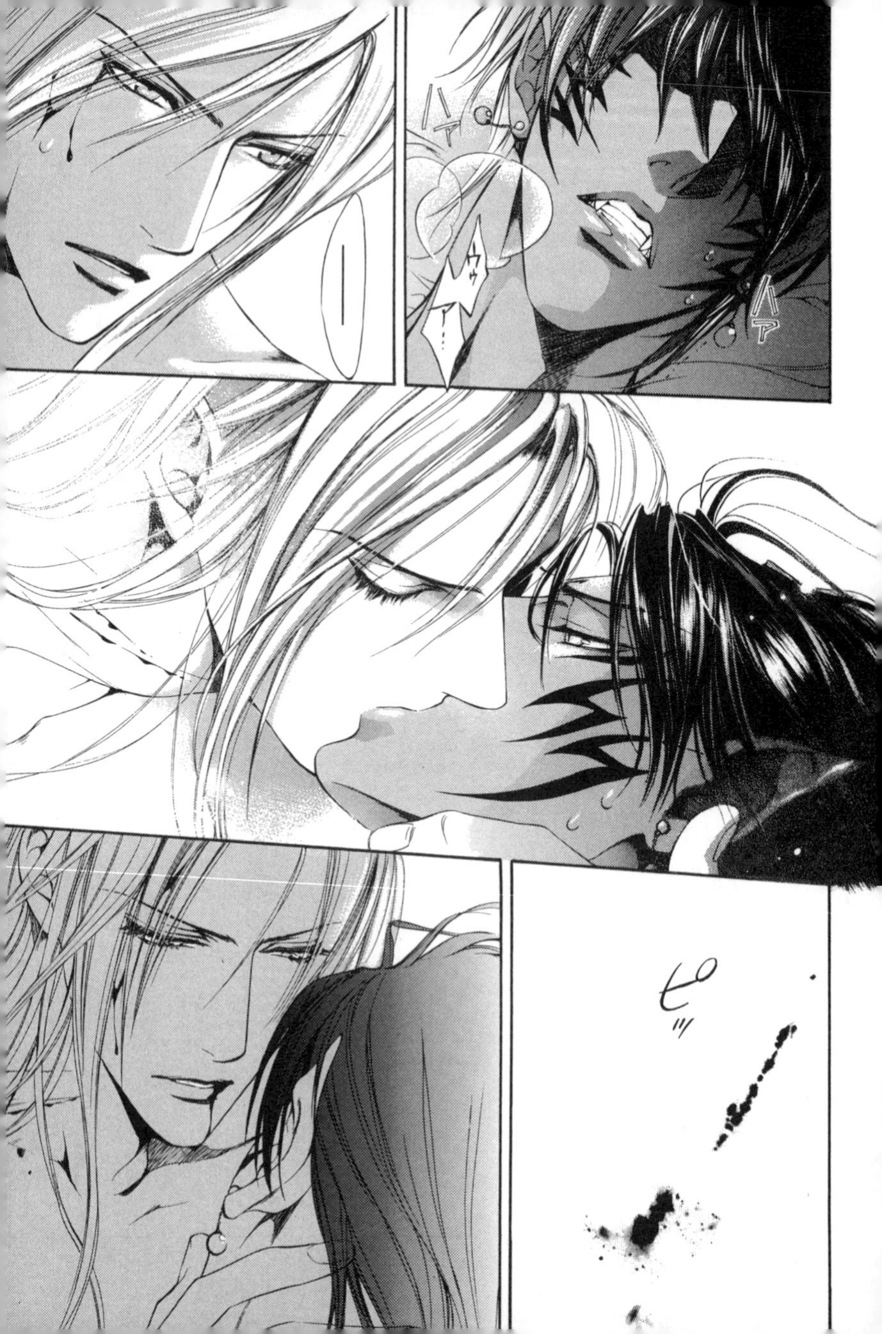
ハァ
ハァ
ウゥ
ー…
―
ピッ

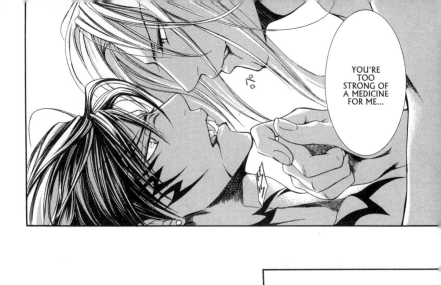

YOU'RE TOO STRONG OF A MEDICINE FOR ME...

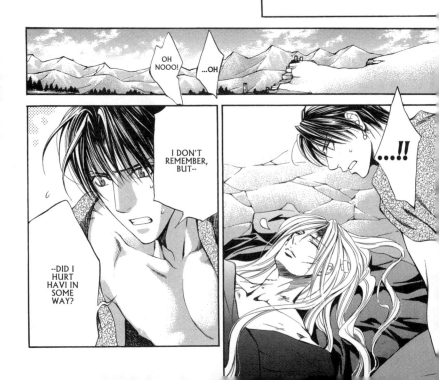

OH NOOO!

...OH

....!!

I DON'T REMEMBER, BUT--

--DID I HURT HAVI IN SOME WAY?

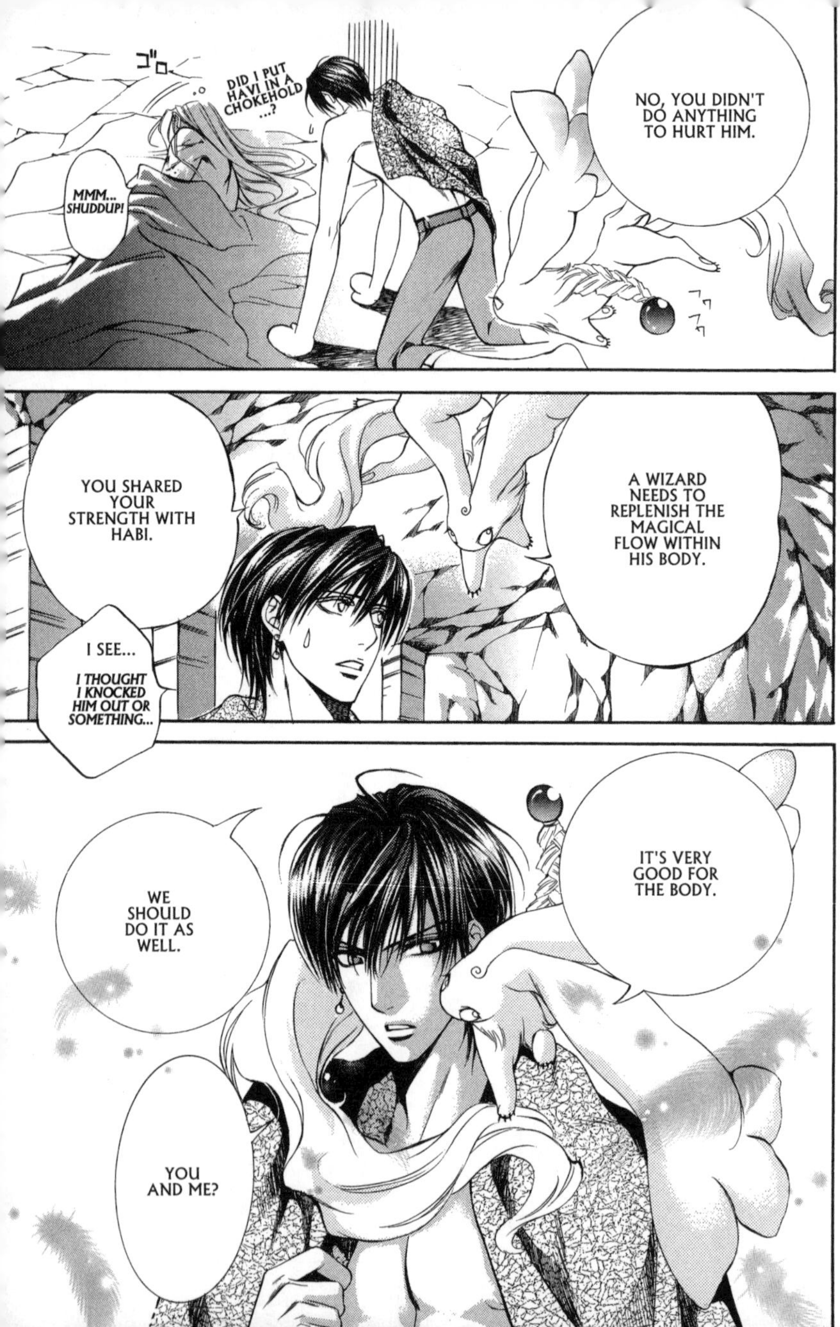
NO, YOU DIDN'T DO ANYTHING TO HURT HIM.
DID I PUT HAVI IN A CHOKEHOLD ...?
ゴロ
MMM... SHUDDUP!
A WIZARD NEEDS TO REPLENISH THE MAGICAL FLOW WITHIN HIS BODY.
YOU SHARED YOUR STRENGTH WITH HABI.
I SEE...
I THOUGHT I KNOCKED HIM OUT OR SOMETHING...
IT'S VERY GOOD FOR THE BODY.
WE SHOULD DO IT AS WELL.
YOU AND ME?

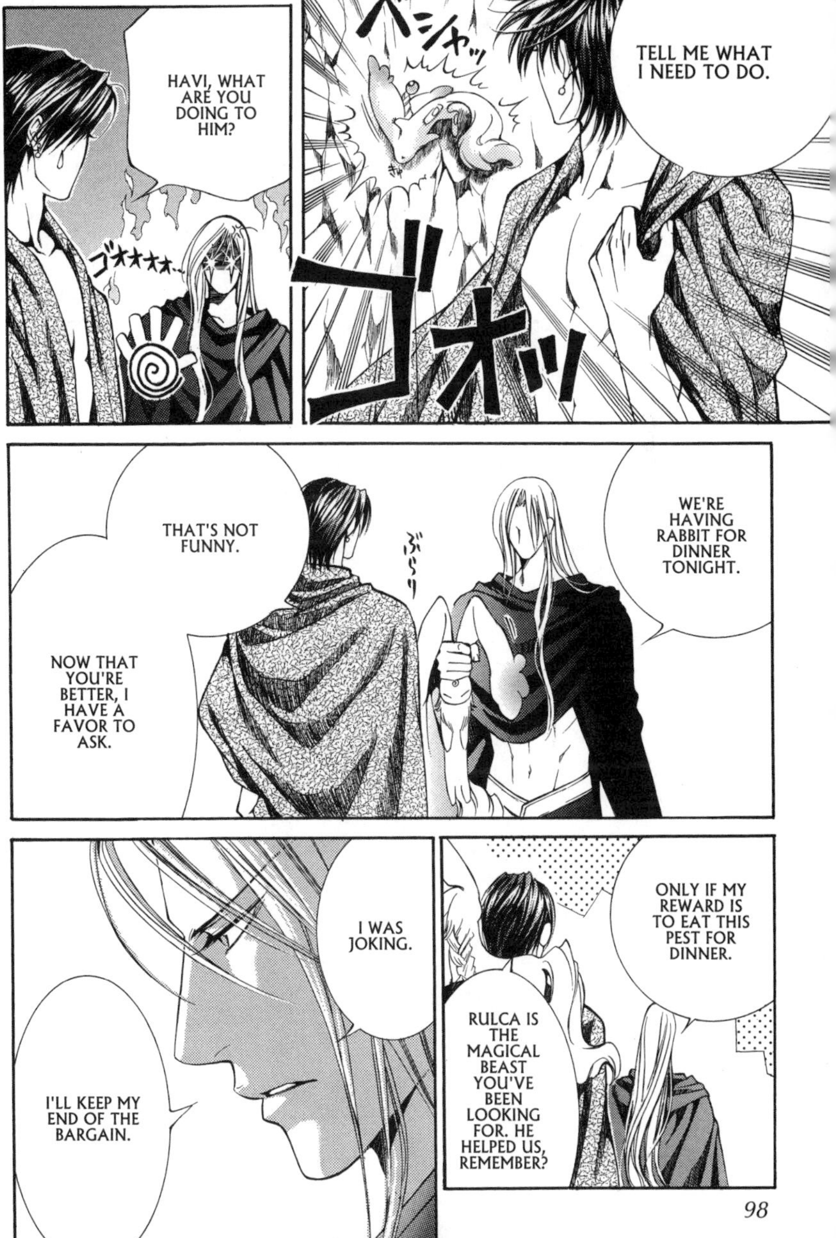
TELL ME WHAT I NEED TO DO.
ベシャッ
ゴオッ
HAVI, WHAT ARE YOU DOING TO HIM?
ゴオオオオ…
WE'RE HAVING RABBIT FOR DINNER TONIGHT.
ぶらり
THAT'S NOT FUNNY.
NOW THAT YOU'RE BETTER, I HAVE A FAVOR TO ASK.
ONLY IF MY REWARD IS TO EAT THIS PEST FOR DINNER.
RULCA IS THE MAGICAL BEAST YOU'VE BEEN LOOKING FOR. HE HELPED US, REMEMBER?
I WAS JOKING.
I'LL KEEP MY END OF THE BARGAIN.

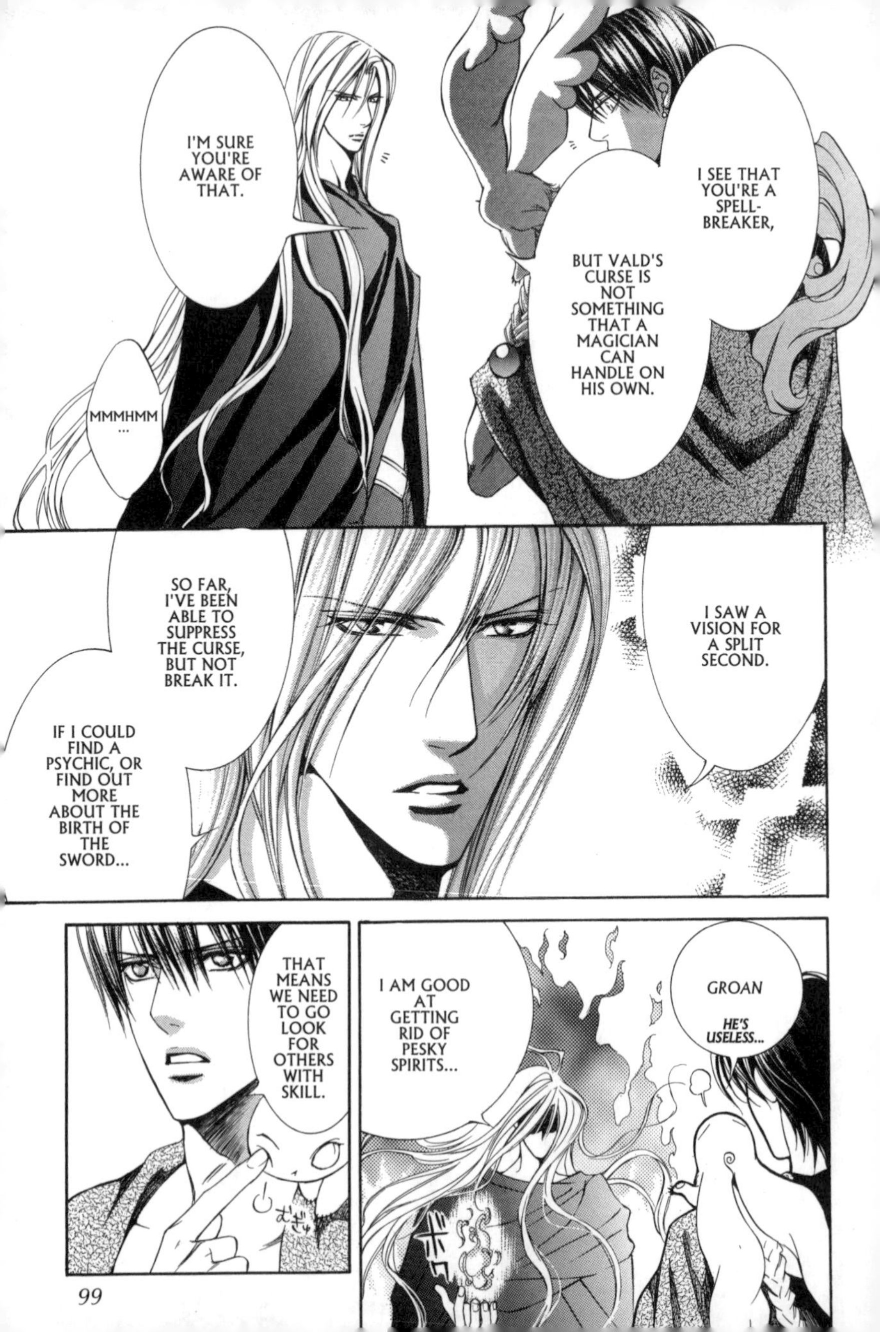
I SEE THAT YOU'RE A SPELL-BREAKER,
BUT VALD'S CURSE IS NOT SOMETHING THAT A MAGICIAN CAN HANDLE ON HIS OWN.
I'M SURE YOU'RE AWARE OF THAT.
MMMHMM...
I SAW A VISION FOR A SPLIT SECOND.
SO FAR, I'VE BEEN ABLE TO SUPPRESS THE CURSE, BUT NOT BREAK IT.
IF I COULD FIND A PSYCHIC, OR FIND OUT MORE ABOUT THE BIRTH OF THE SWORD...
I AM GOOD AT GETTING RID OF PESKY SPIRITS...
GROAN
HE'S USELESS...
THAT MEANS WE NEED TO GO LOOK FOR OTHERS WITH SKILL.
むぎゅ

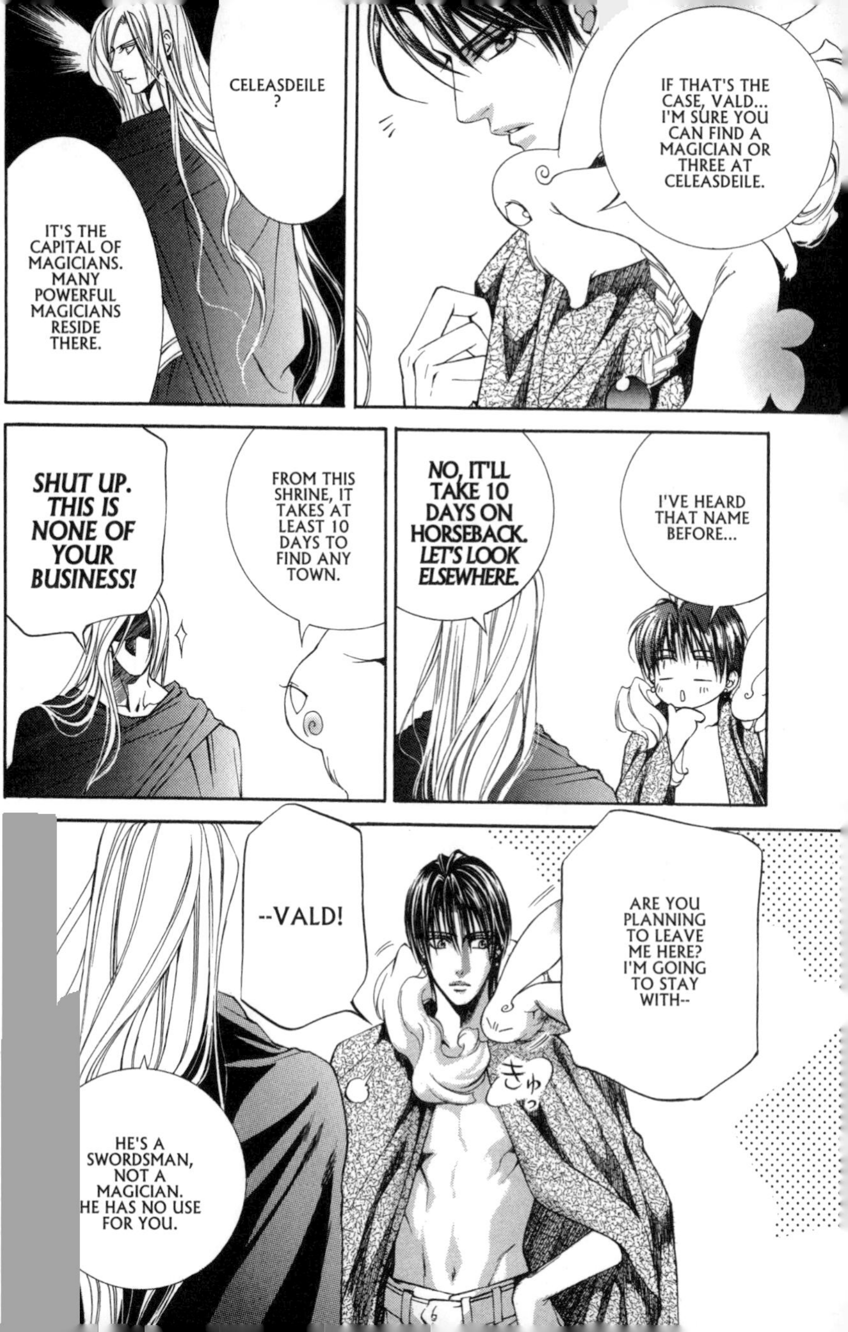
IF THAT'S THE CASE, VALD... I'M SURE YOU CAN FIND A MAGICIAN OR THREE AT CELEASDEILE.
CELEASDEILE?
IT'S THE CAPITAL OF MAGICIANS. MANY POWERFUL MAGICIANS RESIDE THERE.
I'VE HEARD THAT NAME BEFORE...
NO, IT'LL TAKE 10 DAYS ON HORSEBACK. LET'S LOOK ELSEWHERE.
FROM THIS SHRINE, IT TAKES AT LEAST 10 DAYS TO FIND ANY TOWN.
SHUT UP. THIS IS NONE OF YOUR BUSINESS!
ARE YOU PLANNING TO LEAVE ME HERE? I'M GOING TO STAY WITH--
--VALD!
きゅっ
HE'S A SWORDSMAN, NOT A MAGICIAN. HE HAS NO USE FOR YOU.

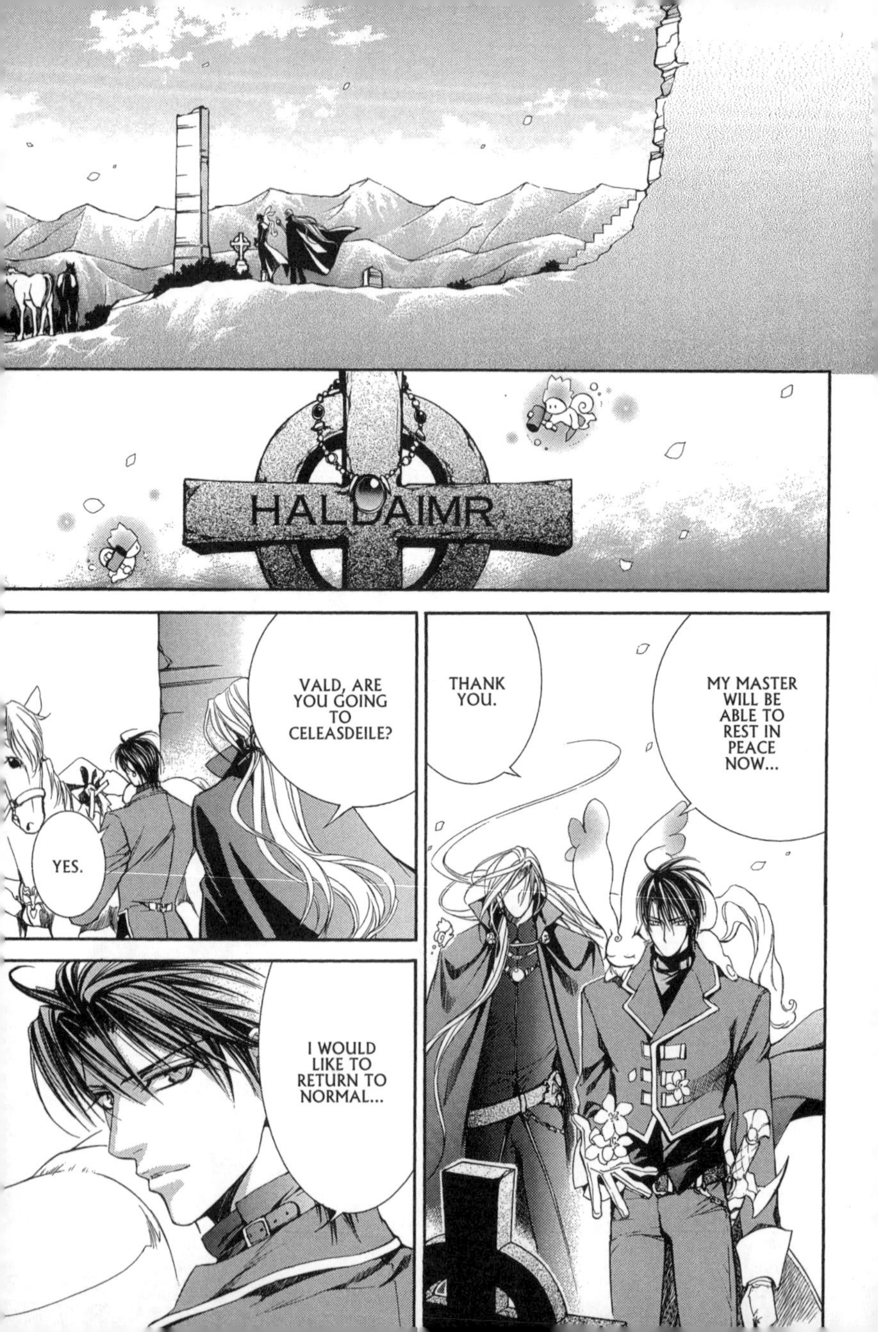
HALDAIMR
MY MASTER WILL BE ABLE TO REST IN PEACE NOW...
THANK YOU.
VALD, ARE YOU GOING TO CELEASDEILE?
YES.
I WOULD LIKE TO RETURN TO NORMAL...

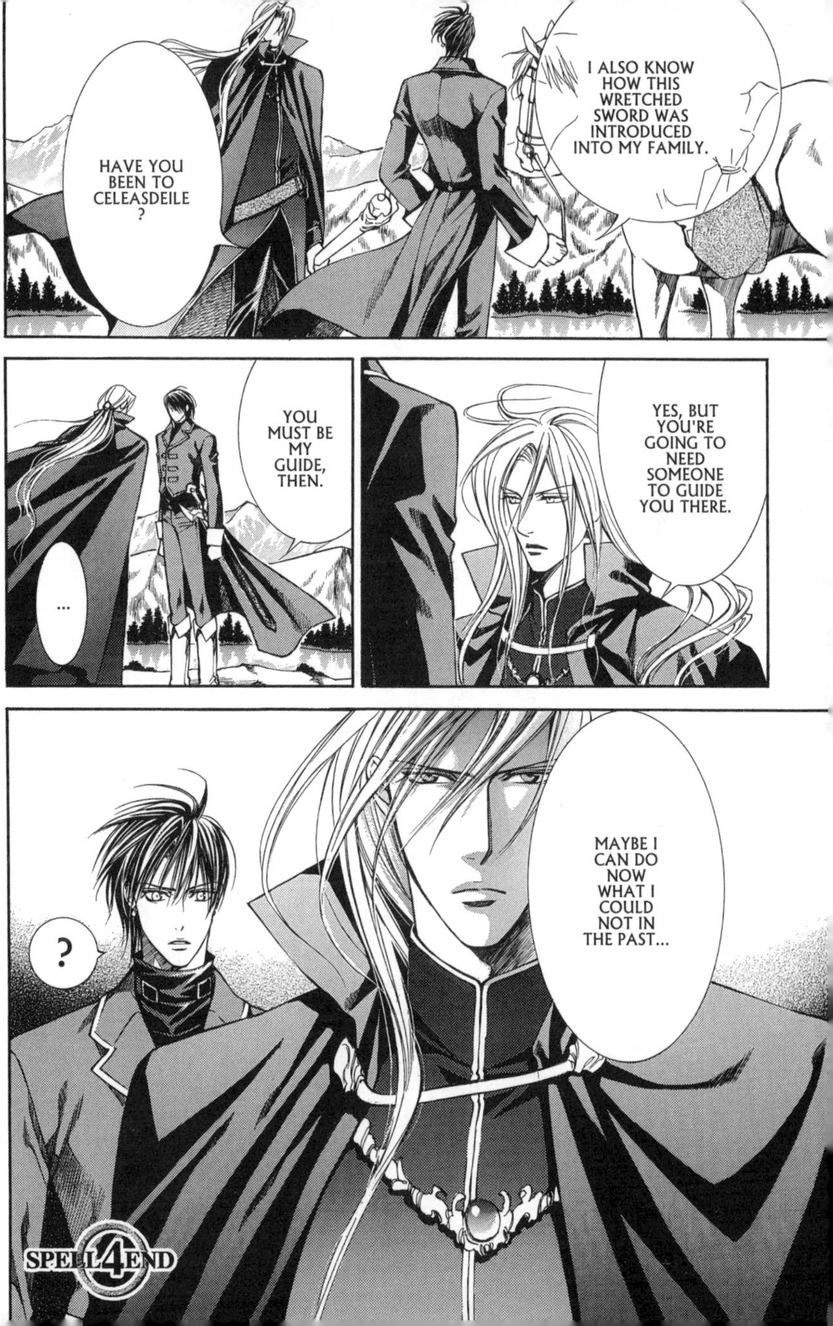
I ALSO KNOW HOW THIS WRETCHED SWORD WAS INTRODUCED INTO MY FAMILY.
HAVE YOU BEEN TO CELEASDEILE ?
YES, BUT YOU'RE GOING TO NEED SOMEONE TO GUIDE YOU THERE.
YOU MUST BE MY GUIDE, THEN.
...
MAYBE I CAN DO NOW WHAT I COULD NOT IN THE PAST...
?
SPELL 4 END

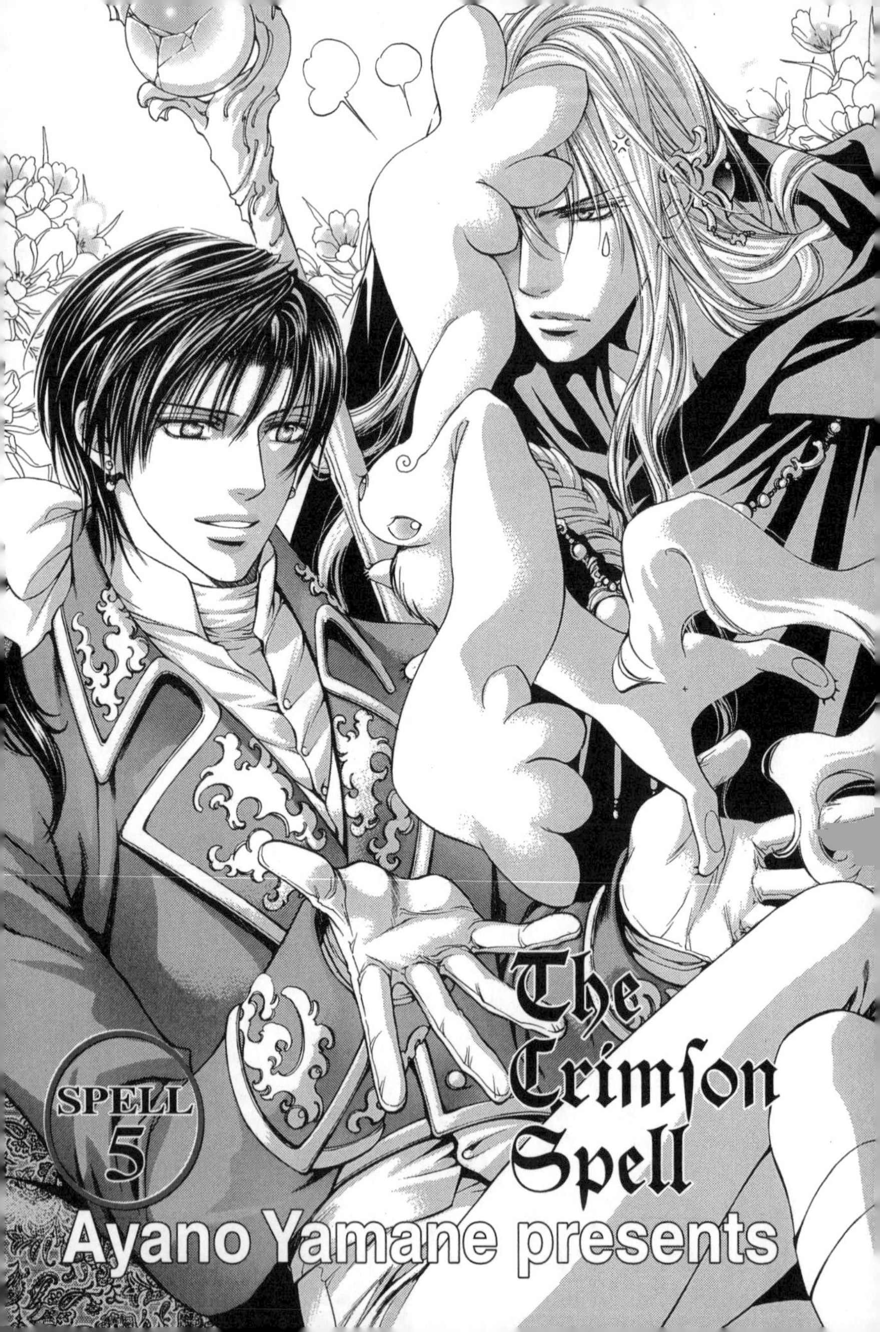
The Crimson Spell
SPELL 5
Ayano Yamane presents

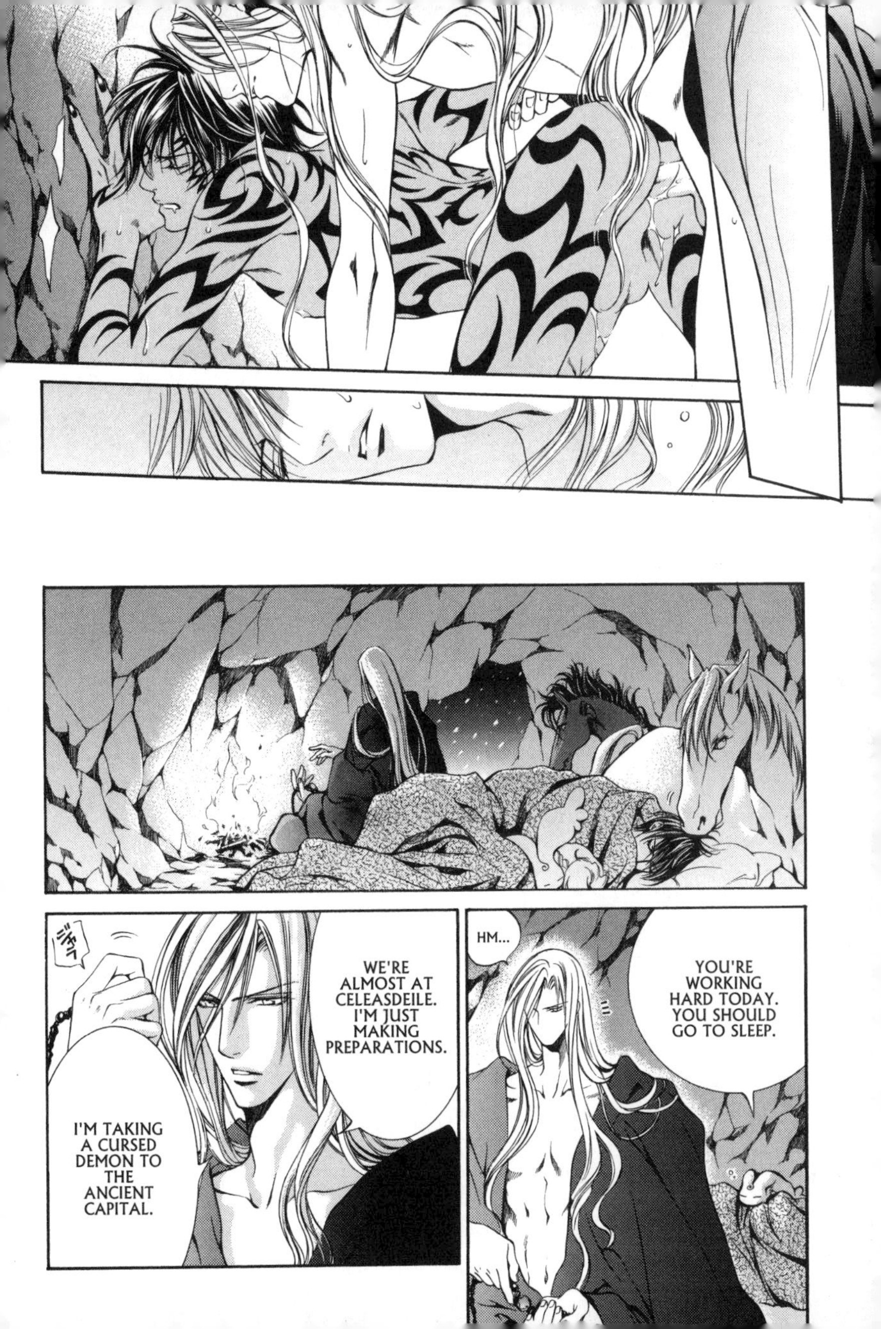
HM...
YOU'RE WORKING HARD TODAY. YOU SHOULD GO TO SLEEP.
WE'RE ALMOST AT CELEASDEILE. I'M JUST MAKING PREPARATIONS.
I'M TAKING A CURSED DEMON TO THE ANCIENT CAPITAL.

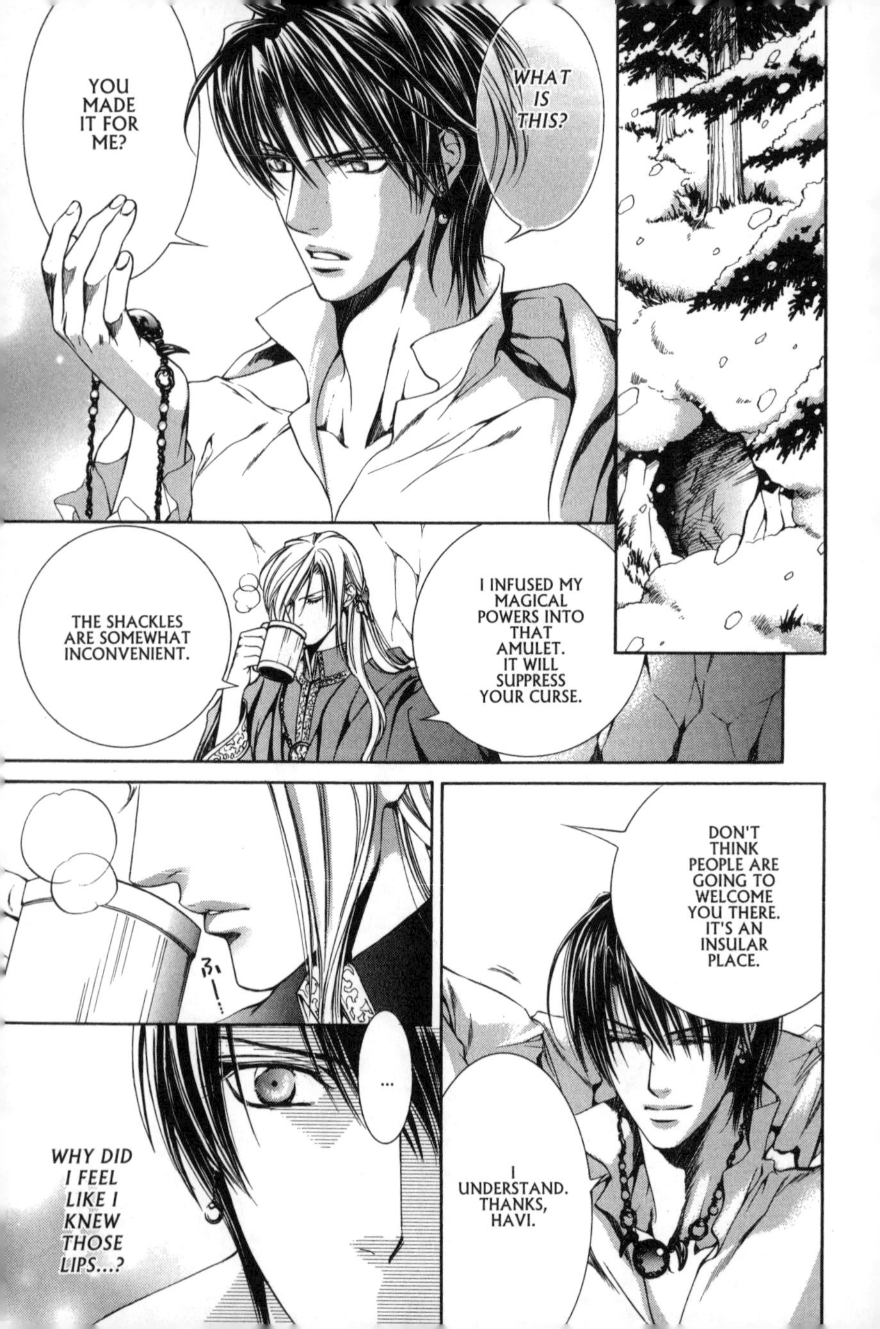
WHAT IS THIS?
YOU MADE IT FOR ME?
I INFUSED MY MAGICAL POWERS INTO THAT AMULET. IT WILL SUPPRESS YOUR CURSE.
THE SHACKLES ARE SOMEWHAT INCONVENIENT.
DON'T THINK PEOPLE ARE GOING TO WELCOME YOU THERE. IT'S AN INSULAR PLACE.
I UNDERSTAND. THANKS, HAVI.
ふー…
...
WHY DID I FEEL LIKE I KNEW THOSE LIPS...?

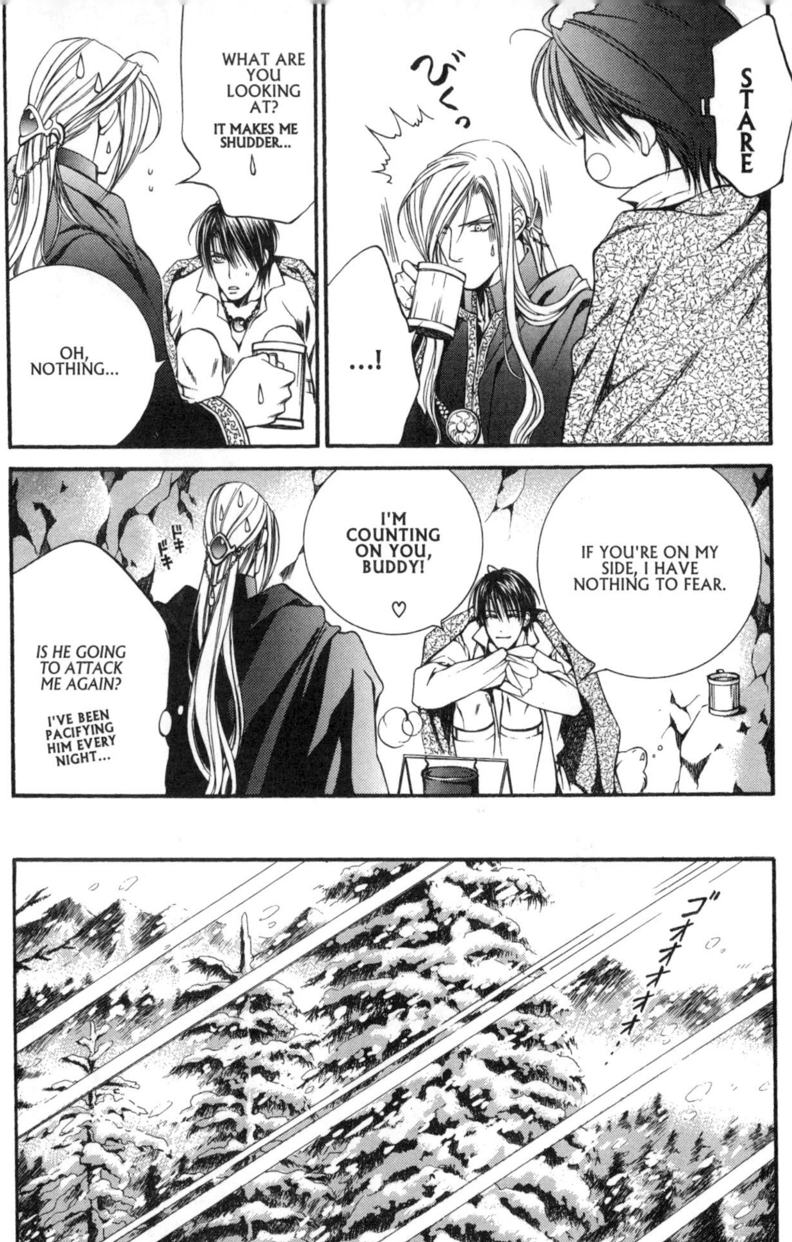
STARE
びくっ
...!
WHAT ARE YOU LOOKING AT?
IT MAKES ME SHUDDER...
OH, NOTHING...
IF YOU'RE ON MY SIDE, I HAVE NOTHING TO FEAR.
I'M COUNTING ON YOU, BUDDY! ♡
ドキドキ
IS HE GOING TO ATTACK ME AGAIN?
I'VE BEEN PACIFYING HIM EVERY NIGHT...
ゴオオオオオ...

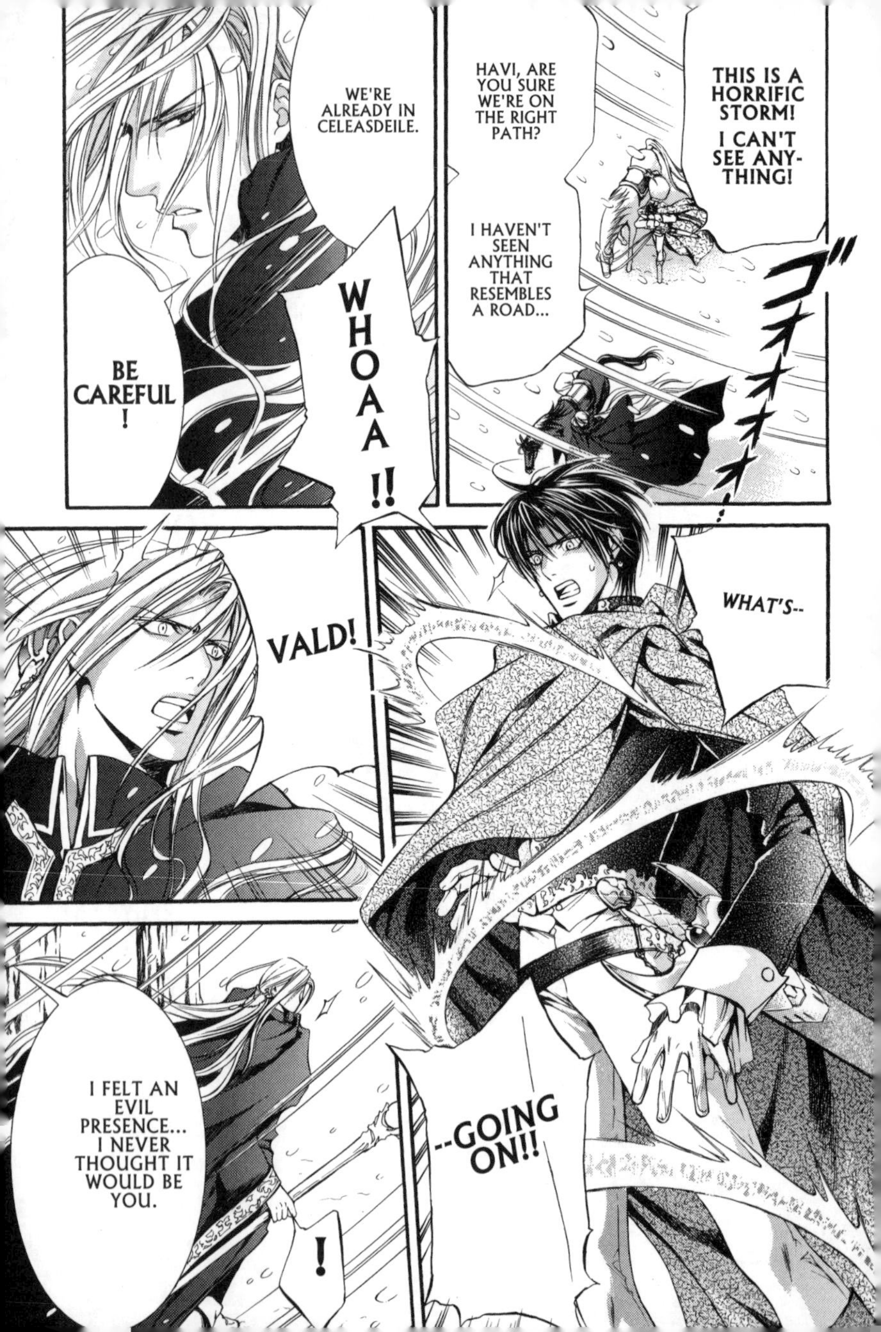
THIS IS A HORRIFIC STORM!
I CAN'T SEE ANYTHING!
HAVI, ARE YOU SURE WE'RE ON THE RIGHT PATH?
I HAVEN'T SEEN ANYTHING THAT RESEMBLES A ROAD...
ゴオオオオ…
WE'RE ALREADY IN CELEASDEILE.
BE CAREFUL!
WHOAA!!
WHAT'S--
VALD!
--GOING ON!!
I FELT AN EVIL PRESENCE... I NEVER THOUGHT IT WOULD BE YOU.
!

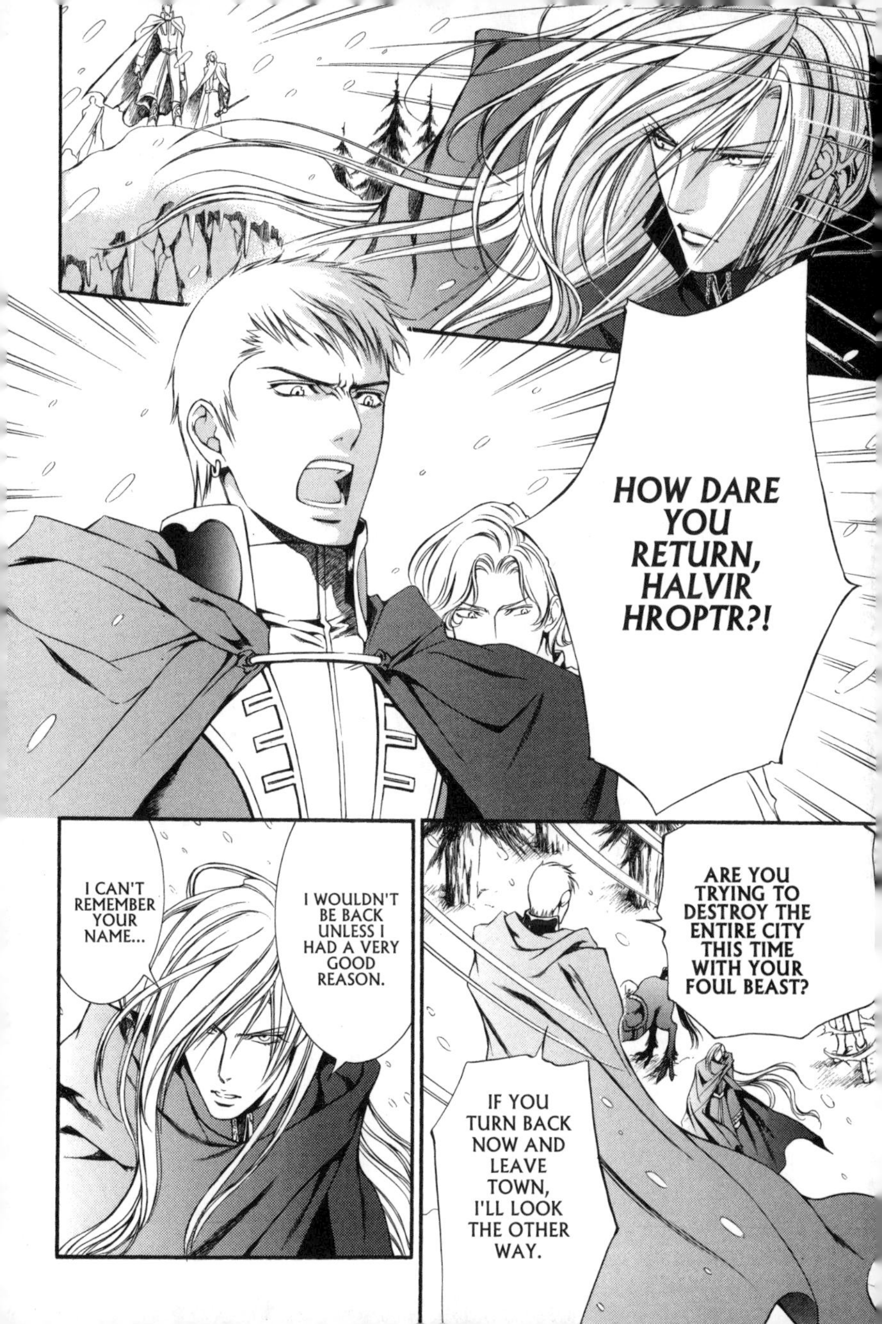
HOW DARE YOU RETURN, HALVIR HROPTR?!
ARE YOU TRYING TO DESTROY THE ENTIRE CITY THIS TIME WITH YOUR FOUL BEAST?
IF YOU TURN BACK NOW AND LEAVE TOWN, I'LL LOOK THE OTHER WAY.
I WOULDN'T BE BACK UNLESS I HAD A VERY GOOD REASON.
I CAN'T REMEMBER YOUR NAME...

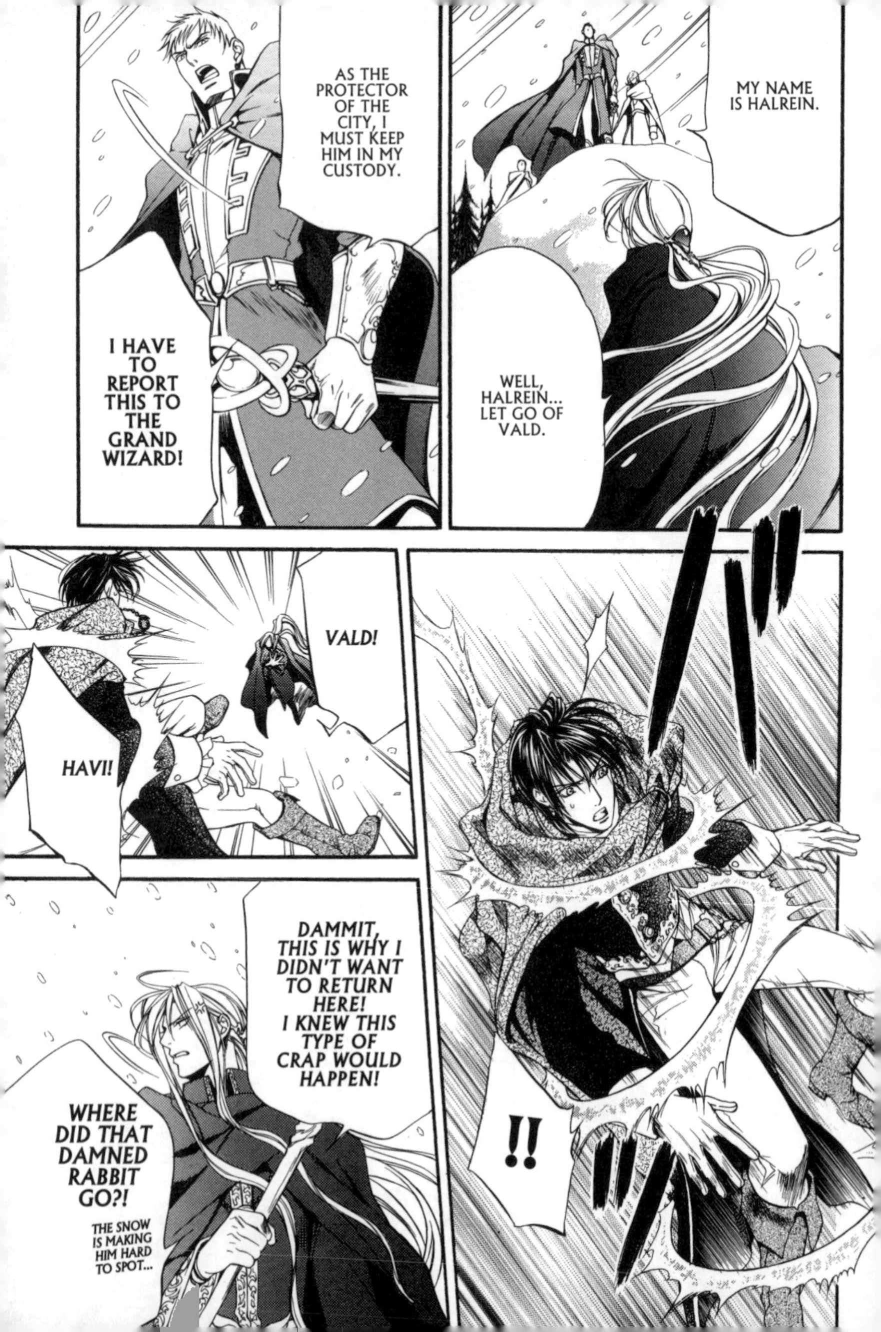
MY NAME IS HALREIN.
WELL, HALREIN... LET GO OF VALD.
AS THE PROTECTOR OF THE CITY, I MUST KEEP HIM IN MY CUSTODY.
I HAVE TO REPORT THIS TO THE GRAND WIZARD!
!!
VALD!
HAVI!
DAMMIT, THIS IS WHY I DIDN'T WANT TO RETURN HERE! I KNEW THIS TYPE OF CRAP WOULD HAPPEN!
WHERE DID THAT DAMNED RABBIT GO?!
THE SNOW IS MAKING HIM HARD TO SPOT...

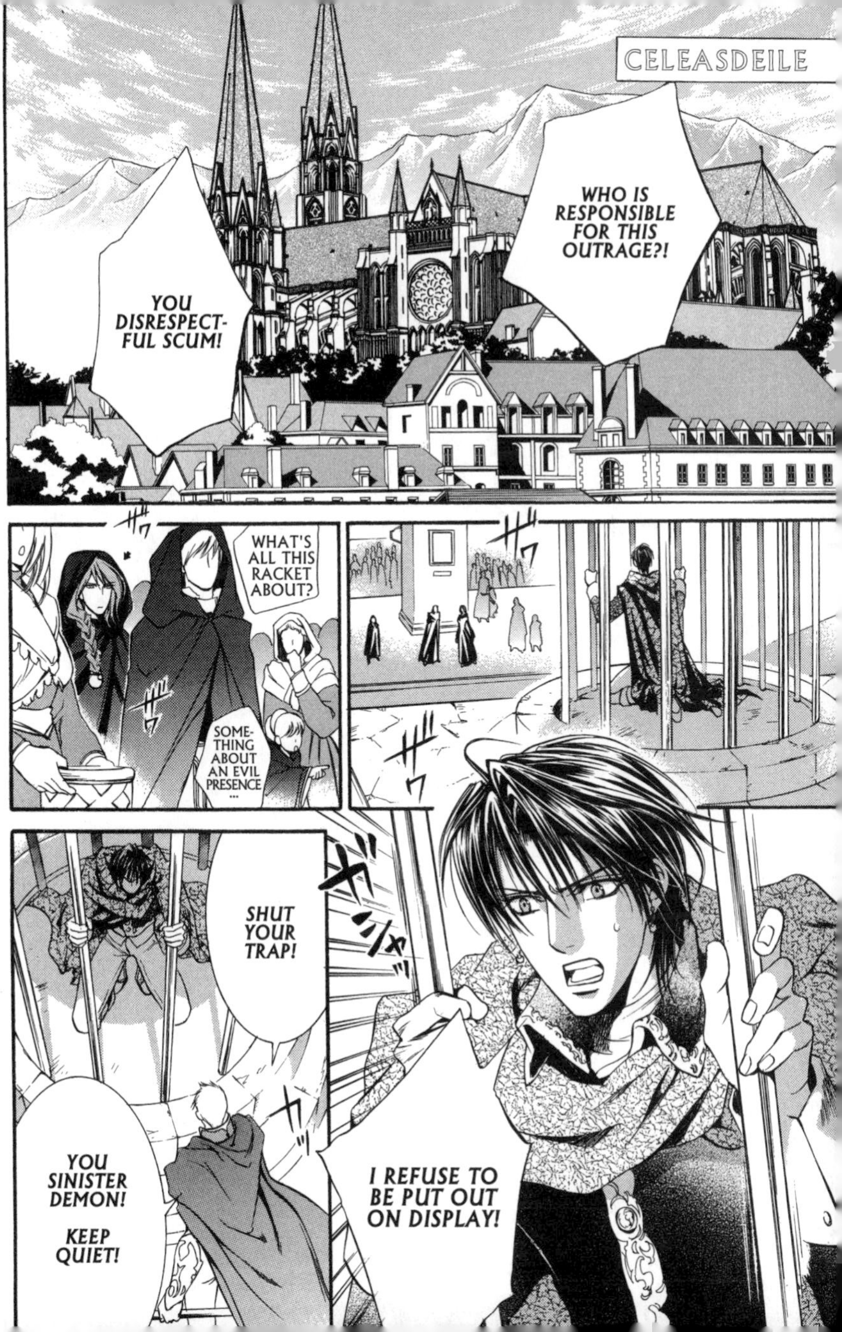
CELEASDEILE
WHO IS RESPONSIBLE FOR THIS OUTRAGE?!
YOU DISRESPECTFUL SCUM!
WHAT'S ALL THIS RACKET ABOUT?
SOMETHING ABOUT AN EVIL PRESENCE...
I REFUSE TO BE PUT OUT ON DISPLAY!
SHUT YOUR TRAP!
YOU SINISTER DEMON!
KEEP QUIET!

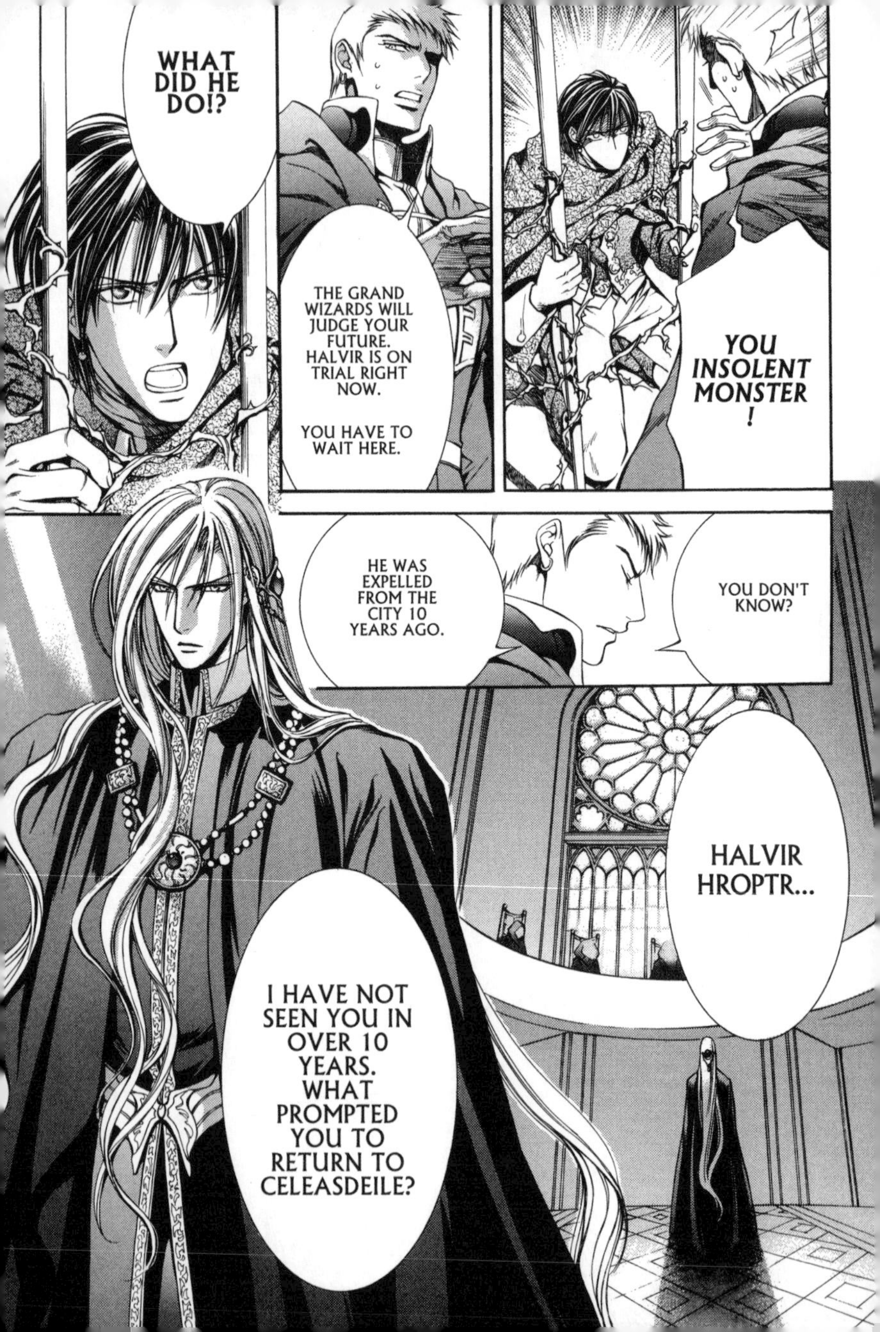
YOU INSOLENT MONSTER!
THE GRAND WIZARDS WILL JUDGE YOUR FUTURE. HALVIR IS ON TRIAL RIGHT NOW.
YOU HAVE TO WAIT HERE.
WHAT DID HE DO!?
YOU DON'T KNOW?
HE WAS EXPELLED FROM THE CITY 10 YEARS AGO.
HALVIR HROPTR...
I HAVE NOT SEEN YOU IN OVER 10 YEARS. WHAT PROMPTED YOU TO RETURN TO CELEASDEILE?

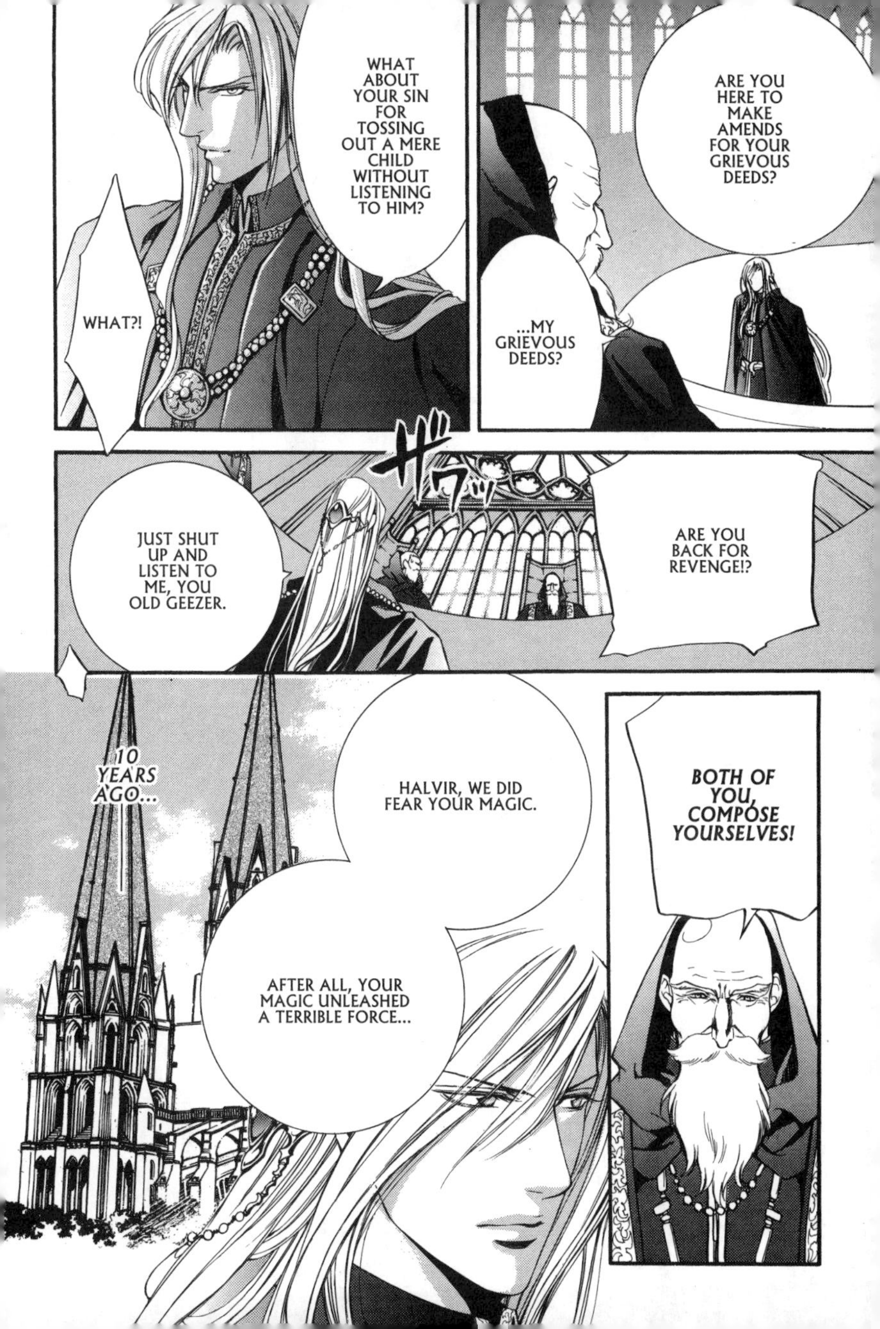
ARE YOU HERE TO MAKE AMENDS FOR YOUR GRIEVOUS DEEDS?
...MY GRIEVOUS DEEDS?
WHAT ABOUT YOUR SIN FOR TOSSING OUT A MERE CHILD WITHOUT LISTENING TO HIM?
WHAT?!
ザワッ
ARE YOU BACK FOR REVENGE!?
JUST SHUT UP AND LISTEN TO ME, YOU OLD GEEZER.
BOTH OF YOU, COMPOSE YOURSELVES!
HALVIR, WE DID FEAR YOUR MAGIC.
10 YEARS AGO...
AFTER ALL, YOUR MAGIC UNLEASHED A TERRIBLE FORCE...

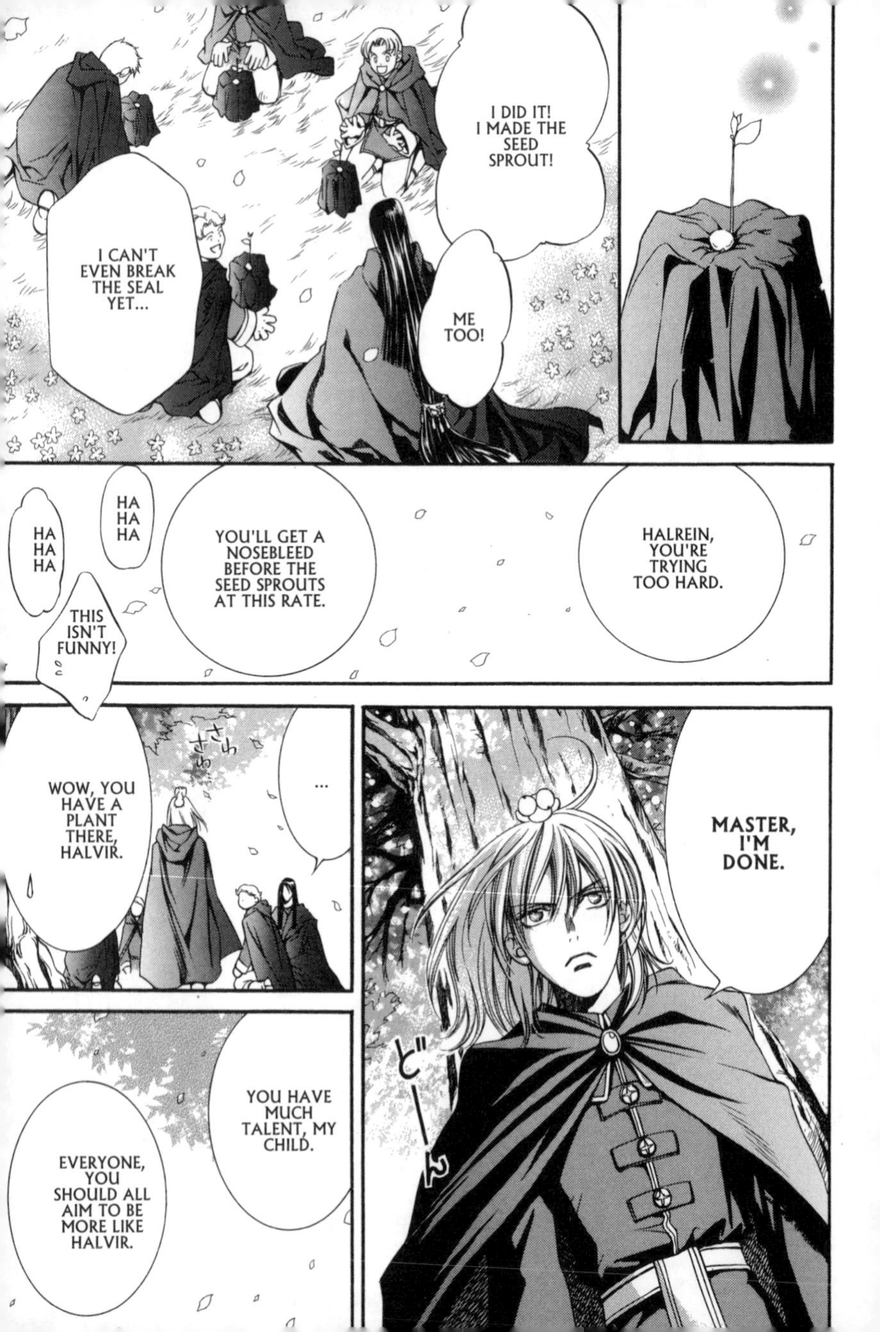
I DID IT! I MADE THE SEED SPROUT!
ME TOO!
I CAN'T EVEN BREAK THE SEAL YET...
HALREIN, YOU'RE TRYING TOO HARD.
YOU'LL GET A NOSEBLEED BEFORE THE SEED SPROUTS AT THIS RATE.
HA HA HA
HA HA HA
THIS ISN'T FUNNY!
MASTER, I'M DONE.
...
WOW, YOU HAVE A PLANT THERE, HALVIR.
YOU HAVE MUCH TALENT, MY CHILD.
EVERYONE, YOU SHOULD ALL AIM TO BE MORE LIKE HALVIR.

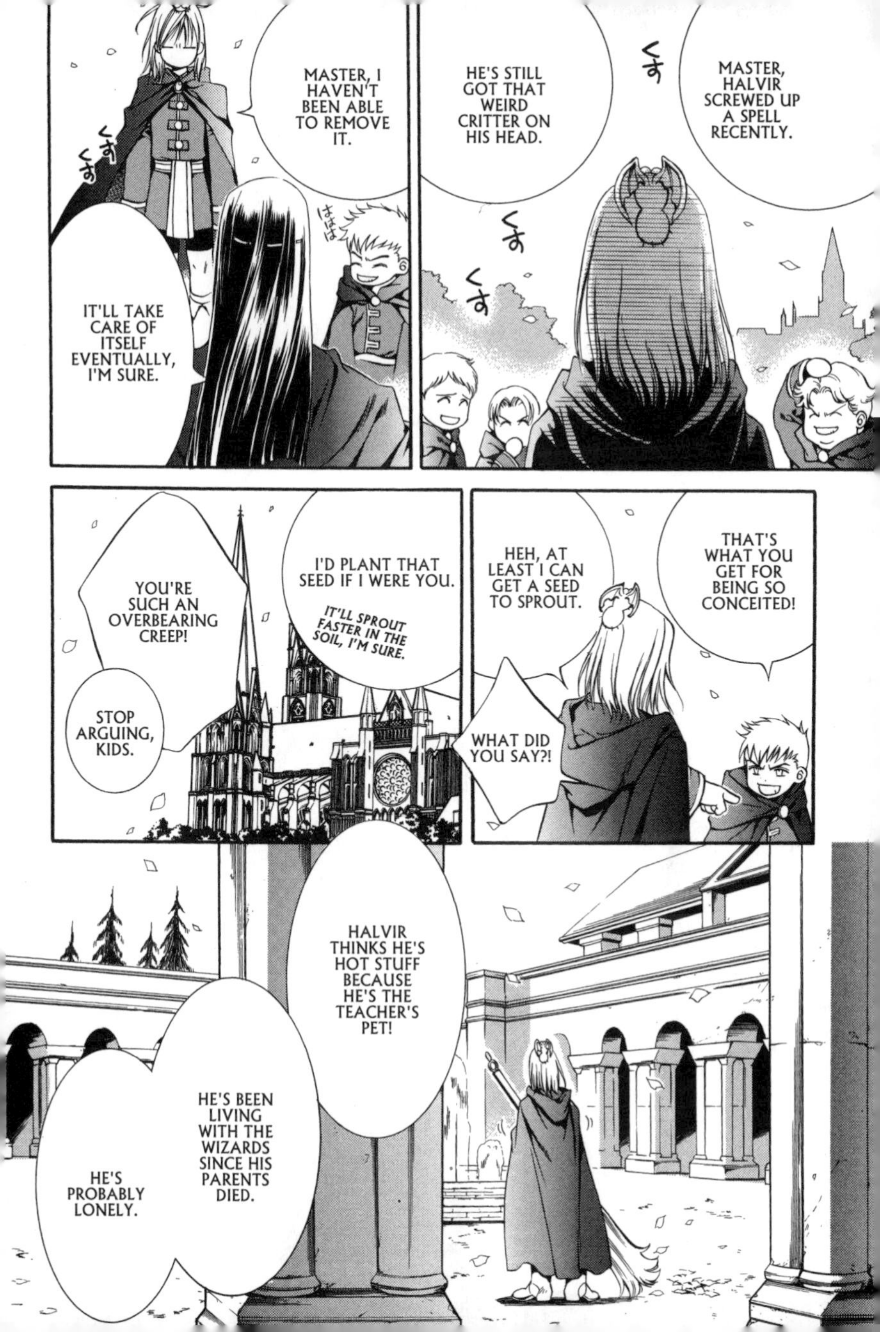
MASTER, HALVIR SCREWED UP A SPELL RECENTLY.
くす
HE'S STILL GOT THAT WEIRD CRITTER ON HIS HEAD.
くす くす
MASTER, I HAVEN'T BEEN ABLE TO REMOVE IT.
ははは
くす くす
IT'LL TAKE CARE OF ITSELF EVENTUALLY, I'M SURE.
THAT'S WHAT YOU GET FOR BEING SO CONCEITED!
HEH, AT LEAST I CAN GET A SEED TO SPROUT.
WHAT DID YOU SAY?!
I'D PLANT THAT SEED IF I WERE YOU.
IT'LL SPROUT FASTER IN THE SOIL, I'M SURE.
YOU'RE SUCH AN OVERBEARING CREEP!
STOP ARGUING, KIDS.
HALVIR THINKS HE'S HOT STUFF BECAUSE HE'S THE TEACHER'S PET!
HE'S BEEN LIVING WITH THE WIZARDS SINCE HIS PARENTS DIED.
HE'S PROBABLY LONELY.

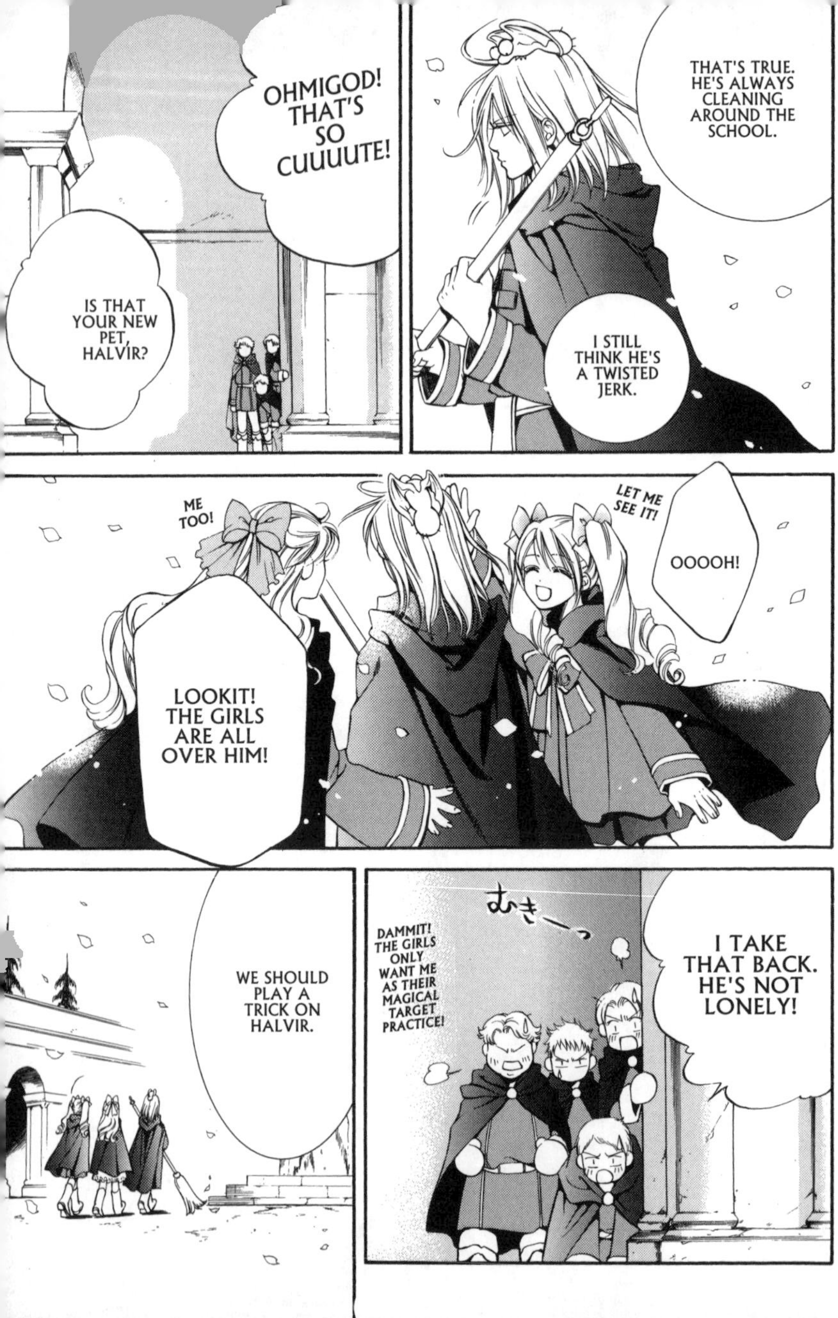
THAT'S TRUE. HE'S ALWAYS CLEANING AROUND THE SCHOOL.
I STILL THINK HE'S A TWISTED JERK.
OHMIGOD! THAT'S SO CUUUUTE!
IS THAT YOUR NEW PET, HALVIR?
LET ME SEE IT!
OOOOH!
ME TOO!
LOOKIT! THE GIRLS ARE ALL OVER HIM!
I TAKE THAT BACK. HE'S NOT LONELY!
むきーっ
DAMMIT! THE GIRLS ONLY WANT ME AS THEIR MAGICAL TARGET PRACTICE!
WE SHOULD PLAY A TRICK ON HALVIR.

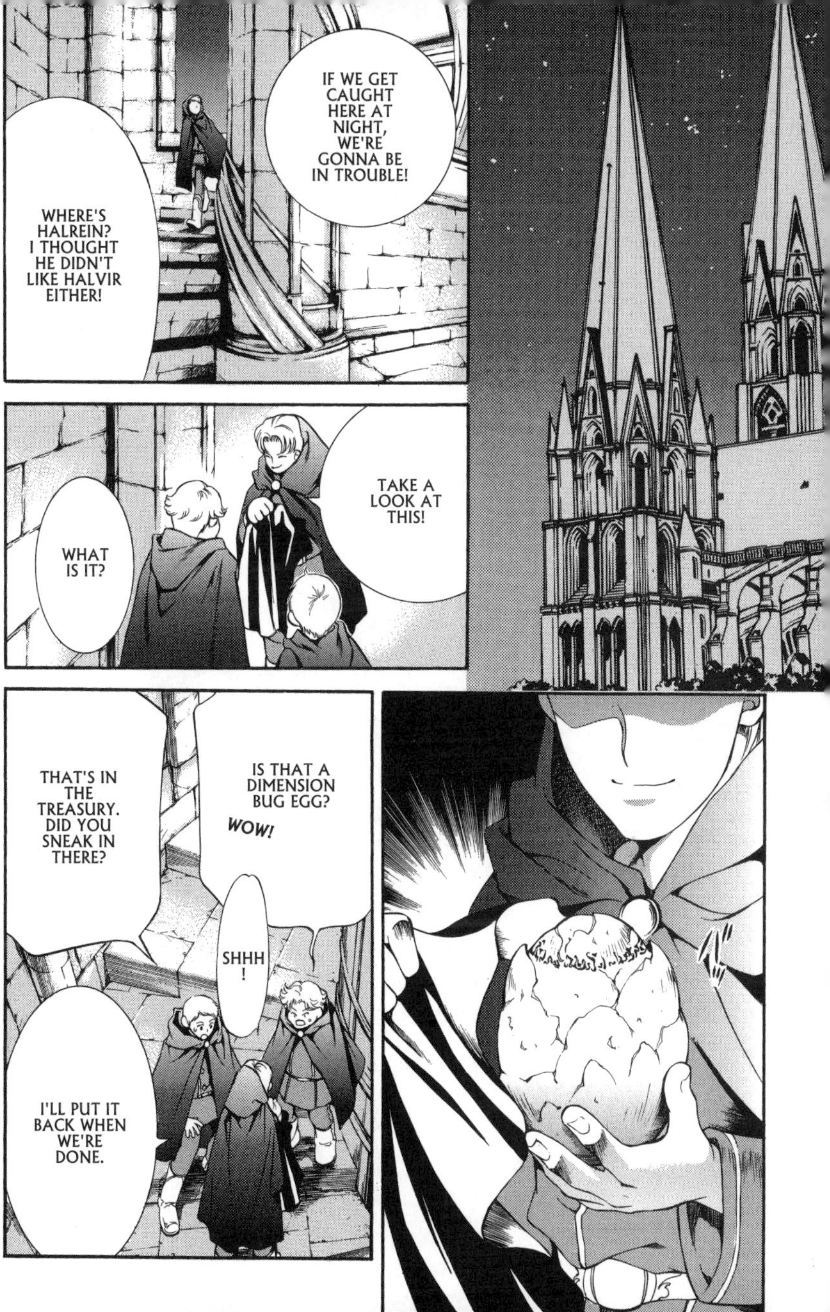
IF WE GET CAUGHT HERE AT NIGHT, WE'RE GONNA BE IN TROUBLE!
WHERE'S HALREIN? I THOUGHT HE DIDN'T LIKE HALVIR EITHER!
TAKE A LOOK AT THIS!
WHAT IS IT?
IS THAT A DIMENSION BUG EGG?
WOW!
THAT'S IN THE TREASURY. DID YOU SNEAK IN THERE?
SHHH!
I'LL PUT IT BACK WHEN WE'RE DONE.

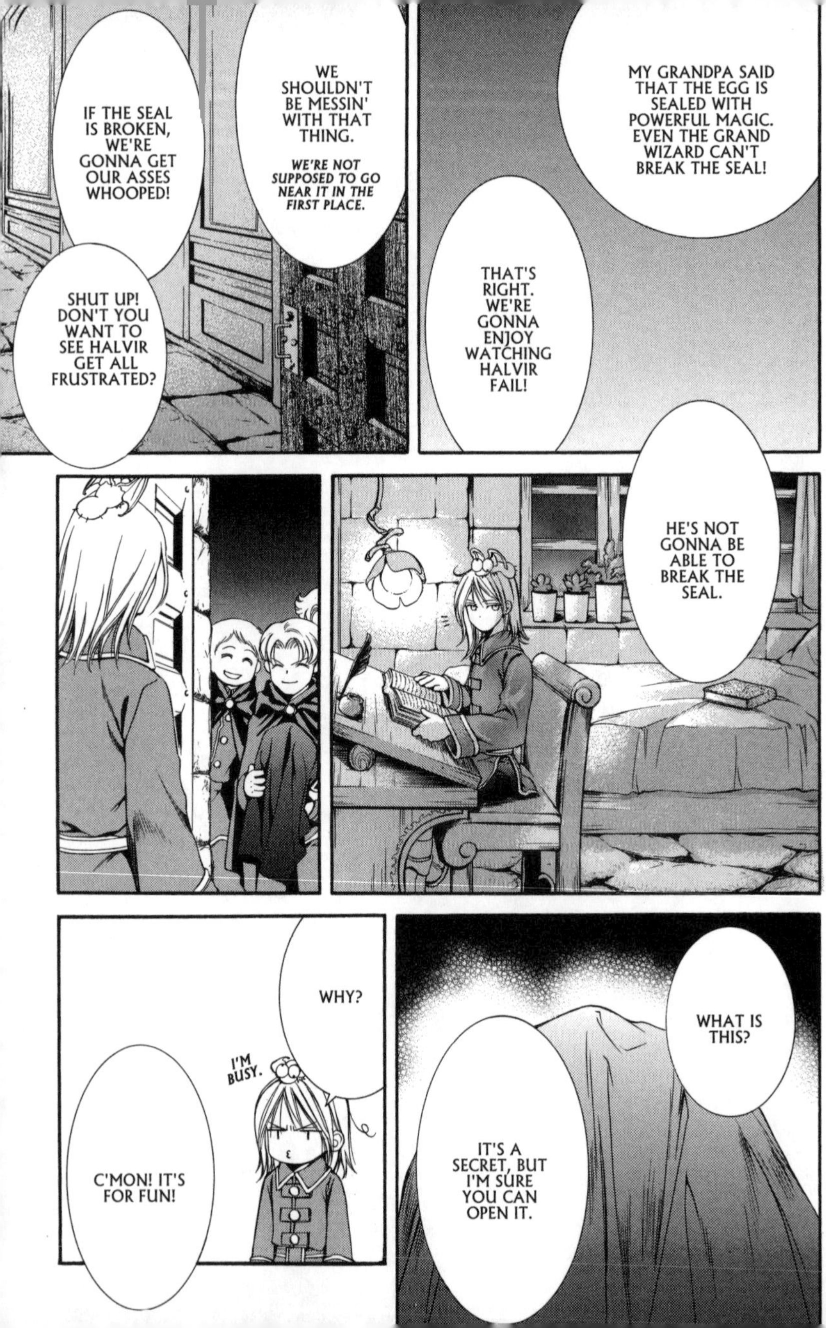
MY GRANDPA SAID THAT THE EGG IS SEALED WITH POWERFUL MAGIC. EVEN THE GRAND WIZARD CAN'T BREAK THE SEAL!
THAT'S RIGHT. WE'RE GONNA ENJOY WATCHING HALVIR FAIL!
WE SHOULDN'T BE MESSIN' WITH THAT THING.
WE'RE NOT SUPPOSED TO GO NEAR IT IN THE FIRST PLACE.
IF THE SEAL IS BROKEN, WE'RE GONNA GET OUR ASSES WHOOPED!
SHUT UP! DON'T YOU WANT TO SEE HALVIR GET ALL FRUSTRATED?
HE'S NOT GONNA BE ABLE TO BREAK THE SEAL.
WHAT IS THIS?
IT'S A SECRET, BUT I'M SURE YOU CAN OPEN IT.
WHY?
I'M BUSY.
C'MON! IT'S FOR FUN!

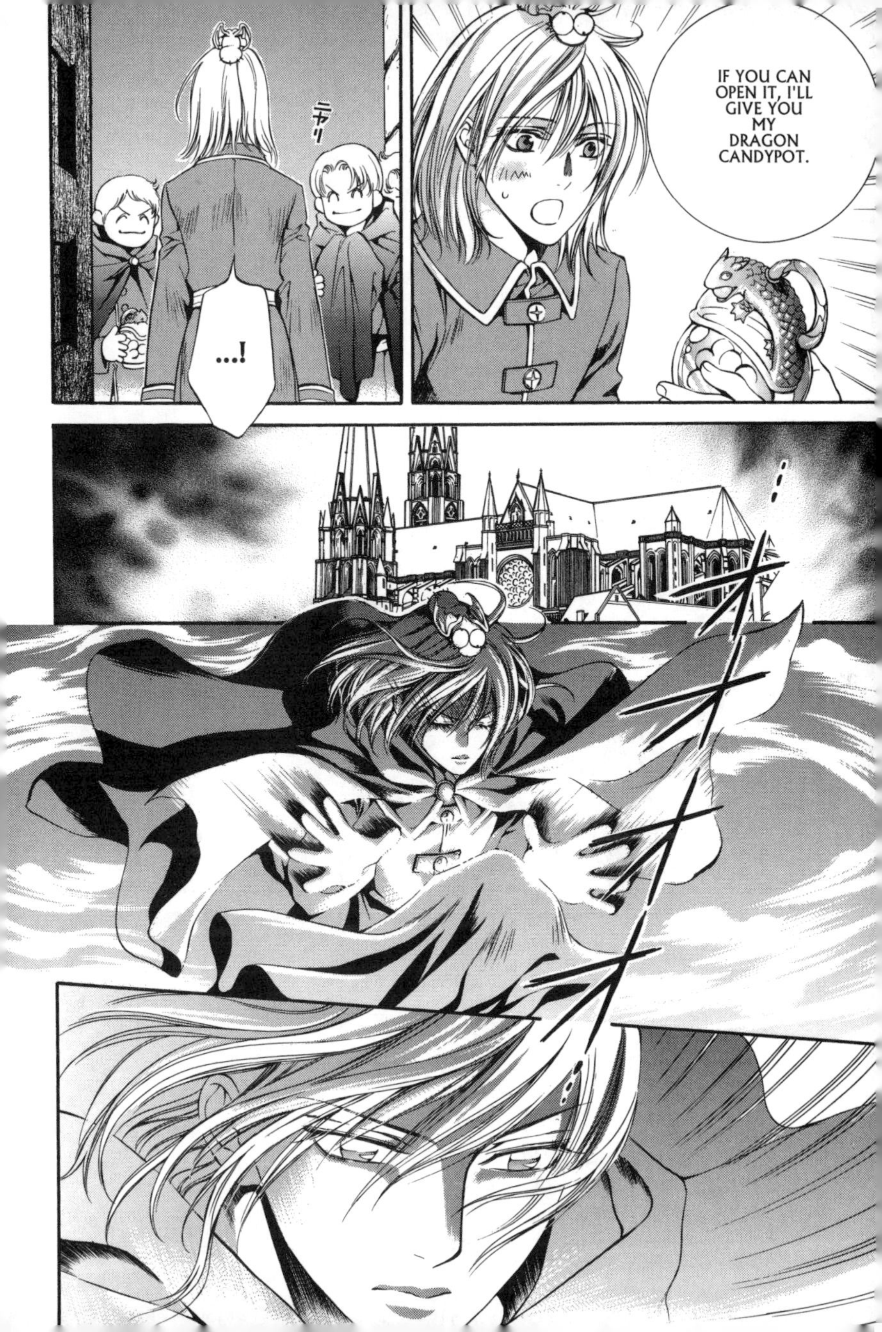
IF YOU CAN OPEN IT, I'LL GIVE YOU MY DRAGON CANDYPOT.
ニヤリ
...!

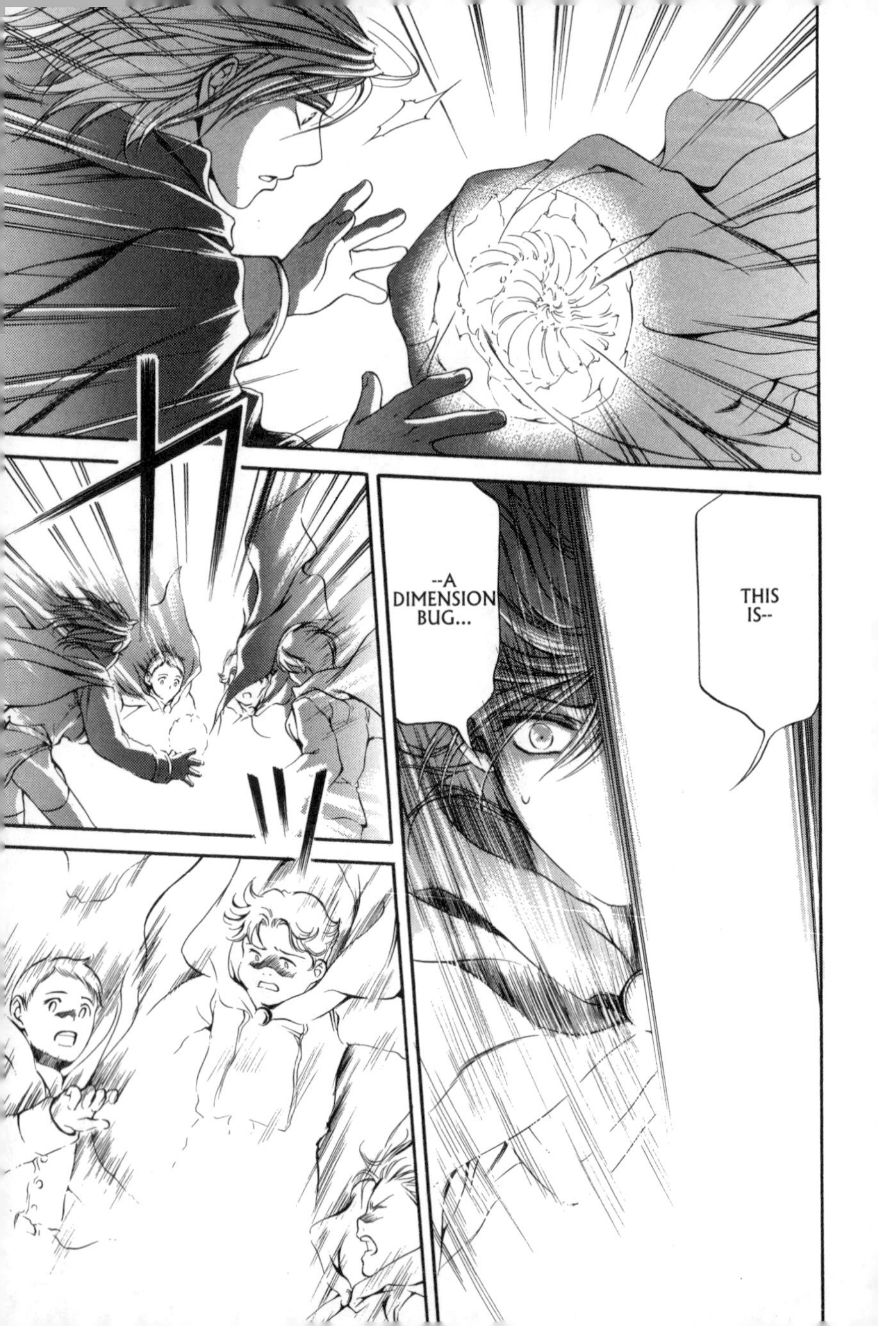
THIS IS--
--A DIMENSION BUG...

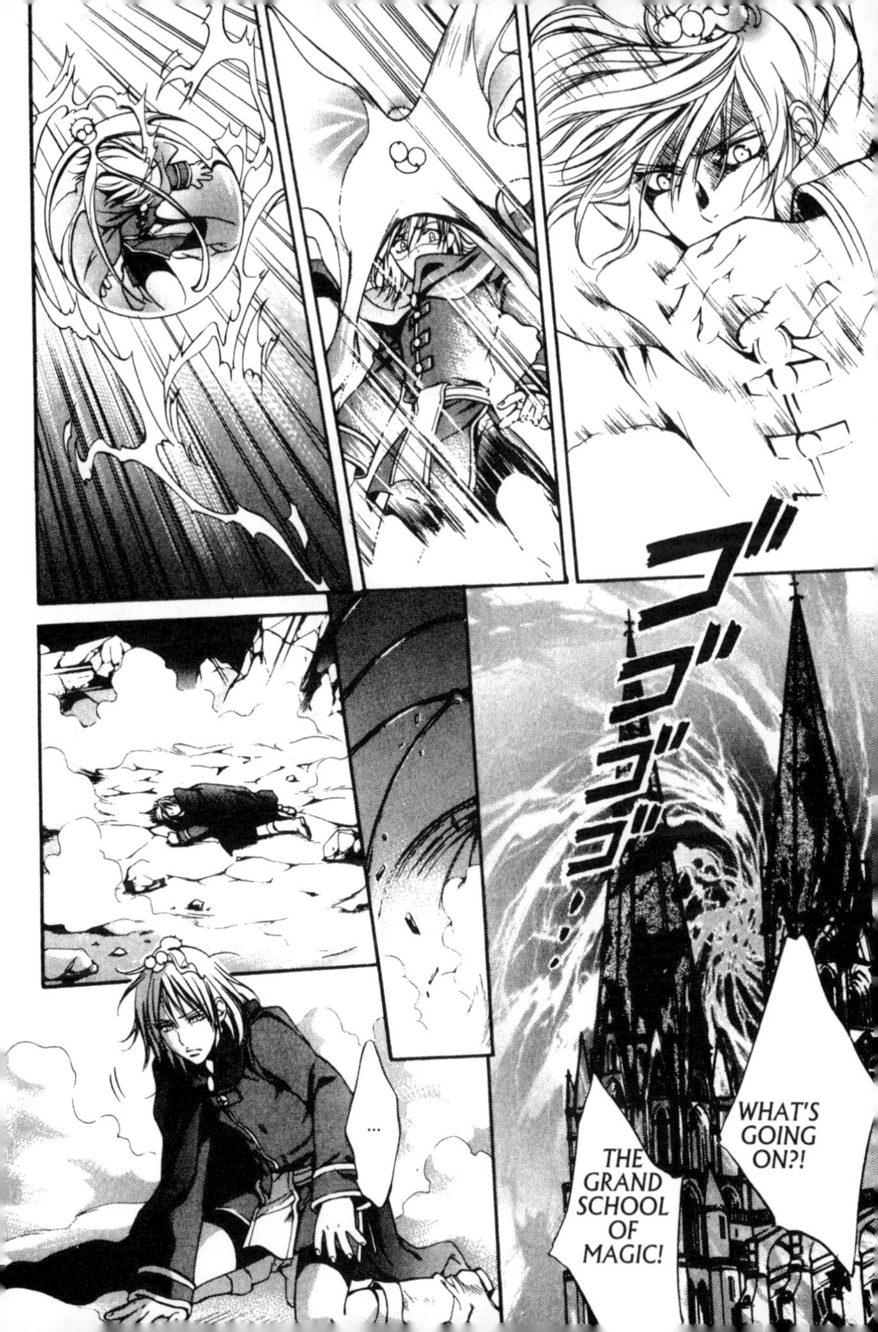
ゴゴゴゴゴ…
WHAT'S GOING ON?!
THE GRAND SCHOOL OF MAGIC!
...

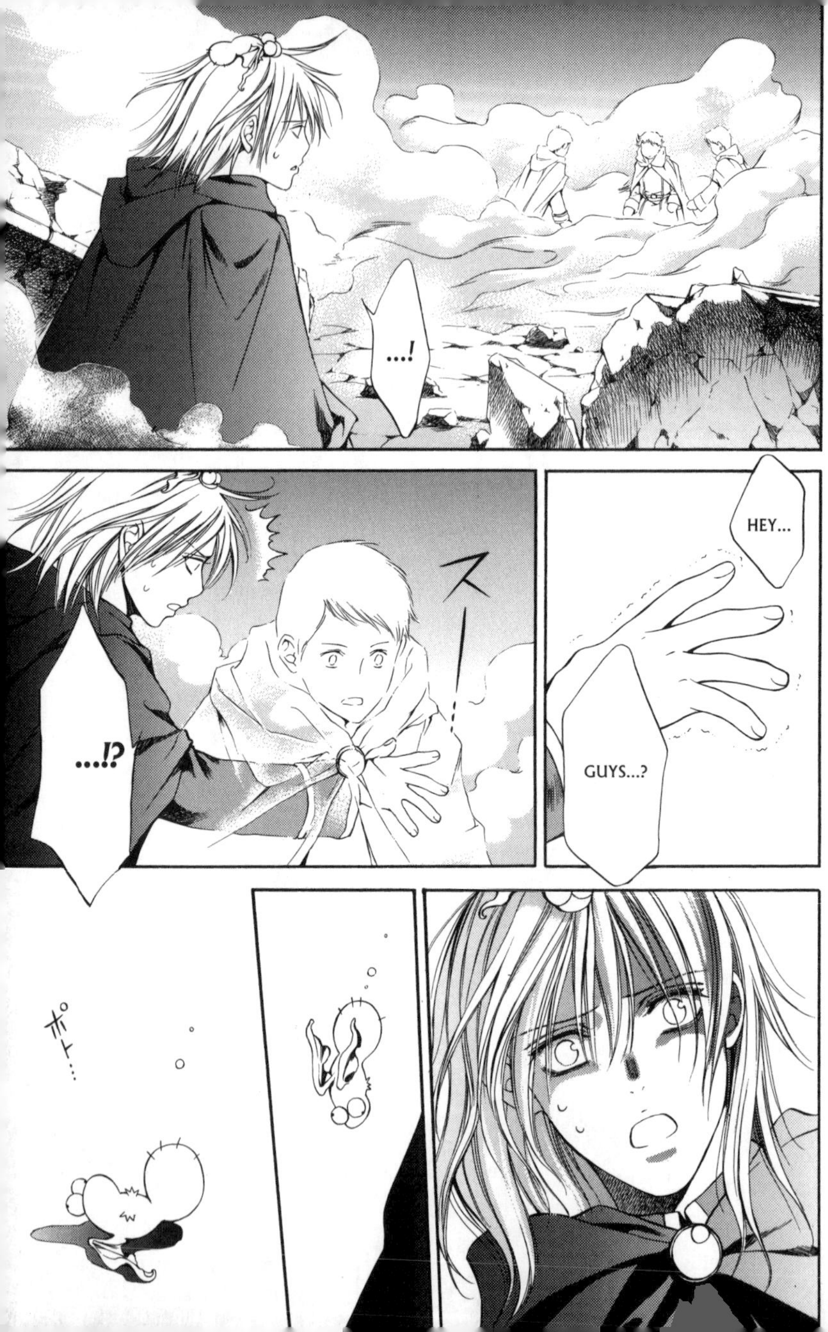
...!
HEY...
GUYS...?
...!?
ス
ポト…

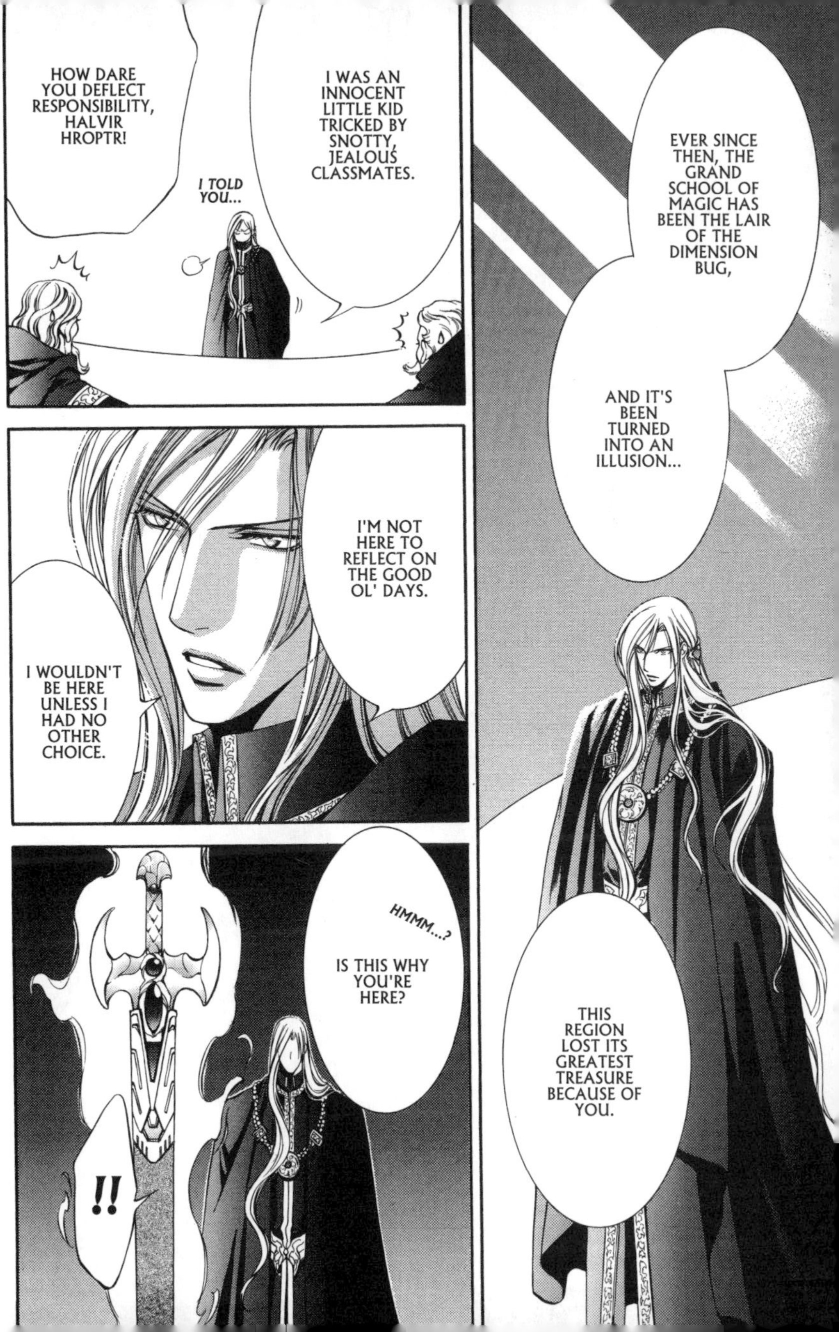
EVER SINCE THEN, THE GRAND SCHOOL OF MAGIC HAS BEEN THE LAIR OF THE DIMENSION BUG,
AND IT'S BEEN TURNED INTO AN ILLUSION...
THIS REGION LOST ITS GREATEST TREASURE BECAUSE OF YOU.
I WAS AN INNOCENT LITTLE KID TRICKED BY SNOTTY, JEALOUS CLASSMATES.
I TOLD YOU...
HOW DARE YOU DEFLECT RESPONSIBILITY, HALVIR HROPTR!
I'M NOT HERE TO REFLECT ON THE GOOD OL' DAYS.
I WOULDN'T BE HERE UNLESS I HAD NO OTHER CHOICE.
HMMM...?
IS THIS WHY YOU'RE HERE?
!!

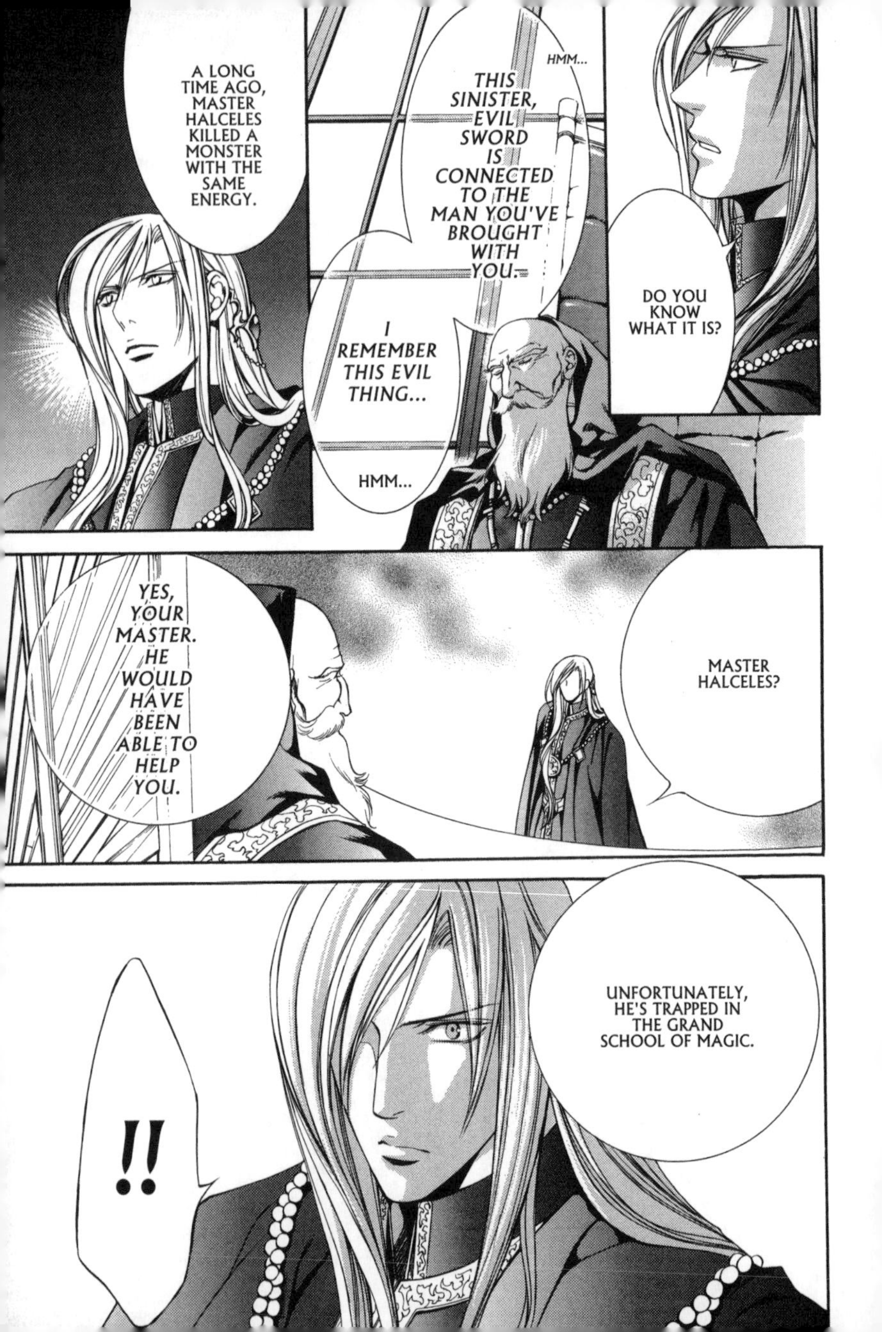
DO YOU KNOW WHAT IT IS?
HMM...
THIS SINISTER, EVIL SWORD IS CONNECTED TO THE MAN YOU'VE BROUGHT WITH YOU.
I REMEMBER THIS EVIL THING...
HMM...
A LONG TIME AGO, MASTER HALCELES KILLED A MONSTER WITH THE SAME ENERGY.
MASTER HALCELES?
YES, YOUR MASTER. HE WOULD HAVE BEEN ABLE TO HELP YOU.
UNFORTUNATELY, HE'S TRAPPED IN THE GRAND SCHOOL OF MAGIC.
!!

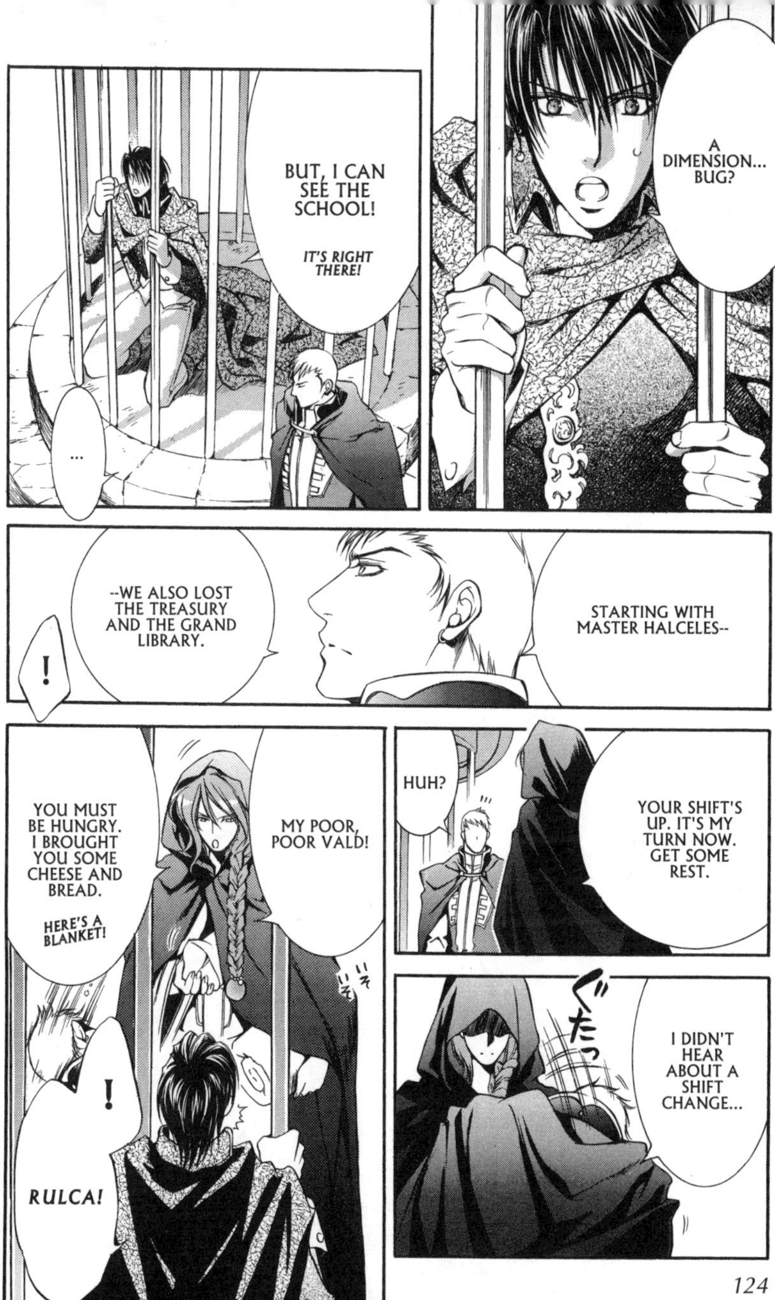
A DIMENSION... BUG?
BUT, I CAN SEE THE SCHOOL!
IT'S RIGHT THERE!
...
STARTING WITH MASTER HALCELES--
--WE ALSO LOST THE TREASURY AND THE GRAND LIBRARY.
!
YOUR SHIFT'S UP. IT'S MY TURN NOW. GET SOME REST.
HUH?
ぐたっ
I DIDN'T HEAR ABOUT A SHIFT CHANGE...
MY POOR, POOR VALD!
YOU MUST BE HUNGRY. I BROUGHT YOU SOME CHEESE AND BREAD.
HERE'S A BLANKET!
いそいそ
!
RULCA!

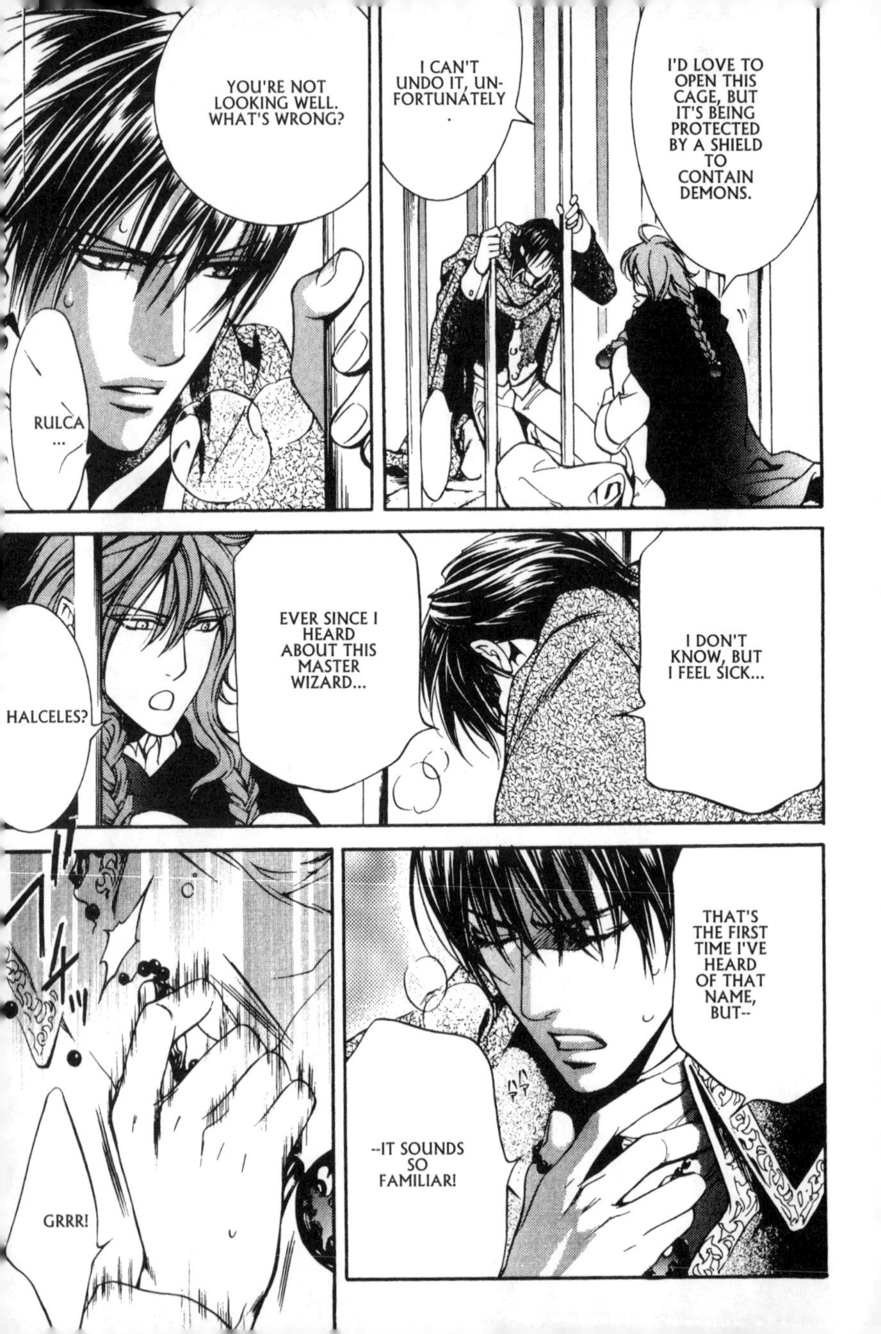
I'D LOVE TO OPEN THIS CAGE, BUT IT'S BEING PROTECTED BY A SHIELD TO CONTAIN DEMONS.
I CAN'T UNDO IT, UN-FORTUNATELY.
YOU'RE NOT LOOKING WELL. WHAT'S WRONG?
RULCA...
I DON'T KNOW, BUT I FEEL SICK...
EVER SINCE I HEARD ABOUT THIS MASTER WIZARD...
HALCELES?
THAT'S THE FIRST TIME I'VE HEARD OF THAT NAME, BUT--
--IT SOUNDS SO FAMILIAR!
GRRR!

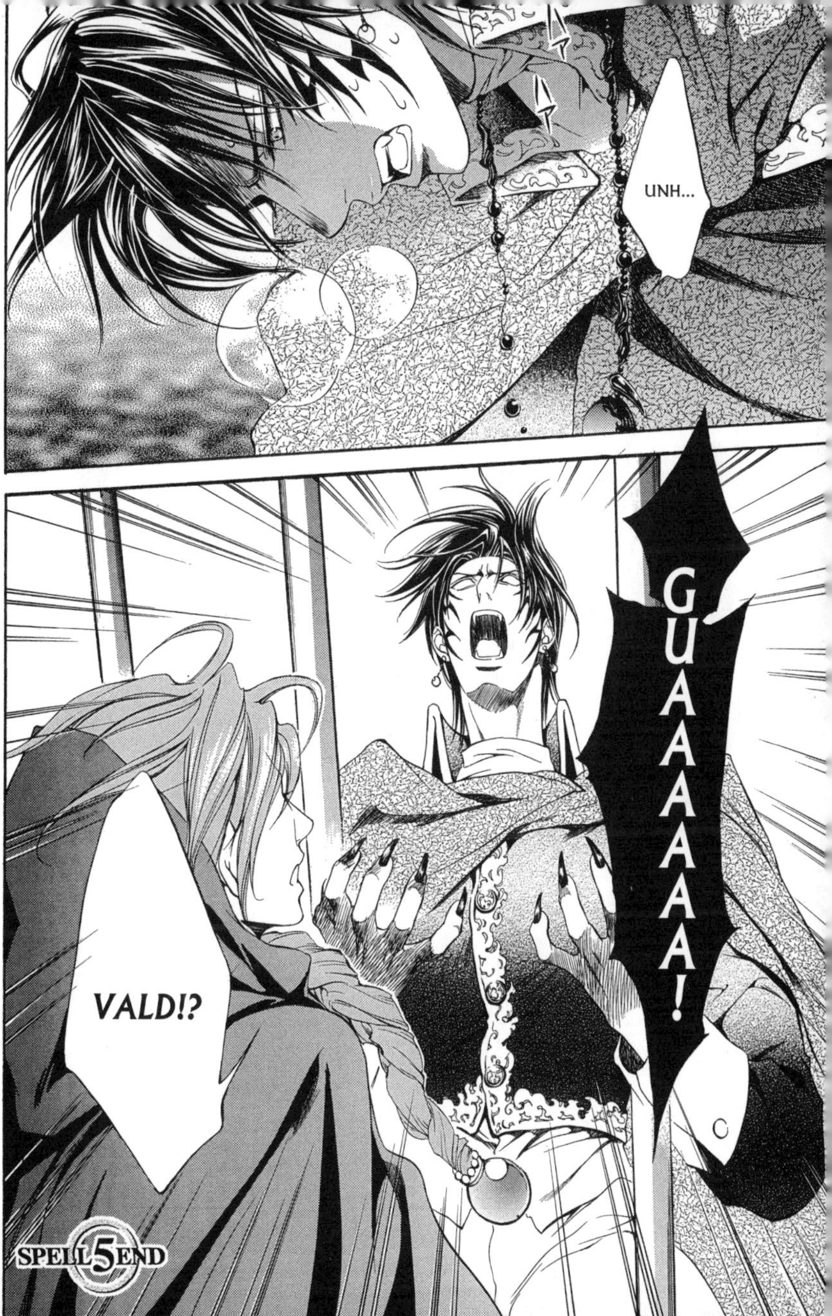
UNH...
GUAAAAAAA!
VALD!?
SPELL 5 END

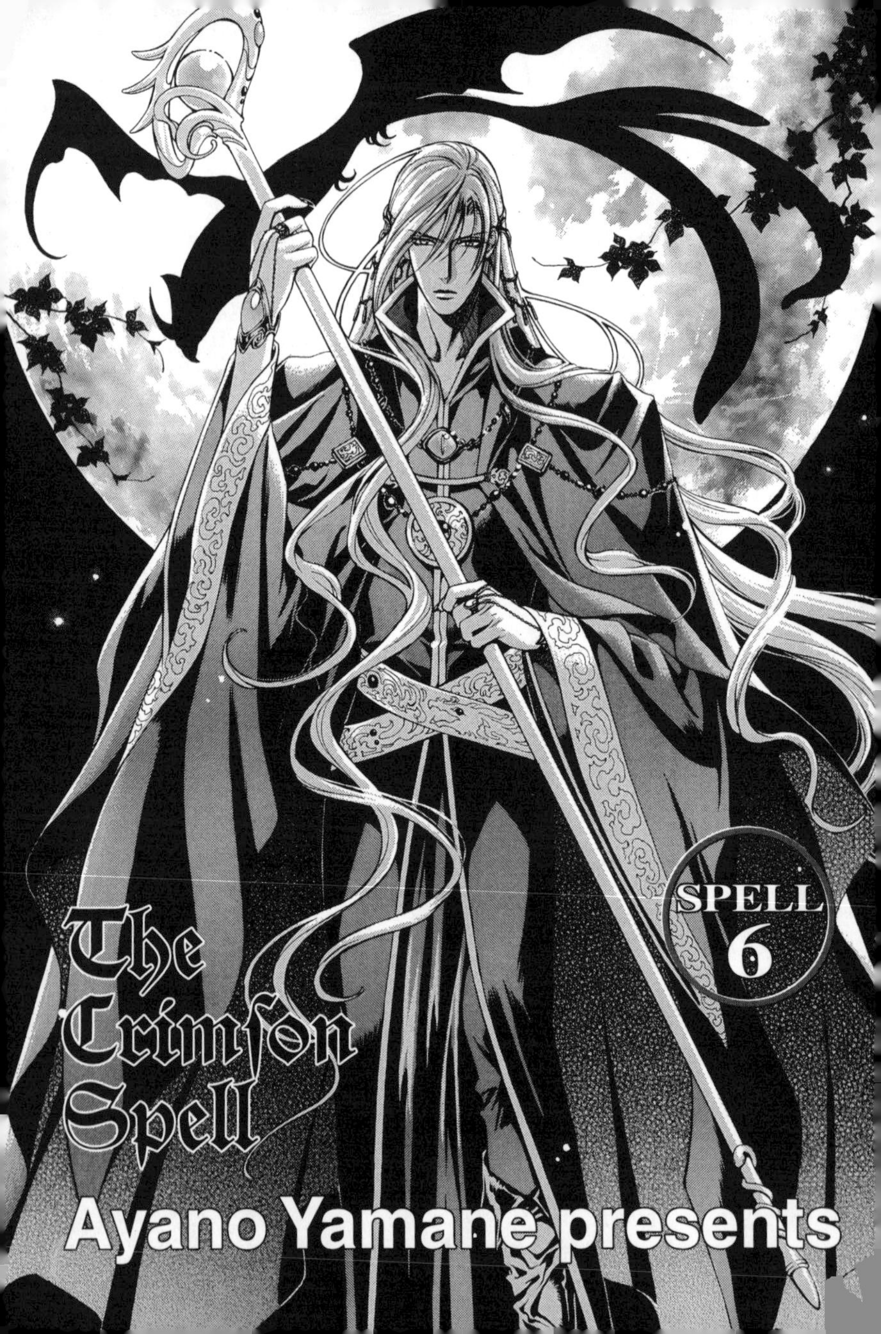
SPELL
6
The Crimson Spell
Ayano Yamane presents

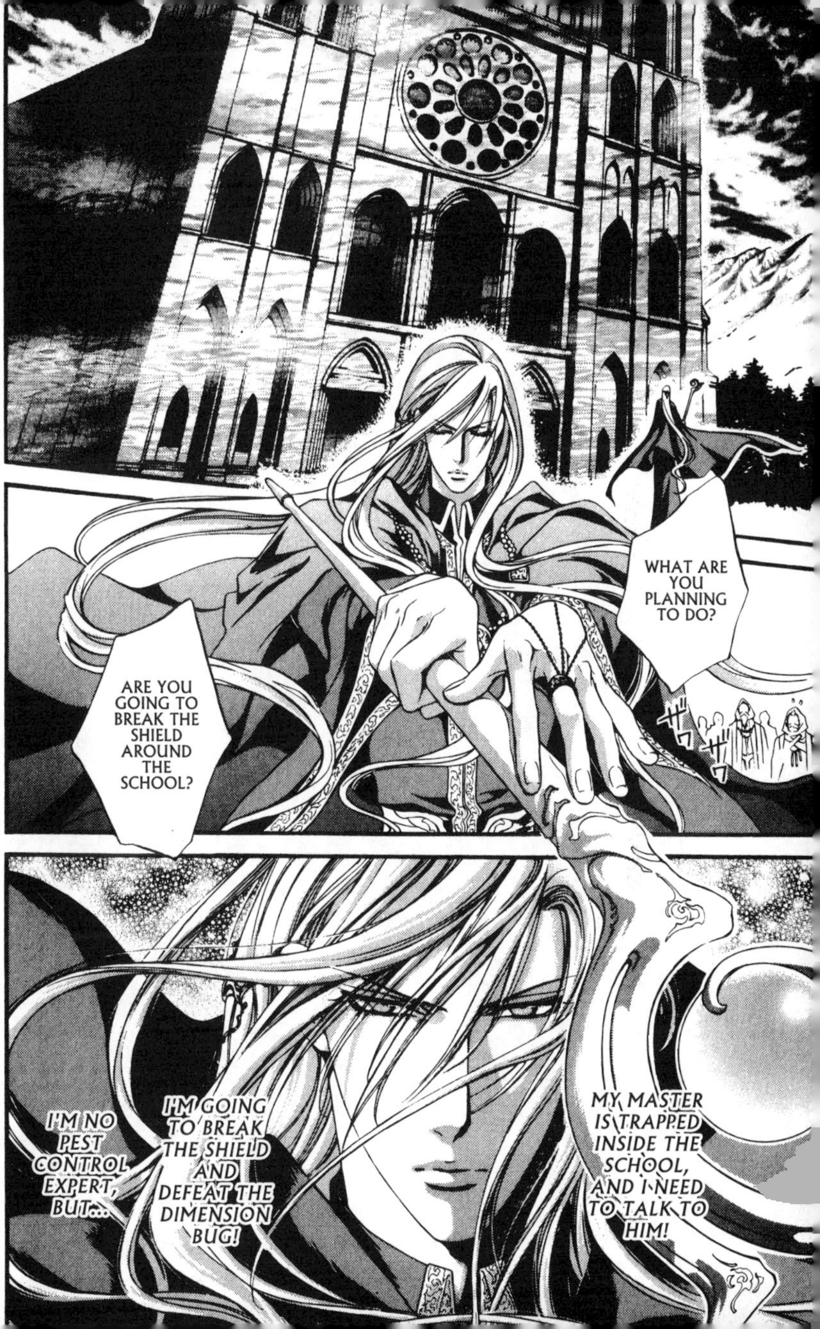
WHAT ARE YOU PLANNING TO DO?
ザワ ザワ
ARE YOU GOING TO BREAK THE SHIELD AROUND THE SCHOOL?
MY MASTER IS TRAPPED INSIDE THE SCHOOL, AND I NEED TO TALK TO HIM!
I'M GOING TO BREAK THE SHIELD AND DEFEAT THE DIMENSION BUG!
I'M NO PEST CONTROL EXPERT, BUT...

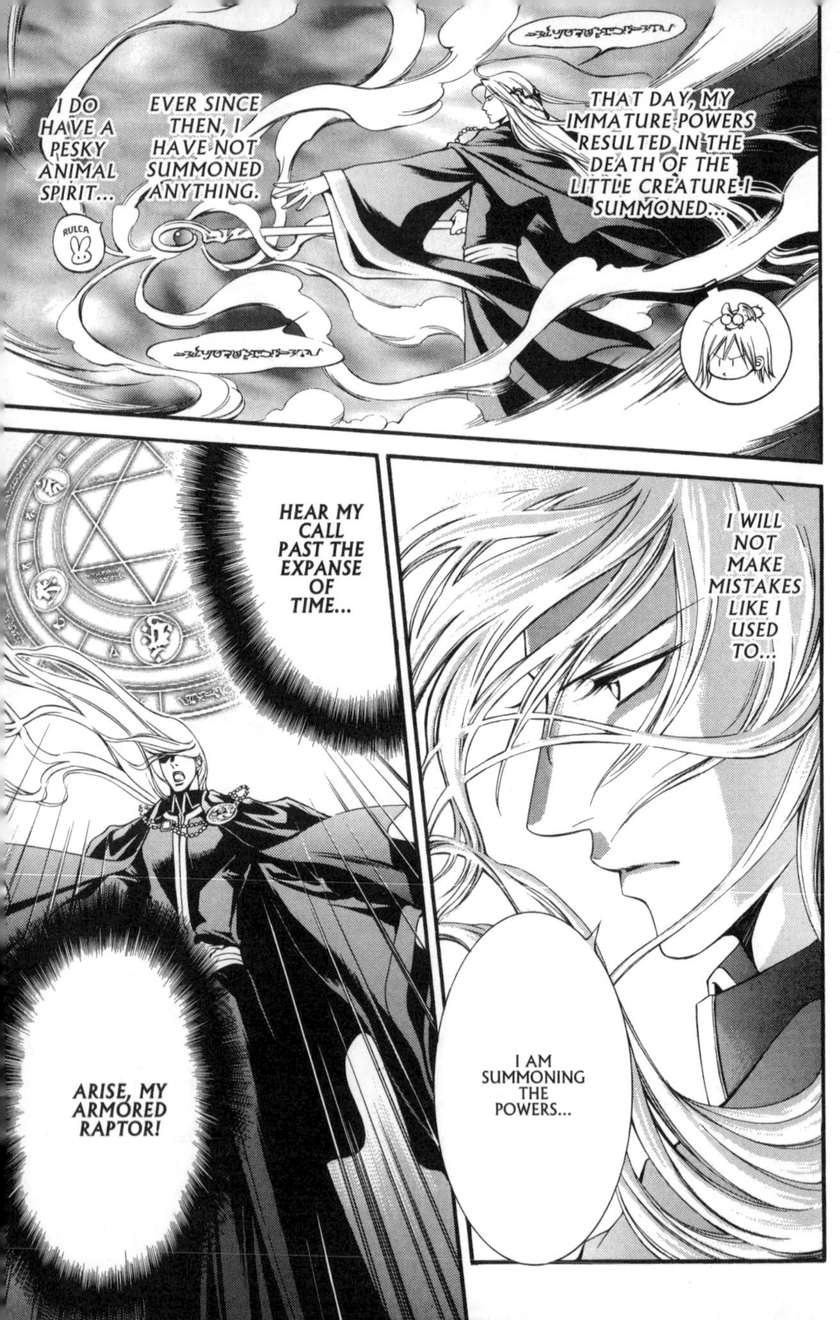
THAT DAY, MY IMMATURE POWERS RESULTED IN THE DEATH OF THE LITTLE CREATURE I SUMMONED...
EVER SINCE THEN, I HAVE NOT SUMMONED ANYTHING.
I DO HAVE A PESKY ANIMAL SPIRIT...
RULCA
I WILL NOT MAKE MISTAKES LIKE I USED TO...
I AM SUMMONING THE POWERS...
HEAR MY CALL PAST THE EXPANSE OF TIME...
ARISE, MY ARMORED RAPTOR!

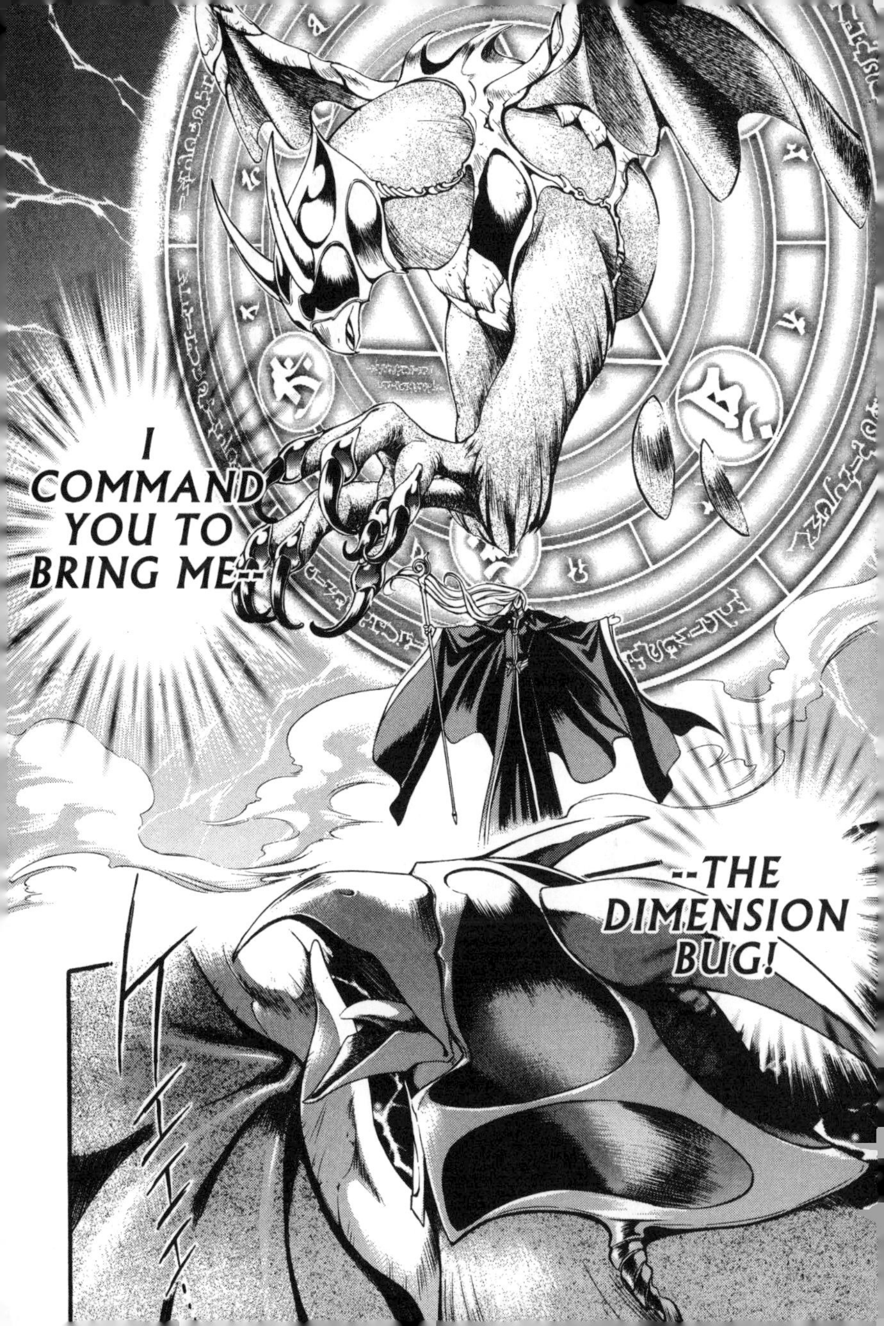
I COMMAND YOU TO BRING ME--
--THE DIMENSION BUG!

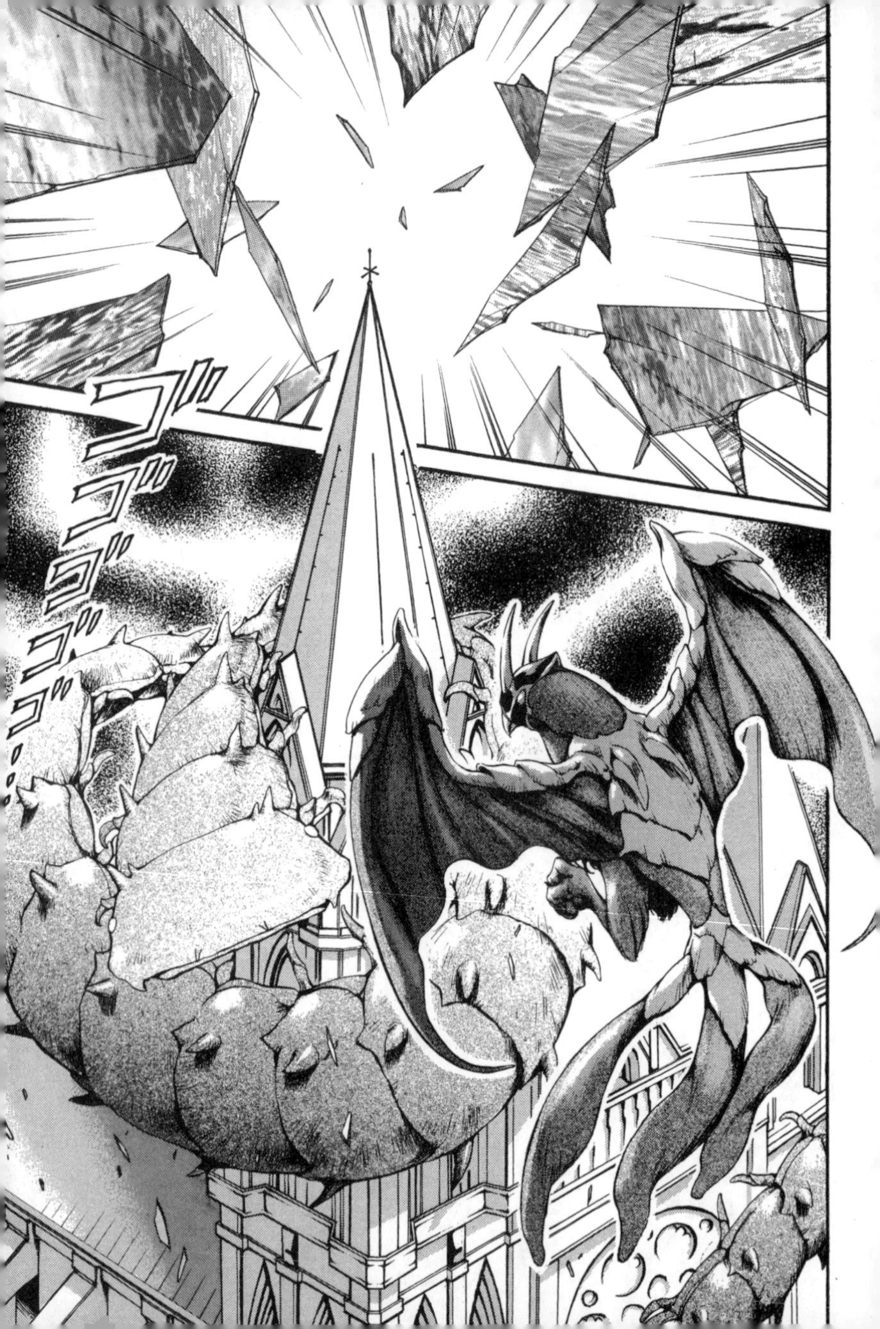
ゴゴゴゴゴゴ…

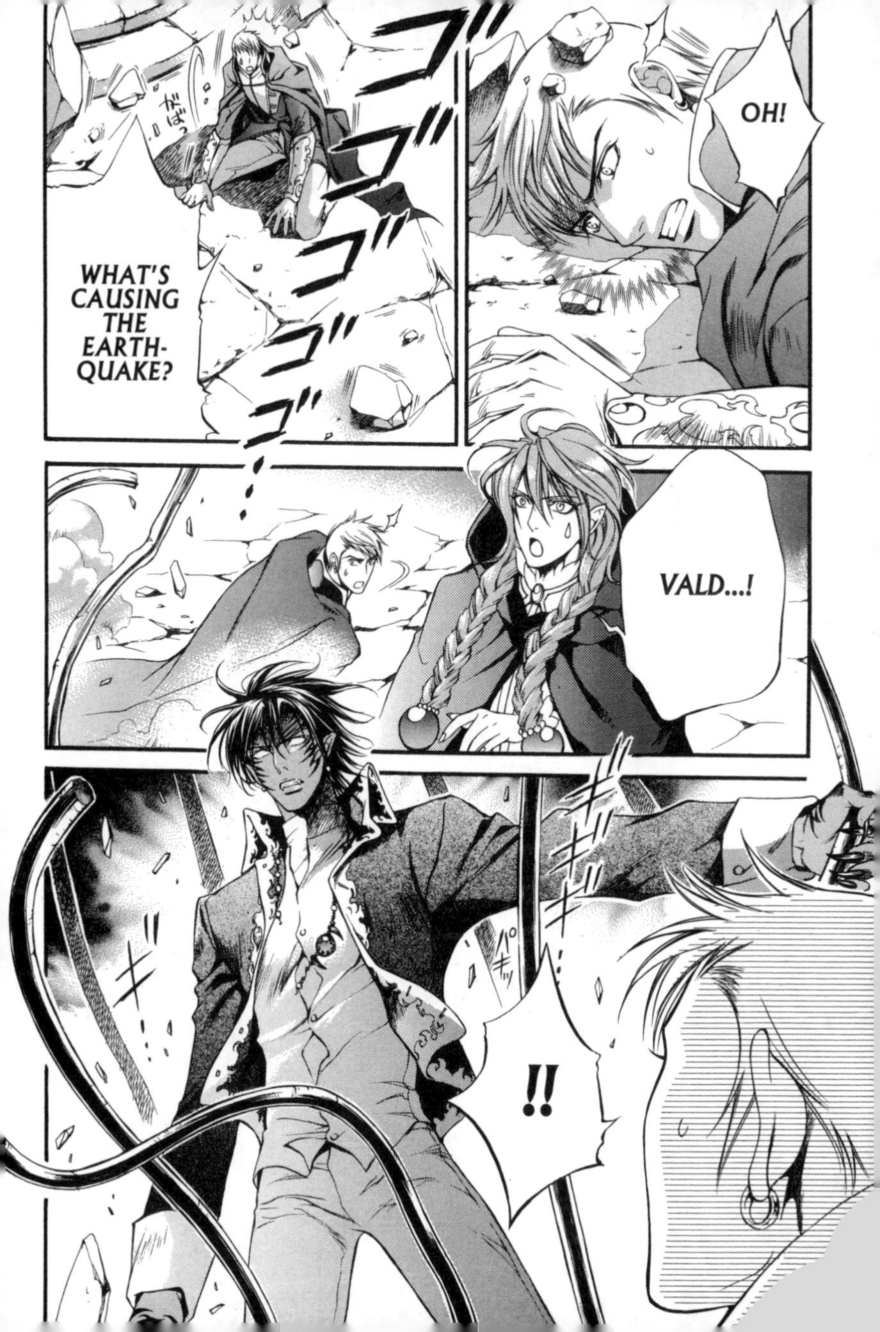
OH!
WHAT'S CAUSING THE EARTH-QUAKE?
がばっ
VALD...!
!!
バキッ

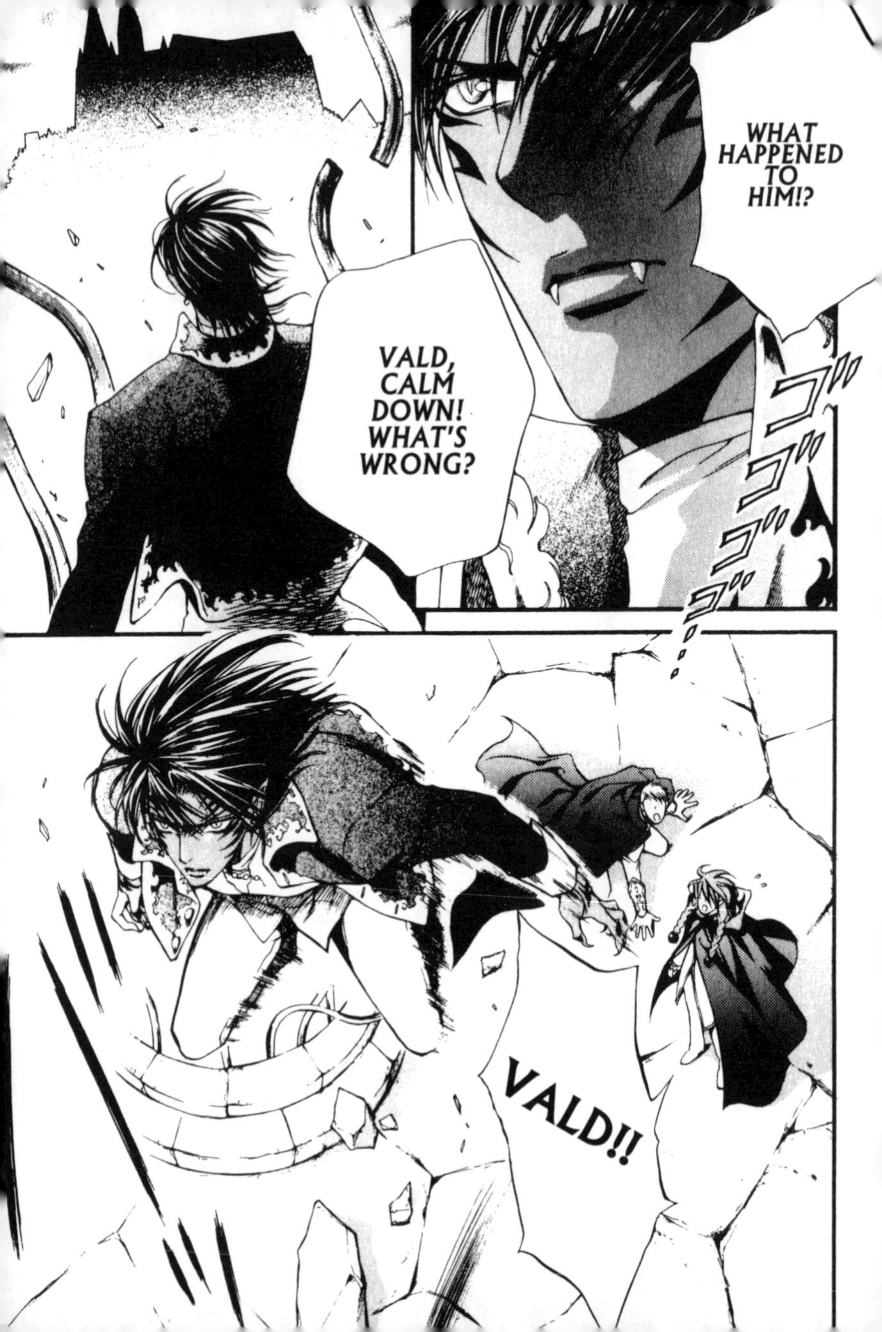
WHAT HAPPENED TO HIM!?
ゴゴゴゴゴ
VALD, CALM DOWN! WHAT'S WRONG?
VALD!!

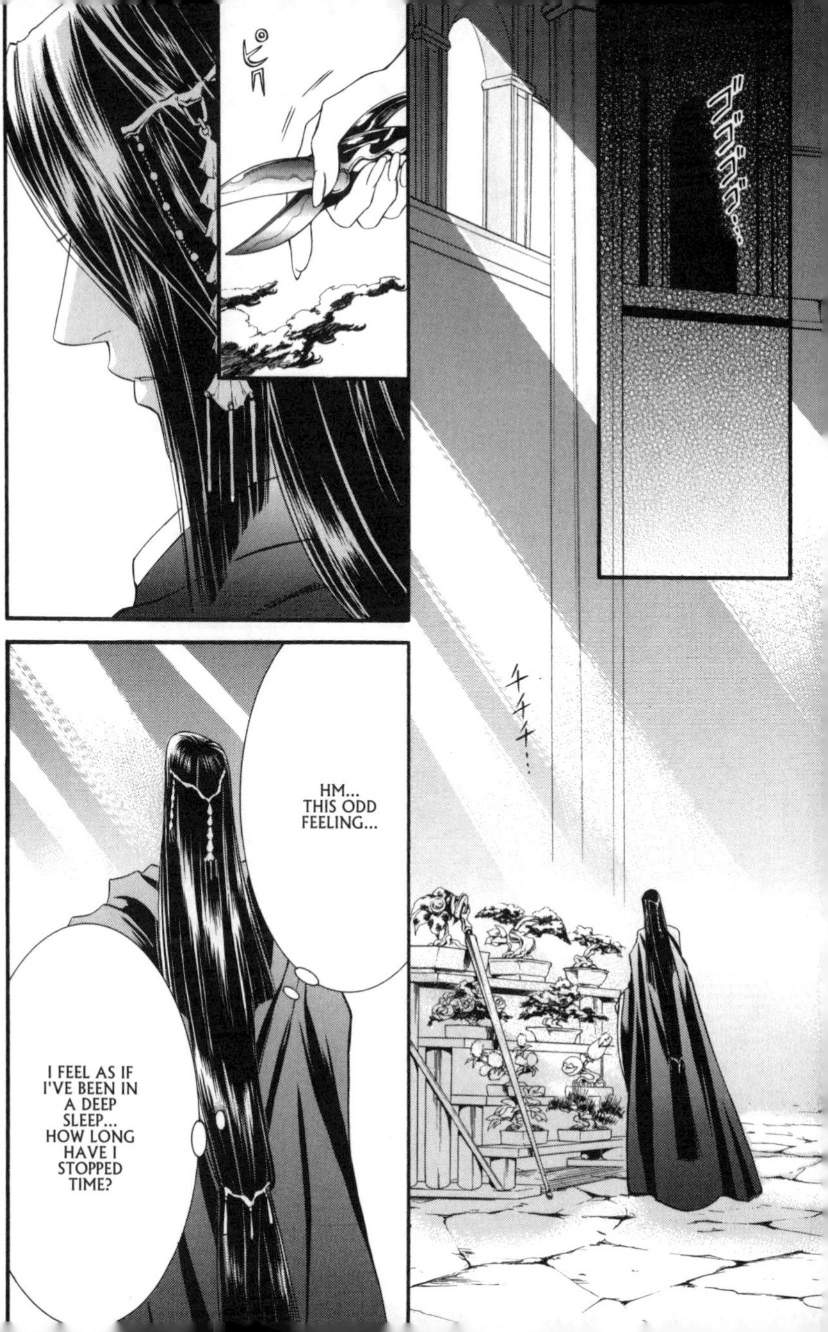
ピク
チチチ…
HM... THIS ODD FEELING...
I FEEL AS IF I'VE BEEN IN A DEEP SLEEP... HOW LONG HAVE I STOPPED TIME?

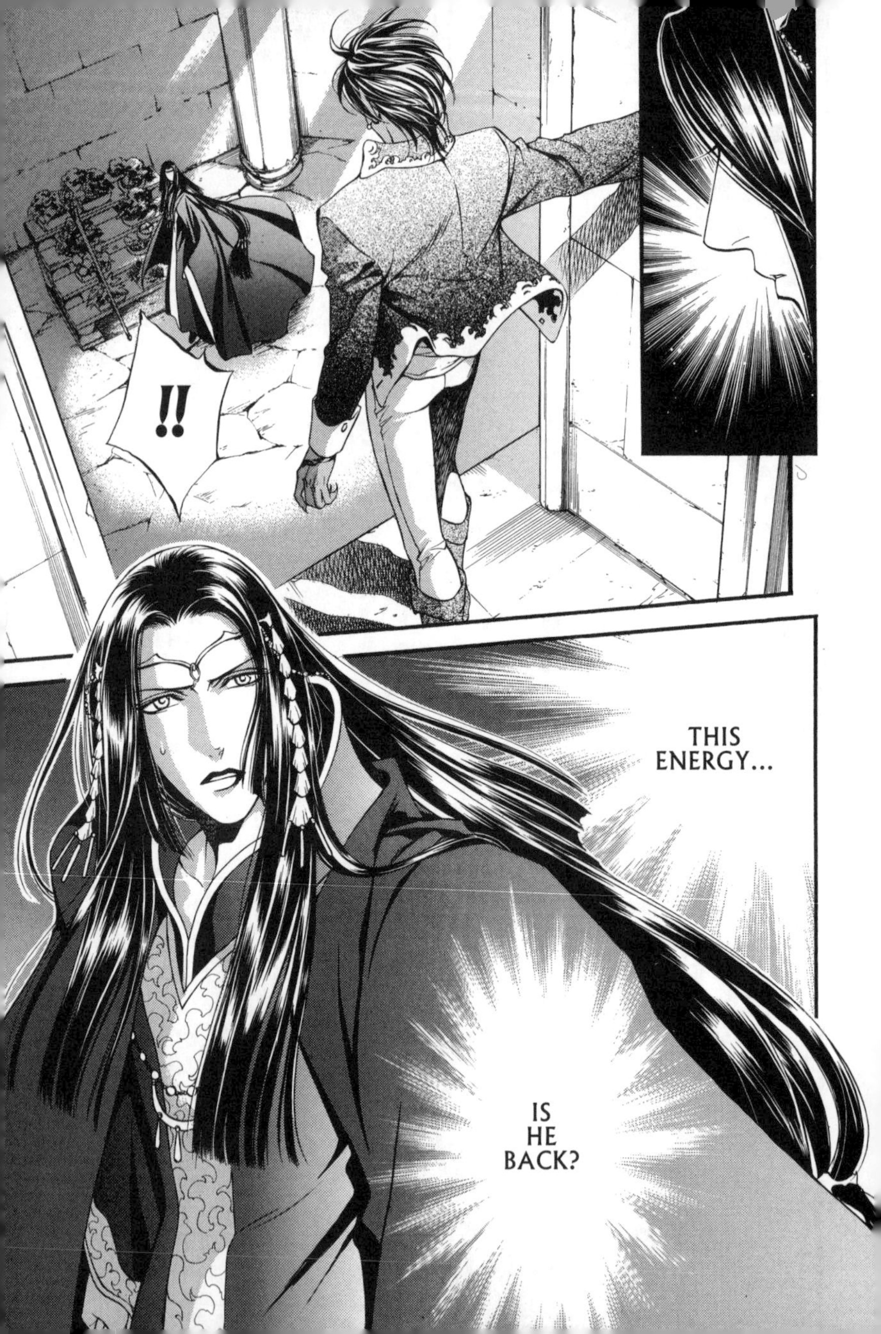
!!
THIS ENERGY...
IS HE BACK?

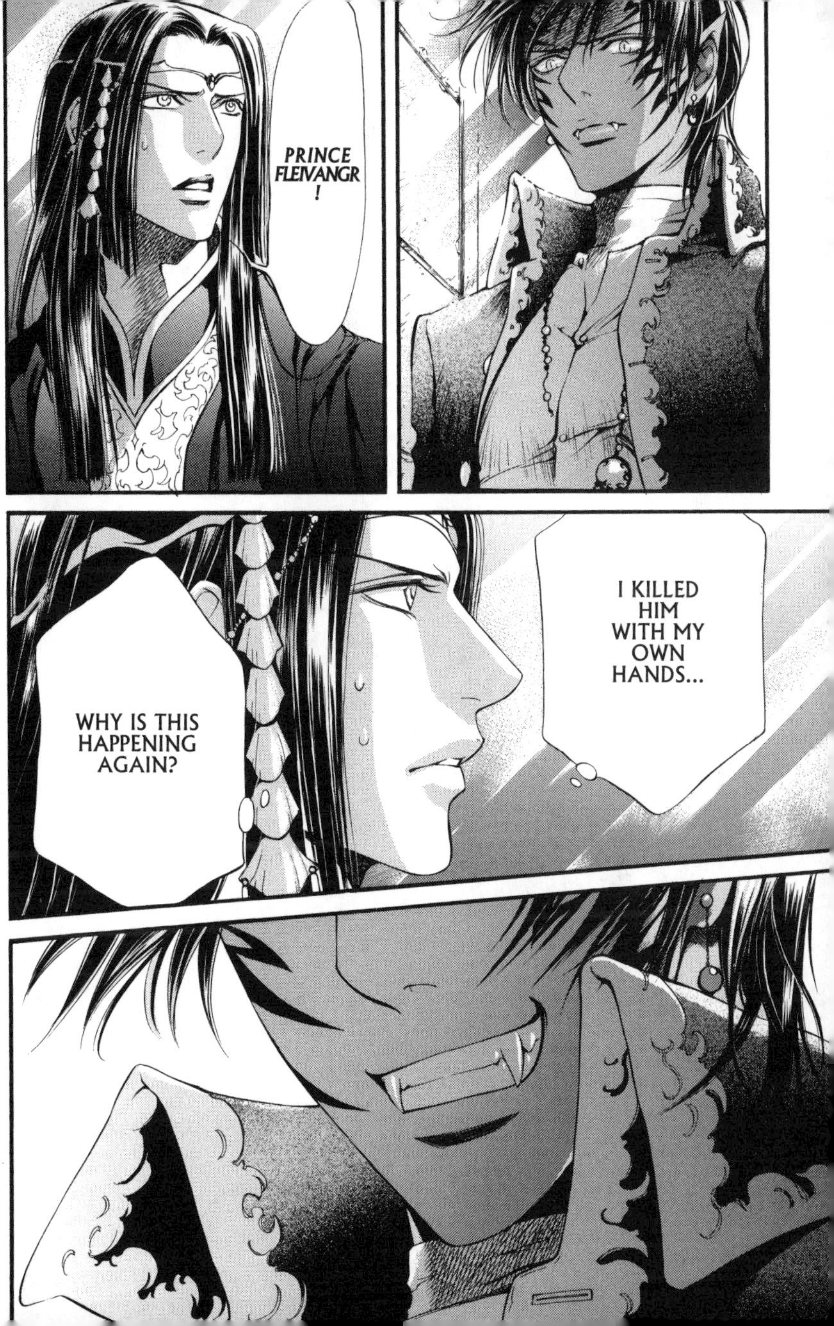
PRINCE FLEIVANGR !
I KILLED HIM WITH MY OWN HANDS...
WHY IS THIS HAPPENING AGAIN?

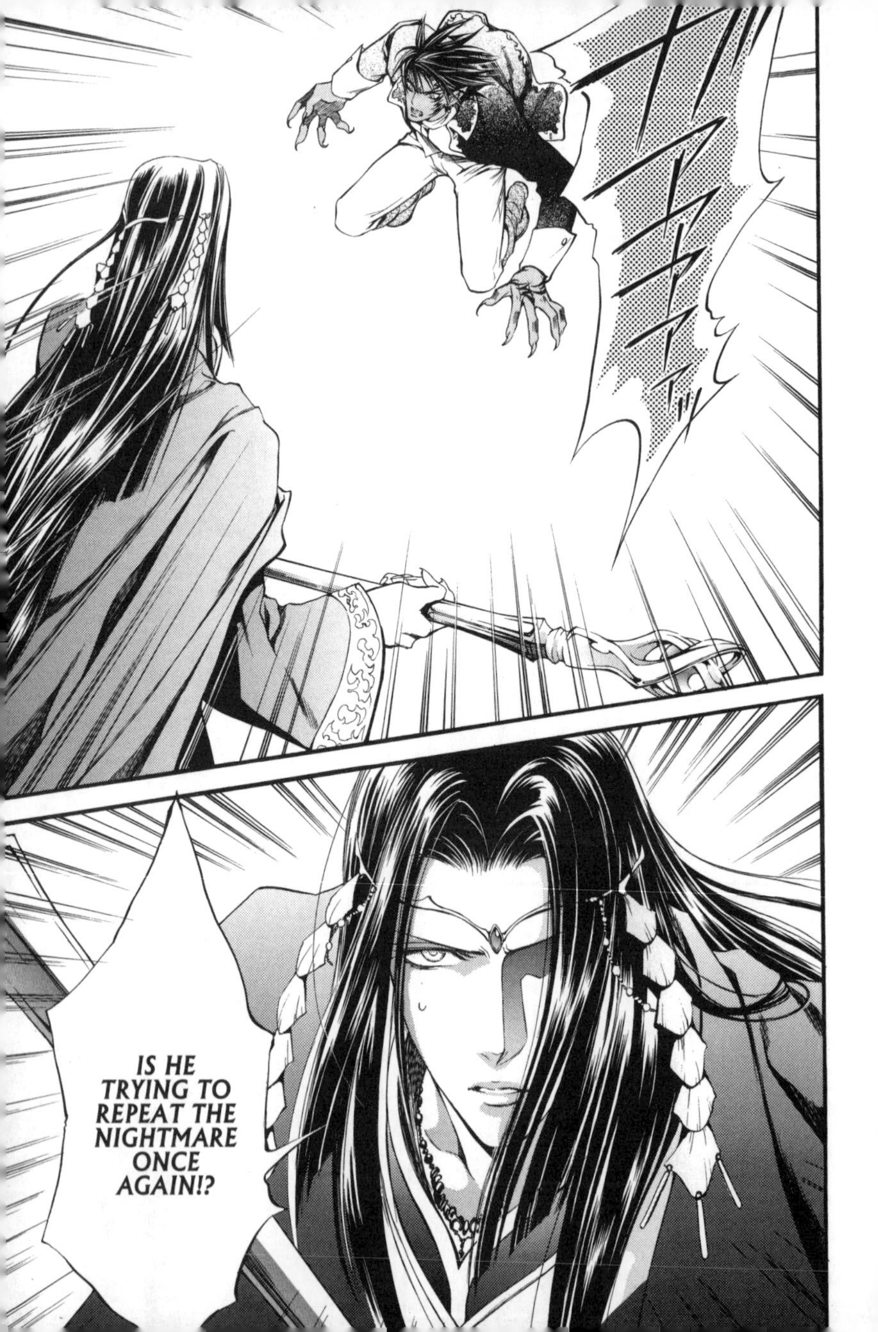
IS HE TRYING TO REPEAT THE NIGHTMARE ONCE AGAIN!?

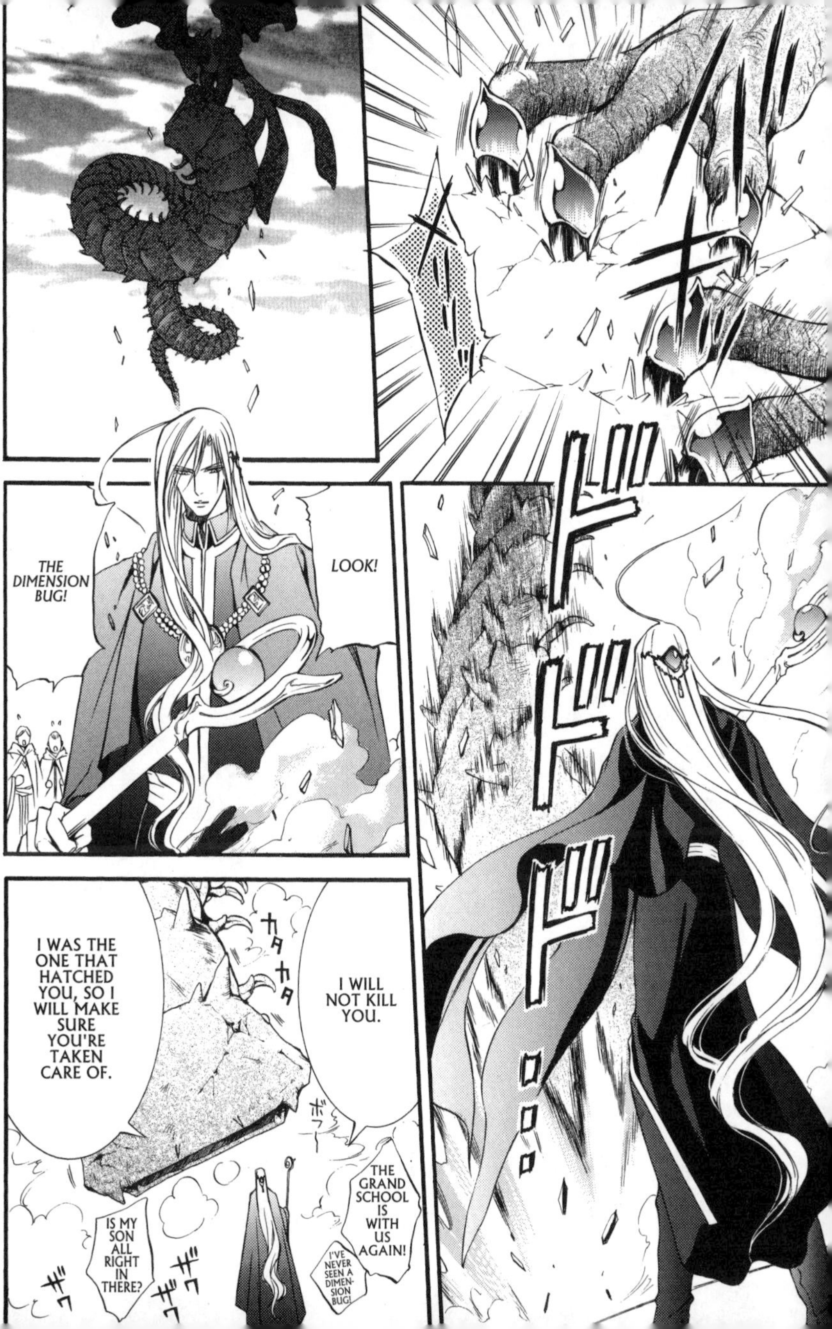
LOOK!
THE DIMENSION BUG!
I WILL NOT KILL YOU.
I WAS THE ONE THAT HATCHED YOU, SO I WILL MAKE SURE YOU'RE TAKEN CARE OF.
カタカタ
THE GRAND SCHOOL IS WITH US AGAIN!
I'VE NEVER SEEN A DIMENSION BUG!
IS MY SON ALL RIGHT IN THERE?

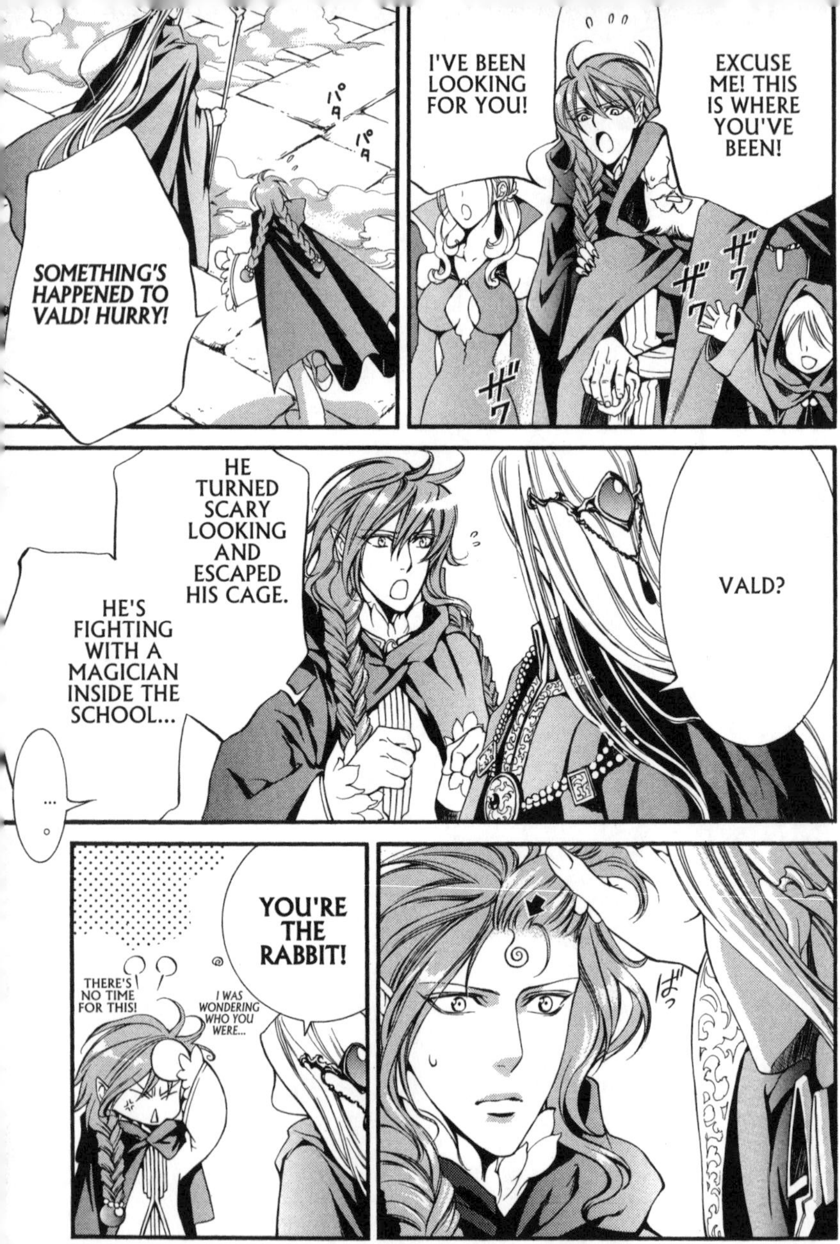
EXCUSE ME! THIS IS WHERE YOU'VE BEEN!
I'VE BEEN LOOKING FOR YOU!
ザワ
ザワ
ザワ
パタ
パタ
SOMETHING'S HAPPENED TO VALD! HURRY!
VALD?
HE TURNED SCARY LOOKING AND ESCAPED HIS CAGE.
HE'S FIGHTING WITH A MAGICIAN INSIDE THE SCHOOL...
...
ばっ
YOU'RE THE RABBIT!
I WAS WONDERING WHO YOU WERE...
THERE'S NO TIME FOR THIS!

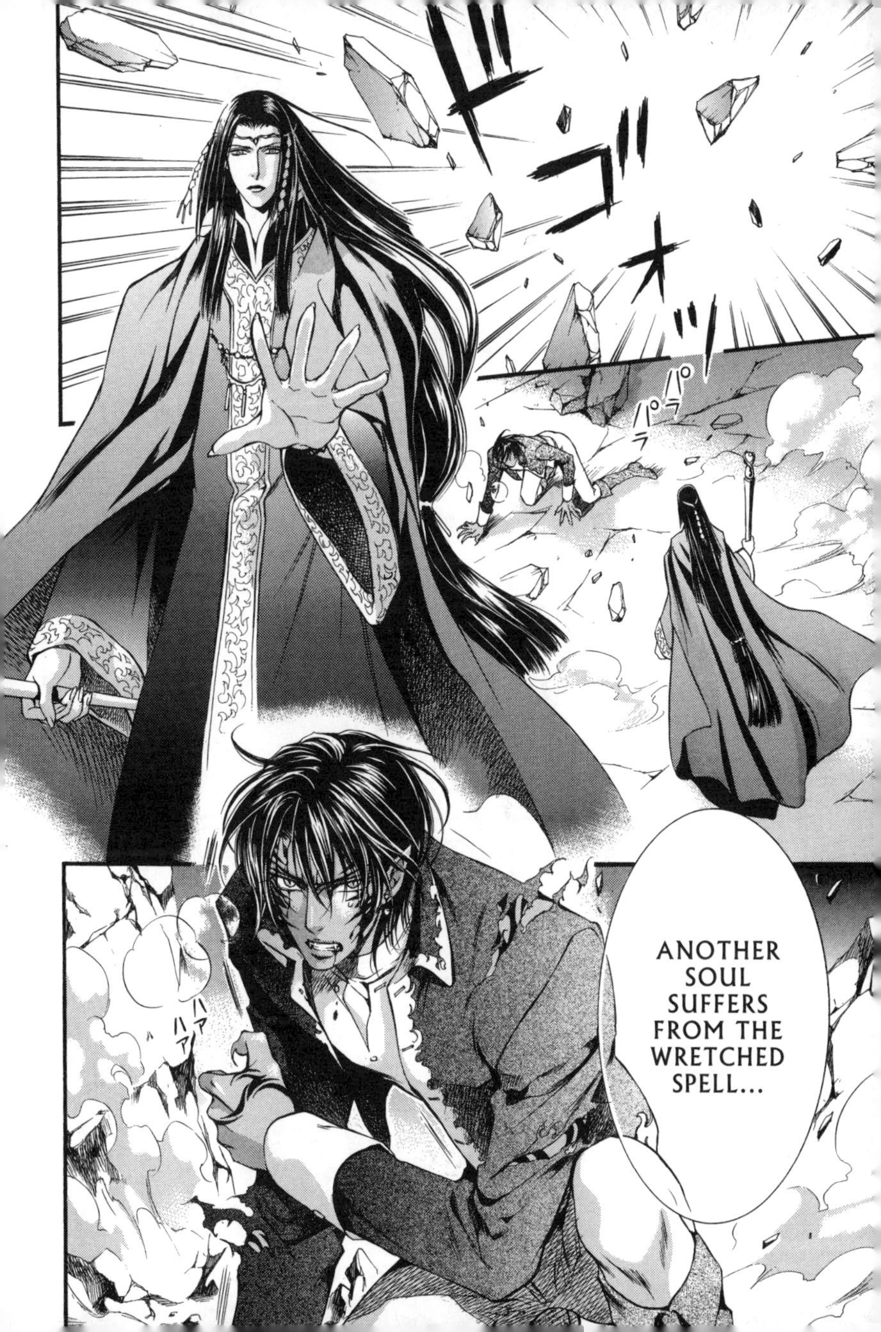

ドゴオッ!
パラパラ
ANOTHER SOUL SUFFERS FROM THE WRETCHED SPELL...
ハァハァ

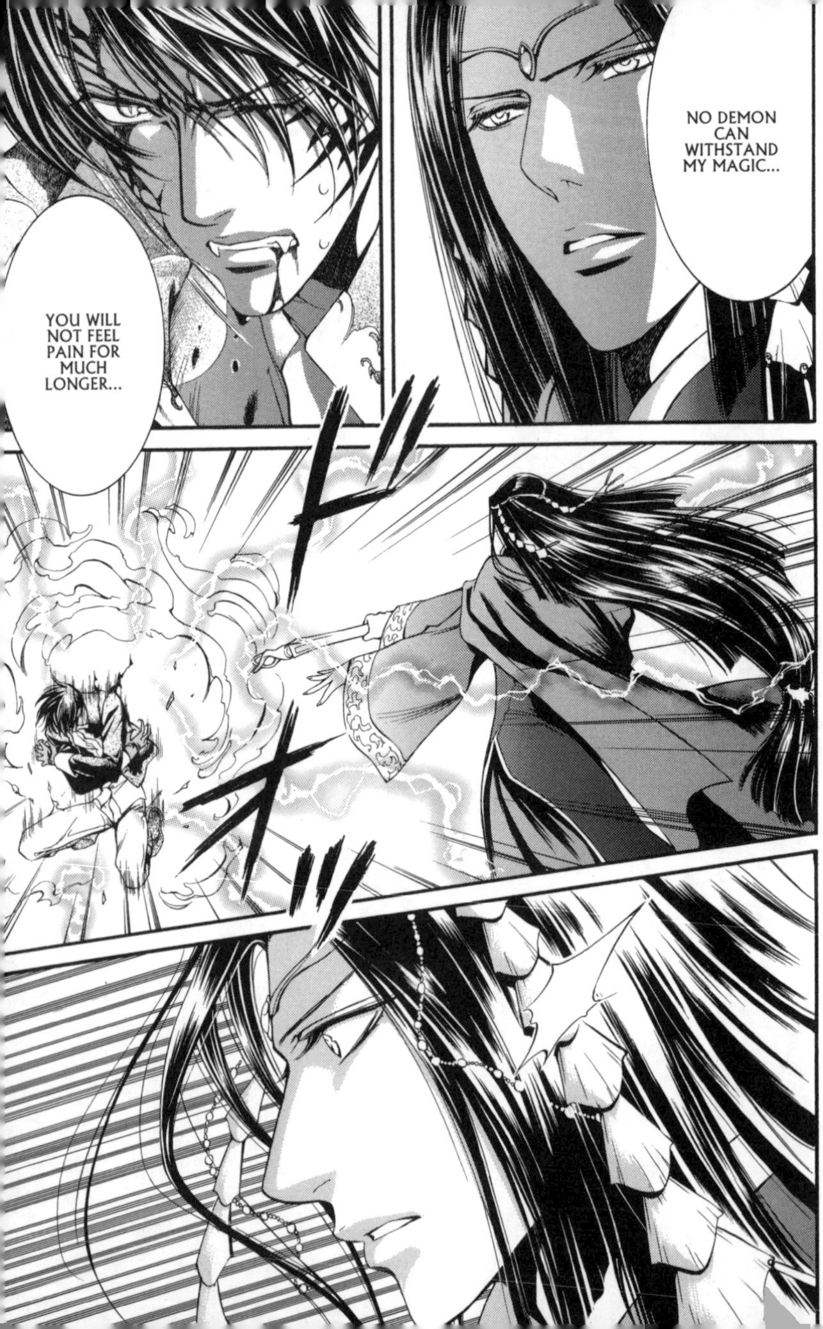
NO DEMON CAN WITHSTAND MY MAGIC...
YOU WILL NOT FEEL PAIN FOR MUCH LONGER...

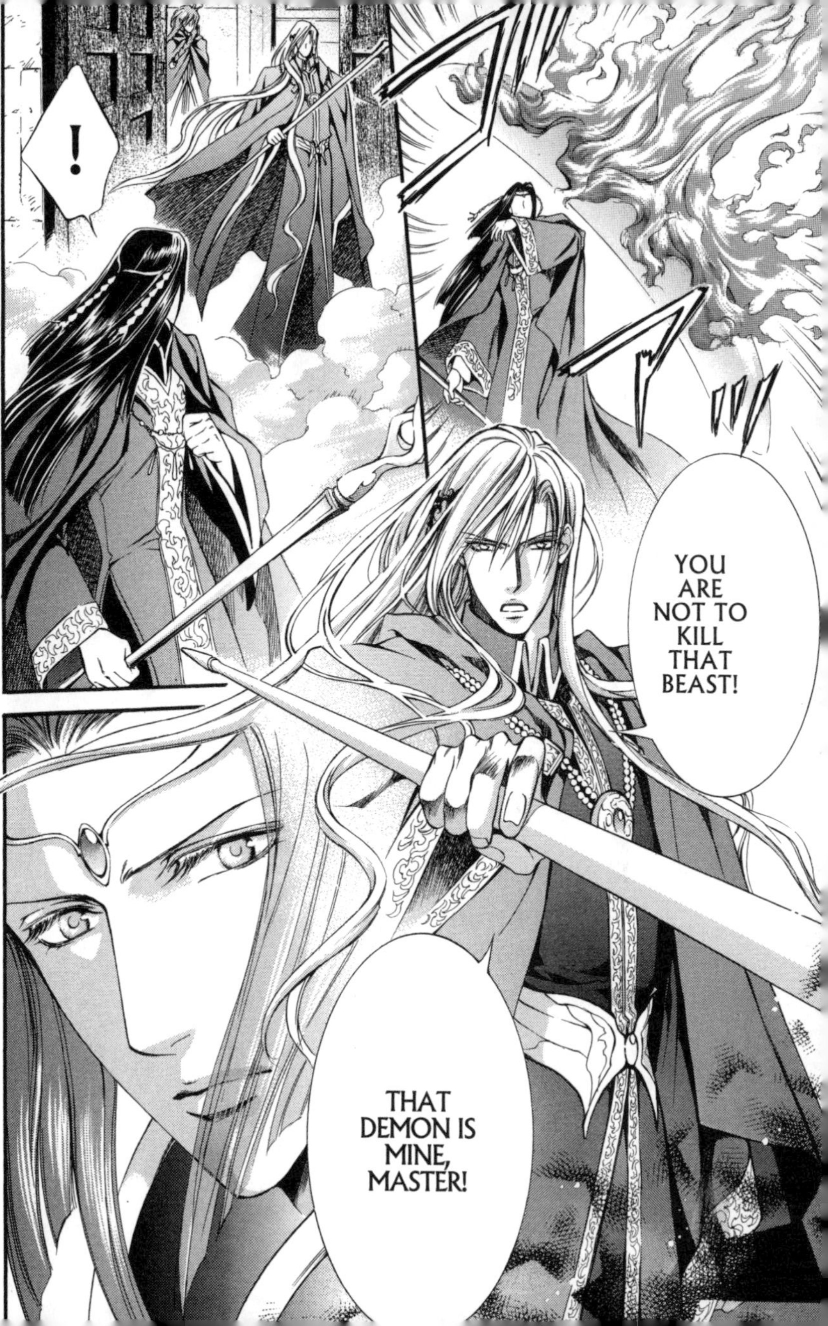
YOU ARE NOT TO KILL THAT BEAST!
!
THAT DEMON IS MINE, MASTER!

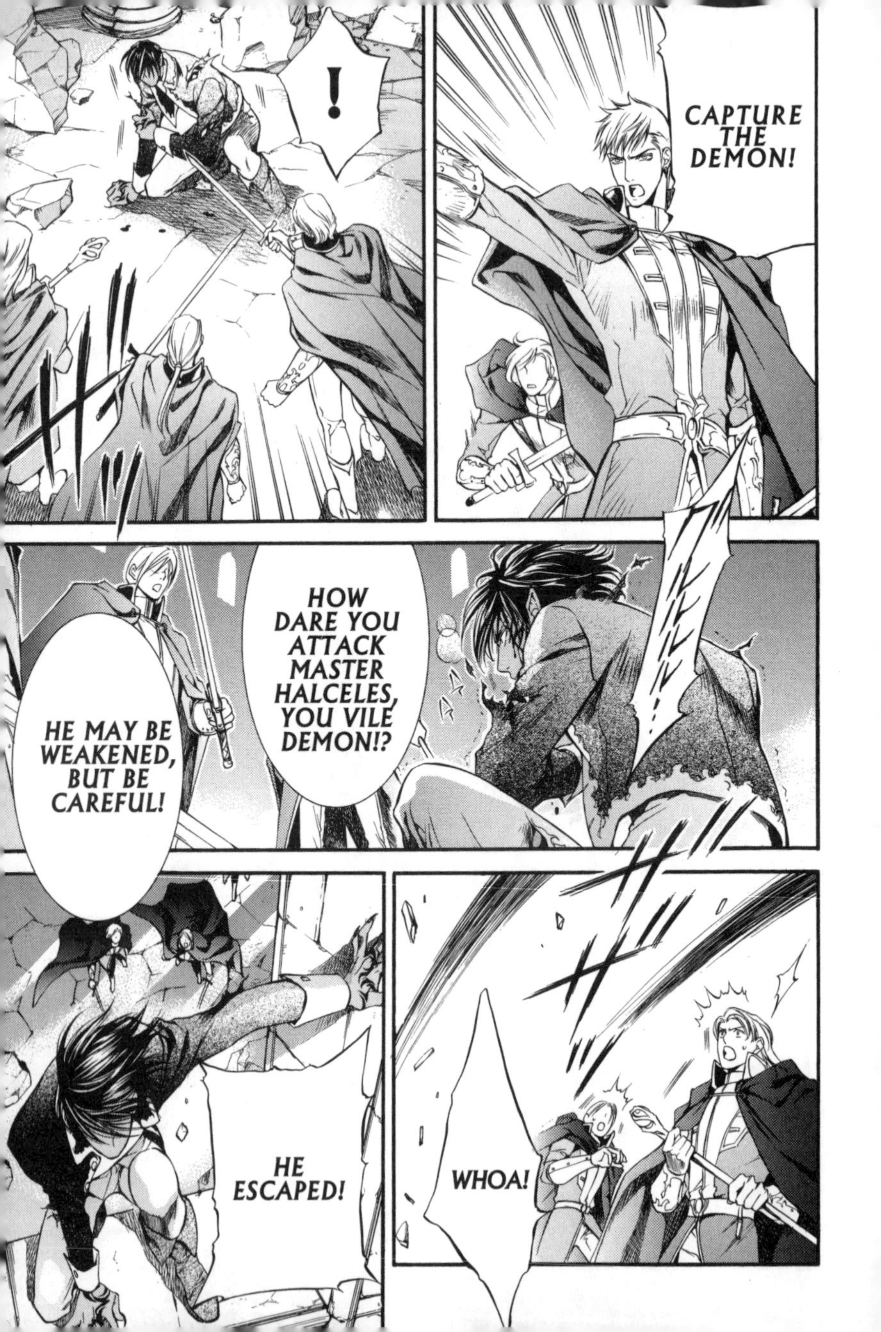
CAPTURE THE DEMON!
!
HOW DARE YOU ATTACK MASTER HALCELES, YOU VILE DEMON!?
HE MAY BE WEAKENED, BUT BE CAREFUL!
WHOA!
HE ESCAPED!

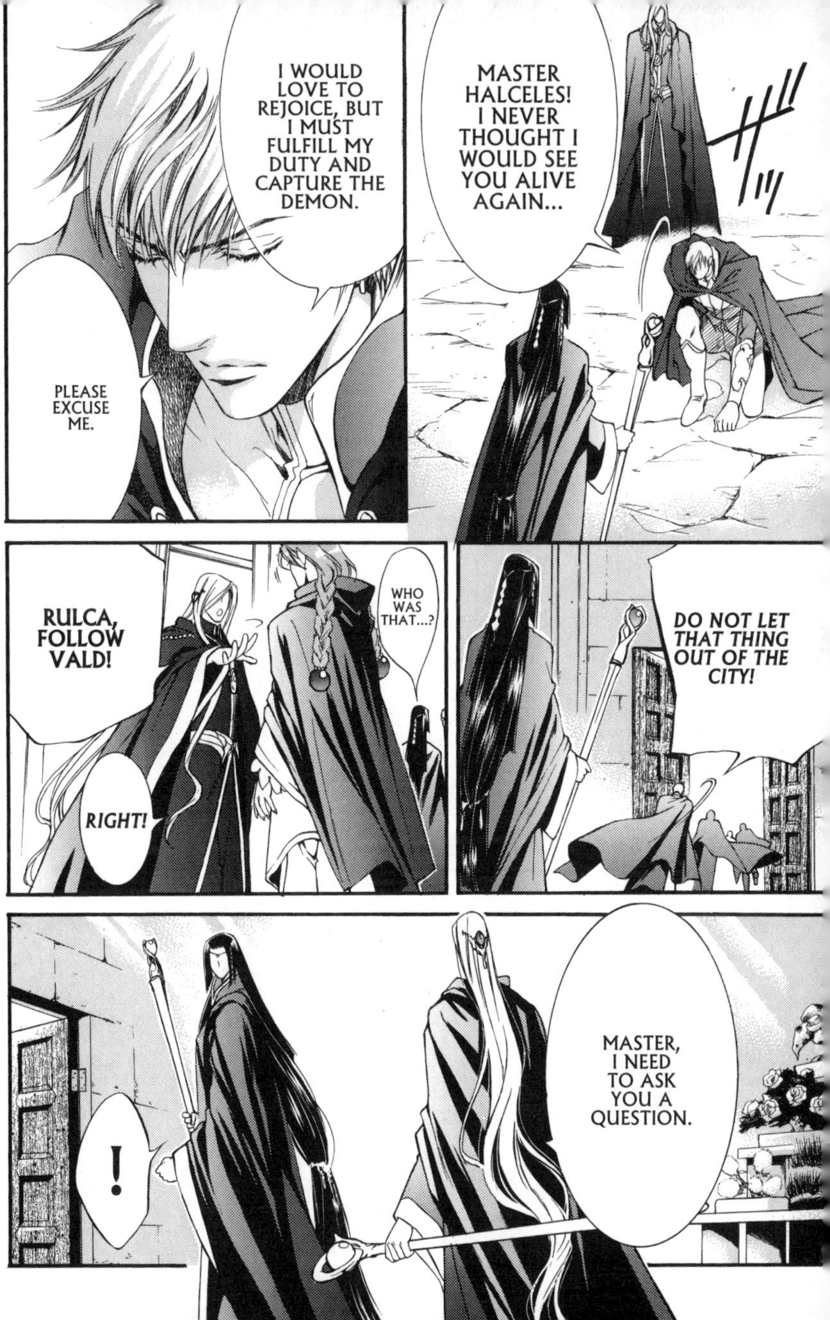
MASTER HALCELES! I NEVER THOUGHT I WOULD SEE YOU ALIVE AGAIN...
I WOULD LOVE TO REJOICE, BUT I MUST FULFILL MY DUTY AND CAPTURE THE DEMON.
PLEASE EXCUSE ME.
DO NOT LET THAT THING OUT OF THE CITY!
WHO WAS THAT...?
RULCA, FOLLOW VALD!
RIGHT!
MASTER, I NEED TO ASK YOU A QUESTION.
!

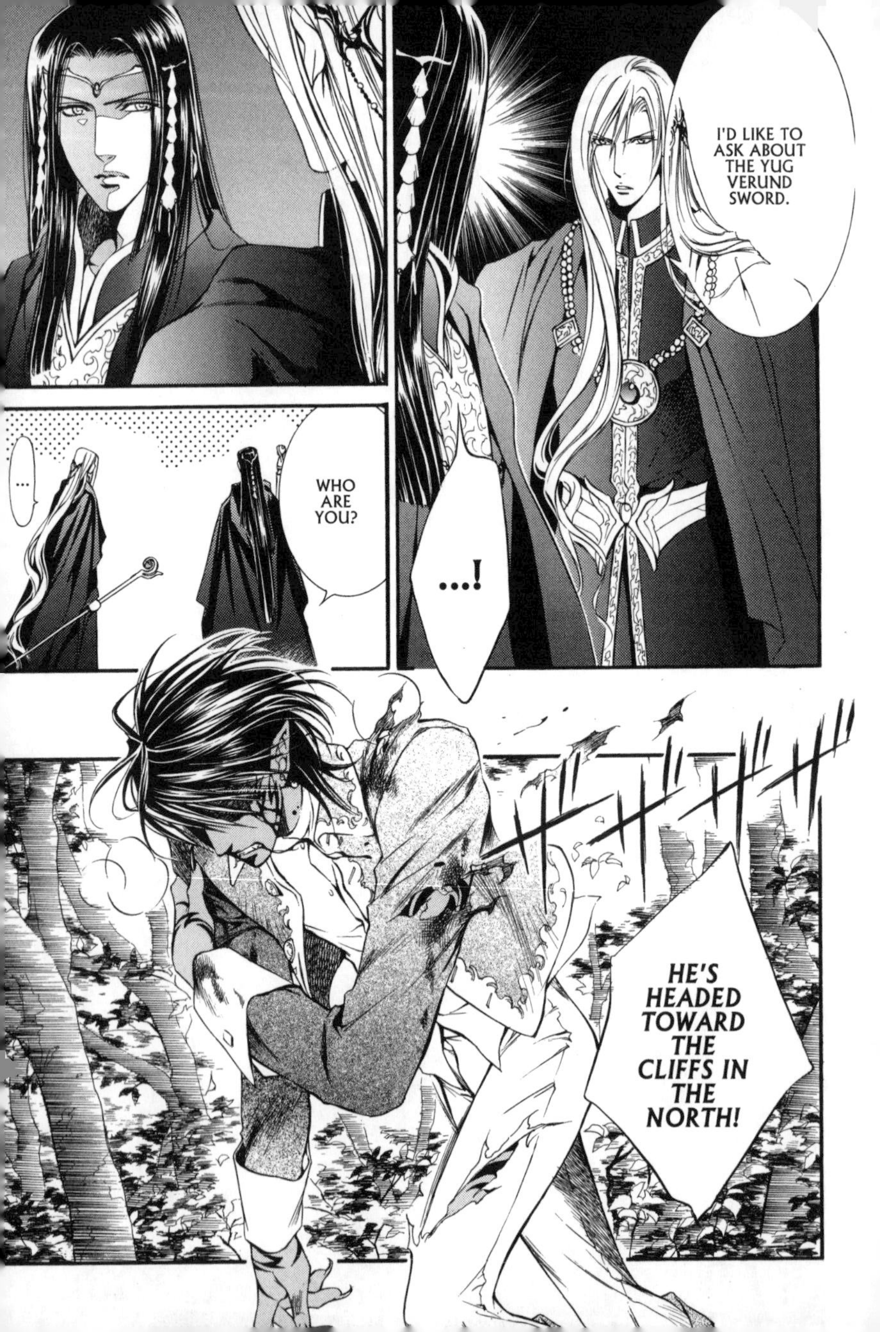
I'D LIKE TO ASK ABOUT THE YUG VERUND SWORD.
...!
WHO ARE YOU?
...
HE'S HEADED TOWARD THE CLIFFS IN THE NORTH!

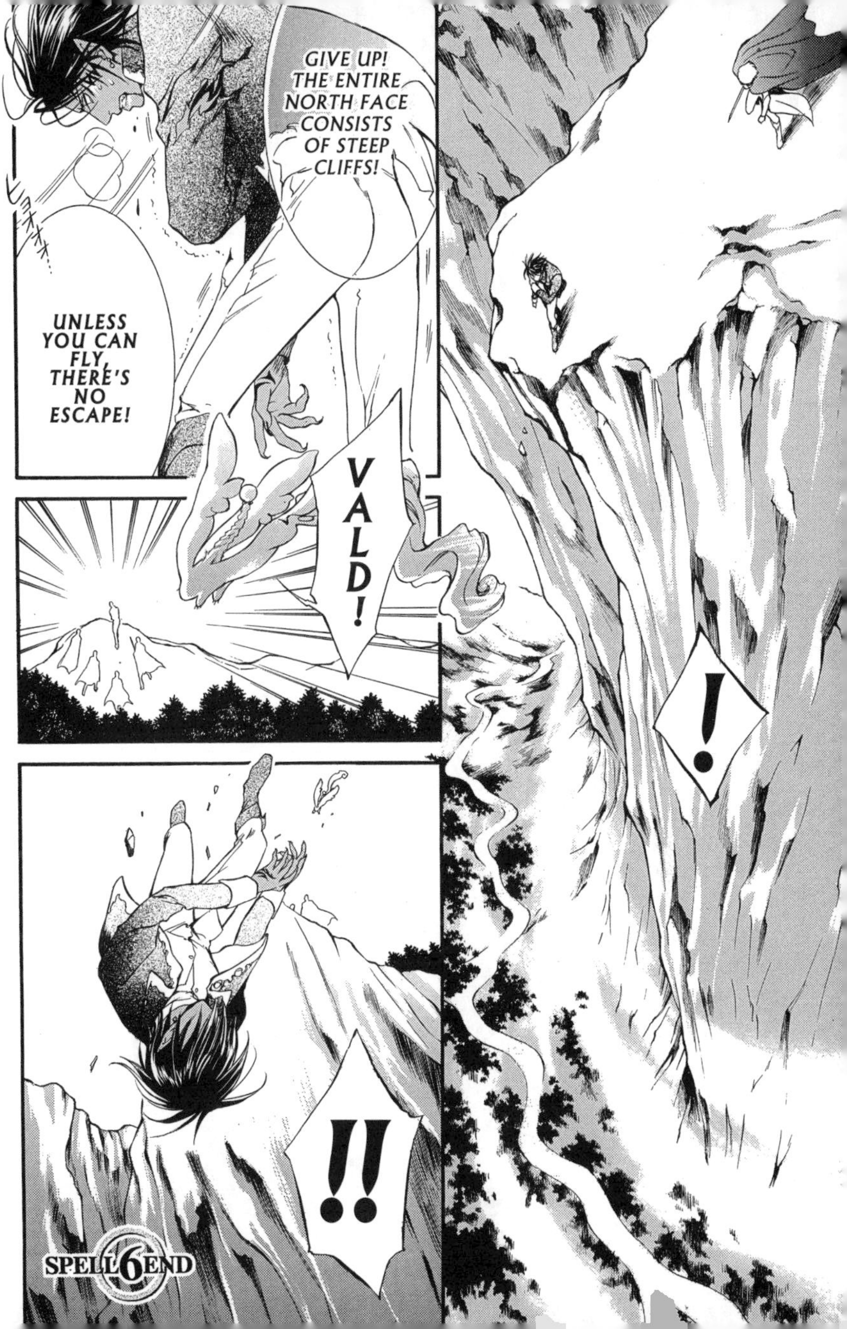
!
GIVE UP! THE ENTIRE NORTH FACE CONSISTS OF STEEP CLIFFS!
UNLESS YOU CAN FLY, THERE'S NO ESCAPE!
VALD!
!!
SPELL 6 END

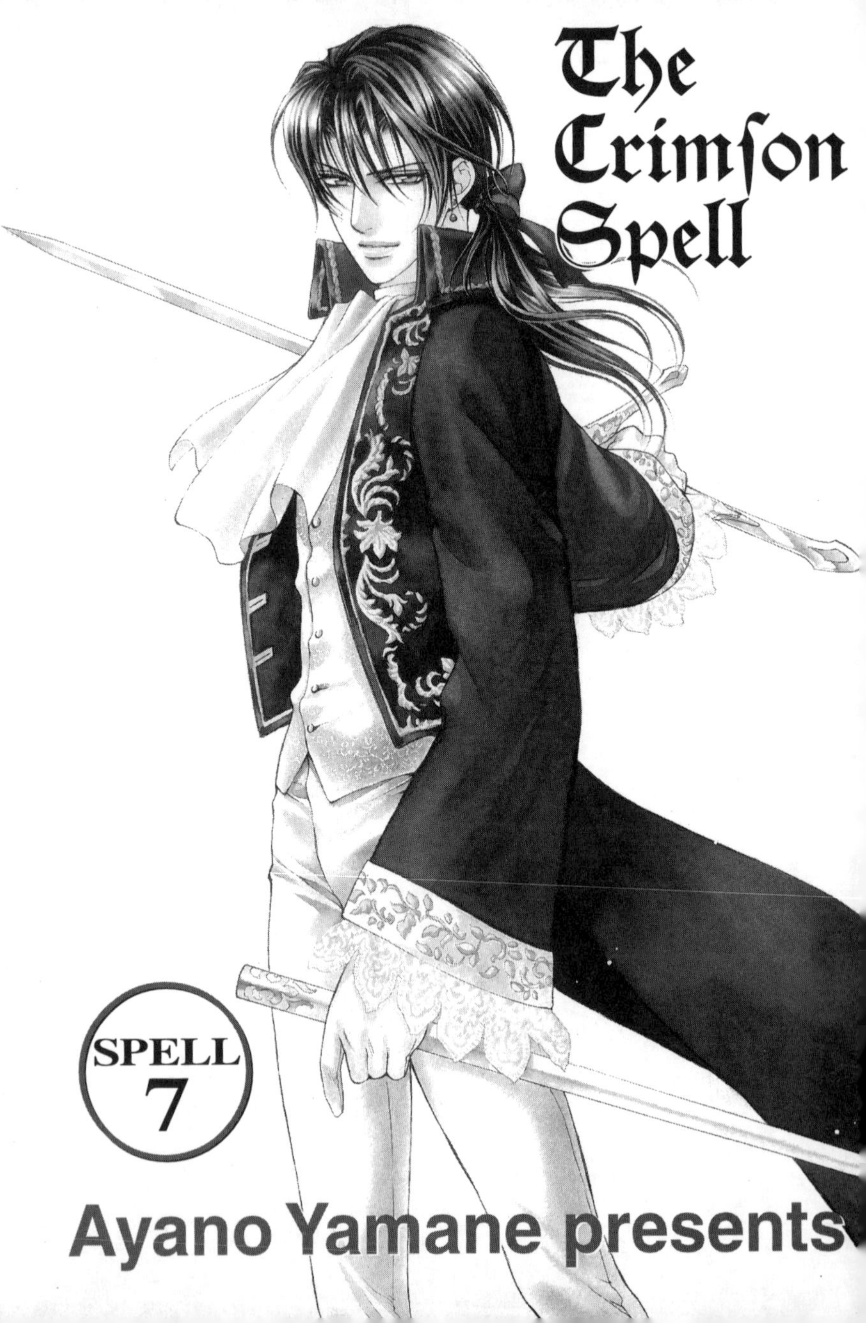
The Crimson Spell
SPELL 7
Ayano Yamane presents

Ayano Yamane Presents

The
Crimson
Spell

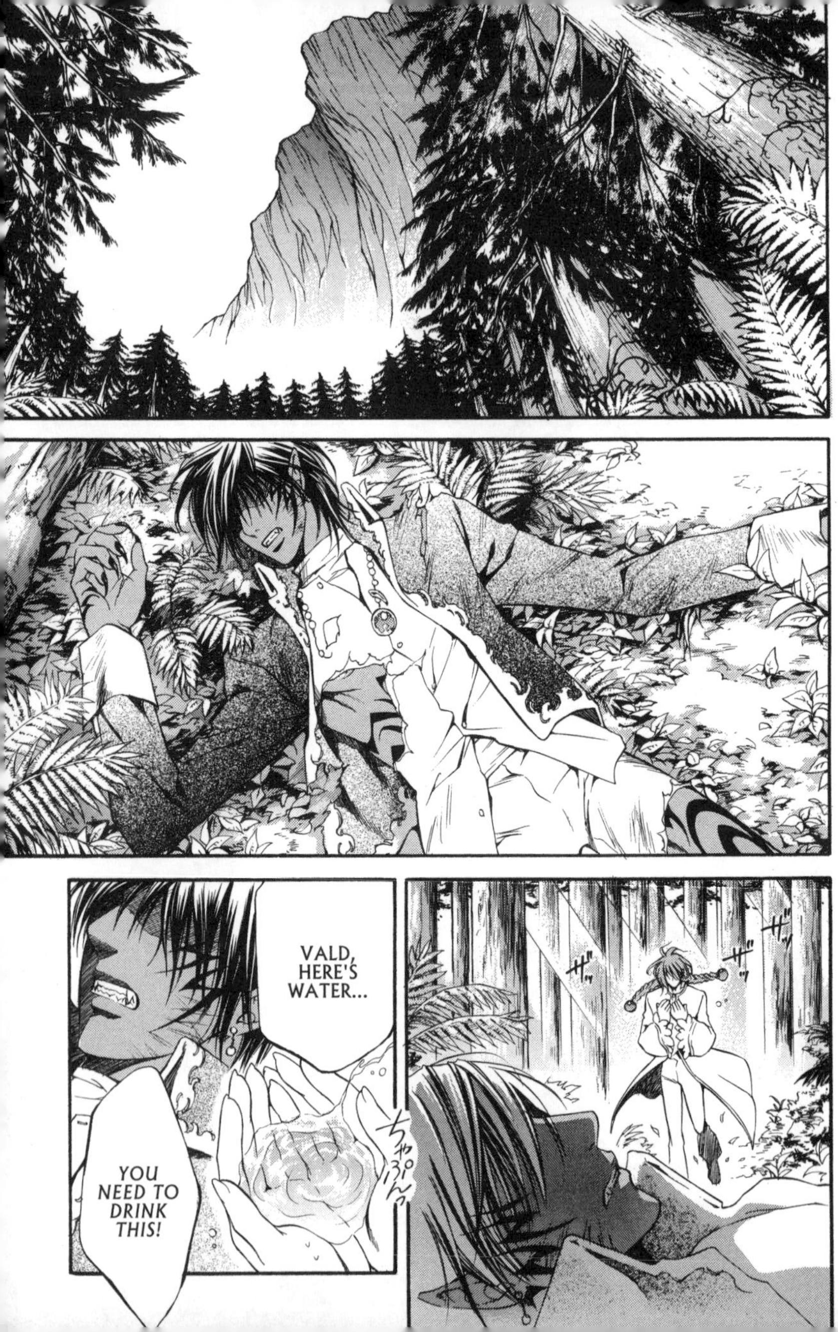
VALD, HERE'S WATER...
YOU NEED TO DRINK THIS!

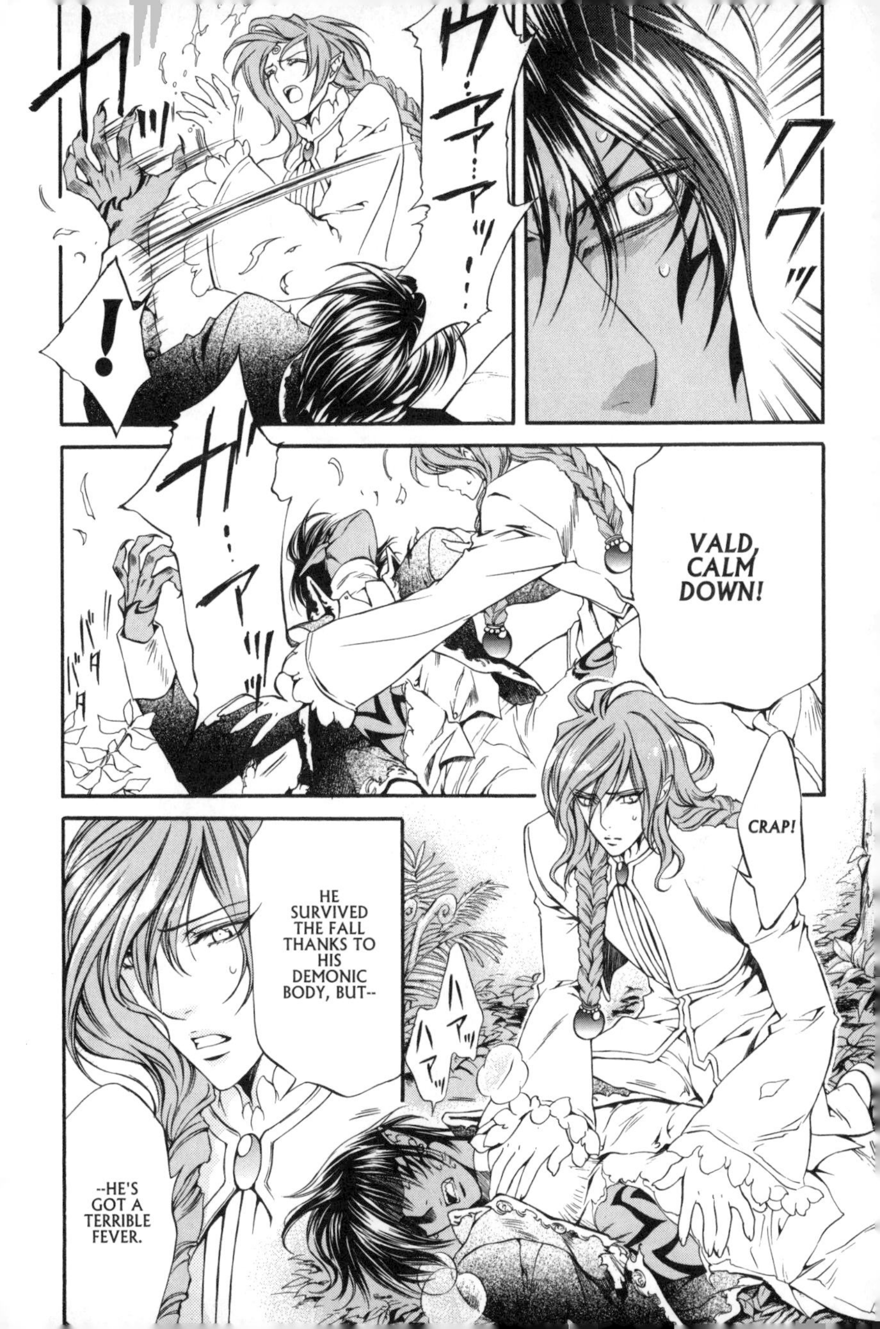
VALD, CALM DOWN!
CRAP!
HE SURVIVED THE FALL THANKS TO HIS DEMONIC BODY, BUT--
--HE'S GOT A TERRIBLE FEVER.

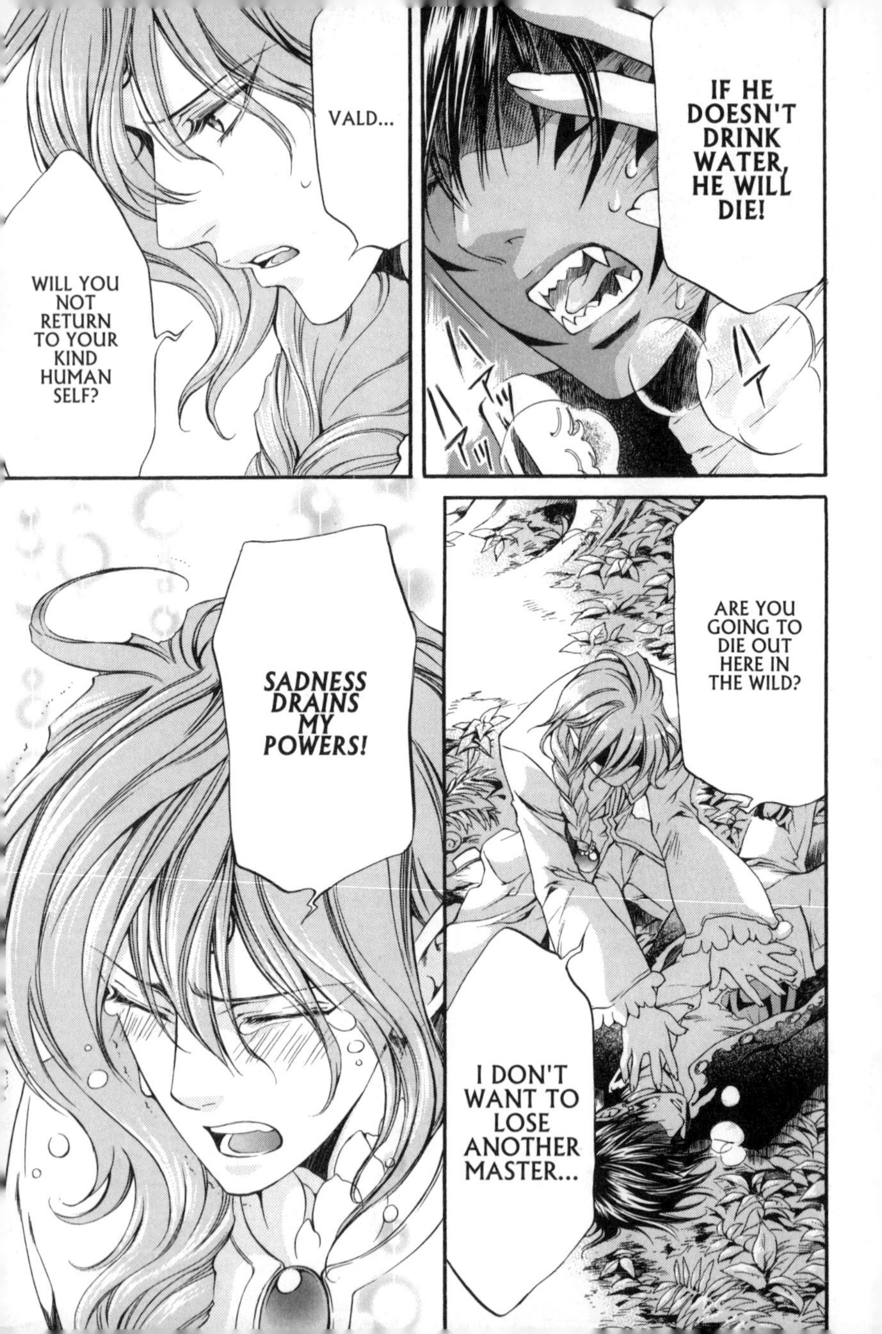
IF HE DOESN'T DRINK WATER, HE WILL DIE!
VALD...
WILL YOU NOT RETURN TO YOUR KIND HUMAN SELF?
ARE YOU GOING TO DIE OUT HERE IN THE WILD?
I DON'T WANT TO LOSE ANOTHER MASTER...
SADNESS DRAINS MY POWERS!

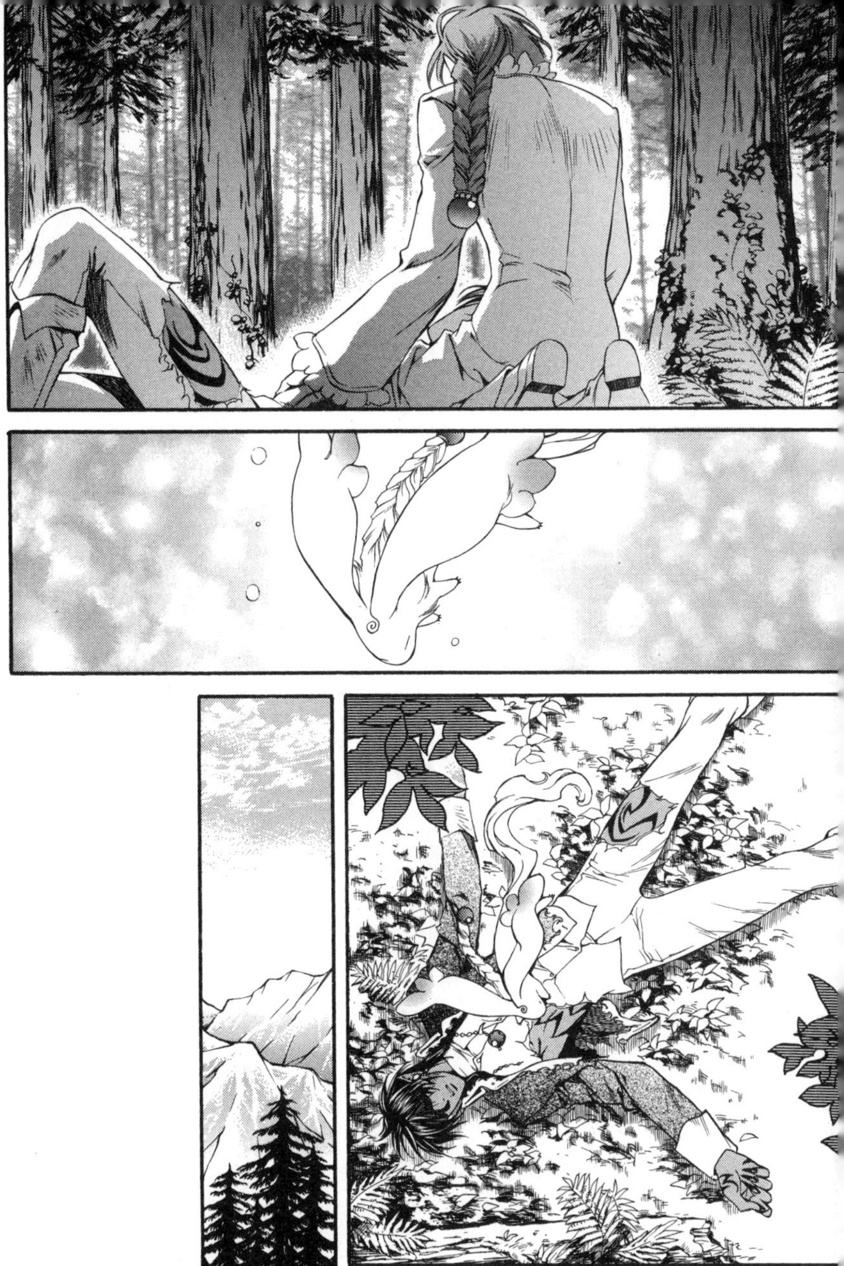

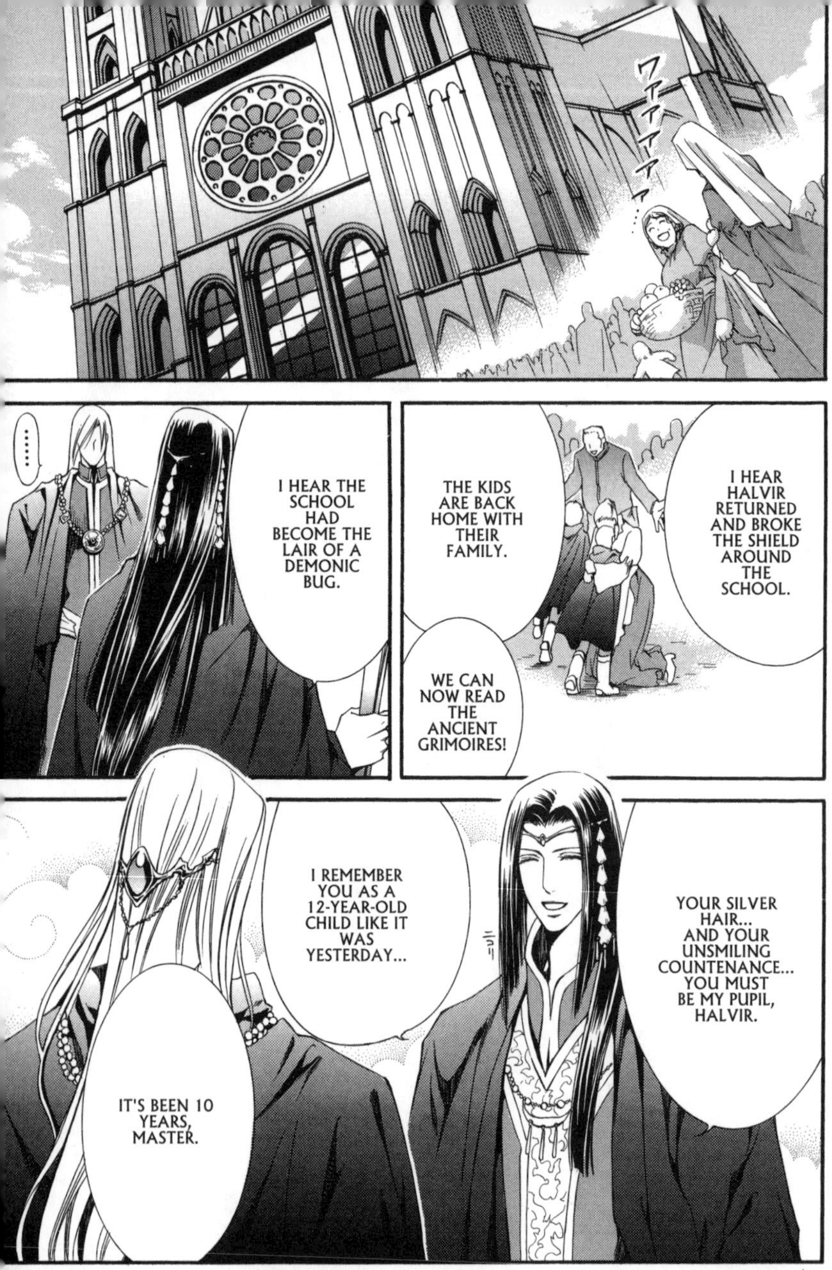
ワアアアアァ…
I HEAR HALVIR RETURNED AND BROKE THE SHIELD AROUND THE SCHOOL.
THE KIDS ARE BACK HOME WITH THEIR FAMILY.
WE CAN NOW READ THE ANCIENT GRIMOIRES!
I HEAR THE SCHOOL HAD BECOME THE LAIR OF A DEMONIC BUG.
……
YOUR SILVER HAIR... AND YOUR UNSMILING COUNTENANCE... YOU MUST BE MY PUPIL, HALVIR.
I REMEMBER YOU AS A 12-YEAR-OLD CHILD LIKE IT WAS YESTERDAY...
IT'S BEEN 10 YEARS, MASTER.

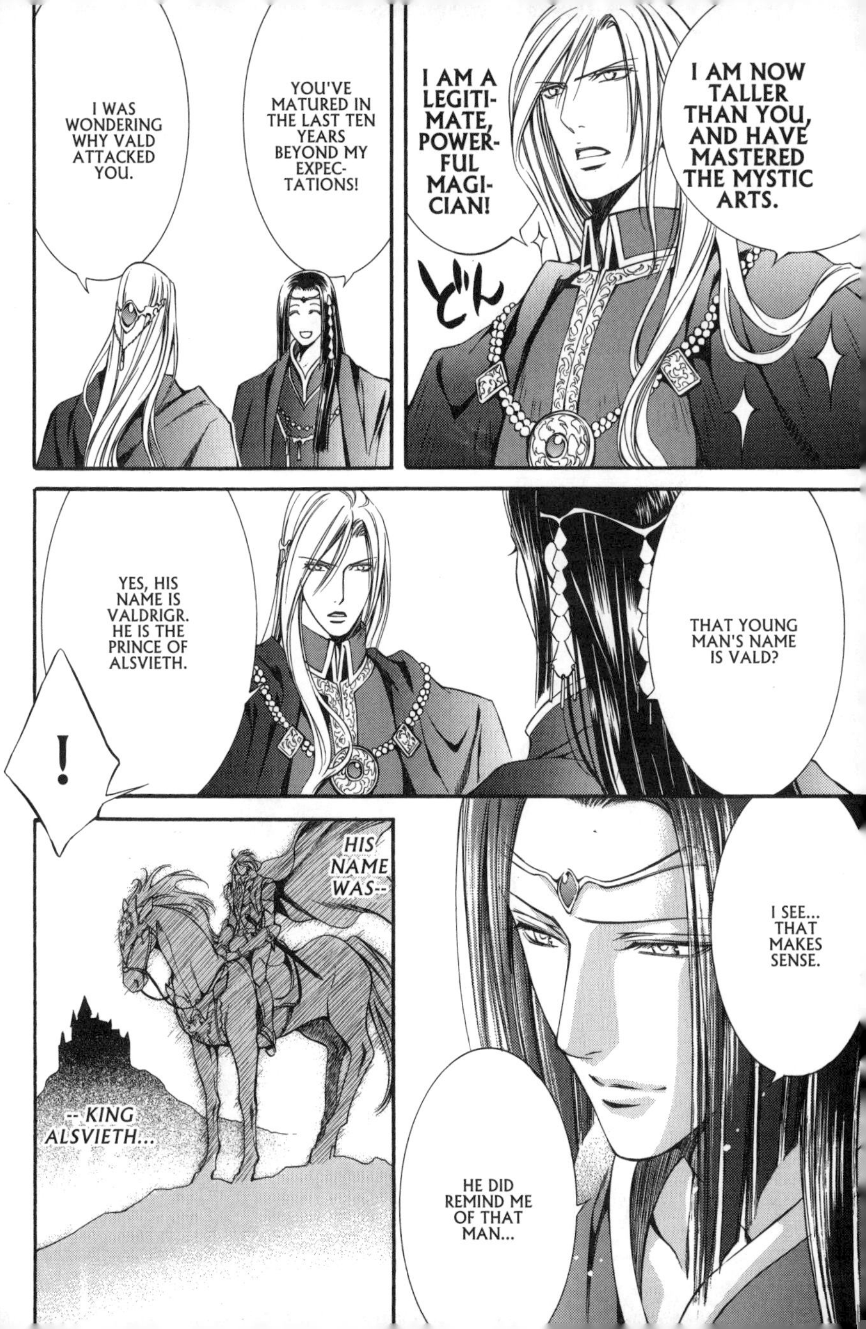
I AM NOW TALLER THAN YOU, AND HAVE MASTERED THE MYSTIC ARTS.
I AM A LEGITIMATE, POWERFUL MAGICIAN!
どん
YOU'VE MATURED IN THE LAST TEN YEARS BEYOND MY EXPECTATIONS!
I WAS WONDERING WHY VALD ATTACKED YOU.
THAT YOUNG MAN'S NAME IS VALD?
YES, HIS NAME IS VALDRIGR. HE IS THE PRINCE OF ALSVIETH.
!
I SEE... THAT MAKES SENSE.
HE DID REMIND ME OF THAT MAN...
HIS NAME WAS--
-- KING ALSVIETH...

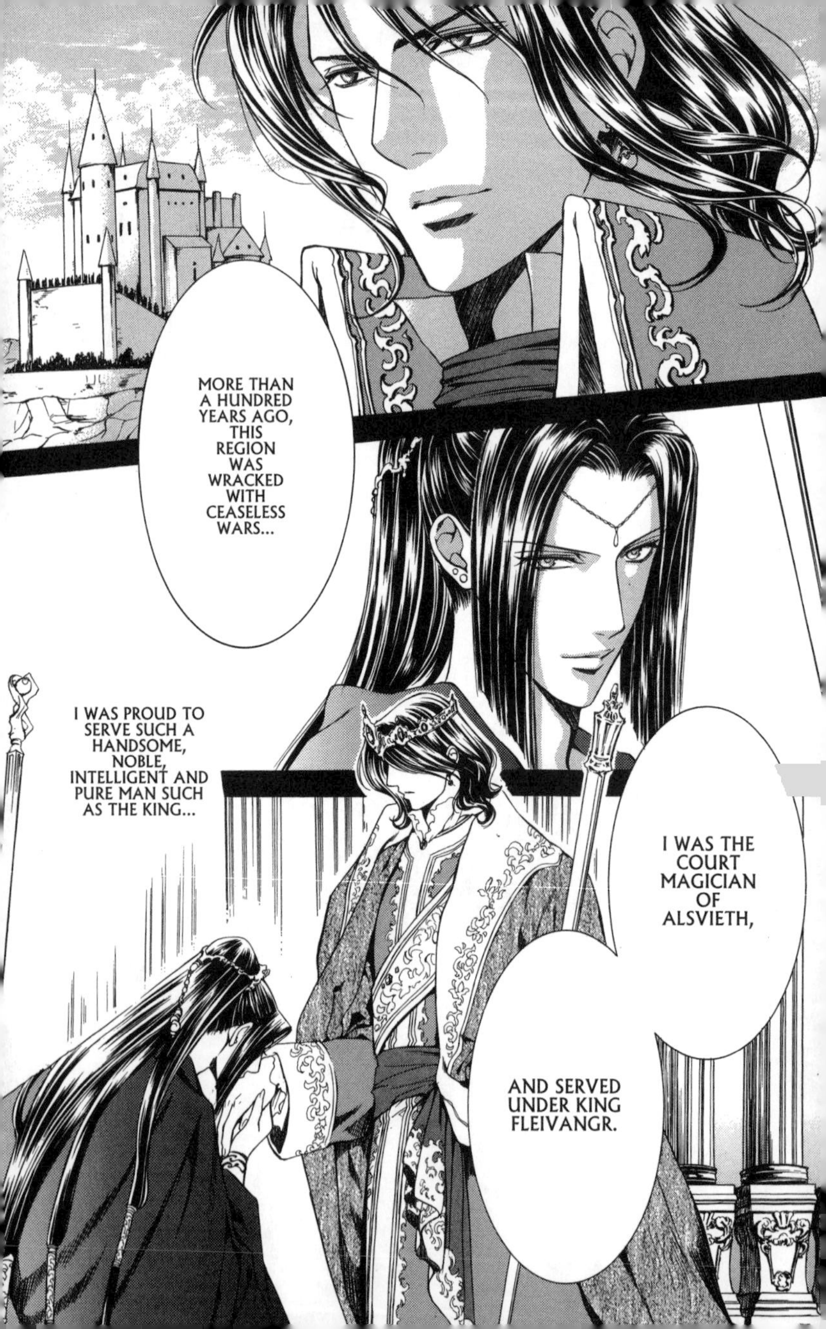
MORE THAN A HUNDRED YEARS AGO, THIS REGION WAS WRACKED WITH CEASELESS WARS...
I WAS THE COURT MAGICIAN OF ALSVIETH,
AND SERVED UNDER KING FLEIVANGR.
I WAS PROUD TO SERVE SUCH A HANDSOME, NOBLE, INTELLIGENT AND PURE MAN SUCH AS THE KING...

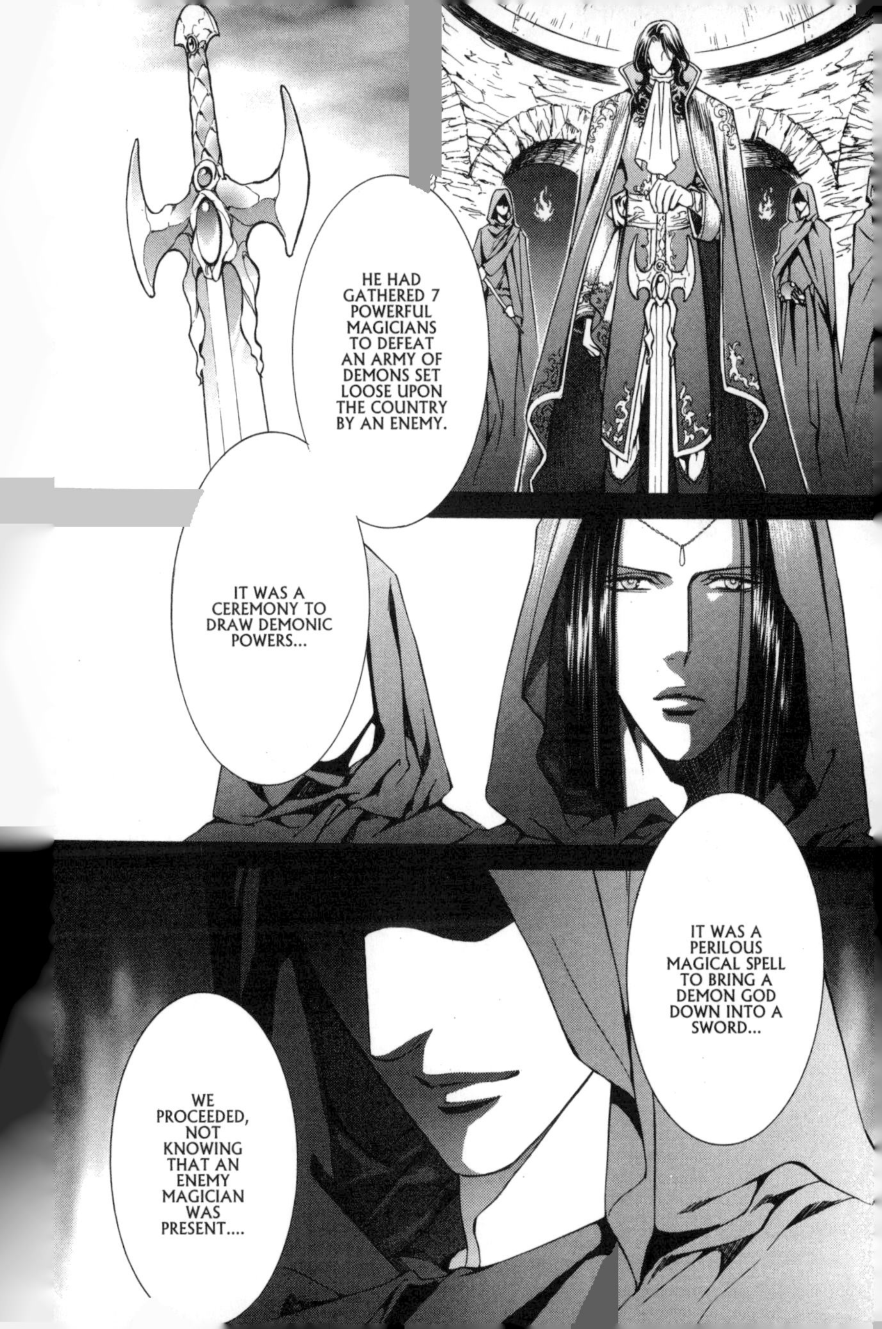
HE HAD GATHERED 7 POWERFUL MAGICIANS TO DEFEAT AN ARMY OF DEMONS SET LOOSE UPON THE COUNTRY BY AN ENEMY.
IT WAS A CEREMONY TO DRAW DEMONIC POWERS...
IT WAS A PERILOUS MAGICAL SPELL TO BRING A DEMON GOD DOWN INTO A SWORD...
WE PROCEEDED, NOT KNOWING THAT AN ENEMY MAGICIAN WAS PRESENT....

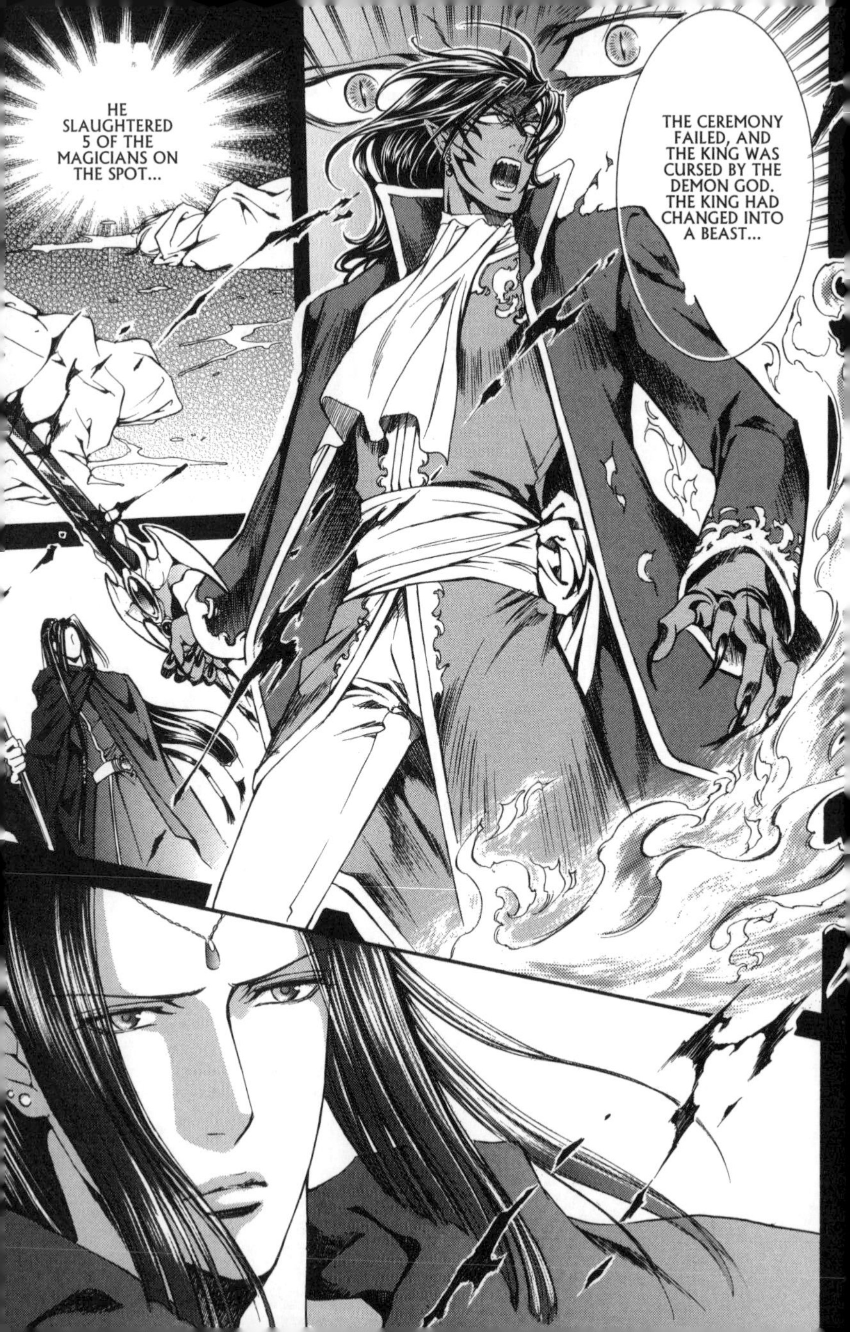
THE CEREMONY FAILED, AND THE KING WAS CURSED BY THE DEMON GOD. THE KING HAD CHANGED INTO A BEAST...
HE SLAUGHTERED 5 OF THE MAGICIANS ON THE SPOT...

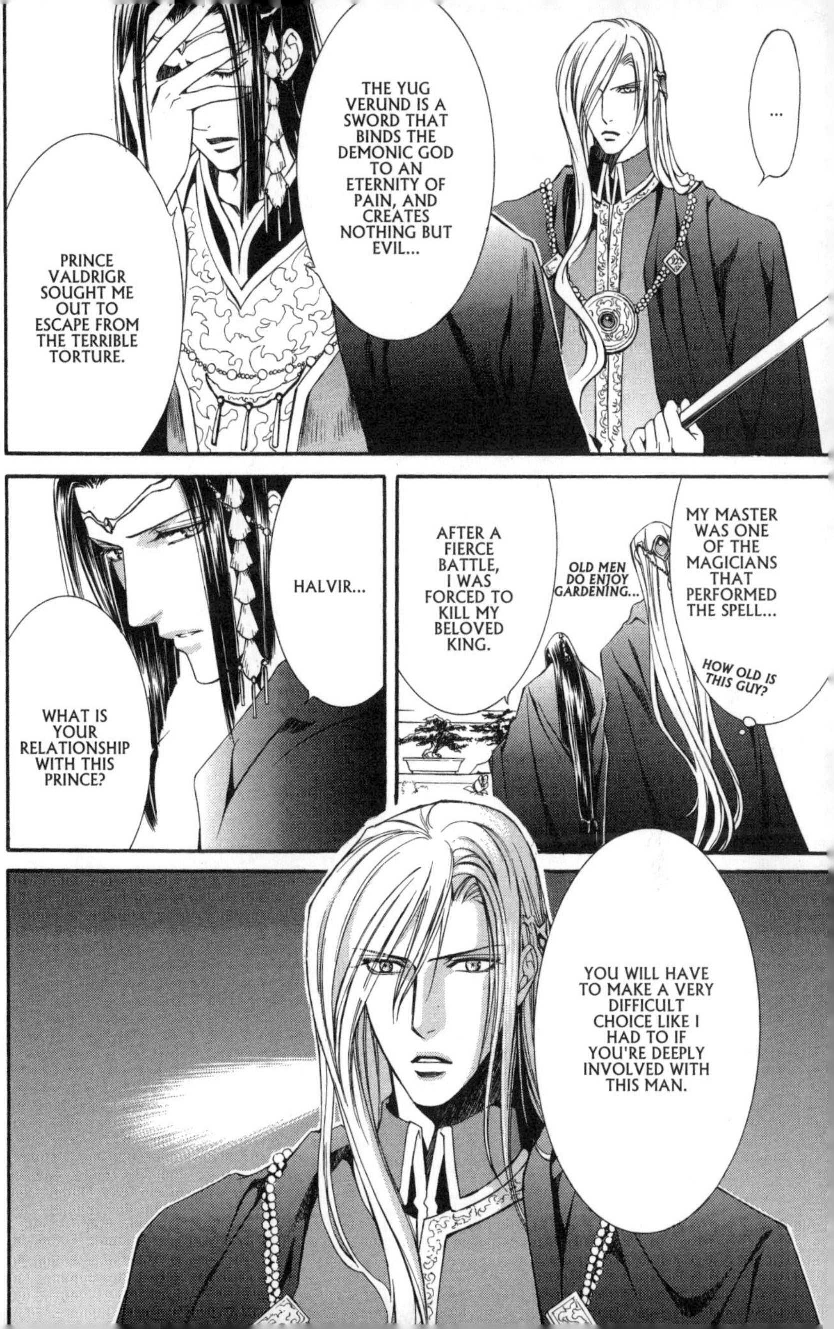
...
THE YUG VERUND IS A SWORD THAT BINDS THE DEMONIC GOD TO AN ETERNITY OF PAIN, AND CREATES NOTHING BUT EVIL...
PRINCE VALDRIGR SOUGHT ME OUT TO ESCAPE FROM THE TERRIBLE TORTURE.
MY MASTER WAS ONE OF THE MAGICIANS THAT PERFORMED THE SPELL...
HOW OLD IS THIS GUY?
OLD MEN DO ENJOY GARDENING...
AFTER A FIERCE BATTLE, I WAS FORCED TO KILL MY BELOVED KING.
HALVIR...
WHAT IS YOUR RELATIONSHIP WITH THIS PRINCE?
YOU WILL HAVE TO MAKE A VERY DIFFICULT CHOICE LIKE I HAD TO IF YOU'RE DEEPLY INVOLVED WITH THIS MAN.

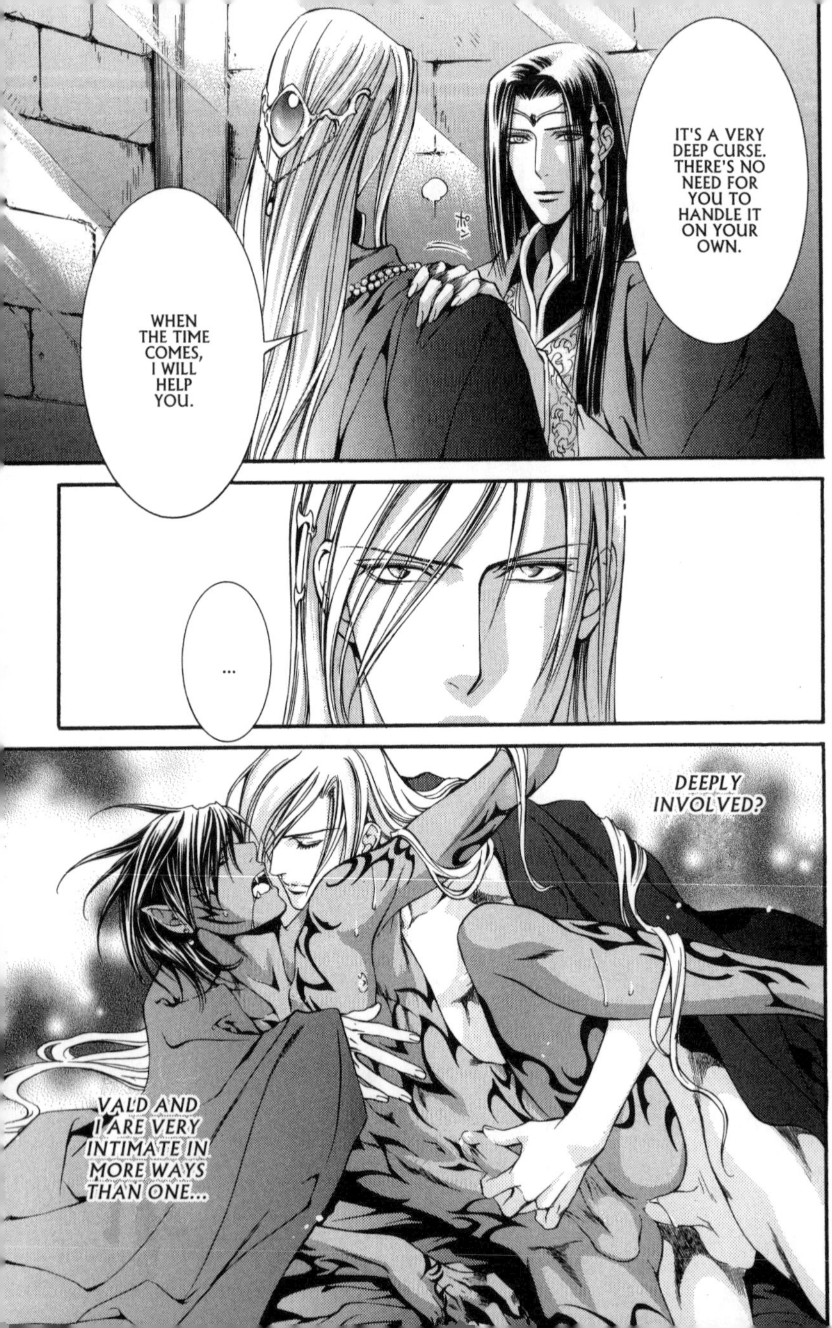
IT'S A VERY DEEP CURSE. THERE'S NO NEED FOR YOU TO HANDLE IT ON YOUR OWN.
WHEN THE TIME COMES, I WILL HELP YOU.
...
DEEPLY INVOLVED?
VALD AND I ARE VERY INTIMATE IN MORE WAYS THAN ONE...

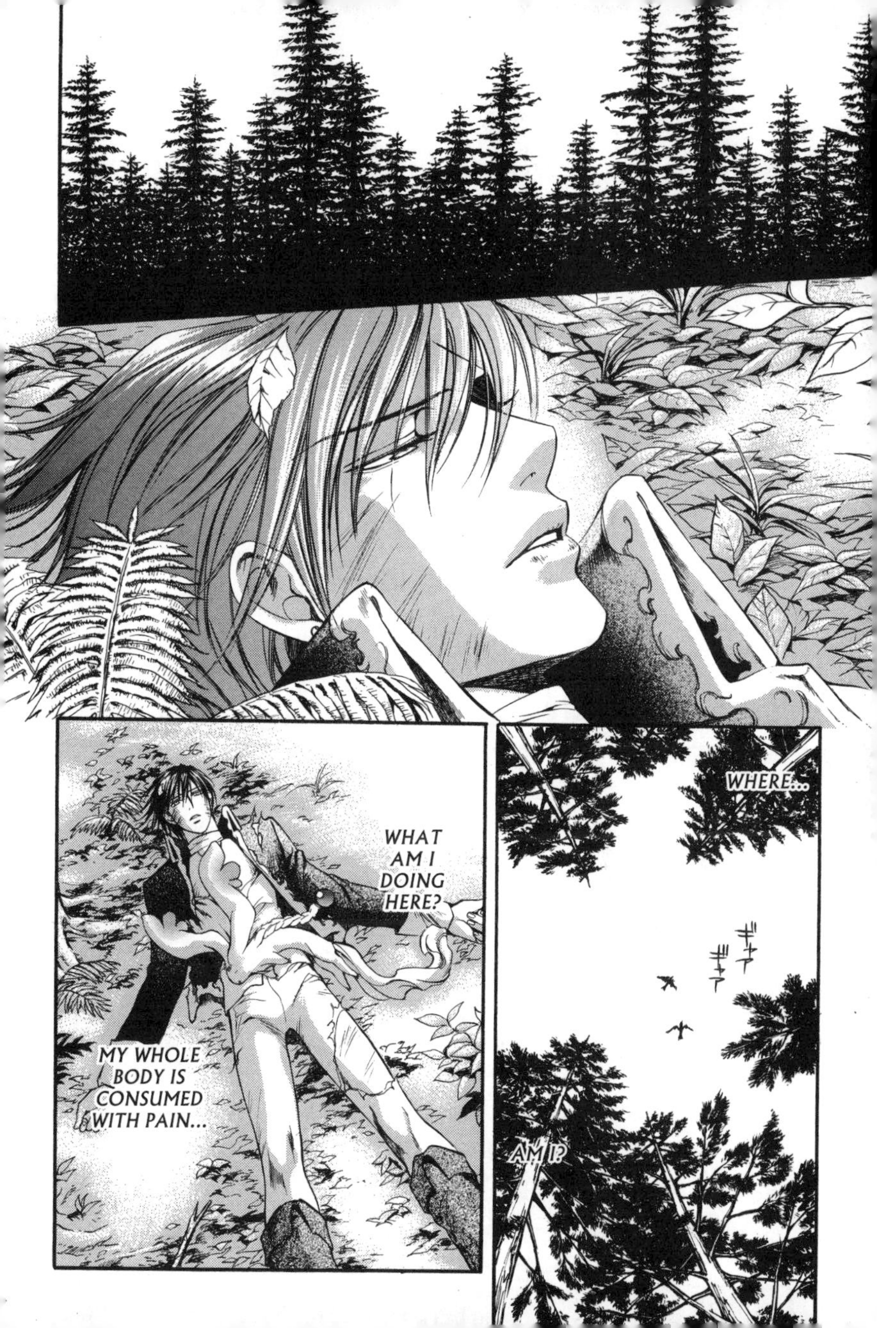
WHERE...
ギャア
ギャア
AM I?
WHAT AM I DOING HERE?
MY WHOLE BODY IS CONSUMED WITH PAIN...

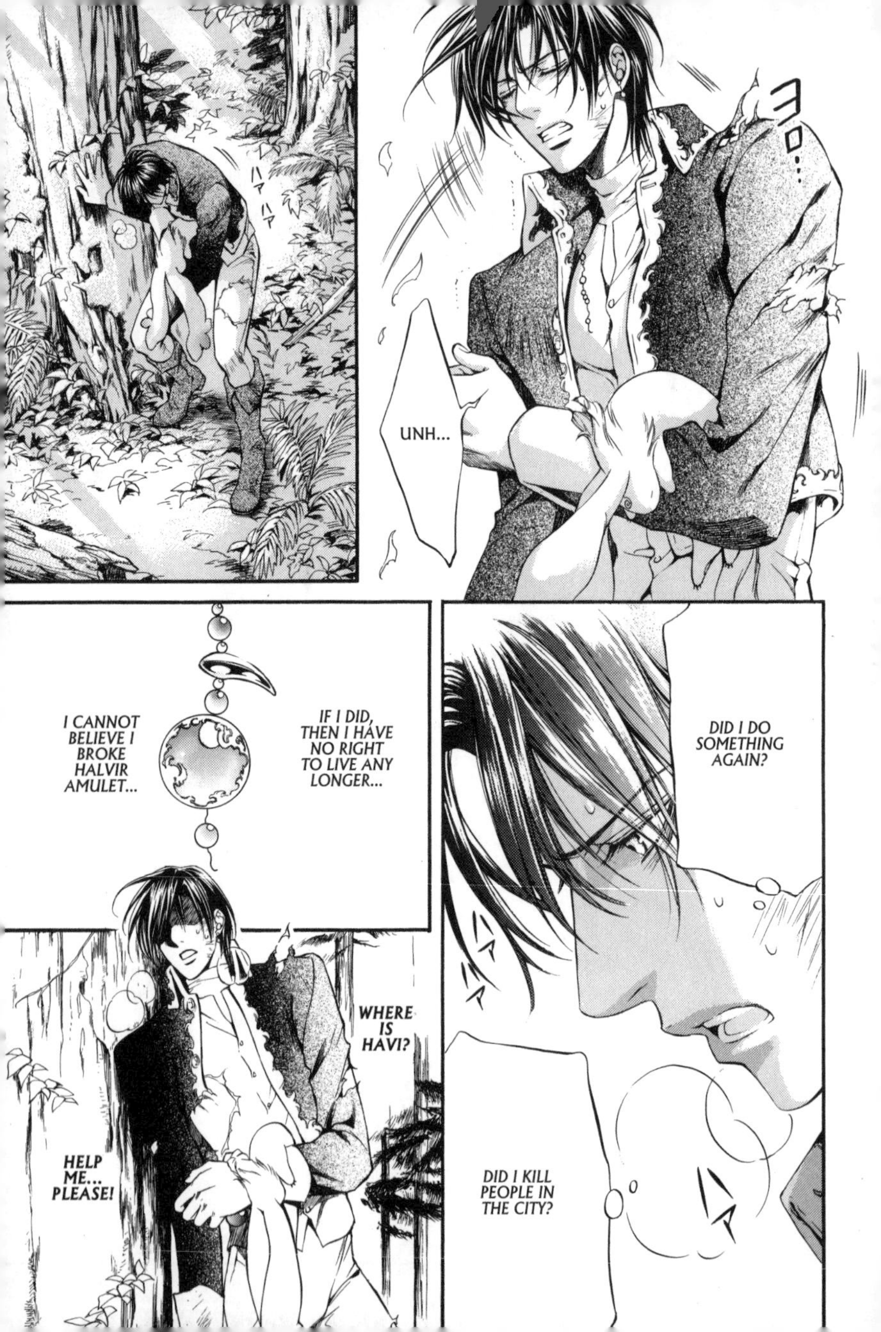

ヨロ…
UNH...
ハァ ハァ
DID I DO SOMETHING AGAIN?
ハァ ハァ
DID I KILL PEOPLE IN THE CITY?
ハァ
IF I DID, THEN I HAVE NO RIGHT TO LIVE ANY LONGER...
I CANNOT BELIEVE I BROKE HALVIR AMULET...
WHERE IS HAVI?
HELP ME... PLEASE!

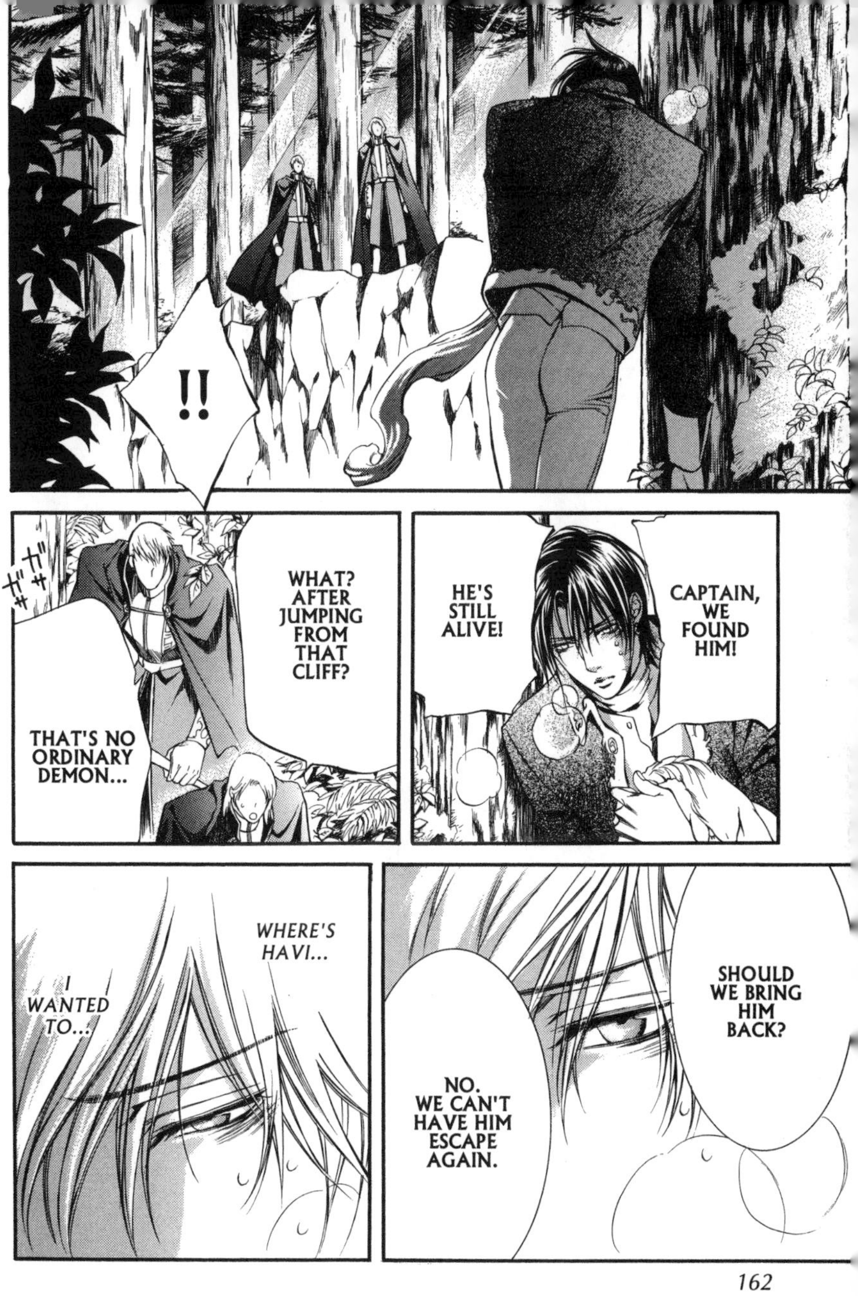
!!
CAPTAIN, WE FOUND HIM!
HE'S STILL ALIVE!
WHAT? AFTER JUMPING FROM THAT CLIFF?
ガヤガヤ
THAT'S NO ORDINARY DEMON...
SHOULD WE BRING HIM BACK?
NO. WE CAN'T HAVE HIM ESCAPE AGAIN.
WHERE'S HAVI...
I WANTED TO...

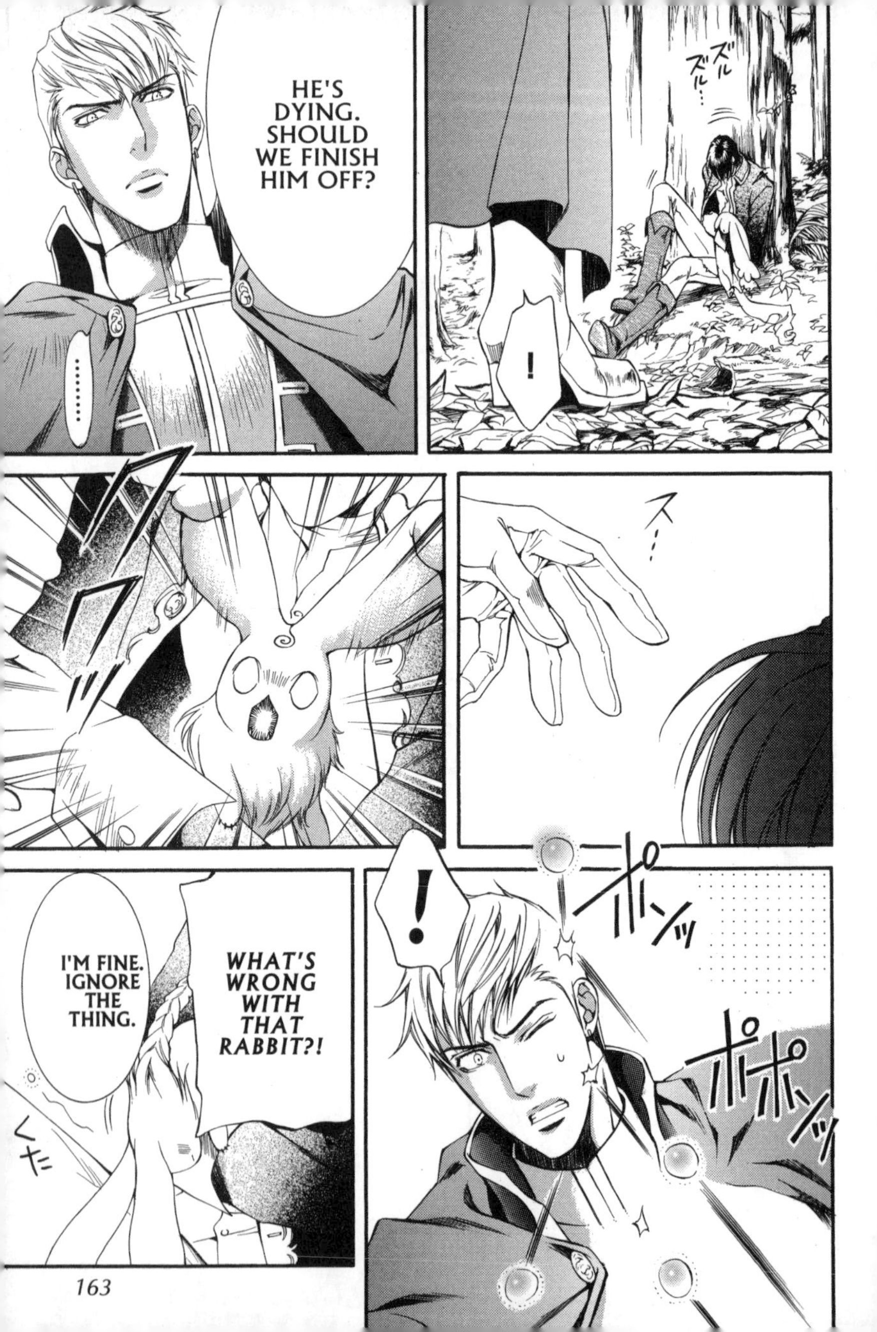
ズルズル…
!
HE'S DYING. SHOULD WE FINISH HIM OFF?
……
ス…
!
ポンッ
ポポンッ
WHAT'S WRONG WITH THAT RABBIT?!
I'M FINE. IGNORE THE THING.
くた

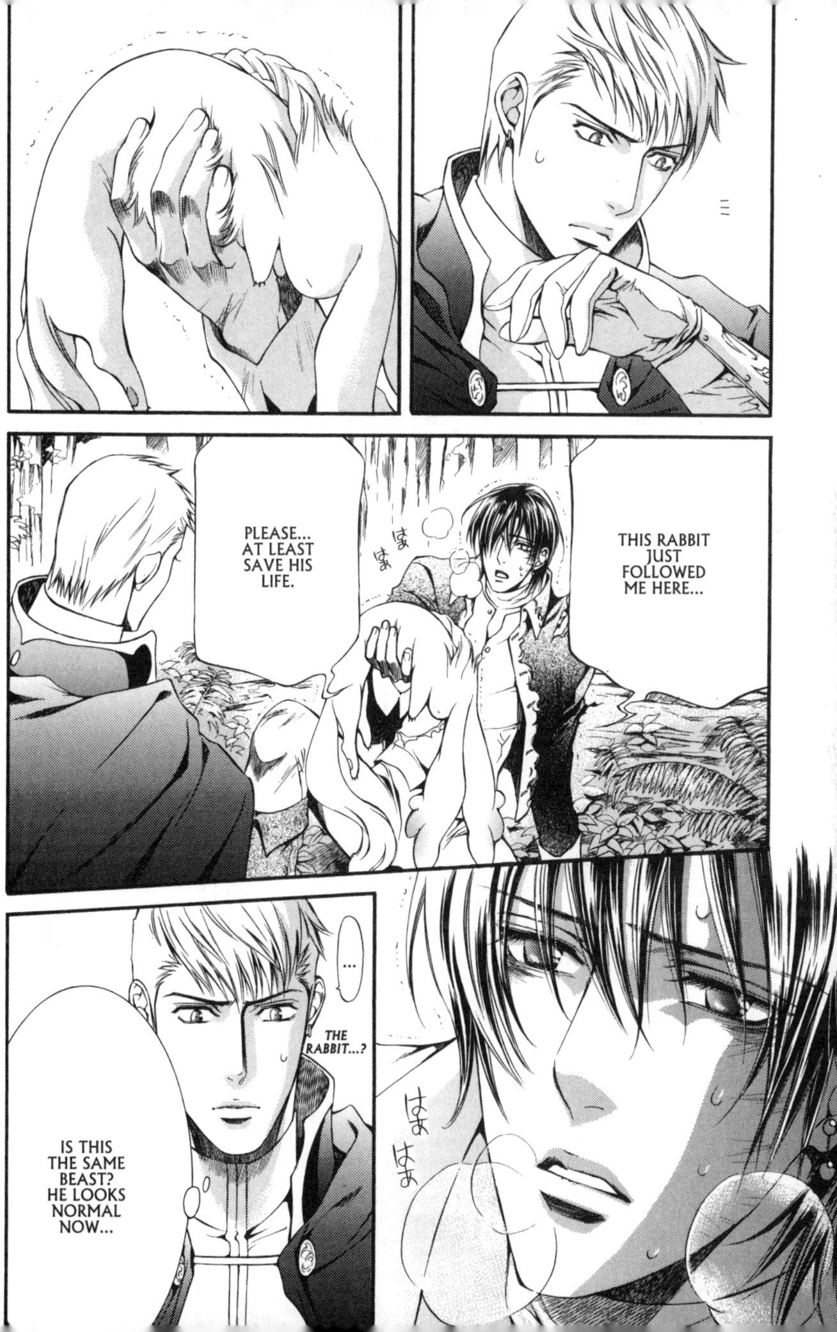
THIS RABBIT JUST FOLLOWED ME HERE...
はぁ はぁ
PLEASE... AT LEAST SAVE HIS LIFE.
はぁ はぁ
...
THE RABBIT...?
IS THIS THE SAME BEAST? HE LOOKS NORMAL NOW...

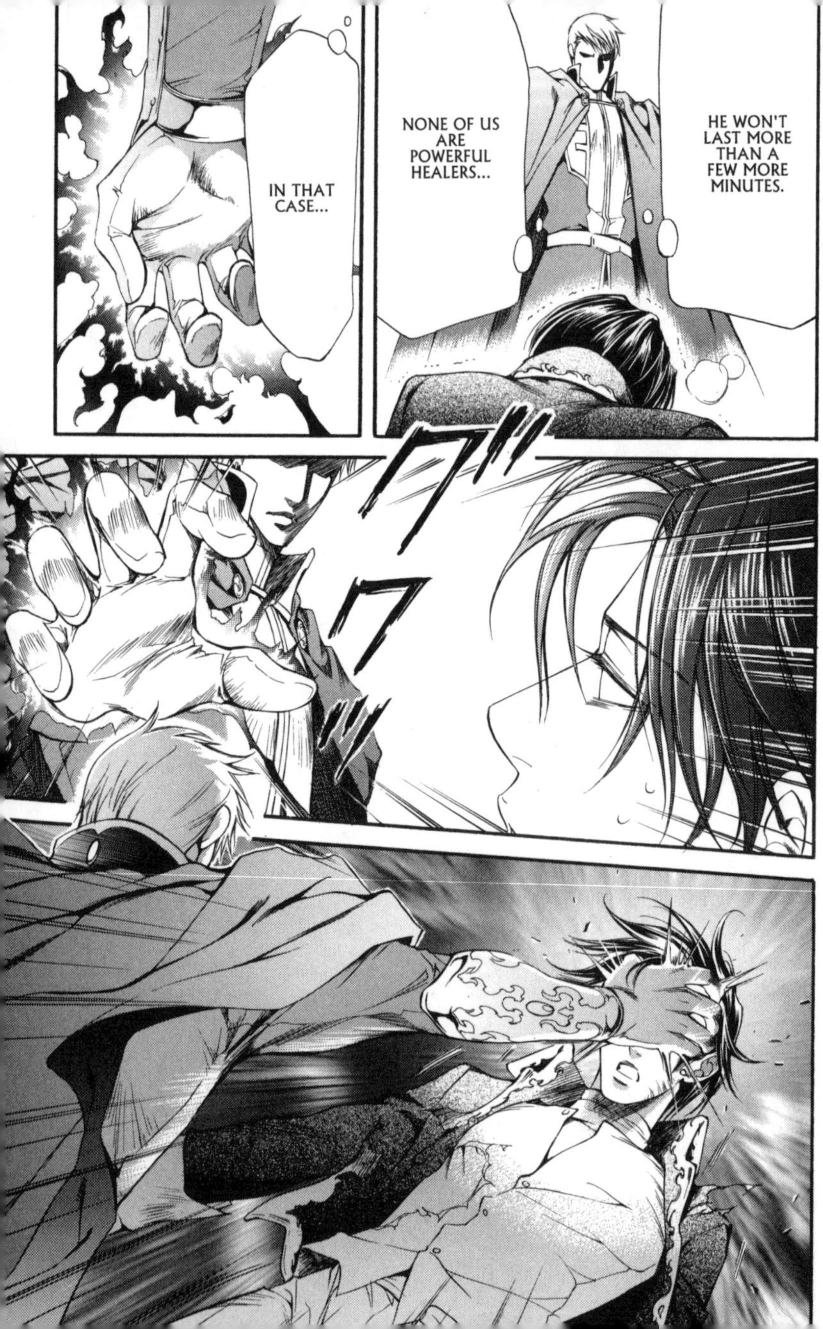
HE WON'T LAST MORE THAN A FEW MORE MINUTES.
NONE OF US ARE POWERFUL HEALERS...
IN THAT CASE...

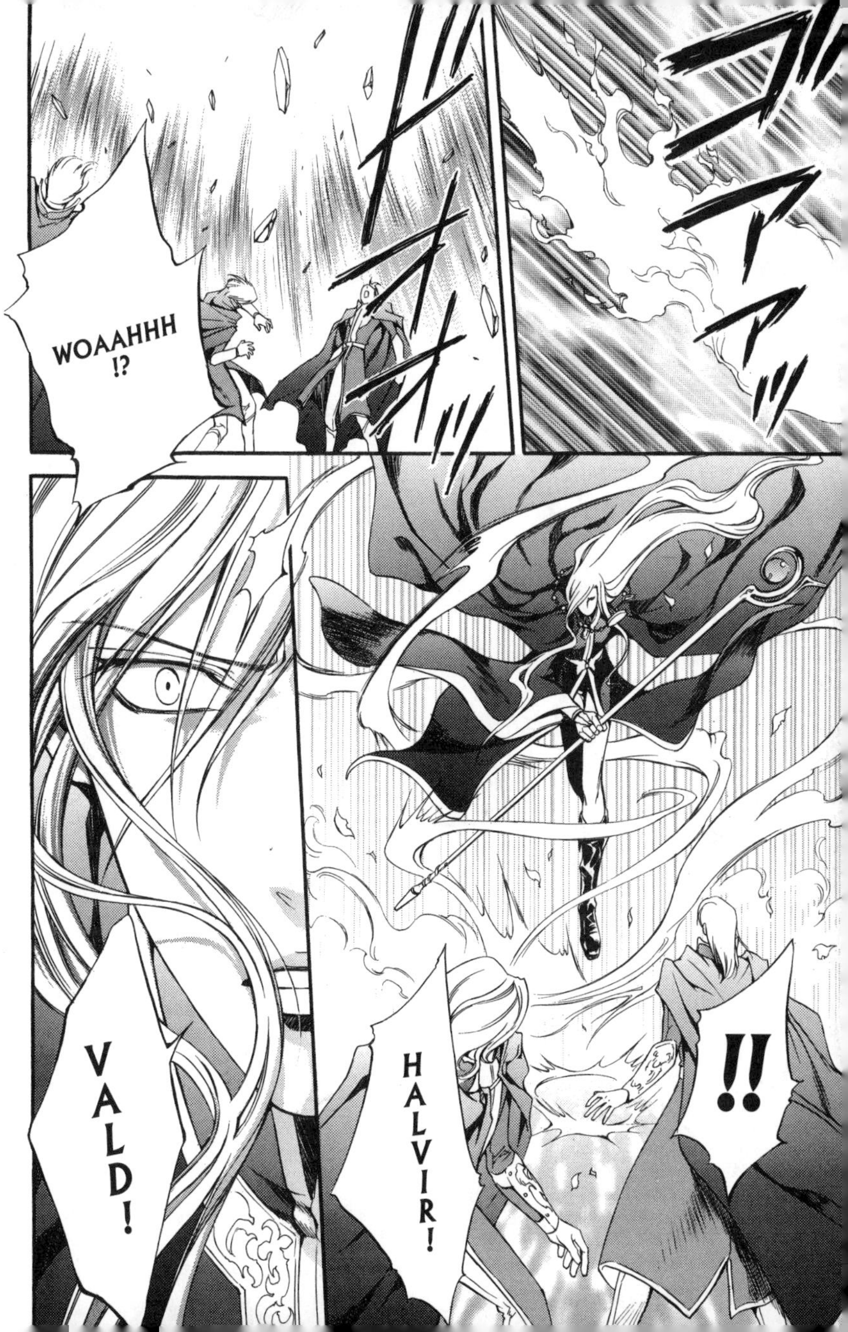
WOAAHHH !?
!!
HALVIR!
VALD!

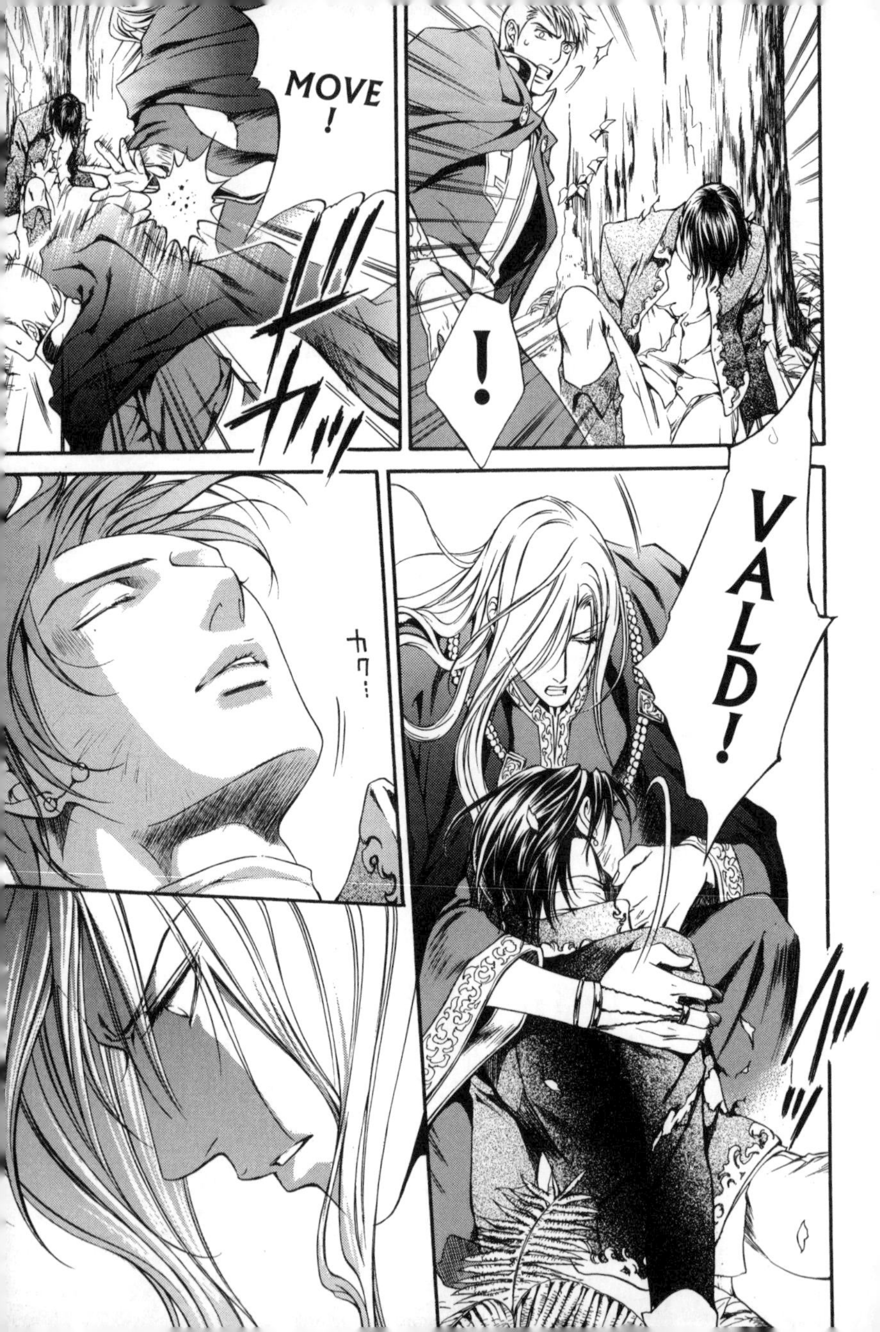
!
MOVE!
VALDI!

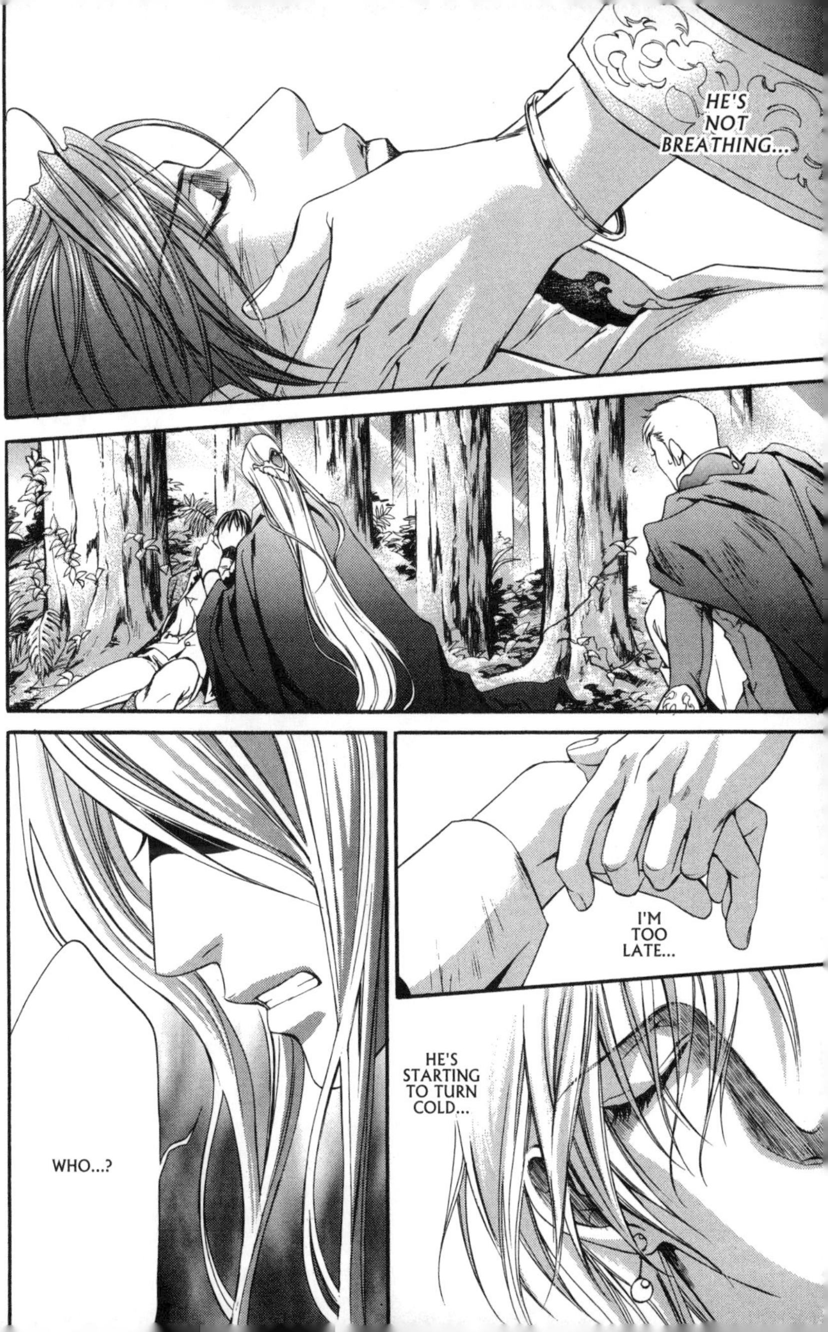
HE'S NOT BREATHING...
I'M TOO LATE...
HE'S STARTING TO TURN COLD...
WHO...?

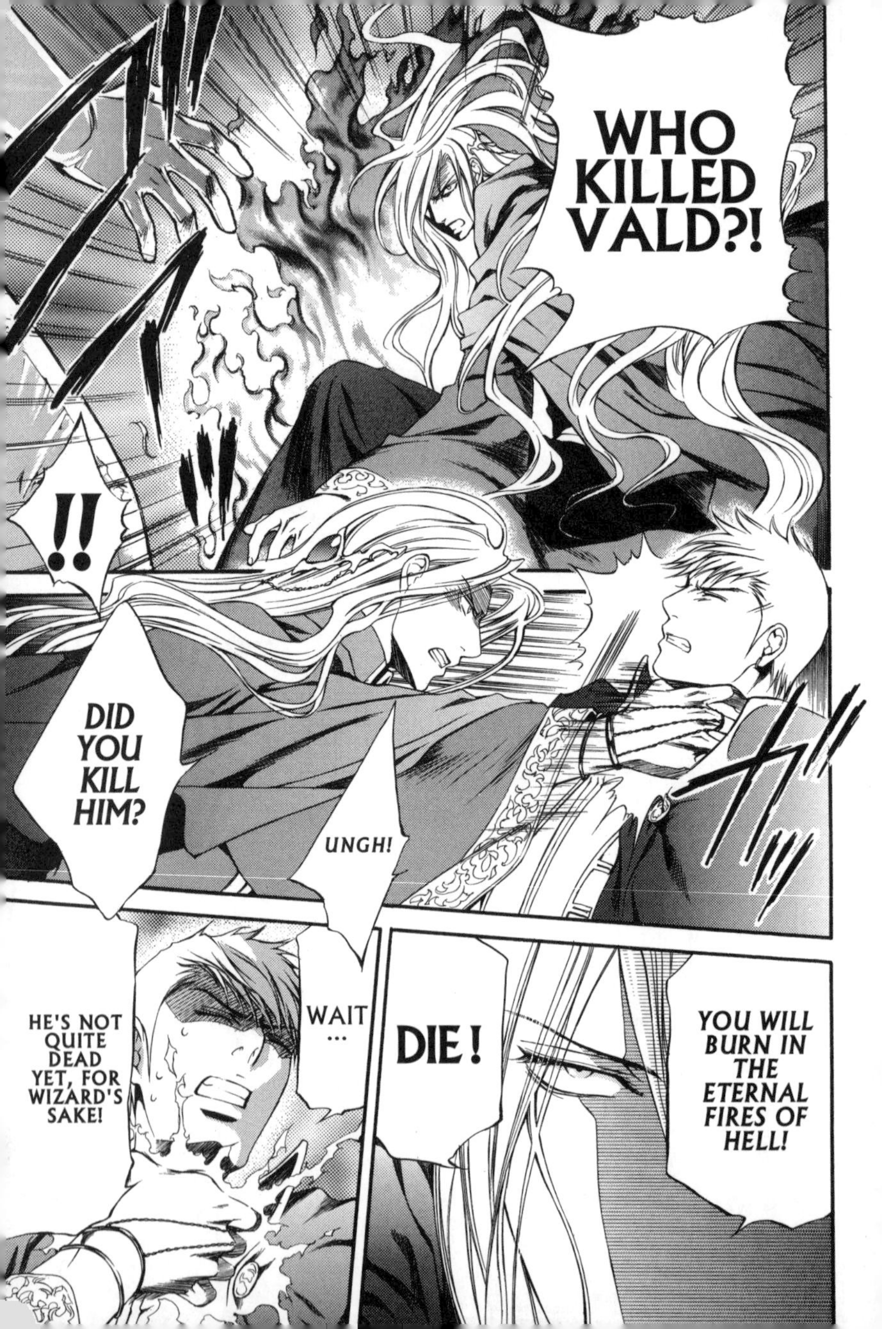
WHO KILLED VALD?!
!!
DID YOU KILL HIM?
UNGH!
YOU WILL BURN IN THE ETERNAL FIRES OF HELL!
DIE!
WAIT ...
HE'S NOT QUITE DEAD YET, FOR WIZARD'S SAKE!

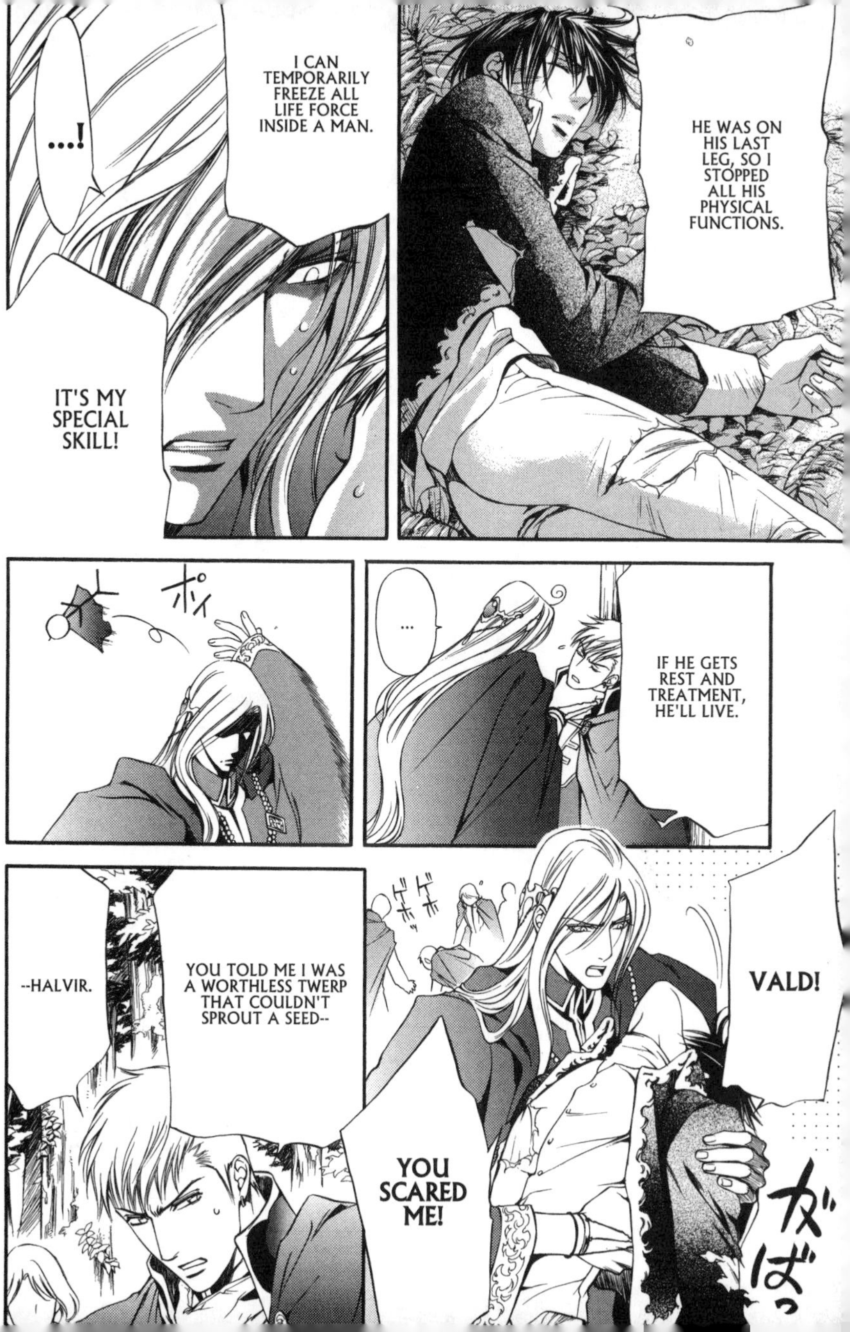
HE WAS ON HIS LAST LEG, SO I STOPPED ALL HIS PHYSICAL FUNCTIONS.
I CAN TEMPORARILY FREEZE ALL LIFE FORCE INSIDE A MAN.
...!
IT'S MY SPECIAL SKILL!
IF HE GETS REST AND TREATMENT, HE'LL LIVE.
...
ポイ
VALD!
ゲホゲホッ
YOU SCARED ME!
がばっ
YOU TOLD ME I WAS A WORTHLESS TWERP THAT COULDN'T SPROUT A SEED--
--HALVIR.

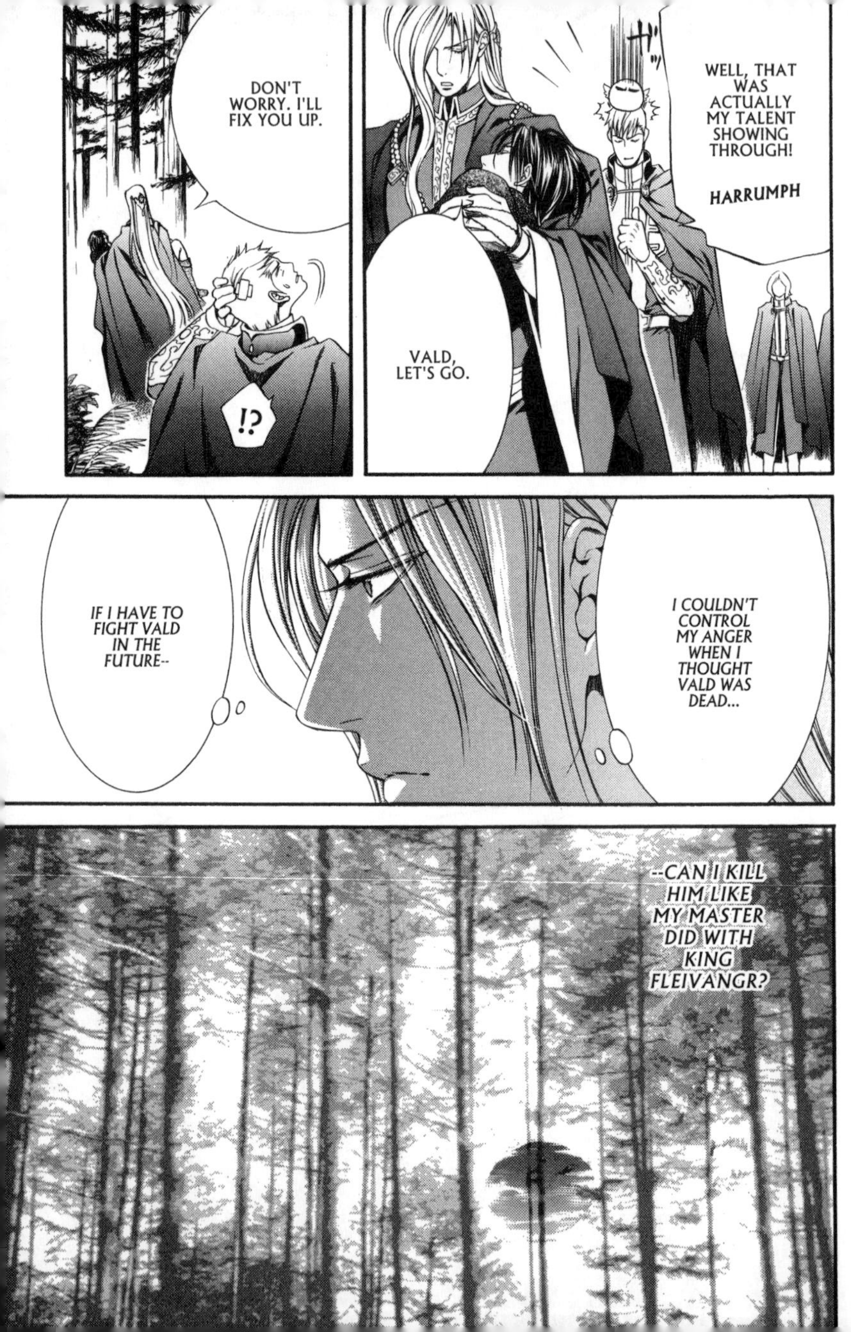
WELL, THAT WAS ACTUALLY MY TALENT SHOWING THROUGH!
HARRUMPH
VALD, LET'S GO.
DON'T WORRY. I'LL FIX YOU UP.
!?
I COULDN'T CONTROL MY ANGER WHEN I THOUGHT VALD WAS DEAD...
IF I HAVE TO FIGHT VALD IN THE FUTURE--
--CAN I KILL HIM LIKE MY MASTER DID WITH KING FLEIVANGR?

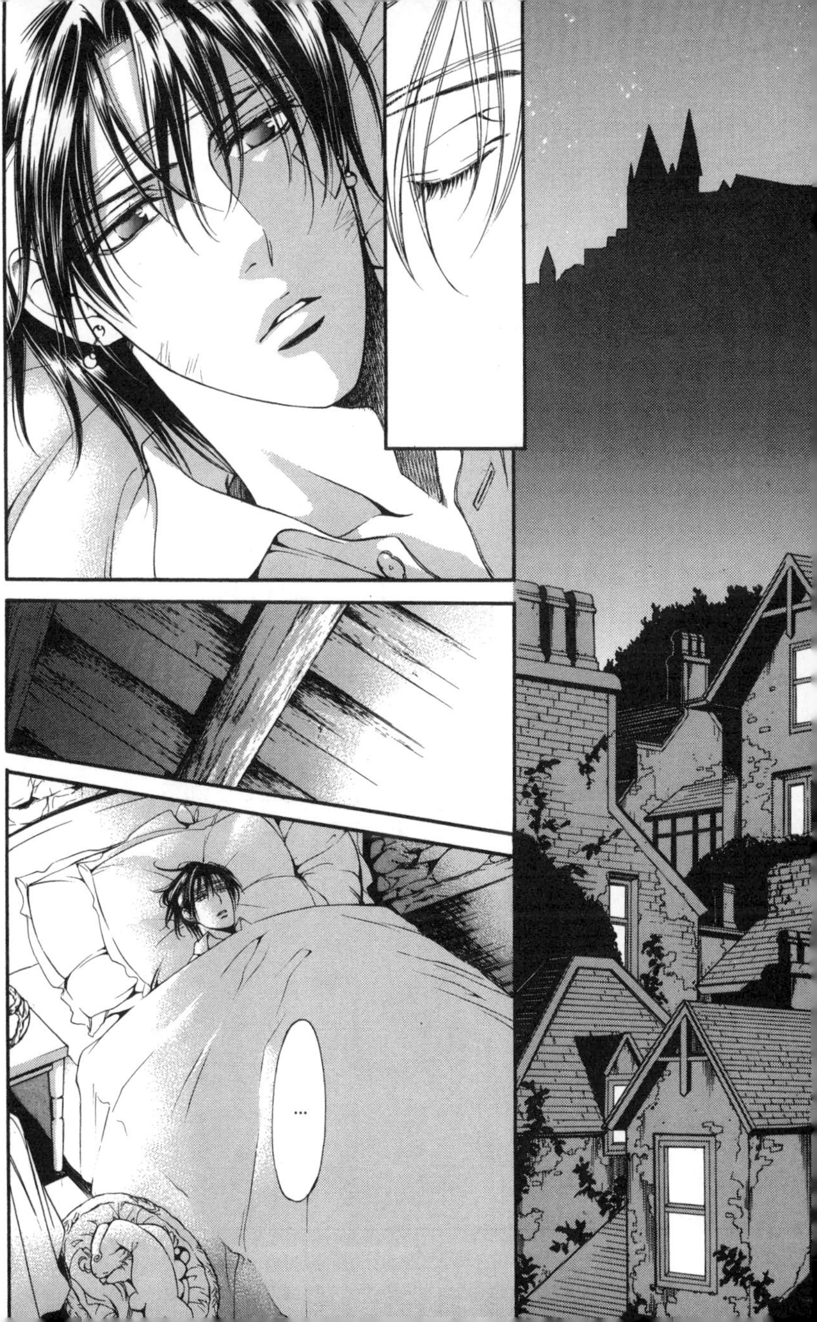
...

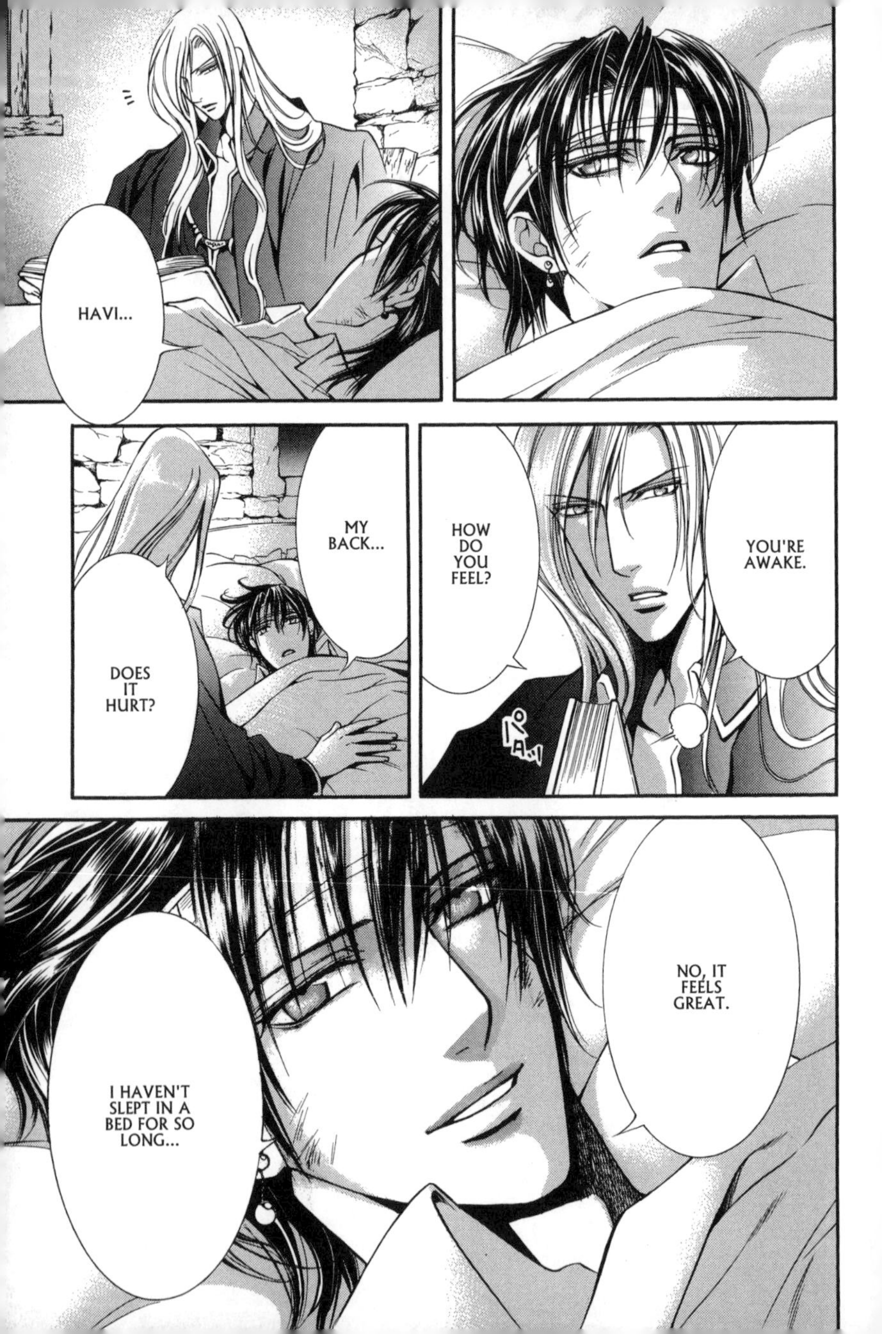
HAVI...
YOU'RE AWAKE.
HOW DO YOU FEEL?
MY BACK...
DOES IT HURT?
NO, IT FEELS GREAT.
I HAVEN'T SLEPT IN A BED FOR SO LONG...

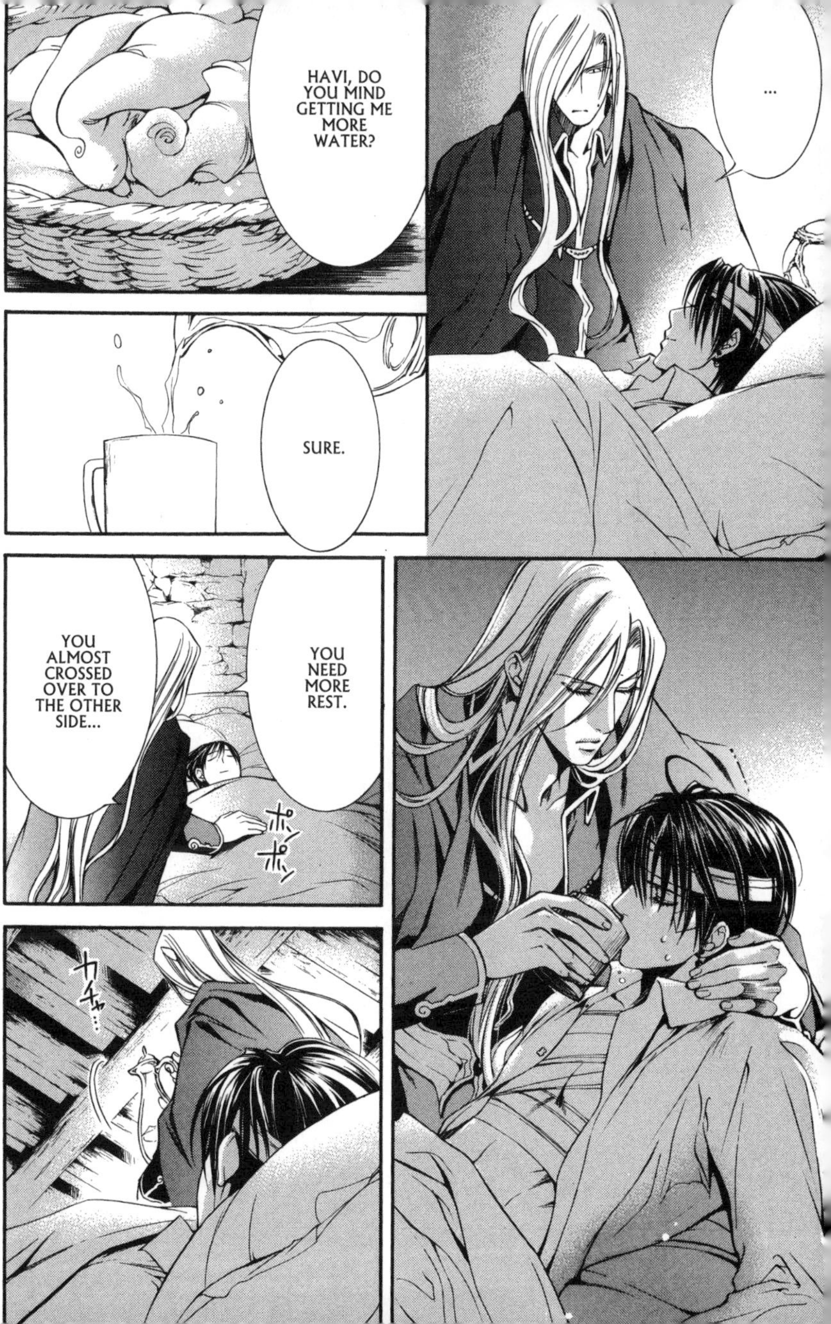
...
HAVI, DO YOU MIND GETTING ME MORE WATER?
SURE.
YOU NEED MORE REST.
YOU ALMOST CROSSED OVER TO THE OTHER SIDE...
ポンポン
カチャ…

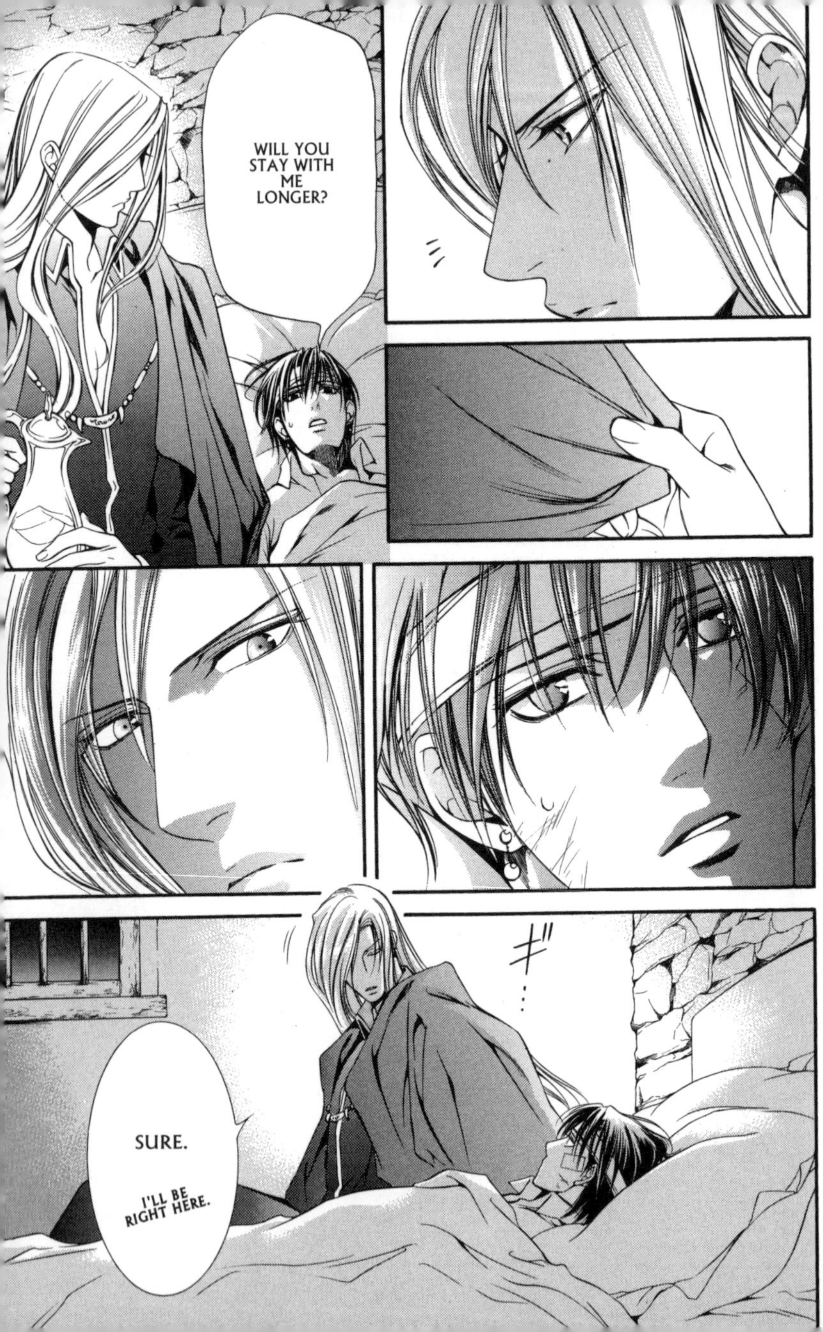
WILL YOU STAY WITH ME LONGER?
ギ
SURE.
I'LL BE RIGHT HERE.

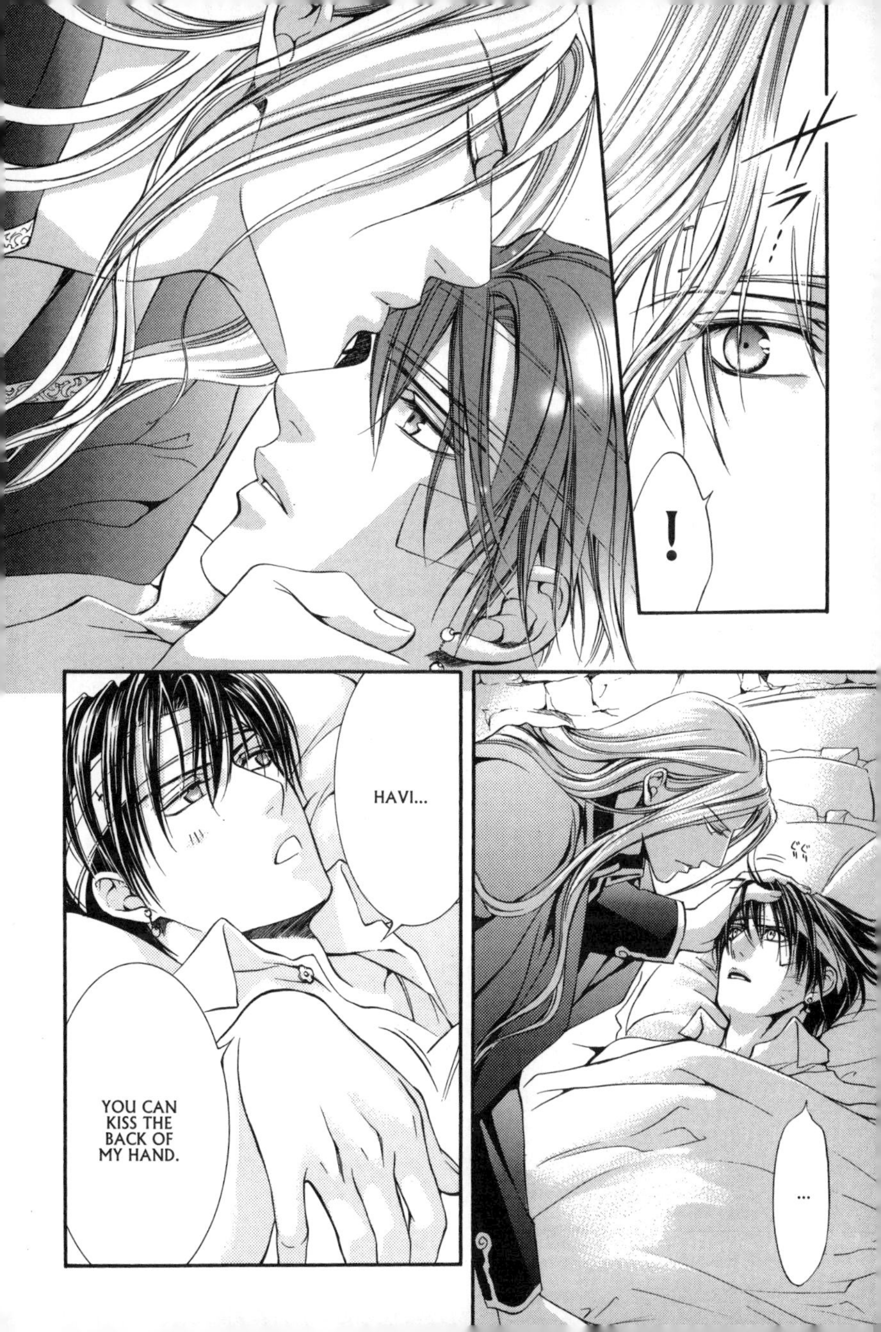
!
...
HAVI...
YOU CAN KISS THE BACK OF MY HAND.

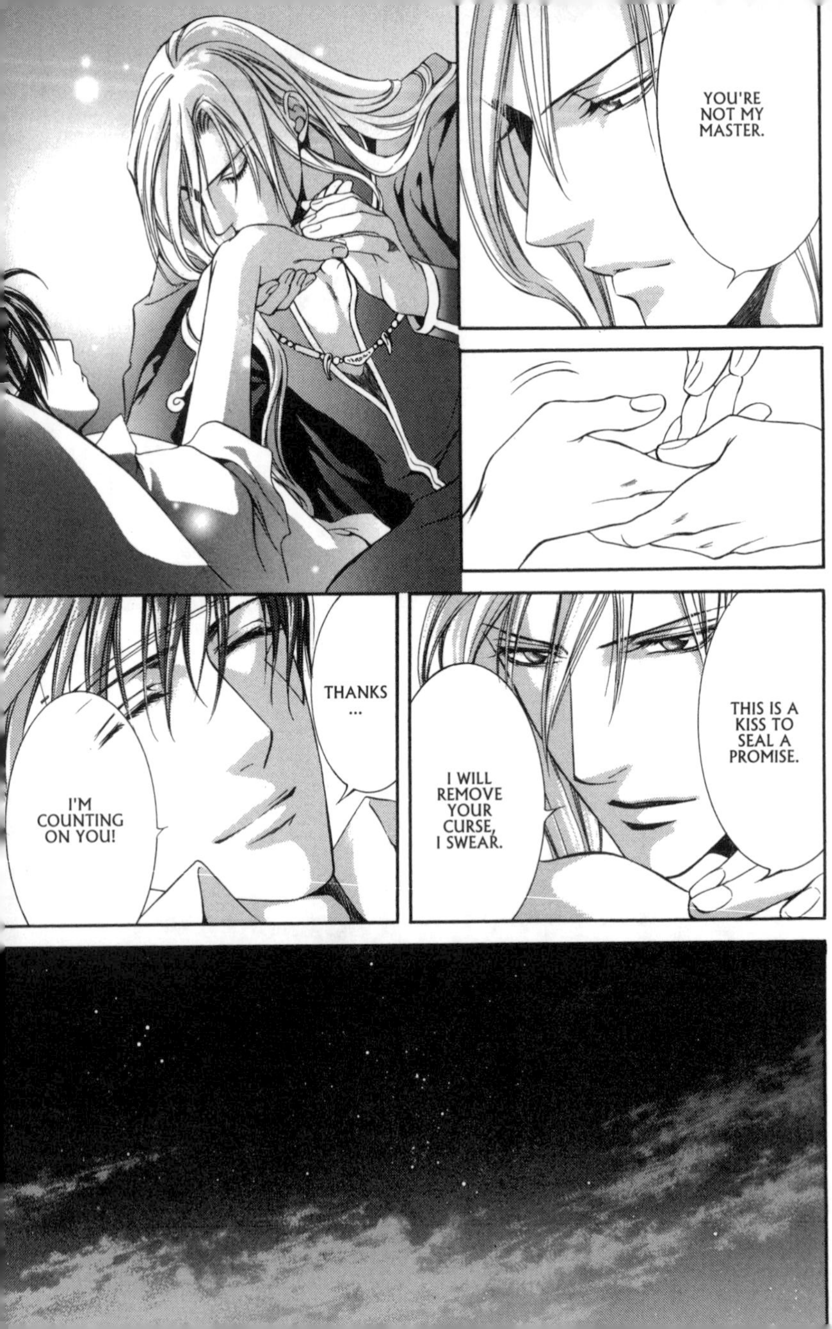
YOU'RE NOT MY MASTER.
THIS IS A KISS TO SEAL A PROMISE.
I WILL REMOVE YOUR CURSE, I SWEAR.
THANKS ...
I'M COUNTING ON YOU!

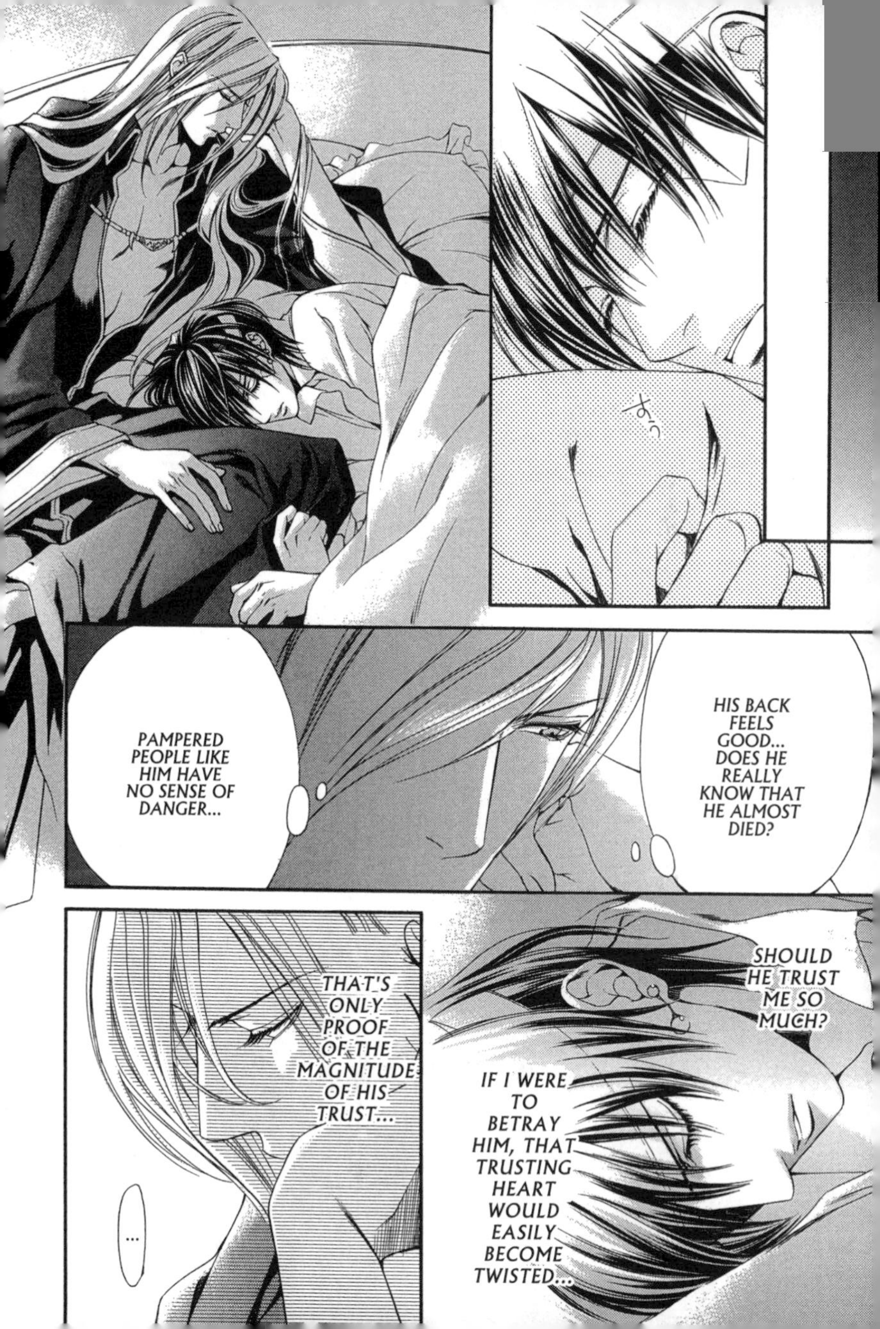
HIS BACK FEELS GOOD... DOES HE REALLY KNOW THAT HE ALMOST DIED?
PAMPERED PEOPLE LIKE HIM HAVE NO SENSE OF DANGER...
SHOULD HE TRUST ME SO MUCH?
IF I WERE TO BETRAY HIM, THAT TRUSTING HEART WOULD EASILY BECOME TWISTED...
THAT'S ONLY PROOF OF THE MAGNITUDE OF HIS TRUST...
...

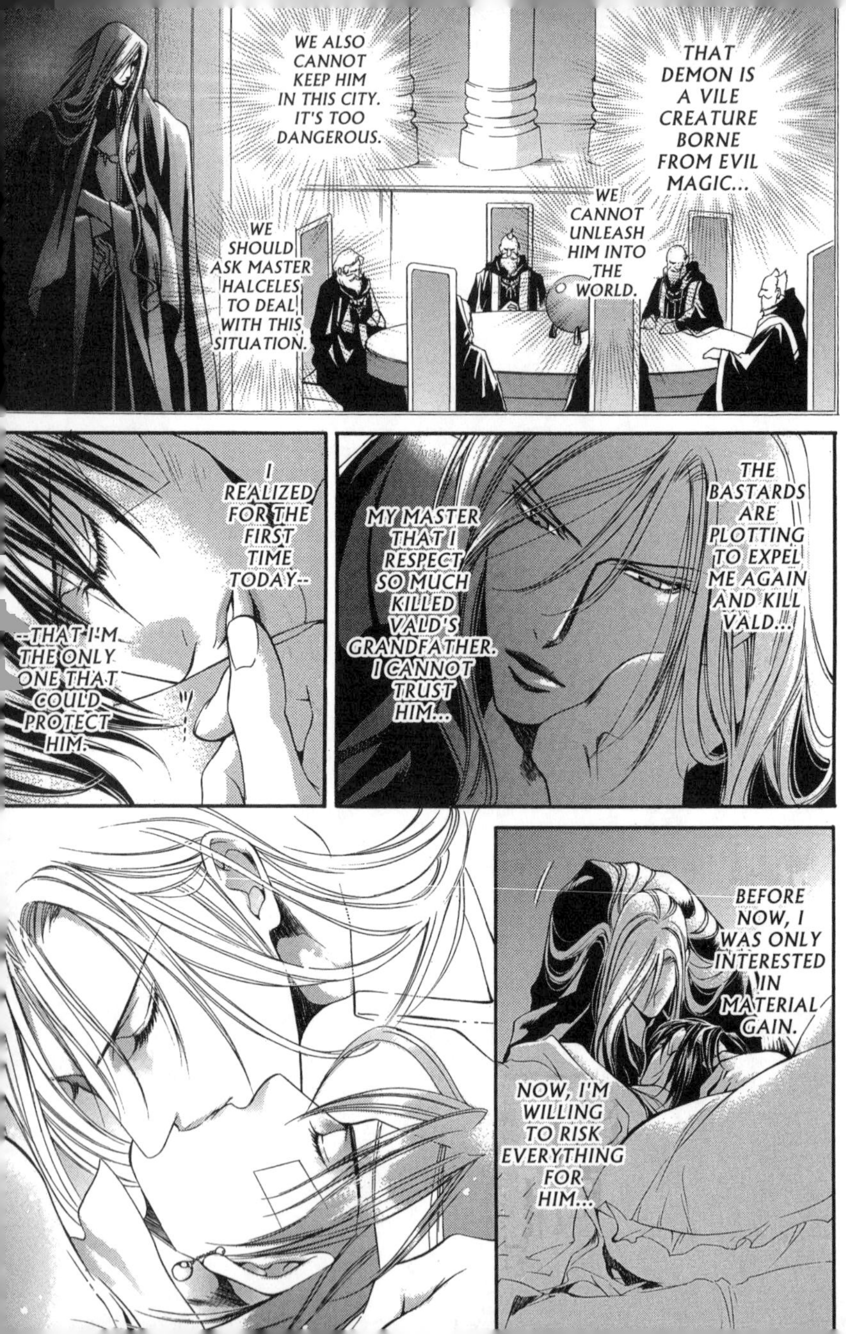
THAT DEMON IS A VILE CREATURE BORNE FROM EVIL MAGIC...
WE ALSO CANNOT KEEP HIM IN THIS CITY. IT'S TOO DANGEROUS.
WE CANNOT UNLEASH HIM INTO THE WORLD.
WE SHOULD ASK MASTER HALCELES TO DEAL WITH THIS SITUATION.
THE BASTARDS ARE PLOTTING TO EXPEL ME AGAIN AND KILL VALD...
MY MASTER THAT I RESPECT SO MUCH KILLED VALD'S GRANDFATHER. I CANNOT TRUST HIM...
I REALIZED FOR THE FIRST TIME TODAY--
--THAT I'M THE ONLY ONE THAT COULD PROTECT HIM.
BEFORE NOW, I WAS ONLY INTERESTED IN MATERIAL GAIN.
NOW, I'M WILLING TO RISK EVERYTHING FOR HIM...

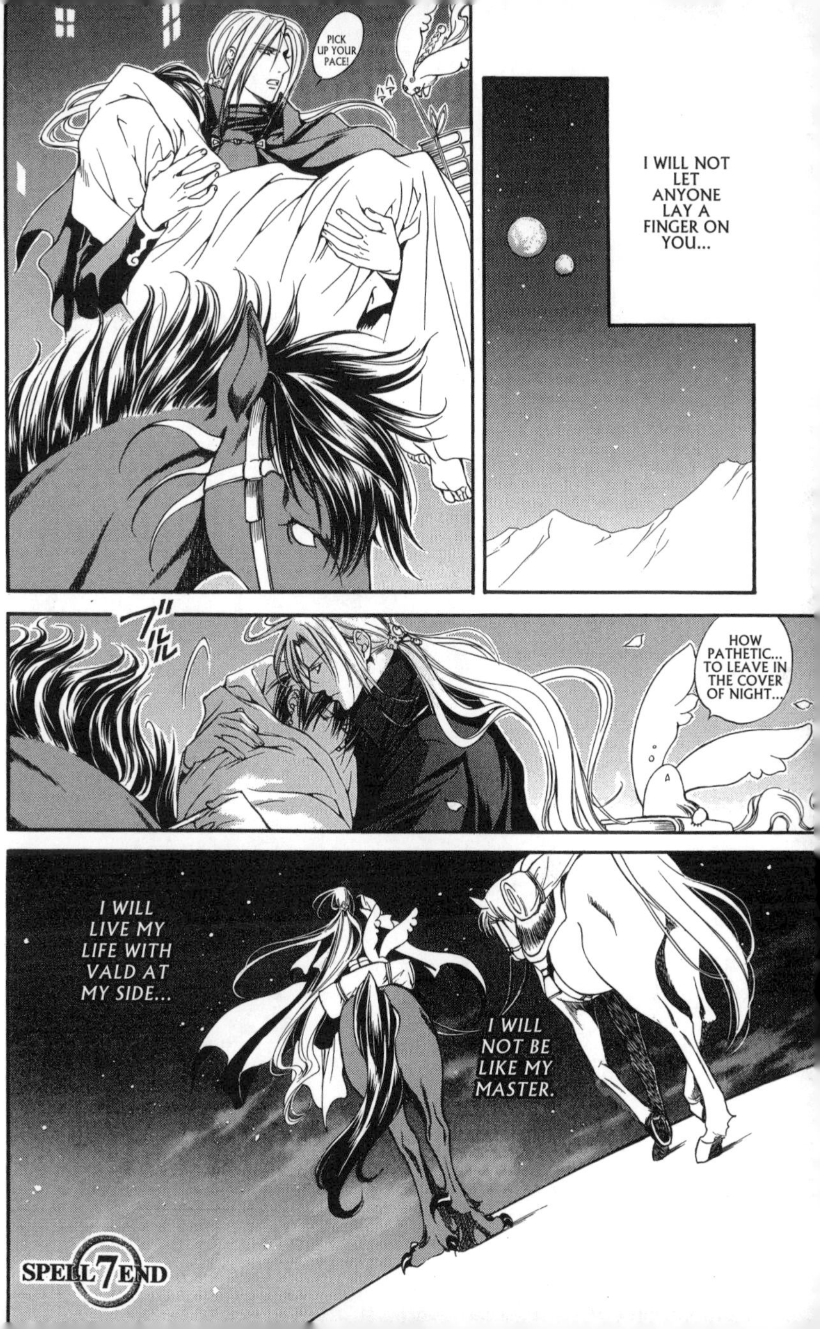
I WILL NOT LET ANYONE LAY A FINGER ON YOU...
PICK UP YOUR PACE!
HOW PATHETIC... TO LEAVE IN THE COVER OF NIGHT...
ブル
I WILL LIVE MY LIFE WITH VALD AT MY SIDE...
I WILL NOT BE LIKE MY MASTER.
SPELL 7 END

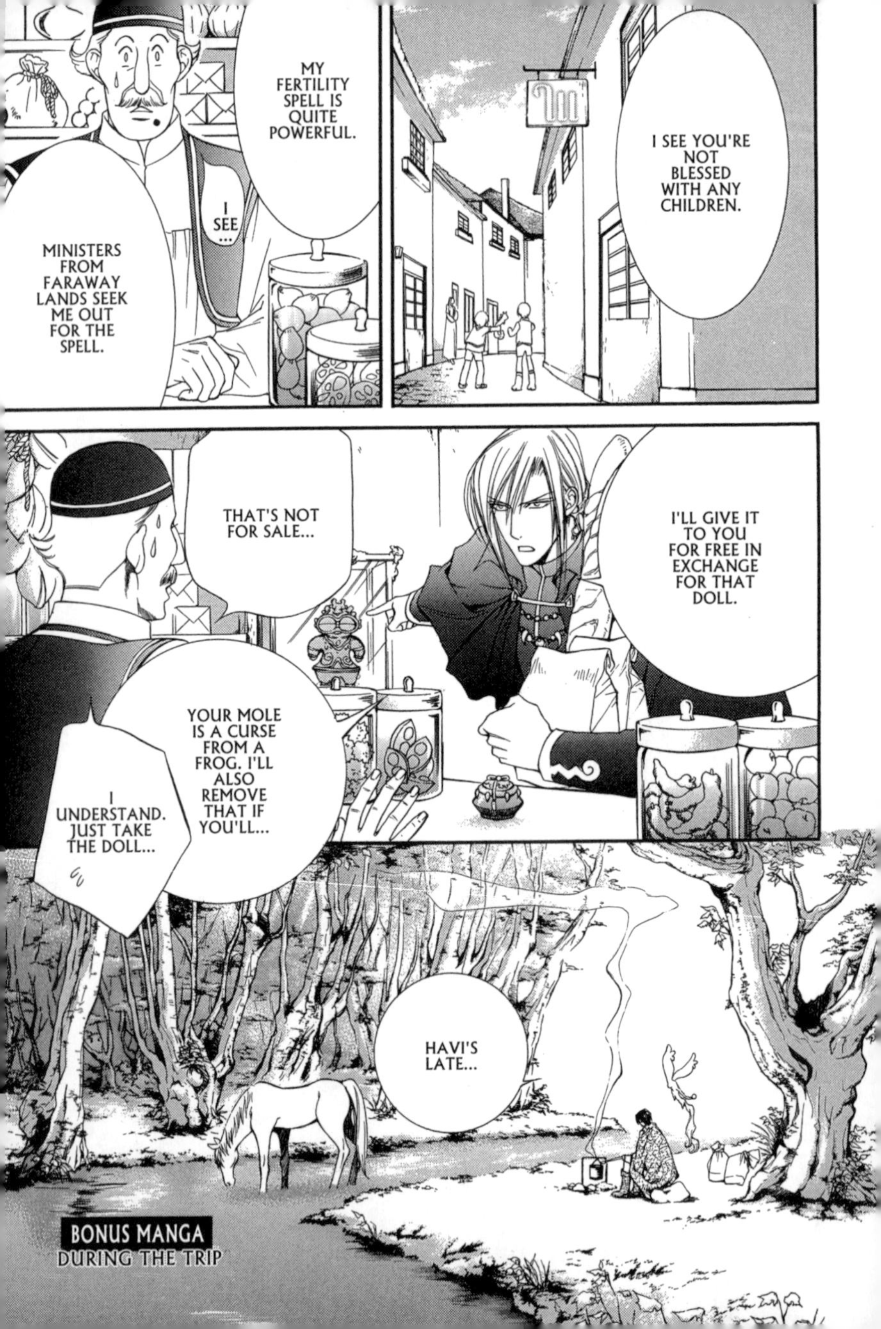
I SEE YOU'RE NOT BLESSED WITH ANY CHILDREN.
MY FERTILITY SPELL IS QUITE POWERFUL.
I SEE...
MINISTERS FROM FARAWAY LANDS SEEK ME OUT FOR THE SPELL.
I'LL GIVE IT TO YOU FOR FREE IN EXCHANGE FOR THAT DOLL.
THAT'S NOT FOR SALE...
YOUR MOLE IS A CURSE FROM A FROG. I'LL ALSO REMOVE THAT IF YOU'LL...
I UNDERSTAND. JUST TAKE THE DOLL...
BONUS MANGA
DURING THE TRIP
HAVI'S LATE...

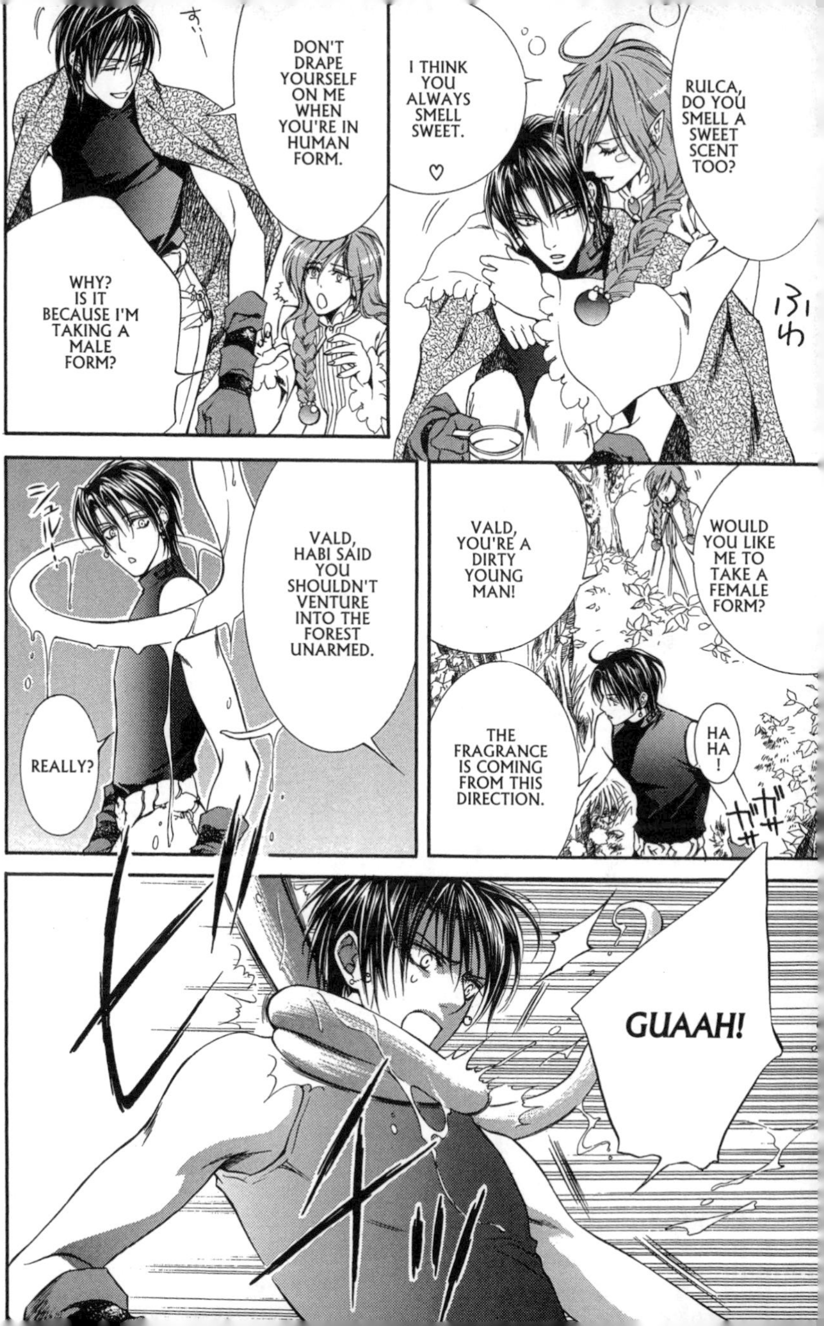
RULCA, DO YOU SMELL A SWEET SCENT TOO?
ふわ
I THINK YOU ALWAYS SMELL SWEET. ♡
DON'T DRAPE YOURSELF ON ME WHEN YOU'RE IN HUMAN FORM.
WHY? IS IT BECAUSE I'M TAKING A MALE FORM?
WOULD YOU LIKE ME TO TAKE A FEMALE FORM?
VALD, YOU'RE A DIRTY YOUNG MAN!
HA HA !
ガサガサ
THE FRAGRANCE IS COMING FROM THIS DIRECTION.
VALD, HABI SAID YOU SHOULDN'T VENTURE INTO THE FOREST UNARMED.
REALLY?
GUAAH!

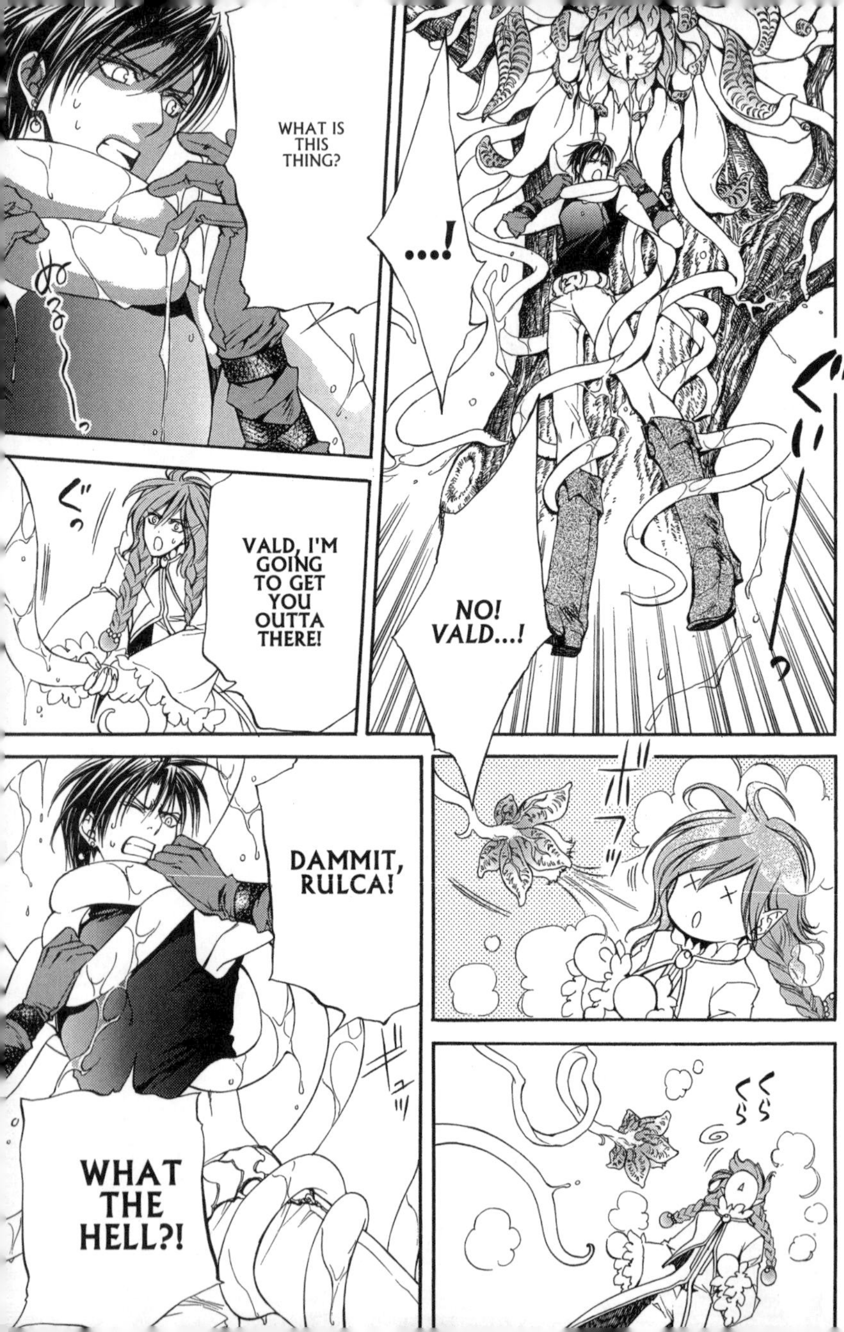

...!
NO! VALD...!
WHAT IS THIS THING?
ぬる
ぐっ
VALD, I'M GOING TO GET YOU OUTTA THERE!
くらくら
DAMMIT, RULCA!
WHAT THE HELL?!

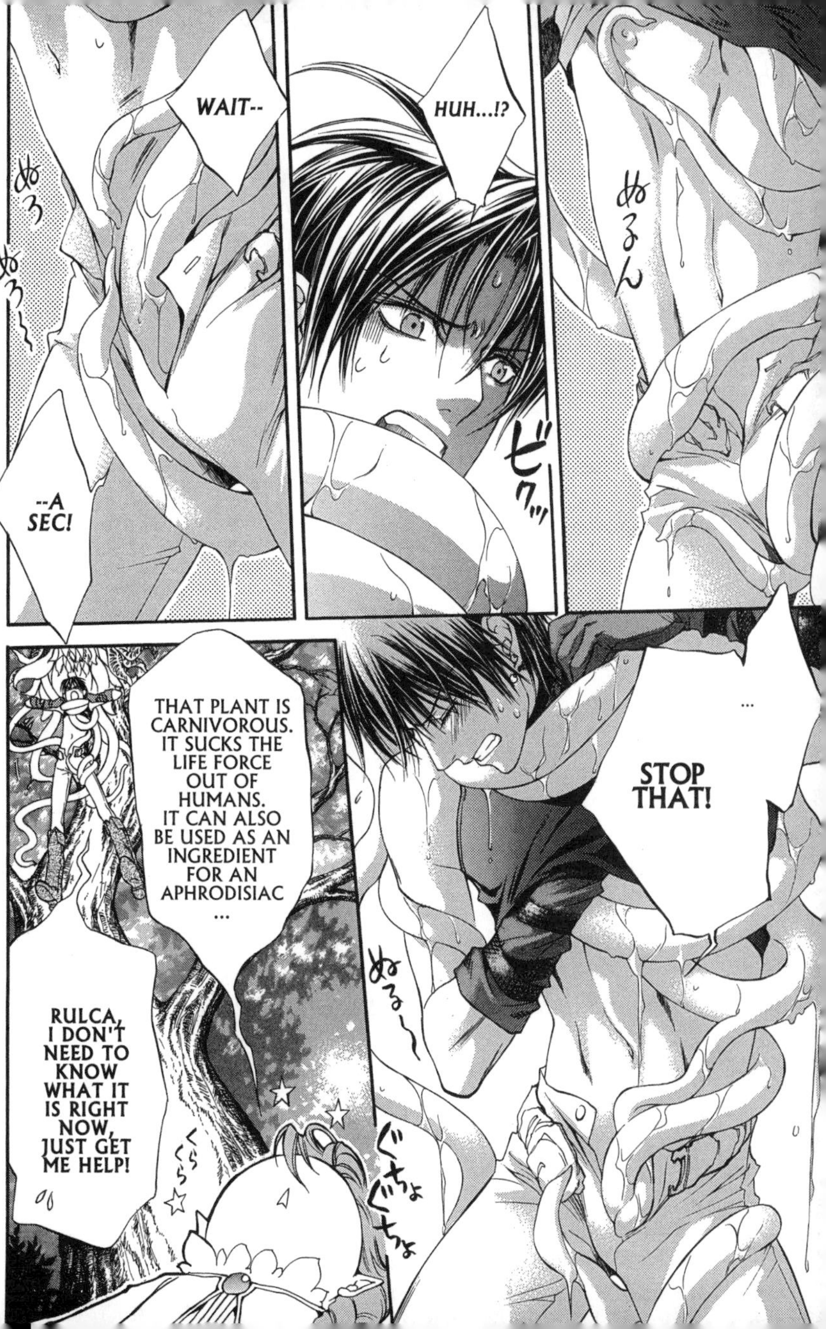
ぬるん
HUH...!?
ビクッ
WAIT--
ぬろ
ぬろ〜
--A SEC!
...
STOP THAT!
ぬる〜
ぐちょ
ぐちょ
THAT PLANT IS CARNIVOROUS. IT SUCKS THE LIFE FORCE OUT OF HUMANS. IT CAN ALSO BE USED AS AN INGREDIENT FOR AN APHRODISIAC ...
RULCA, I DON'T NEED TO KNOW WHAT IT IS RIGHT NOW, JUST GET ME HELP!
くら
くら

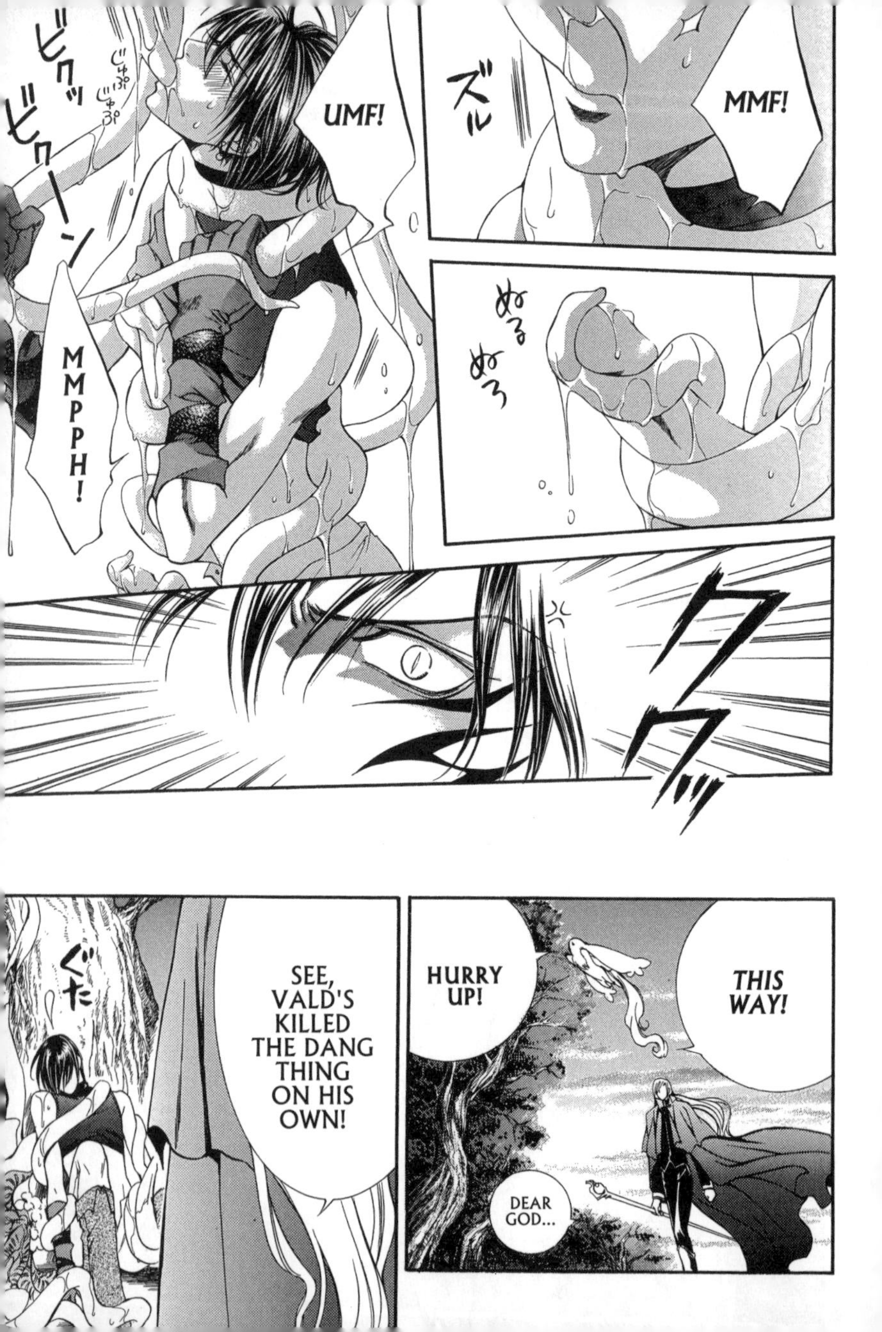

ズル
MMF!
ぬるぬる
UMF!
ビクッ
ビクーン
じゅぷじゅぷ
MMPPH!
ククッ
THIS WAY!
HURRY UP!
DEAR GOD...
SEE, VALD'S KILLED THE DANG THING ON HIS OWN!
ぐた

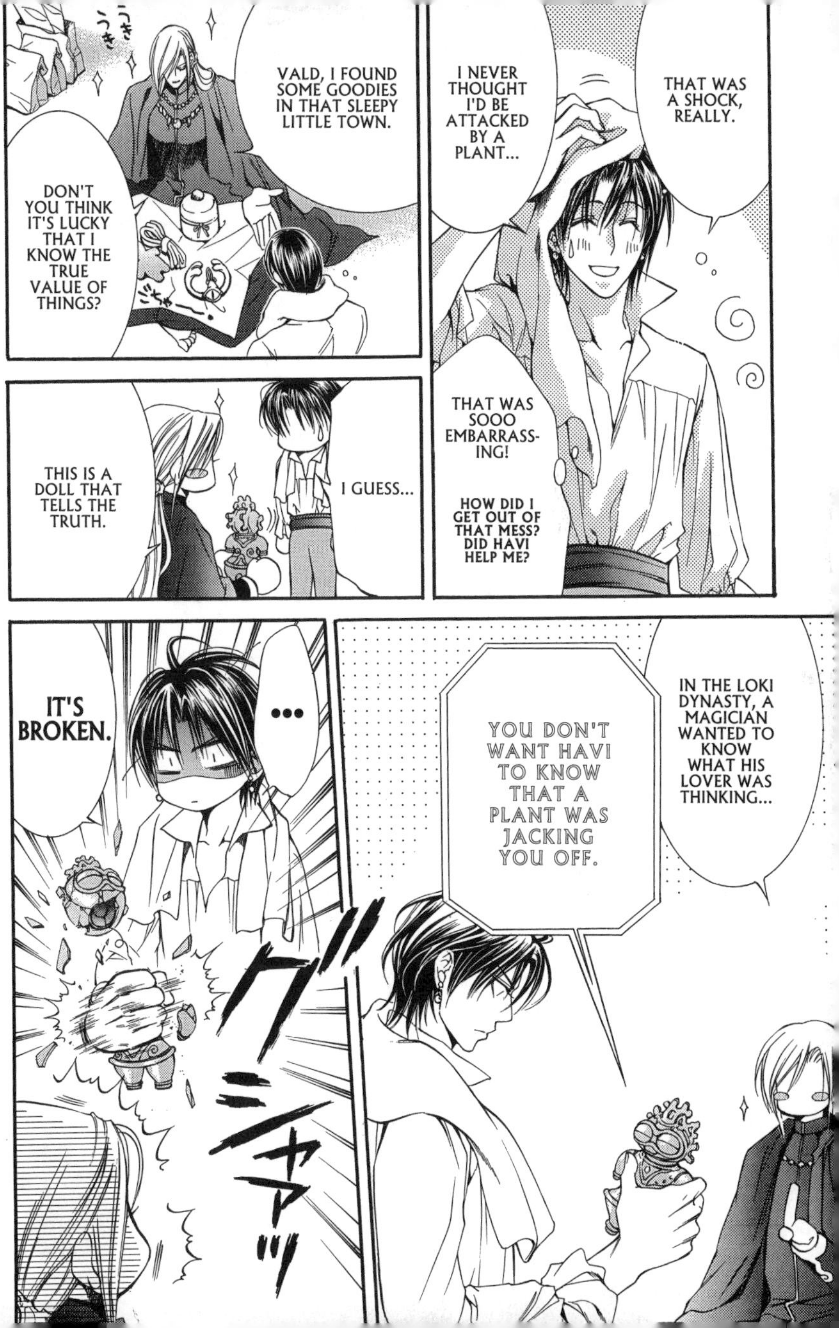
THAT WAS A SHOCK, REALLY.
I NEVER THOUGHT I'D BE ATTACKED BY A PLANT...
THAT WAS SOOO EMBARRASSING!
HOW DID I GET OUT OF THAT MESS? DID HAVI HELP ME?
うきうき
VALD, I FOUND SOME GOODIES IN THAT SLEEPY LITTLE TOWN.
DON'T YOU THINK IT'S LUCKY THAT I KNOW THE TRUE VALUE OF THINGS?
I GUESS...
THIS IS A DOLL THAT TELLS THE TRUTH.
IN THE LOKI DYNASTY, A MAGICIAN WANTED TO KNOW WHAT HIS LOVER WAS THINKING...
YOU DON'T WANT HAVI TO KNOW THAT A PLANT WAS JACKING YOU OFF.
...
IT'S BROKEN.
グシャアッ

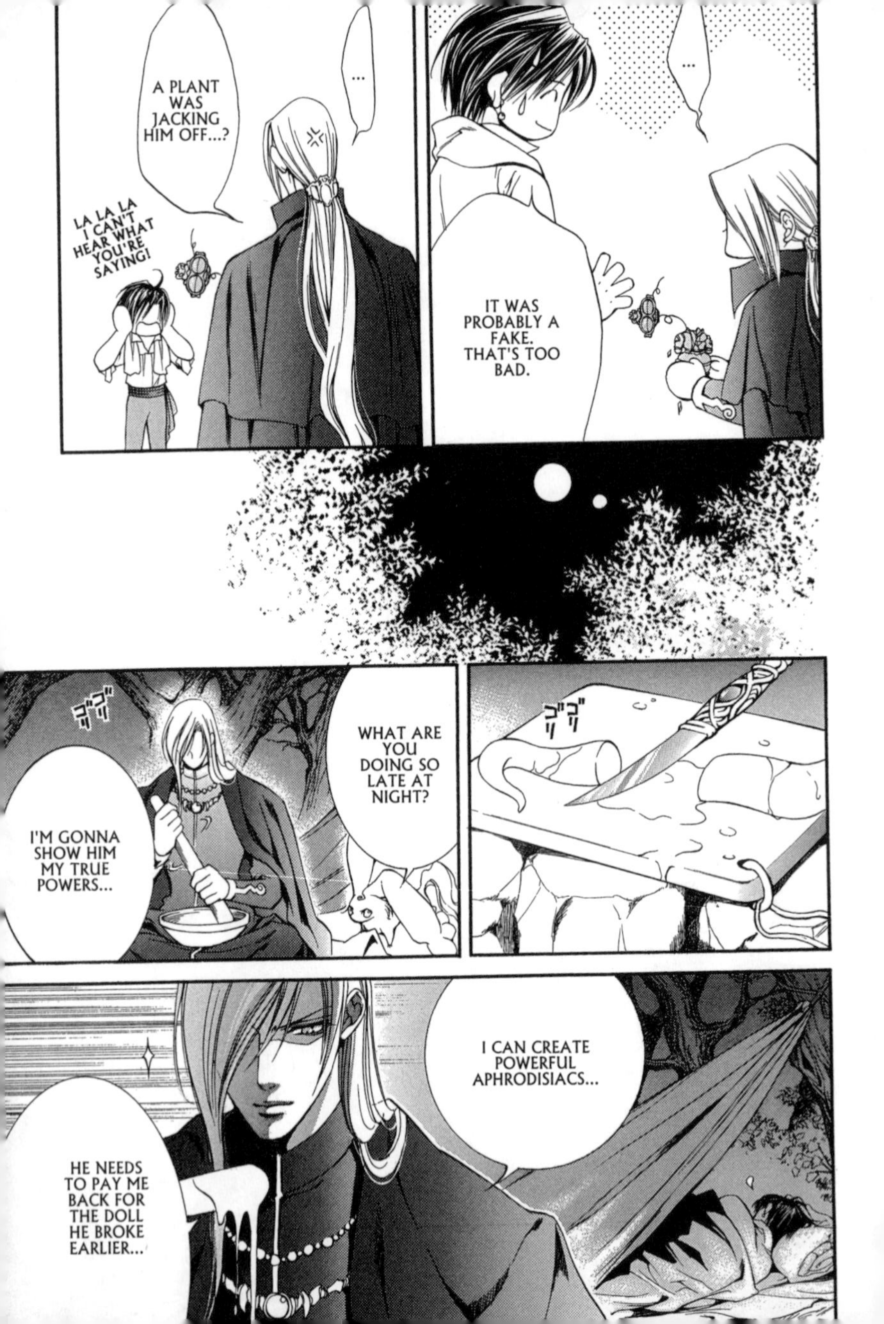
...
IT WAS PROBABLY A FAKE. THAT'S TOO BAD.
...
A PLANT WAS JACKING HIM OFF...?
LA LA LA I CAN'T HEAR WHAT YOU'RE SAYING!
ゴゴ
ゴゴ
WHAT ARE YOU DOING SO LATE AT NIGHT?
I'M GONNA SHOW HIM MY TRUE POWERS...
I CAN CREATE POWERFUL APHRODISIACS...
HE NEEDS TO PAY ME BACK FOR THE DOLL HE BROKE EARLIER...

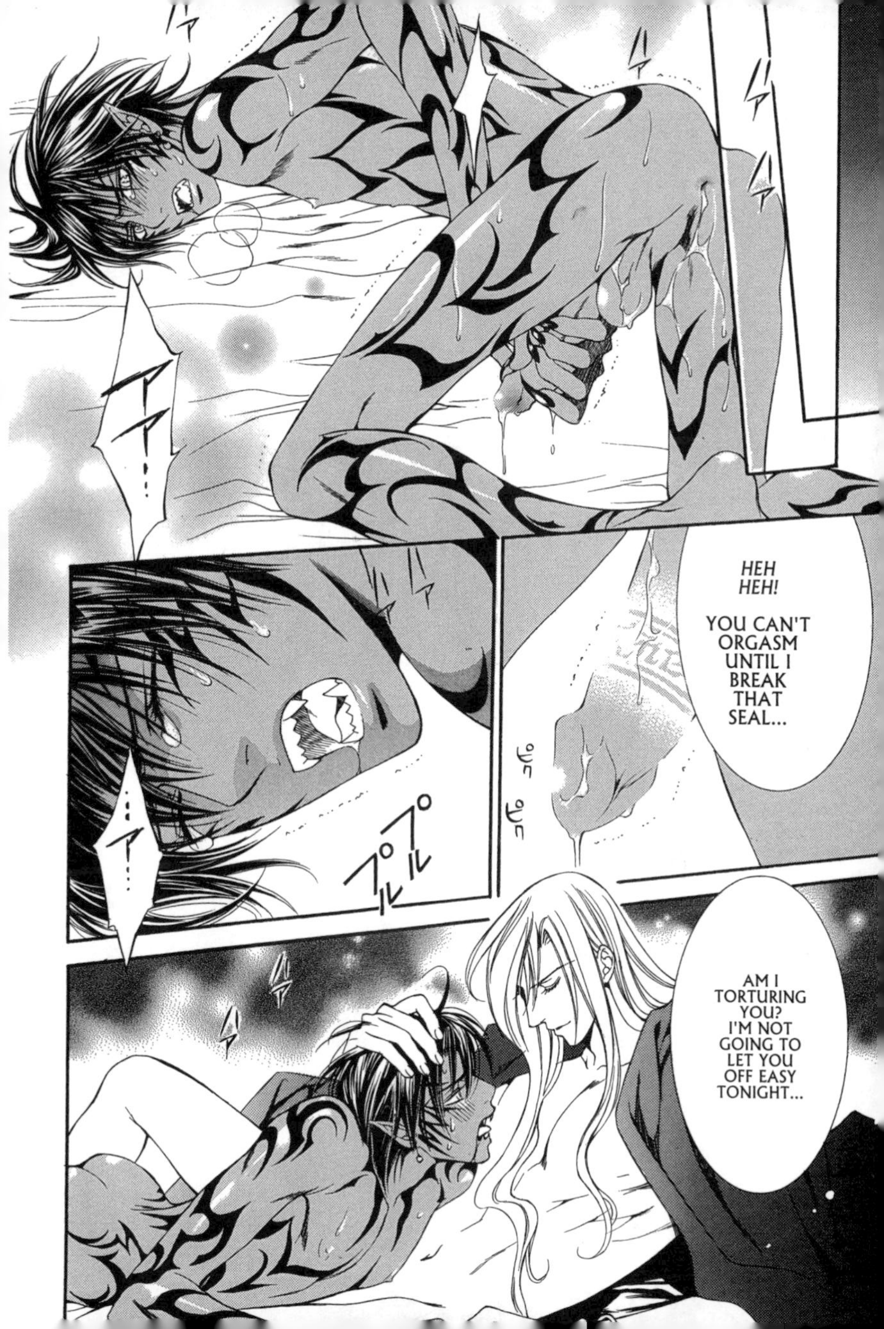
HEH HEH! YOU CAN'T ORGASM UNTIL I BREAK THAT SEAL...
AM I TORTURING YOU? I'M NOT GOING TO LET YOU OFF EASY TONIGHT...

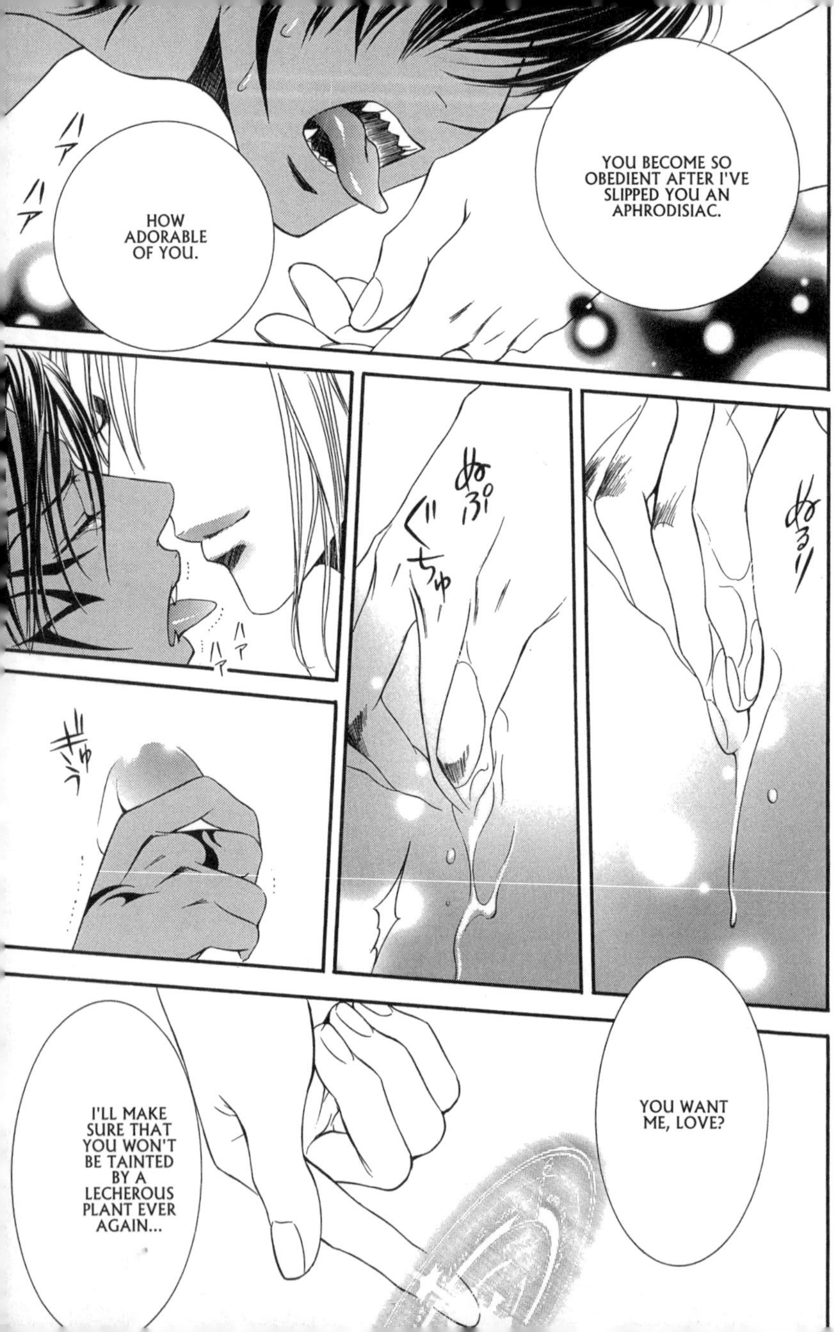
YOU BECOME SO OBEDIENT AFTER I'VE SLIPPED YOU AN APHRODISIAC.
HOW ADORABLE OF YOU.
ハァハァ
ぬるり
ぬぷ
ぐちゅ
ハァハァ
ぎゅっ
YOU WANT ME, LOVE?
I'LL MAKE SURE THAT YOU WON'T BE TAINTED BY A LECHEROUS PLANT EVER AGAIN...

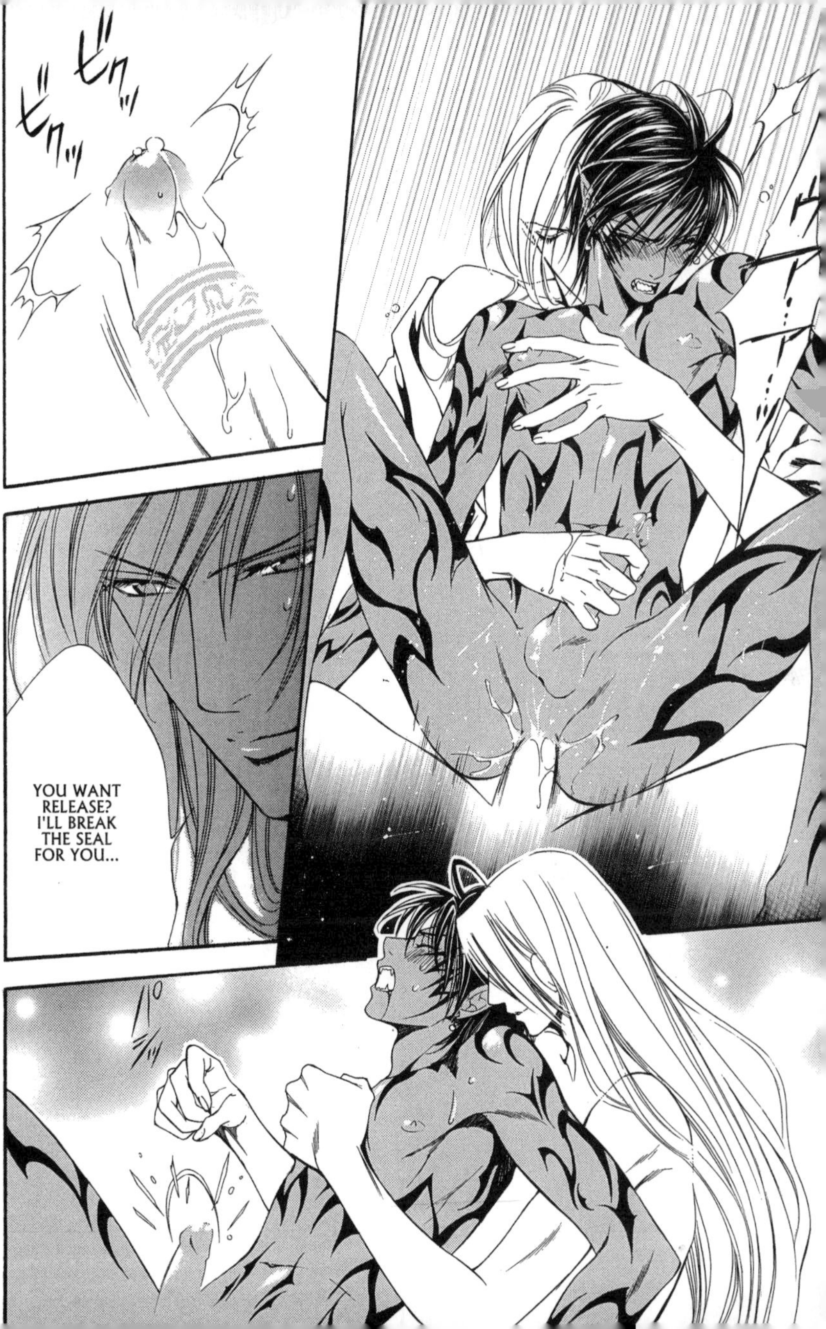
YOU WANT RELEASE? I'LL BREAK THE SEAL FOR YOU...

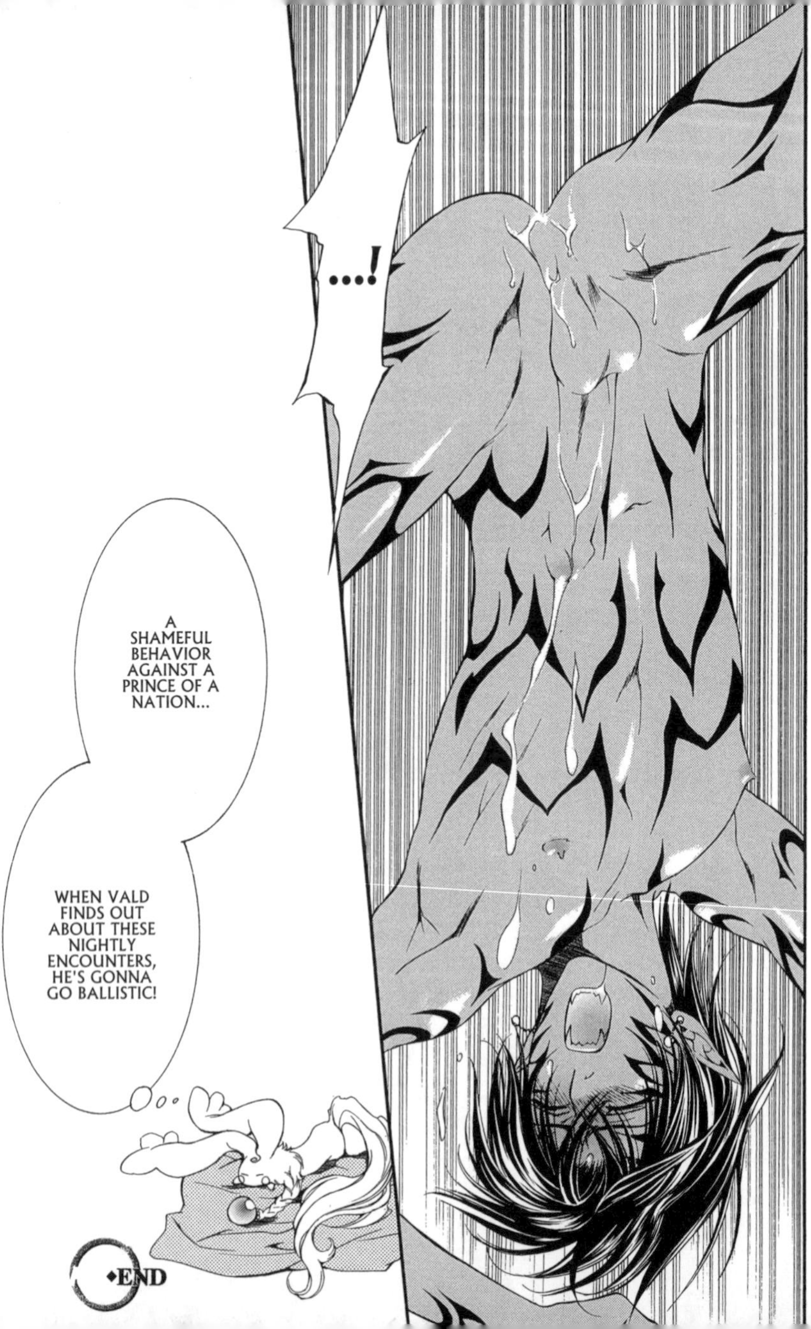

...!
A SHAMEFUL BEHAVIOR AGAINST A PRINCE OF A NATION...
WHEN VALD FINDS OUT ABOUT THESE NIGHTLY ENCOUNTERS, HE'S GONNA GO BALLISTIC!
END

Hello! This is Ayano Yamane! This is my first comic with this publisher! Thank you for purchasing this volume! 💜

As you can see, I've been working on this fantasy fiction for about a year. At first, when they asked me what I wanted to work on, I said "oh, a high school drama, maybe..." They replied with, "what about fantasy? You seemed interested in the genre for a while." So, that's how this project got started... Many people told me that yaoi and fantasy don't mix, but my publisher allowed me to work on this project! Thank you for all the fans that voted in the comic polls and sent fan letters. Your support means the world to me! Thanks to you, I have enough material for the first volume!

I've been a fantasy fan for a while, so I had a great time thinking about the storyline. Everything I've worked on has been based on my interests. This story is no exception! I had been alternately working on other projects from other publishers every other month, so I had a very tight deadline. I know each story wasn't very long, so let me apologize for that! This is nothing new, but I wish I could draw faster! Sigh...

This story has a whole bunch of long-haired characters! Long-haired characters are almost essential in fantasy stories, so I really didn't have a choice (laughs). I also love designing different costumes and arms. The sword and castle design was definitely influenced by Takaruza Theater! It may not be appropriate, but let's ignore that! I admit writing this story has brought up weird questions, like do people in fantasyland wear underwear, and what does their underwear look like (maybe I'm not alone)? I admit Vald has changed costumes throughout the story, although I understand if the readers are puzzled about where his wardrobe came from. I can assure you that he doesn't have a wardrobe staff following him around (laughs). I have to admit that whenever I'm drawing costumes, I always enjoy drawing the backside. Heh heh.

← Continued

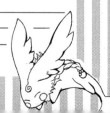

◀ Crimson Spell Preview Illustration

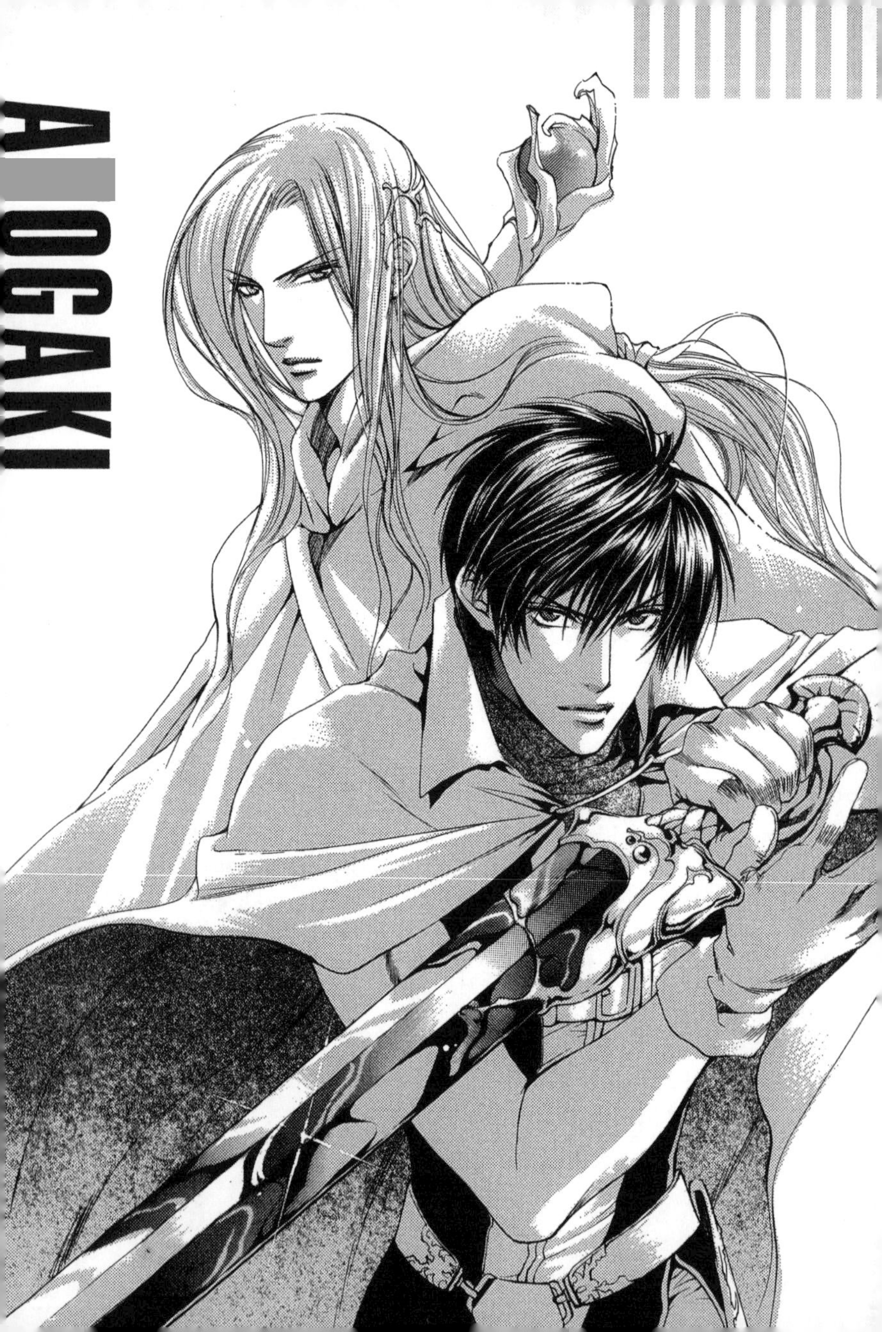
AOGAKI

I admit that this story isn't always pleasant to the female vision- since it has close-ups of monsters and unattractive robbers. Please forgive me! I do enjoy drawing them...! I've always loved drawing dragons and horses. I may not be any good, but I enjoy drawing them as much as school uniforms and nice suits!

When I was in grade school, I loved drawing pictures of dragons featured on my favorite game packaging. I think this is kind of a continuation of that... I'm getting a bit emotional...

I suppose the bonus can be summed up as tentacle sex. Well, I suppose it's not too unusual within the fantasy genre... I've also added several pages to the main story as a bonus for people who have read this series in magazines!

Havi almost lost Vald to a tentacled plant monster! However, their journey still continues. I'd love to continue with this story. Both fantasy and non-fantasy fans, I'd love to hear your opinion! I hope to see you in the next issue! ♥
Again, thank you for our support!

2005.7.吉日
やまねあやの拝.
Ayano Yamane

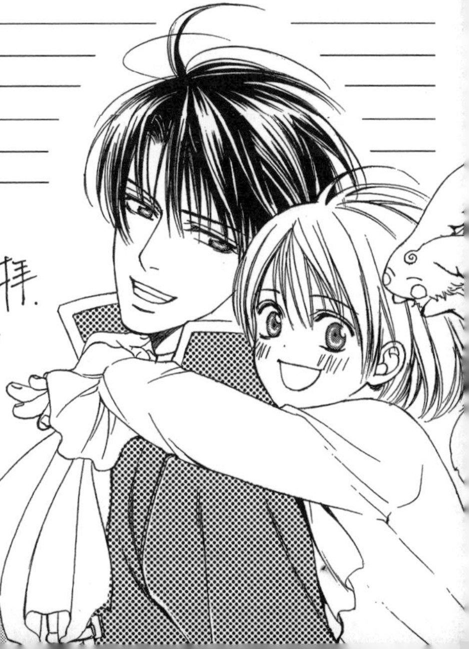

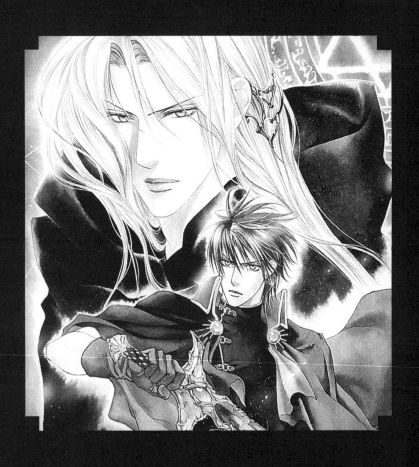

COMING SOON: A KING'S LESSON

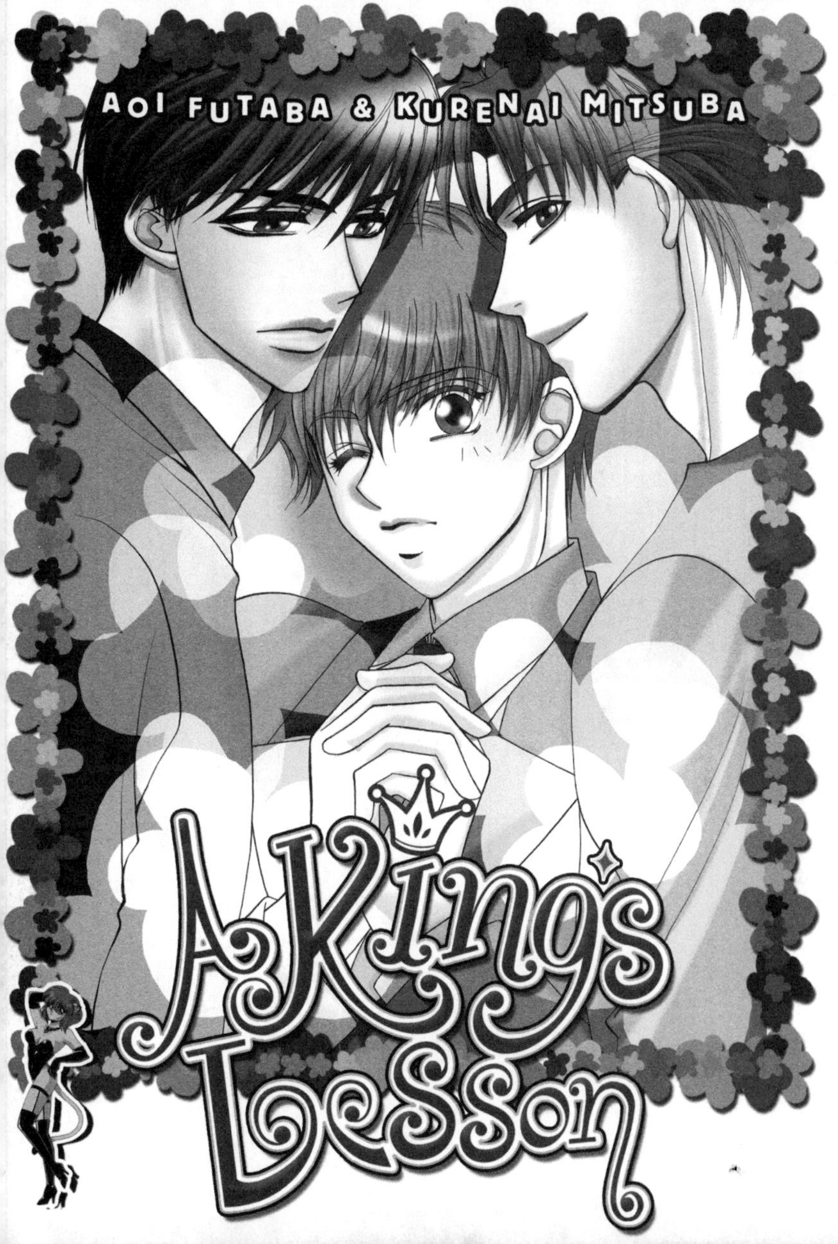
AOI FUTABA & KURENAI MITSUBA
A King's Lesson